COMMUNICATIONS
TOOLKIT 5TH ED.

JANE **GRELLIER**   VERONICA **GOERKE**   KATIE **FIELDING**

T0364000

CENGAGE

Communications Toolkit
5th Edition
Jane Grellier
Veronica Goerke
Katie Fielding

Publishing editor: Fiona Hammond
Developmental editor: Emily Spurr
Project editor: Alex Chambers
Project designer: Nikita Bansal
Cover designer: Studio Regina (Regine Abos)
Text designer: Watershed Art & Design (Leigh Ashforth)
Editor: Lauren McGregor
Permissions/Photo researcher: Wendy Duncan
Indexer: Julie King
Proofreader: Jennifer Bulter
KnowledgeWorks Global Ltd

Any URLs contained in this publication were checked for
currency during the production process. Note, however, that
the publisher cannot vouch for the ongoing currency of URLs.

Fourth edition published in 2018

© 2022 Cengage Learning Australia Pty Limited

Copyright Notice
This Work is copyright. No part of this Work may be reproduced, stored in a
retrieval system, or transmitted in any form or by any means without prior
written permission of the Publisher. Except as permitted under the
Copyright Act 1968, for example any fair dealing for the purposes of private study,
research, criticism or review, subject to certain limitations. These limitations
include: Restricting the copying to a maximum of one chapter or 10% of this
book, whichever is greater; providing an appropriate notice and warning with the
copies of the Work disseminated; taking all reasonable steps to limit access to
these copies to people authorised to receive these copies; ensuring you hold the
appropriate Licences issued by the Copyright Agency Limited ("CAL"), supply a
remuneration notice to CAL and pay any required fees. For details of CAL licences
and remuneration notices please contact CAL at Level 11, 66 Goulburn Street,
Sydney NSW 2000, Tel: (02) 9394 7600, Fax: (02) 9394 7601
Email: info@copyright.com.au
Website: www.copyright.com.au

For product information and technology assistance,
in Australia call **1300 790 853**;
in New Zealand call **0800 449 725**

For permission to use material from this text or product, please email
aust.permissions@cengage.com

National Library of Australia Cataloguing-in-Publication Data
ISBN: 9780170452052
A catalogue record for this book is available from the National Library of
Australia.

Cengage Learning Australia
Level 7, 80 Dorcas Street
South Melbourne, Victoria Australia 3205

Cengage Learning New Zealand
Unit 4B Rosedale Office Park
331 Rosedale Road, Albany, North Shore 0632, NZ

For learning solutions, visit **cengage.com.au**

Printed in China by 1010 Printing International Limited.
2 3 4 5 6 7 25 24 23 22

↘ BRIEF CONTENTS

↘ CONTENTS

↘ FOREWORD

In Australia's near universal higher education (HE) system, students enter our institutions with great diversity in academic preparedness, with varying social and cultural capital, and with differing, often ill-formed, expectations of what is involved in tertiary study. In their first weeks and months, students report that they are frequently confounded by a lack of clarity about what is required for learning engagement and success. Many also find our institutional and academic language impenetrable and have difficulty in understanding disparate discipline conventions. For too many commencing students, the transition to their first year in HE is an anxious and unsupported journey, in which they move from the known and familiar to the unknown and indecipherable. And now, in the 2020s, this system vulnerability has been significantly exacerbated by a rapid pivot to emergency remote teaching.

The fifth edition of this important toolkit for learner success publishes in the midst of a global pandemic and at a time when the future of learning and work in a disrupted world is more uncertain than ever before. As COVID-19 swept around the world and into our institutions, HE's capability for flexibility and responsiveness to meet the changing needs of diverse cohorts has been severely stress tested. How do we equip learners with the skills they need to participate and succeed in rapidly changing educational and work environments; learners whose ranks now include a new influx of freshly displaced workers? Particularly, how do we assure the learning and growth mindset necessary for foundational skills' development, and as the basis on which a lifelong commitment to iterative up- and re-skilling can be built?

This is the context to which this book speaks. Students' successful transitions into, through and out of HE have been issues of concern and dedicated research nationally and internationally for decades. It is clear that the cost and impact of student departure are highest in the first year – for government, institutions, individuals, their communities and society at large, across a spectrum of reputational, ethical, personal, economic and legal dimensions. COVID-19 has laid bare long-standing educational inequities, chief amongst which is the compounding impact on participation and attainment of digital disadvantage, financial precarity and fragile mental wellbeing. The sector imperative to be clear about what works for inclusive learning, success and retention, in the context of pervasive student heterogeneity, must be freshly (re)prioritised.

Put simply, online learning is very different from the face-to-face learning experience and the risk of cognitive overload for first-year students is very real. We should consider carefully what the COVID-19 generation of HE learners *need to do* in order to learn. They must: 'learn how to learn' online; wrangle an associated array of tools, technologies, activities, supports and resources presented with more or less coherence; seek to manage their multiple first-year transitions across a myriad of institutional communications; and (eventually) engage with the content and skills of their new discipline. Many will need help and guidance to buttress their mental wellbeing. A number of commencing HE students will arrive straight from school having suffered learning loss due to disadvantage and challenges experienced over periods of home schooling in the pandemic.[1] As we reflect on the lessons learned from our online upscaling of HE teaching and support in aid of commencing students' online learning, the need to embrace enabling ('transition') pedagogies[2] and their principles of universal design is more critical than ever. The new edition of this book steps through many of the essential elements to which explicit curricular attention should be directed to scaffold early student success and build learning confidence for emerging discipline competence.

Higher education providers cannot claim to have been caught completely unawares by the challenges they faced in response to the COVID-19 pandemic. Over the course of the last decade, as the scale of online teaching for online learning has grown, there has been considerable government and regulatory interest in providers' performance on student attrition, retention and success metrics.[3] In Australia, the national regulator, the Tertiary Education Quality and Standards Agency (TEQSA), has a mandate under the *Higher Education Standards Framework*[4] to hold providers accountable for assuring successful student transition into, and progress through, courses of study regardless of 'educational background, entry pathway, *mode or place of study*' (Standard 1.3.6, emphasis added). Higher attrition rates in online learning had already been identified as a cause for significant concern: '*external students are around 2½ times more likely to withdraw from higher education than internal students*'.[5] Relatedly, the issue of how to provide transition and learning support for COVID-19 remote learners became problematic when traditional, on-campus, 9 am–5 pm weekday services were forced to close. Equitable support service provision had also attracted specific regulatory attention. In 2017, the Australian Higher Education Standards Panel (HESP) warned that '[i]nstitutions should pay particular attention to ensuring their support services are meeting the needs of external students who are not regularly attending campus because these students are identified as at risk of not completing their studies'.[6]

In this context, an important aspect of equitably unpacking for all students the culture of HE and its disciplines is to be explicit in the learning design about the expectations of tertiary study and the criteria for successful engagement with it. Specifically, early and contextualised development of enabling academic skills and literacies, including digital literacy, is critical for learning success. Attention to assuring such supported skills acquisition by way of inclusive curriculum design builds self-efficacy and competence and develops self-regulatory capability. This in turn has been found to support student mental wellbeing.[7] Given the foreseeability of transition

1   For example, Lamb, S., Maire, Q., Doecke, E., Macklin, S., Noble, K., & Pilcher, S. 2020. 'Impact of learning from home on educational outcomes for disadvantaged children: brief assessment.' https://www.vu.edu.au/sites/default/files/submission-government-impact-learning-from-home.pdf
2   For example, Kift, S. 2015. 'A decade of Transition Pedagogy: A quantum leap in conceptualising the first-year experience.' *HERDSA Review of Higher Education*, 2, 51–86.
3   For example, Tertiary Education Quality and Standards Agency. 2017. 'Characteristics of Australian Higher Education Providers and Their Relation to First-year Student Attrition.' Melbourne: Australian Government Department of Education and Training.
4   *Higher Education Standards Framework (Threshold Standards) 2015* https://www.legislation.gov.au/Details/F2015L01639
5   Higher Education Standards Panel (HESP). 2017. 'Final Report - Improving Retention, Completion and Success in Higher Education' at 14 https://www.dese.gov.au/uncategorised/resources/higher-education-standards-panel-final-report-improving-retention-completion-and-success-higher
6   HESP, note 3, at 9, Recommendation 7.
7   Baik, C., Larcombe, W., Wyn, J., Allen, L., Brett, M., Field, R., James, R. & Brooker, A. 2016. 'A Framework for Promoting Student Mental Wellbeing in Universities'. http://unistudentwellbeing.edu.au/wp-content/uploads/2016/11/MCSHE-Student-Wellbeing-Framework_FINAL.pdf

hurdles, there is an onus on us as educators to articulate, clearly and consistently, the hidden rules, expectations and behaviours fundamental to successful learning engagement, whatever 'the mode or place of study' (as the *HE Standards Framework* mandates). This is especially important in the online environment where there are fewer opportunities for teacher and peer interactions. If we expect first-year students to become independent and self-managing learners, they must be supported in their early development and acquisition of the tools they need to engage productively with the learning and assessment tasks we design for them. Communication and academic study skills are integral to early student achievement in this regard.

But this is a lifelong and life-wide imperative now also. Acquisition of the education staples of basic skills and literacies is essential to realising individualised success in learning journeys across the lifespan. Industry 4.0's automation, in tandem with COVID-19, has created a 'double-disruption scenario'[8] for learners and workers, which has only heightened the consequential nature of mastering essential skills and literacies so that barriers to lifelong learning participation are proactively dismantled. The fourth industrial revolution has focused particular attention on the development of the uniquely human skills that do not lend themselves easily to automation. Amongst this latter category, communication skills are often most frequently mentioned.[9] Learners need to develop these skills – active listening, effective verbal and non-verbal communication, presentation skills, teamwork, intercultural communication and the ability to communicate across genres – as they are integral to lifelong engagement in education and training. Employers expect employees to have these skills, both in their own right and as a subset of other highly valued interpersonal skills; for example, as a basis for negotiation and conflict resolution, emotional intelligence, for inquiry and information management, and for project management.

This book makes clear for all students, whatever their background or prior learning, the substance of the academic skills and literacies in which they must be proficient for workforce entry and then continuing engagement in lifelong learning. It does so comprehensively and accessibly, in a manner that is direct, inclusive, motivational and learner-centric. The practical advice, tips and strategies that are presented provide novice learners with the opportunity to acquire the threshold skills and literacies many degree programs assume already exist. Critically, for the current generation of students, the book also focuses on the scaffolding of online learning and engagement with the digital student experience. In this way, the book makes explicit the rules and expectations of the hidden curriculum, while also surfacing the potential for disciplinary difference. Crucially for first-year success, the authors acknowledge early the importance of the social context

---

8 World Economic Forum. 2020. 'The Future of Jobs' at 5 http://www3.weforum.org/docs/WEF_Future_of_Jobs_2020.pdf
9 See, for example, data on the National Skills Commission website https://www.nationalskillscommission.gov.au/resource-centre/latest-data. See also Burning Glass & Business Higher Education Forum. (2018). The New Foundational Skills of the Digital Economy. https://www.burning-glass.com/research-project/new-foundational-skills/

of learning and seek to normalise the predictable anxiety many new learners will encounter over the course of their early engagement in the student lifecycle.

But students are only one half of the equation for effective transition pedagogy. Many higher education teachers also require assistance to unpack and scaffold the acquisition of these foundational skills for diverse cohorts; assistance which is not predicated on a deficit view of entering student ability. This is another great value of this book – the ways and means for empowering student learning are made explicit for both students *and* their teachers, whether the mode of delivery is face-to-face, blended or wholly online. To have maximum impact on student success, substantive references to this book should be embedded in core first-year curricula; across all of the planned learning experiences in organised and sequenced design that is contextualised to the discipline and provides support for just-in-time student access. The research in this regard is clear: to be most effective, language and learning skills' development should be integrated into the curriculum and the context of discipline learning – their acquisition cannot be left to chance. I commend the authors on the obvious care, expertise and respect for students and their learning they bring to this task. The book is a valuable contribution to the effective deployment of transition pedagogies and should be harnessed in aid of intentional first-year curriculum design. I recommend this book as an invaluable learning support for diverse first-year student cohorts and for those who seek to engage with them for learning success. Both students and teachers will be grateful for the learning it facilitates, whatever the mode or place of study.

Professor Sally Kift PFHEA FAAL
President, Australian Learning and Teaching Fellows
ALTF Senior Fellow, Discipline Scholar: Law
February 2021

↘ ABOUT THE AUTHORS

Dr Jane Grellier is a coordinator in the first-year Communications Program in the Faculty of Media, Society and Culture at Curtin University in Perth, Western Australia. She works with a team of teachers who provide communications units to more than 4000 first-year students each year across various internal faculties, as well as online and offshore. Jane worked initially as a secondary English teacher in Western Australian schools, and then spent 15 years as an educational writer and curriculum developer for a range of secondary and tertiary education sectors. She has a strong commitment to teaching writing, especially to encouraging students to write in clear and concise English, which she sees as essential in the university setting. Jane's own research currently focuses on reflective practice – both in her own writing and in developing reflective thinking among first-year students.

Veronica Goerke (PhD) is a senior lecturer at Curtin University who lives with her husband near her children and their families on Whadjuk Noongar Country in Boorloo (Perth, Western Australia). Her ancestors all come from the Valtellina in northern Italy and her first language was a dialect from that region. Like Jane and Katie, Veronica first worked as a secondary school teacher, before moving into universities, where she taught and coordinated communication skills, as well as holding leadership roles in academic development and curriculum design. She has worked with Australian First Nation colleagues to co-create and deliver reconciliation-related projects including intercultural staff training and on-country subjects for students. She has completed research into the first-year experience, communication skills and students' use of tablets for learning. However, her key research focus is reconciliation in Australian universities. She believes we are all continually learning how to better communicate with each other, so we can be more inclusive and respectful and thus enact real reconciliation and peace across the world.

Katie Fielding is a teacher at Curtin University in Perth, Western Australia, where she works predominantly with first-year students in the faculties of Media, Culture and Social Inquiry (MCASI), and Education. She began her teaching career in secondary school English, and later moved into the tertiary education space where her passions for teacher education and language have been indulged. She has a particular interest in the ways that online learning can be harnessed to provide students with opportunities to access education. Katie's own research focuses on the role that digital technologies can play in helping young children develop their capacities for creative thinking, innovation and problem solving.

↘ ACKNOWLEDGEMENTS

Many of our colleagues at Curtin University have continued to be supportive and generous with their time and ideas as we have been working on this fifth edition. We acknowledge that our text builds on the work of those who have come before us and those who work beside us, not just at Curtin, but across the higher education sector. In this section, we say thank you to our colleagues and the many students we have taught or encountered over the years who have made us better teachers and communicators.

We start by thanking those involved in the development of the first four editions, whose feedback and contribution are the foundation of this new text: Trish Dooey, Carol Igglesden, Katie Scott, Cathryn Wilkinson, Cathy Cupitt, Lyn Payne, Gabby Barrett, Sue Denham, Katalin Dobos, Deborah Hunn, Richard Liston, Robyn Mayes, Chris Nagel, Hugh Rayner, Nari van Der Zanden, Sue Grey-Smith, Pippa Beetson, Paula Beck, Karen Rickman, Katherine Bathgate, Melanie Griffiths, Michelle Carey, Jeannie Morrison, Geoff Cody, Lyn Komarzynski, Liam Lynch, Joy Scott and Helen Rogers (the Communications Program); Lara Mackintosh (the Department of Architecture); Ann Kosovich, Beatrice Tucker, Kuki Singh, Raelene Tifflin and Allan Goody (Office of Teaching and Learning); Aaron Matthews, Michelle Webb and Brenda Larsen (Centre for Aboriginal Studies); Jim Elliott (Student Transition and Retention Team); Lynne Vautier (the TL Robertson Library); Simon Forrest (Office of the Elder in Residence) and Courtenay Harris (Faculty of Health Sciences). We also thank Anne Harris (Honorary Senior Lecturer, Edith Cowan University).

As with previous editions, this toolkit would be impoverished without the many examples of written work and ideas students have allowed us to include. Delighting in their success as communicators, we thank all these students: Tashia Abeyasinghe, Sanan Al Abbasi, Esther Adeney, John Aldridge, Aidan Ashwin, Geoff Barnes, Sharon Beale, Crystal Beaini, Tammy Beven, Simon Blyth, Jonathon Borrello, Barbara Bozsik, Paul Britton, Cameron Broad, Ben Caracciolo, Alex Cardell-Oliver, Alex (Ping Hei) Chan, Ebony Clare Chang, Rebecca Chang, Justin Colangelo, Mariko Collins, Ebba Collinson, Anna Dewar-Leahy, Aden Dielesen, Sean Dixon, Seamus Dobbs, Hursh Dodhia-Shah, Khush Dodhia-Shah, Marcia Doolan, Sarah Edmiston, Sarah N. Falzon, Naomi Fisher, Daniel Flynn, Kristie Foenander, Daniel Frewer, James Gibson, Alannah Goerke, Megan Goerke, Olivia Hamblin, Samuel Hammond, Fiona Harvey, Jacqui Holub, Annaliese Hunt, Ashley Hunt, Matt Hunter, Stephanie Huynh, Fiona Jones, Joel Kandiah, Sigrid Kautzner, Tim Kenworthy, Mortigou Labunda, Damian Lay, Sarah Lazzaro, Jasmine Lei, Jonathan Lendich, Chris Lodge, Jessica Matthews, Robert McLeod, Amado Mendoza, Alina Morelli, Ashleigh Morris, Khin Myint, Kathleen Nelly, Alan Ng, Lars Nielsen, Alex Ogilvie, Lane O'Refferty, Niamh O'Sullivan, Grant Perkins, Samantha Petri, Ryan Pinto, Lisa Podbereski, Christine Polowyj, Sally Potsch, Abbey Prentice, Ryan Quinn, Zeik Rafferty, Christine Regan, Jason Robards, Carol Rusch, Samia Scott, Melissa Settineri, Kelley Shaughnessy, Lala Sheikh, Kaylene Schutz, Lewis Stewart, Shaun Sullivan, Freyja Taverner, Kristy Taylor, Dawit Tesfaye, Steve Trudgian, Alex VanderPlas, Marelize Venter, Ella Wakeman, Stephanie Walker, Kathleen Ward, Emily Webb, Wei Wei, Lavinia Wehr, Ellie Willoughby, Jennifer Zeven and Alex Zuniga. A special thank you to Courtnee Nichols for her narrative and photograph of group processes in Chapter 15.

Jane would like to thank her husband Warren for his continuing support through this writing process. Their shared passion for teaching and for language lies at the heart of all her work, and their teaching experiences together over the past years have kept her grounded and enthusiastic. Her current work with online learners of all ages has sparked her enthusiasm for this form of learning – to all those wonderful online students, seeking to change and enrich their lives through studies, she conveys her enormous respect.

Veronica again thanks her beloved husband and sometimes editor, Mark, as well as children, Damien, Alannah and Megan. She enjoys – most of the time – learning from her children, their partners and friends about how to play with new online communication tools. She always enjoys watching her toddler grandchild, Madeline, mimicking her grandmother shouting on the smartphone! Veronica also acknowledges that from working closely with First Nations, she has learned good communication is more about the many ways of listening, rather than the words spoken.

Katie would like to publicly acknowledge the love, patience and understanding of her family, which has given her the space to follow her dreams and achieve her goals. She particularly thanks her husband, Nick, with whom she frequently engages in passionate intellectual arguments about all manner of topics (about which they are often in furious agreement!) and her children, Lucy, Jacqui and Maggie, who daily provide her with the inspiration to be a strong, smart and capable woman: she hopes that she will be always be a positive example for them. Be anything you want to be, girls.

To the staff at Cengage Learning, especially Fiona Hammond, Emily Spurr, Sarah Payne, Natalie Orr and Ronald Chung, who have supported us in this venture 'fifth time around', we say thank you for your patience, helpful encouragement and regular email 'nudges'.

Much of the work in this fifth edition was done during 2020 while people were trying to cope with the COVID-19 pandemic. It was a time when many of us were quickly forced to work, study and stay connected with others online, without being in their physical presence. Thus, we had to find online apps that allowed us to continue to communicate in ways that were meaningful to us. Also, many of us had to become proficient with the new apps used in the online learning environments at our study and work places. We realise that some students and teachers had to use communication tools they didn't – and maybe still don't – particularly like! Whatever is happening in our world as you read this, and whether you are a student or a teacher, we hope our text will help you. This text contains the fundamental tools for a student to communicate in an academic environment. Just like our first edition, it is a 'toolkit', so if you are a student, dive in, rummage around and find whatever you need to help you successfully complete your studies!

The authors and Cengage Learning would also like to thank the following reviewers for their incisive and helpful feedback:

↘ Thomas Sim, Australian Institute of Professional Counsellors

↘ Linda Robyn Stirling, Federation University

↘ Neelu Sharma, University of South Australia

- Kolleen Miller-Rosser, Southern Cross University
- Tanya Weiler, University of South Australia
- Steven Howard, University of Wollongong
- Sharon Leca Elizabeth Stanton, Central Queensland University
- Carol Crevacore, Edith Cowan University
- Karen Felstead, Federation University Australia
- Shelly Abbott, Flinders University
- Michael Gardiner, University of Southern Queensland
- Tanya Weiler, University of South Australia
- Linda Stirling, Federation University
- Rebecca Gilroy, Southern Cross University.

↘ BEFORE YOU READ THIS BOOK

Students, past and present, are the characters in this book. They come from Curtin University in Perth, Western Australia; Open Universities Australia and Miri, Sarawak; Notre Dame University, Fremantle; Edith Cowan University; and the University of Western Australia. They are enrolled in a wide range of courses, including fine arts, design, social sciences, commerce, health sciences, science, law, engineering, nursing, computer science, geology, spatial sciences, architecture, planning, construction management, cultural studies, Australian Indigenous studies, journalism, screen arts and education courses. Most are first-year students, taking a unit that focuses on the learning processes they will need for university study – in research, academic writing, teamwork and oral presentations. These students have provided models for this book, and stories of effective (and not-so-effective) academic practice.

Our experience teaching and coordinating units for such students has played a major part in shaping this book:

↘ We have chosen to write informally throughout the book, addressing you, the current student, directly, and speaking personally about our own experience.

↘ We address both individual students and those working in seminar or workshop groups, and provide activities for both types of student throughout the book.

↘ We also emphasise some of the language processes you will need in your future professional careers in order to communicate successfully with clients, employers and colleagues. You can't start to develop these processes too soon!

↘ The book is applicable to all undergraduate courses at university, particularly to first-year students in these courses. You will be able to apply our advice and models to whatever discipline you are studying.

↘ The book will be useful for any student studying at a tertiary or a secondary level. Developing academic communications is a major educational focus in the 21st century, and the book is our contribution to this.

Although the book focuses on language development, we want to emphasise that education, both tertiary and secondary, is about much more than this. We like this quote from Allan Luke, Professor of Education at Queensland University of Technology, from his public address at the Brisbane Ideas Festival on 30 March 2006:

66 Although they always have and will continue to serve the national economic interest, universities must remain seedbeds for basic intellectual work, for speculative theory and experimental practice. They must perpetually strive to become more open environments where students are encouraged to engage with historical, scientific and narrative knowledge, to debate these matters freely and speculatively, and to apply these understandings to the complex worlds of new economies, new technologies and new cultures. 99

This quote sums up our approach to education. While we focus in this book on helping you develop the processes you will need to be successful students, we believe that these processes are means rather than ends in themselves. If you learn well to think, research, write, reflect, work collaboratively and deliver presentations, then you can benefit from the 'seedbeds' and 'open environments' that are universities, and you can play your part in making them such rich places. We wish you joy in your studies, and hope that this book will enhance them.

Guide to the text

As you read this text you will find a number of features in every chapter to enhance your study of communications and help you understand how the theory is applied in the real world.

CHAPTER-OPENING FEATURES

Identify the key concepts that the chapter will cover with the **Chapter contents** at the start of each chapter.

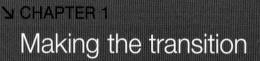

↘ CHAPTER 1
Making the transition

CONTENTS

→ Your first months as a tertiary student
Connecting online
Connecting with peers
Connecting with faculty
The library
Academic learning support
Course and unit/subject outlines
Calendars and study plans
Overview of the semester or study period

FEATURES WITHIN CHAPTERS

Read authentic **Student Reflection** examples of real student communication efforts that illustrate theory in practice. These come from students across a wide range of disciplines.

 Student reflection 1.1   **Participating in Orientation Week is key**

Orientation Week is a key to success! You learn everything during this week especially as a first year, For example, my university takes Academic Integrity very seriously, and so in O-Week, I attended workshops on referencing and made sure to ask questions while I was there. Learn what is offered to you in your faculty. Where do you go for help? Best parking zones? Finding out all these things helps you be less stressed when the teaching week starts – so you don't have to worry about learning about the campus and instead can start learning your new subject. You can focus on one thing at a time!

Kath Nelly, Commerce student

FEATURES WITHIN CHAPTERS

Explore **Examples** of real communication that highlight good practice as well as **Annotated examples** that provide guidance and advice to help you self-evaluate and improve your own communication.

Example 1.1   An inappropriate formal email

> Hey
>
> I just want to know what the physics labs are worth. Coz i missed the last one, coz the car broke down and i came too late to the next one. Just thinking if there's any chance of doing a makeup test or something. Anyhow, why aren't the tests done at the end of the lab rather than at the start. Coz if your late even slightly u'll miss the test. Anyway hope you can assist my query, cheers.
>
> Anthony

Test your understanding as you go via the **Activity boxes** which include questions to help you review, integrate, and comprehend information.

ACTIVITY 2.2   Make a post to your group discussion board

If you are already enrolled in an online unit, navigate to your group discussion board (or relevant collaborative area of the LMS) and make a post introducing yourself.

In your post, you might include:

- Where in the world you are located.
- Why you have chosen to study online.
- Something that you are excited about or looking forward to.
- Something that you are nervous about.

These ideas have not been suggested arbitrarily: sharing this kind of information is beneficial for you and your classmates. Noting where you are broadly located (e.g. in regional Western Australia, Dubai or suburban Auckland) can help your tutor understand

Learn How to identify the most common mistakes and errors students make and how to address or improve on them through the **How to spot and fix tables**.

How to spot and how to fix flowery language

How to spot a flowery thesis statement	How to fix it with a clearer, stronger verb-based sentence
There is a role for technology to continue to be adopted, developed and embraced by teachers in primary school classrooms in the pursuit of allowing teaching and learning to experience enhancement, excitement and being relevant to students.	Primary school teachers must continue to use technology in their teaching in order to enhance their students' learning, excitement and sense of relevance in their studies.
It is an indisputable fact that a part in the development, maintenance and promotion of safety on their construction sites should always be played by construction managers. But nowadays, in this day and age, importance and fundamental emphasis is also placed by them on the daily and perpetual promotion of healthy habits, emotional attitudes, good gender relationships, beneficial	While construction managers have always promoted safety on construction sites, in the 21st century these construction managers must now focus on the mental and physical wellbeing of their workers, which will in turn help create a healthy and equitable society.

FEATURES WITHIN CHAPTERS

Hint boxes in each chapter give you simple tips and suggestions for more effective communication

You get out what you put in!

Your tutors are there to guide and assist you, but they are not mind readers! If you need help with a concept or skills, make sure you ask questions. Put up your (virtual) hand frequently and get involved right from the start. In our experience, students who are active participants on the group discussion boards are usually the ones who are able to achieve their potential. Remember that discussion boards are for interaction between students, too – if you know the answer to a classmate's question, go ahead and reply!

Challenge yourself to:
- be the first to make a post
- respond to at least three other people's posts each week
- share your response to an activity
- give another student feedback, advice, or answer their question.

END-OF-CHAPTER FEATURES

At the end of each chapter you will find several tools to help you to review, practise and extend your knowledge.
- Review your understanding of the key chapter topics with the **Revision Activities**.

REVISION TOOLS

↘ Revision activity: Revise these ideas

1 The first few months of tertiary studies, whether online or on campus, are likely to be disorienting; students need to allow themselves time to become familiar with their new learning environment. All students need to develop healthy study habits relevant to their life situation.

2 Students should first become familiar with their teachers, fellow students and the faculty or department structure in which they are studying.

3 There are many additional resources available to tertiary students, including resources within the LMS at their institution (e.g. Blackboard, Moodle), the library and academic learning support and counselling services.

4 Students find calendars and study plans useful tools for keeping on top of the demands of different parts of the semester.

5 It is important to start work on assignments early as many assignment tasks are complex and require research. Beginning such assignments the week before they are due is likely to mean they cannot be completed for given deadlines.

6 Communication with teachers, coordinators and fellow students must be semi-formal and always respectful.

7 There may be several reasons why students are not doing as well as they would like. It's important for students to quickly recognise when they need help, and for them to take advantage of the many strategies available to

END-OF-CHAPTER FEATURES

- Process and apply content to current issues or personal experience using the critical and reflective **Thinking activities**

↘ Thinking activity: Critical and reflective questions

1 Do I know where to get help at my tertiary institution so I can be successful in my studies? Specifically, do I know where to get help if I ever experience difficulties (for example with mental health, body health or student life generally)?

2 Have I explored the LMS before classes start to ensure I will not miss out on crucial information? Am I confident with my level of digital literacy? If not, have I checked where I can get help?

- Use the **Useful weblinks** to extend your understanding and explore online resources.

↘ Useful weblinks

The University of Western Sydney has basic, introductory resources about navigating the web, discerning good from bad websites and developing and maintaining a digital identity. See the 'Digital literacy' link: **https://www.westernsydney.edu.au/studysmart/home/ digital_literacy**.

The University of Adelaide has a 'Wellbeing Hub' with excellent information for tertiary level students including study tips, mental health and making a successful transition to university. See: **https://www.adelaide.edu.au/student/wellbeing/**

Guide to the online resources

Cengage is pleased to provide you with a selection of resources that will help you prepare your lectures and assessments. These teaching tools are accessible via cengage.com.au/instructors for Australia or cengage.co.nz/instructors for New Zealand.

MINDTAP

Premium online teaching and learning tools are available on the *MindTap* platform - the personalised eLearning solution.

NEW

MindTap is a flexible and easy-to-use platform that helps build student confidence and gives you a clear picture of their progress. We partner with you to ease the transition to digital – we're with you every step of the way.

The *Cengage Mobile App* puts your course directly into students' hands with course materials available on their smartphone or tablet. Students can read on the go, complete practice quizzes or participate in interactive real-time activities.

MindTap for Grellier's *Communication Toolkit 5th edition* is full of innovative resources to support critical thinking, and help your students move from memorisation to mastery! Includes:

• *Communication Toolkit 5th edition* eBook
• Student communication examples
• Communication templates and checklists
• Communication activities

MindTap is a premium purchasable eLearning tool. Contact your Cengage learning consultant to find out how MindTap can transform your course.eLearning tool. Contact your Cengage learning consultant to find out how *MindTap* can transform your course.

⁙ CENGAGE | MINDTAP

INSTRUCTOR'S GUIDE

The **Instructor's Guide** is packed with content that helps you set up and administer your class: Chapter essential points, activities and suggested responses and more.

COGNERO® TEST BANK

A bank of questions has been developed in conjunction with the text for creating quizzes, tests and exams for your students. Create multiple test versions in an instant and deliver tests from your LMS, your classroom, or wherever you want using **Cognero Test Bank**.

POWERPOINT™ PRESENTATIONS

Use the chapter-by-chapter **PowerPoint slides** to enhance your lecture presentations and handouts by reinforcing the key principles of your subject.

ARTWORK FROM THE TEXT

Add the digital files of graphs, tables, pictures and flow charts into your course management system, use them in student handouts, or copy them into your lecture presentations.

FOR THE STUDENT

MINDTAP

Premium online teaching and learning tools are available on the *MindTap* *MindTap* is the next-level online learning tool that helps you get better grades! *MindTap* gives you the resources you need to study – all in one place and available when you need them. In the *MindTap Reader*, you can make notes, highlight text and even find a definition directly from the page.

If your instructor has chosen *MindTap* for your subject this semester, log in to *MindTap* to:

- Get better grades
- Save time and get organised
- Connect with your instructor and peers
- Study when and where you want, online and mobile
- Complete assessment tasks as set by your instructor
  When your instructor creates a course using MindTap, they will let you know your course link so you can access the content. Please purchase MindTap only when directed by your instructor.
  Course length is set by your instructor.

PART ONE

TRANSITIONING TO TERTIARY STUDIES

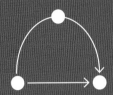

Kaya! Hello from Jane, Veronica and Katie, who have written this text for you from where we live in Noongar Country. 'Kaya' is a word that means a combination of 'hello' and 'yes'. It is a happy greeting in the language of the Whadjuk Noongar, who are the original custodians of the area that now includes Perth, Western Australia. Wherever you are in the world as you read this, dive into our toolkit and scan the chapters to find what you need to be a successful student.

Over the past few decades, the digital revolution has caused disruption in how tertiary institutions create and deliver education. These institutions have been working hard to transform how they help you learn skills to enhance how innovative, entrepreneurial and collaborative you will be when you graduate. In fact, your university or college is actively a part of this 'profound social and economic transformation that has been catalysed by breathtaking advances in automation and artificial intelligence, and unprecedented access to data and computation' (Jahanian, 2020).

Every tertiary institution is committed to helping you stay and succeed in whatever you have chosen to study with them, and so they make big investments to help you have a smooth transition. They have noted, as Professor Sally Kift stated, 'it is clear that first year students face unique challenges as they make very individual transitions to study; particularly academically and socially, but also culturally, administratively and environmentally' (2015, 53). In Australia, the Tertiary Education Quality and Standards Agency (TEQSA) monitors the standards of these higher education institutions to ensure you receive a quality learning experience. The first few chapters of our text should help you get off to a good start.

Part 1 will be useful if you are beginning your higher education studies – whether you are a recent school-leaver or are returning to study after doing other things. Many of you will make a smooth transition to tertiary studies, adapting to new expectations and approaches to learning; some of you, however, will experience challenges. You may have difficulties organising yourself, adjusting to the course you have chosen or developing the particular communication skills required for success at this level.

You may be an older student (i.e. who has not come straight from school) who hasn't done extended writing for 20 years and may feel overwhelmed by the apparent expectations around digital literacy. Or you might be a student who is very confident with mathematics, but not so sure of your oral-presentation skills. You may even be the first person in your family to enrol in higher education. Whoever you are, this section contains hints that will be useful for you.

Part 1 has two chapters. The first introduces you to some key aspects of life in higher education, while the second outlines some reading, note-making and exam-preparation skills that you may find beneficial. If you already feel confident in both of these areas, go straight to Part 2.

→ **Chapter 1:**   Making the transition

→ **Chapter 2:**   Online learning

Making the transition

CONTENTS

> ❝ Surviving university is actually a great experience! Nearing to the end of my degree, I now realise and value the time and effort I put in since first-year. I got through uni by setting little goals for myself each semester regarding achievement of learning outcomes and assignments. It's important to remember that you are responsible for your own learning. Draw upon what motivates you to complete tasks – think of your life in a bigger picture. ❞
>
> *Rebecca Chang, Health Sciences student*

Your first months as a tertiary student

Whether you are a recent school-leaver or someone returning to study after a break of several years, and whether you have chosen to study mostly by attending classes on a physical campus or completely online, it is important that you develop a toolkit of strategies to help you survive – and, indeed, thrive – as a tertiary student. So, before you get into the chapters on communication skills, read through this chapter for some ideas you may find useful during those first months of study.

Connecting online

Your first task is to find your way around your institution's *learning management system* (or LMS), such as Blackboard, Moodle or Canvas. Even if you are someone who is very confident in the online environment, make time to explore the LMS at the institution where you are now studying to see how your lecturers have used it for their subjects. If this way of working is completely new to you, look for help either on campus or online, attend sessions organised by the library and ask other students for help.

Another reason for becoming familiar with, and regularly using, your institution's LMS is that this is likely to be the place where you will submit your assessments. Even if you do not submit all your assessments through the LMS, the assessment marking requirements are likely to be outlined and recorded in the LMS.

We have included some points to help you – especially if you are someone who is studying only online:

- Read the 'welcome packs', introductory information and study guides, and then re-read them. View any introductory videos provided by your lecturers.
- Check all the links in your unit website so that you become familiar with how the unit is set up.
- Search for your unit outline or calendar to find all the due dates for assignments. (Download it, and consider printing a copy for your study desk.)
- If your unit includes a discussion board or other means of communicating with your tutor and fellow students, introduce yourself in that forum as soon as you can. We find that those students who put off doing this task for several weeks often feel awkward 'arriving late', and so have more challenges participating.
- You will know best how to organise yourself. There is plenty of advice online about how to ensure you organise your life appropriately, but only you know what will work for you.

See Chapter 2 for more detailed information, but to start with, here are some helpful websites to guide you as you study online:

- Online Study Australia – 'How to Succeed in Online Courses (18 Tips)': **https://onlinestudyaustralia.com/courses/how-succeed-tips**
- TAFE Queensland – 'Eight Tips to Prepare You for Online Study': **https://tafeqld.edu.au/news-events/news-blogs/2018/eight-tips-for-online-study.html**
- Northeastern University – 'Tips for Taking Online Classes: Eight Strategies for Success': **https://www.northeastern.edu/graduate/blog/tips-for-taking-online-classes**

Our last piece of advice should possibly have come at the beginning; but, after thinking through some of the points above, you may now be in a better position to receive it. Think again about your commitment to online study and, more importantly, about how much you will be able to undertake. Studying online is not a method of 'rushing through' a course while applying less effort than in face-to-face learning. In fact, it can sometimes be more time-consuming than on-campus study, and it can be more difficult to maintain your commitment to study when you are working physically alone. Its value is that it usually allows you to be flexible in time and space; but it will still make large demands on your time.

If you are someone who prefers to study on campus and are now studying online only, take care not to overload yourself with many units. Take your time, be patient with yourself and focus on developing good online study habits.

Connecting with peers

Once you have joined a class, whether you are studying online or on a campus, and whether you prefer working alone or with others, the first thing we advise you to do is to connect with people and hopefully make new friends. Connecting with people should be easier in the first few weeks, since your lecturer(s) will set up a number of activities that encourage you to introduce yourself. Take any such opportunities to get to know other students.

Do not rely solely on personal social media spaces, but quickly access the online meeting platforms provided within your courses and become an active participant on them as soon as possible. This will enable you not only to get to know your peers but also to see who you might prefer to work with (i.e. on future group assignments). Whether or not you get involved in extracurricular activities, these online spaces allow you to easily and naturally make links with peers within your course. In your course, you will meet people who have chosen the same subjects as you, and with whom you therefore already have something in common. Also, make use of opportunities to work in groups (see Chapter 15 for specific advice on this), since this can help you make friends more quickly, and thus you will feel supported as you study. Whatever you do, keep looking for ways to meet and connect with other students. You will note we repeat this advice throughout the text – often using quotes from our student contributors!

Connecting with faculty

Get to know your faculty or discipline area as soon as you can. You will need to know the answers to these questions:

- Who are my lecturers and how do I contact them?
- Where is the main office for my faculty or department?
- Where is the key information about my course located on the website and in the LMS? (This includes the contact details for whomever is responsible for my course if I cannot contact my lecturer, as these may be different people.)
- How do I submit assignments?
- Does my area have a special room or online space for first-year students or students studying my course?

Even if you are a student who has been studying for a while, if you don't yet know the answers to these questions, don't be afraid to go now and find the answers. After all, you're likely to be studying within the same area for at least three years, so this information is still very useful.

The library

More than ever before, higher education libraries – including their websites – are the places to go to learn all you need to know about succeeding in tertiary environments. As a tertiary student, you will need to use more than just general websites for your research; lecturers will generally expect you to use a range of sources, including discipline-specific e-journals, which can often only be accessed via the library. Don't forget to communicate with the librarians themselves, because they are usually at the forefront of digital technology, making them invaluable when you are conducting secondary research at this level. (See Chapter 3 for further details.) Whatever resources are available at your institution's library, access and use them.

Thus, as soon as you are enrolled, whether you're studying on campus or online, you should do a tour of your library's website so that you will know what your library can offer you.

Academic learning support

If you would like some extra support or you are having difficulties with any aspects of your studies, the best place to go for help, in the first instance, is your institution's website. Most, if not all, tertiary institutions have clear links from their homepage to such support. These websites are 'one-stop shops' for students, and we encourage you to explore them as soon as you can so you know what your institution can offer you.

In addition to online support, every university or college will have places where students can go to get free assistance with their studies. This may include help with essay writing, academic study skills seminars and help with developing English-language proficiency for academic purposes. Explore what is available now so that if you need some help one day, you will know where to get it. As noted, most tertiary institutions house this information 'one click away' from the homepage, such as at Swinburne University (**https://www.swinburne.edu.au/life-at-swinburne/ student-support-services/study-learning-support**) and at Queensland University of Technology (see the 'QUT cite/write' link at **https://www. citewrite.qut.edu.au**). If you're having problems, especially in areas such as organising your life or writing your assignments, go and ask for help. It is there!

If you are an Australian Aboriginal or Torres Strait Islander student – and especially if you are from a remote community – you may choose to seek out the areas of your campus that are especially for Indigenous Australian students. Search the website and you will find information such as Nura Gili at the University of New South Wales (see **https://student.unsw.edu. au/additional-support**).

Whoever you are, you should find out what your institution can offer you.

Course and unit/subject outlines

The way in which programs and parts of programs are named differs across tertiary institutions. In this book, we will use the word 'course' to describe a full program lasting three or more years (e.g. Medical Imaging, Psychology) and 'unit' or 'subject' for one subject within that course, lasting a semester or perhaps a year.

Read your course and unit outlines as soon as you receive them. The unit outline contains essential information about the unit, such as learning outcomes, assessment details and the topics for each class. Make time to check every outline carefully – especially before you start assignments – because your success will depend on knowing exactly what you are required to do.

Calendars and study plans

Use an online calendar to organise how and when you will study. Create a study plan as soon as possible, and refer to the official *academic calendar* (available through the website of your place of study) as you do this. You can then make a weekly study plan, as well as a semester study plan.

Set up calendar alerts to remind you of key dates. Place all your deadlines in your calendar, as well as weekly times to prepare for classes and then to review after each class. Set aside time in Week 3 or 4 of semester to reassess your study plan to see if it is realistic, and reorganise if you need to.

Check your study timetable and work commitments, as well as the demands of 'the rest' of your life, and get organised about how you want to live it. If you don't have a plan, you will be more likely to fall behind in your work and get stressed. Making your plan public, at least to the important people in your life, is also a good idea, so that they will support you rather than sabotage your plans.

The key dates in your study plan will be the assessment due dates. It is likely that several assessments will be due around the same time, but you are expected to start working on them well in advance. You won't be able to complete them all in the week they're due. Even if you were a person who could start and finish an assignment in one night at secondary school, you will not be able to do this with tertiary-level studies.

When you prepare your study plan in the first week of semester, indicate the blocks of time that you will spend on each assignment. If the assignments are all due in Week 12, setting aside only Week 11 to work on them is highly risky. Here are some more tips to help you:

- Talk to your peers about how they organise their homework and study time (but ignore people who say they don't do any work and 'wing it' the night before). See the section later in this chapter about the value of study groups.
- If you need to submit a hard copy of your assignment, don't leave the printing until 'the night before'. There may be problems (e.g. a printer breaking down) so organise your printing well in advance of the due date.
- If everything gets too much and you are behind on an assignment, speak to the relevant lecturer (in person, by email or other method of communication they have instructed you to use) as soon as possible. If possible, it's a good idea to indicate what you have completed so far and how much more you plan to do.
- You may need a short extension on the submission date. Remember that you usually need to apply for this *before* the assignment is due. Check your unit outline for the rules about extensions. Some students leave it until it's too late to apply for an extension, and then they might have marks deducted for making a late submission.
- Another option is to use your institution's academic learning support services or visit its counselling service. Counsellors are not just there to assist you when life is difficult; they are there for students who simply get tired, stressed or disorganised. So, don't forget to check out the relevant information on your institution's website.

Whatever you decide to do, *do something*. Your lecturers can't read your mind and, even if you don't believe you have a valid excuse, if you are not coping and are having difficulty meeting an assessment deadline, speak to someone about it.

Overview of the semester or study period

Though all institutions and courses vary in how and when they conduct their first year, they all follow similar processes. The following sections provide a summary of what is likely to happen during your first semester or study period.

Orientation Week

For most tertiary institutions, Orientation Week (or 'O Week') is the time when students are introduced to their study environment and, more specifically, to their course. You will be introduced to key staff members, receive information about your course and be expected to familiarise yourself with the campus or online environment. You will confirm your class timetable, check course and unit/subject information online, explore on-campus (or online) classrooms and create a study plan.

It's normal to experience information overload during this time. However, you'll soon start to feel familiar and more at ease.

Student reflection 1.1 **Participating in Orientation Week is key**

Orientation Week is a key to success! You learn everything during this week especially as a first year. For example, my university takes Academic Integrity very seriously, and so in O Week, I attended workshops on referencing and made sure to ask questions while I was there. Learn what is offered to you in your faculty. Where do you go for help? Best parking zones? Finding out all these things helps you be less stressed when the teaching week starts – so you don't have to worry about learning about the campus and instead can start learning your new subject. You can focus on one thing at a time!

Kathleen Nelly, Commerce student

Early weeks of semester

The first two to three weeks of a course will often seem easy, since little may be expected of you and you will be given plenty of information (often too much!). This will include information about assessment requirements.

Hint from a recent graduate

'Completing assignments and fulfilling the obligations of your degree well before the due dates will grant you the gift of ultimate freedom to experience the joys of university, like friends, partying, sports and other events, to their fullest potential.'

Hursh Dodhia-Shah, Bachelor of Commerce graduate

The last day for *enrolling* in a new unit/subject to your course is usually within the first week of semester. You may be overwhelmed with expectations and information, but if you are starting to feel unsure about your current course and you think you may want to study something else, get advice now before the deadline.

The last day for *withdrawing* from a unit/subject without paying fees often occurs within the first weeks of semester. If you are not sure whether you want to study all the subjects you are enrolled in, get advice before this payment deadline. You may need to withdraw from one unit or get help to create a viable study plan.

If you're having problems understanding the assessments in your course, ask lecturers for help and use websites such as those named throughout this chapter.

Tuition-free weeks

Throughout the academic year, every institution will have breaks from course delivery – but not from learning. During these tuition-free weeks, use your time away from class contact wisely by catching up on assessments and study notes.

Lecturers will be available during these periods, but their contact times may be more restricted than in other weeks, so check their availability in advance.

Later weeks of semester

In the final weeks of a study period, course delivery continues and more assessments are due. You should work consistently on assignments during this time. Remember that, although major assignments are often due late in the semester, you should start working on them early so that you won't feel overwhelmed in the last weeks.

Maintain your class attendance and regular study. Contact with your peers and lecturer is invaluable to your learning experience, so make a consistent effort to attend classes.

Lecturers often give advice about exams in the last weeks of a course, so you can't afford to miss these classes! (In our experience, students sometimes fail exams because they don't know the exam requirements, such as materials they need to take into the exam rooms.)

Study Week

In the period between the end of scheduled classes and the start of exams, there is a block of time, often called 'Study Week', during which you will have time to study for your exams.

Lecturers are available for help during this time. Contact them if you're feeling desperate or if you need to clarify any last-minute issues.

Examination weeks

It's your responsibility to check when and where your exams are to be held. Be careful to check the final timetable on your institution's website. Don't rely on the draft timetable, as details can change.

If you cannot attend an exam because of illness or another major crisis, contact your lecturer or your institution's counselling services *before* the exam. They will help you resolve your issue.

If you have attended an exam but have major concerns about your performance (e.g. your car broke down on the way and you missed half the exam or you had a migraine and could not complete the paper), communicate with your lecturer or your institution's counselling services *immediately after* the exam. Don't wait until you receive your results.

Class formats – virtual and physical

The delivery format of your classes may vary widely: from online classes in a standard LMS or via a meeting application (e.g. Zoom), to an on-campus seminar with desks and chairs, to an augmented-reality learning experience outdoors. Below, we provide explanations for learning experiences given within these delivery formats, but note that these may be different from what your institution uses:

- In *lectures*, a lecturer presents information to a mass audience of students. See Chapter 4 for information about how to take notes in lectures.
- *Tutorials* support lectures. In them, small groups of students get together with tutors to discuss the ideas presented in lectures and in set readings. During the semester, students often complete a tutorial presentation of some kind – generally, a formal oral presentation, sometimes with an accompanying tutorial paper.
- *Seminars* stand alone, rather than supporting a lecture. They can be of any size, but are generally small enough to allow students to interact with each other. They are likely to involve informal group activities, and students may be required to complete readings or other activities before they attend class.
- In *workshops*, *studios* and *laboratories*, students complete particular activities (e.g. scientific experiments, filmmaking, painting, writing tasks, architectural drawing, computer programming) with the support of professionals from their discipline. Unless the classroom is locked (or timed, as for a synchronous online session), enter, sit and wait for the tutor. Once the class begins, behave respectfully and in the same way you would if you were sharing a space with any group. If you are using digital devices (e.g. tablets or smartphones) to participate in the class,

be careful how you position the camera lens; unless advised otherwise, if you wish to record a class, you must always check with the lecturer first, since there may be privacy concerns. If you are in an on-campus class and not using your device, make sure you have it in silent mode.

Is your class 'flipped'?

Many classes – whether they are lectures, tutorials or seminars – are taught in what some call a 'flipped' classroom mode, where the expectation is on you, the student, to complete specific activities (e.g. watch a video) before the class. In 'flipped' classrooms, activities are interactive and built on the premise that these pre-class activities have been done, so arriving prepared is vital for learning.

Study groups

As already stated, even if you have always preferred to work alone, you shouldn't underestimate the importance of making connections with other students. Research has shown that students who do this are more likely to 'hang in there' and complete their course than those who work alone.

Get to know others in your course as soon as possible, and schedule a regular time to meet with them. The aim is to create a group where you can freely discuss your course and student life more broadly outside of class time. An online discussion space, such as a Facebook group, may already exist for your course, and there may also be a study room on campus especially for your faculty. If these resources exist, use them to help you get started on the road to becoming a successful tertiary student. (For more ideas about how to use a study group effectively, see the 'Using Study Groups' webpage at **http://www.educationcorner.com/study-groups.html**.)

Respecting diversity

Consider for a moment the fact that you and other students in your classes all have different backgrounds, as well as different expectations of what student life in a tertiary institution could – or should – be like. There is no *one* right way to be a successful higher education student. However, all students deserve the same respect from their peers and from higher education staff members.

A basic organising principle of Australian higher education campuses is that all people deserve respect, equal rights and opportunities. Look, for example, at this excerpt explaining how to relate to others, which is connected to one of Curtin University's (2020) core values – respect:

❝ At Curtin, relating to others involves demonstrating respect. Respect includes accepting that people are different, with different ideas and opinions, and that they are as entitled to have their views heard as you are. Respecting others means acknowledging their views and refraining from actions which may insult, devalue or degrade them. Respecting yourself means appropriately expressing your own views and opinions, and refraining from unworthy conduct. 99

If there is a right place to discuss any imaginable subject, it's within a tertiary education environment. So, go for it! Freely debate and explore all sorts of issues and views, but always behave with deep respect for each other.

Mature-aged students

Many students go directly from high school to further studies; however, in this section we are referring to those of you who have been away from study long enough to question whether or not you 'have what it takes' to succeed at university. If you are in this category, you may experience some of the following issues as you adapt to university study:

- You are 'out of practice' at being a student.
- You lack confidence in your ability to study successfully because you haven't demonstrated it recently.
- You have a limited knowledge of technology, the Internet and databases.
- You have many demands on your time outside university – you may have children or older parents who need attention, or be in full-time employment.

Some courses attract many mature-aged students, and at some tertiary institutions there are more mature-aged students than school-leavers. If you are such a student, our experience shows you are likely to be more focused and organised in your studies than younger students. However, if you have been away from formal study for a number of years, starting a higher education degree can be rather daunting. Be realistic, and consider carefully how many units you should study. If you take on too much, get advice as soon as you can about the possibility of reducing your study load.

It is very important for you to regularly communicate with fellow students who can help you develop your confidence and your sense of being a student, as well as give you perspectives on how other students are working. Some of our mature-aged students, for example, start by working unnecessarily long hours on their assignments because they don't have a good sense of what is required. An informal chat over coffee or online can help you gain perspective on what others are doing.

Life can be more complex for mature-aged students, and for this reason, most tertiary institutions offer special services for them, from free assistance about how to use technology to childcare support. The different needs of mature-aged students are commonly acknowledged, so if you are one, check out what your place of study offers you.

English-language proficiency

In Australia, most tertiary courses are taught in English, and, even if you are very clever, you will need to have a good level of proficiency in academic English to succeed in them. Australian tertiary institutions have staff members and resources to help students develop their English-language proficiency. If you are a student who struggles with writing, speaking or reading English, and/or if Australian Standard English is an additional language for you, make sure you know where you can get that support. Most places offer support in the form of group workshops and individual consultations as well as downloadable practical writing resources (see, for example, the University of New South Wales: **https://student.unsw. edu.au/skills**). Some tertiary institutions give you the opportunity to get an indication of whether you need help with your English-language skills through post-entry assessments, such as the University of Melbourne's Diagnostic English Language Assessment (DELA) (see **https://students. unimelb.edu.au/academic-skills/english-language-development**).

New international students

If you are new to studying at an Australian tertiary institution, note that there will be many resources specifically designed to support you, and you should make time to explore these as soon as you can. Adjusting to a new culture, and maybe even a different way of learning, can be challenging, so take advantage of the help available. The Australian Government's 'Study Australia' website is a good place to start (see **https://www. studyinaustralia.gov.au**). The place you have chosen to study at will also help you; one example is the University of Adelaide's 'International Students' page (see **https://international.adelaide.edu.au**).

Communicating with tertiary staff

The first thing you may notice about your contact with higher education staff members is that it may appear casual. Teaching, research and administration staff members will probably be happy to be addressed by their first names, and to communicate with you in informal conversation. However, do not let this lull you into becoming overfamiliar or too informal in all your communications with them. Your lecturers will tell you how they prefer you to communicate with them – for example, by email, during synchronous chat times, after classes or during set consultation times. If you are unsure about their preferences, ask them. When in an email dialogue with a lecturer regarding one issue, do not delete the previous emails from the current email you are sending. Also, if you are emailing two or more lecturers with the same question, cc (i.e. copy) them in on the same email rather than sending them separate emails. This will save both people from answering the question when you only require one response.

Example 1.1 is an example of an email from a student to the head of the Physics department. Not only is it too informal – almost impolite – in both its word choices and tone, it also uses terms you would use in a casual text message to a friend, and which are inappropriate in a formal email message.

Example 1.1   An inappropriate formal email

> Hey
>
> I just want to know what the physics labs are worth. Coz i missed the last one, coz the car broke down and i came too late to the next one. Just thinking if there's any chance of doing a makeup test or something. Anyhow, why aren't the tests done at the end of the lab rather than at the start. Coz if your late even slightly u'll miss the test. Anyway hope you can assist my query, cheers.
>
> Anthony

If an email is your first communication with a staff member, it should look more like Example 1.2.

Example 1.2   An appropriate formal email

> SUBJECT: Physics 100 laboratory – classes missed (Anthony Lee, Physics 100: Tutorial Group 6)
>
> Dear Professor Scott,
>
> I apologise for missing the last two Physics labs – I had unavoidable transport problems on both days. As I have now missed one of the in-class tests, can you please advise if there is an opportunity for me to do a makeup test or another replacement assignment to make up for any marks I may have lost?
>
> If you would prefer me to make a time to meet with you to discuss this matter (either online or in your office), please let me know how you would prefer me to contact you.
>
> Kind regards,
> Anthony Lee
> (Physics 100: Tutorial Group 6. Student ID #12345)

Some higher education staff members allow students to communicate with them via text message to either their mobiles or email addresses. If you text rather than use voice messages or emails, remember to keep a formal tone and be restrained in your use of abbreviations. Even if you have given your mobile number to your lecturer, don't assume they have a record of it or of your name. Always sign off with your name and student details to help the lecturer identify you (see Example 1.3).

Example 1.3 An appropriate text message

Sorry, not submitting essay today as I'm sick. Will email ASAP. James Brown, 321432X, Physio 230; Group 3A.

Once you have established a rapport with your lecturers (e.g. exchanged a few emails or phone calls), you can take their cues as to how to continue future correspondence. If they start writing 'Hi [student]' as a salutation, you too could do the same. However, remember the basic principle of all good communication: always consider the audience, purpose and context. If you are unsure, note that when communicating with staff members, it is better to be overly formal and polite than too casual.

Finally, if you are given a student email address, use this instead of your private email address – and get into the habit of checking your student account regularly, since your lecturers might use it to pass on important last-minute messages.

Formal emails

Unless you are emailing friends or people with whom you have already established a rapport, consider these basic emailing rules before you hit the 'Send' button:

- Write a brief but informative word or phrase in the subject box.
- Include a greeting such as 'Dear ...', 'Good morning/good afternoon ...' (most formal) or 'Hi ...', 'Hello ...' (commonly used, especially once you have established some rapport).
- Use plain English. Aim to use short sentences and short paragraphs.
- Check that you have said what you want to say and that there is nothing ambiguous. Be succinct, but include any relevant, important information.
- Maintain a polite and appropriate tone. Consider your audience. Even if you are annoyed about something, be restrained in what you write. Remember that emails can be used in a court of law. If you've written an email while feeling emotional, do not send it immediately; instead, check it again at a later time and ask a wise friend to check it also, before you send it.
- If you need a response to a question, make your request clear.
- Remember to include your name (and, usually, your student number, class group and the unit you are enrolled in) when you sign off.
- Check what you have written and edit spelling or grammatical mistakes.
- Don't assume your lecturers can check their emails immediately. In particular, don't expect instant responses to last-minute assignment enquiries on weekends.

Challenges you might face

Becoming a successful tertiary student is hard work, and we acknowledge that life can be complex. In the following sections, we offer our advice about some common challenges.

Dissatisfaction with assessment results

You will have assessment guides and marking criteria before you start each assignment, so when you get your results and any feedback, these should be self-explanatory. If, however, you don't understand the feedback, discuss this with the lecturer concerned. It is often useful to first go away and examine the feedback carefully before meeting. However, be mindful of any institutional deadlines in case you then want to question your results and make a formal appeal. Some first-year students can be shocked when they do not immediately achieve the high marks they received in secondary school; for example, in a tertiary assignment 60 per cent is often considered a satisfactory result. However, all students have the right to question their results, so check your institution's website to see how the appeal process works, and respectfully take action if you feel you want further explanation of a mark.

Falling behind in your studies

If you start to fall behind in your class preparation or starting your assignments, don't ignore the problem. Everyone knows that study is only one part of your life. However, your lecturers assume it is a very important part of your life and expect you to submit assessments on or before the due dates. You need to find the best way to blend all the parts of your life into one healthy mix so that you can meet all the course requirements.

Every year, some of our students find that their lives don't go as smoothly as they'd planned – for example, they may have to change their accommodation unexpectedly or become unwell. Often, these students don't communicate quickly with their first-year coordinators to get help to potentially modify their enrolment or restructure their course. If you don't know who your first-year coordinator is, ask the staff members in the main office of your faculty and they can direct you to the best person.

Even if you're very busy, try to find time to interact with your fellow students outside of your classes. If you find you have no time to do this, you are probably overloading yourself and you should reduce your study load by withdrawing from a unit. You should be able to complete it later. Dropping a unit can be a good strategy for getting better marks, while at the same time keeping the rest of your life (and your family's lives) calm and content. Remember to check the unit outlines and notices in your student portal for information about 'census dates' and 'last days for withdrawal without penalty' before you do any of this.

The course is too difficult or your motivation is low

You may gain entry into the degree of your choice, then find it is too difficult or that your motivation is plummeting, and begin to wonder if you're going to cope. During the semester, pay attention to any serious doubts you have, and don't wait until the end of semester to get help.

If you're finding your course difficult or you feel like you are studying the wrong course, there are several things you can do:

- Withdraw from one or two units and study part-time for a while to give yourself a better chance to succeed in the remaining units.
- Remain enrolled in all your units, but immediately get some academic support to manage them.
- If you want to change courses, organise to do this as soon as possible. Talk to the undergraduate coordinator of the course you are keen to enrol in, and discuss with them how you can best salvage something from the current semester. You may get credit in a new course for some units you are currently studying.
- Whatever you are experiencing, do not ignore how you are feeling. Speak to peers and other significant people in your life, make an appointment with a counsellor and speak to the course coordinator. Tertiary study is not meant to be done alone, and, no matter how trivial you think your problem is, just remember that if you do nothing, not only will you still have the problem, but you may end up wasting money.
- An Australian study found the key reason for students' ongoing persistence in their studies is that the students who 'hang in there' past first year are those who have life goals (Kinnear et al., 2008). Simply put, you need to have long-term – not just short-term – goals for why you are studying in higher education. These goals are likely to change over the years, and they could be very different to your friends' goals, but you need to have them. If you don't have one or two stated goals, you will find it difficult to stay motivated whenever a subject gets a little boring or difficult. So, if you have not yet articulated your long-term goals, set aside some time (perhaps with a friend) and do this now. It will not only help you survive your first year but also keep you going until the end of your degree.

As already stated, the best place to start looking for help is your institution's website, often within a section of the website especially designated for current students. Also remember to check the 'Useful weblinks' list at the end of this chapter.

REVISION TOOLS

↘ Revision activity: Revise these ideas

1 The first few months of tertiary studies, whether online or on campus, are likely to be disorienting; students need to allow themselves time to become familiar with their new learning environment. All students need to develop healthy study habits relevant to their life situation.

2 Students should first become familiar with their teachers, fellow students and the faculty or department structure in which they are studying.

3 There are many additional resources available to tertiary students, including resources within the LMS at their institution (e.g. Blackboard, Moodle), the library and academic learning support and counselling services.

4 Students find calendars and study plans useful tools for keeping on top of the demands of different parts of the semester.

5 It is important to start work on assignments early as many assignment tasks are complex and require research. Beginning such assignments the week before they are due is likely to mean they cannot be completed for given deadlines.

6 Communication with teachers, coordinators and fellow students must be semi-formal and always respectful.

7 There may be several reasons why students are not doing as well as they would like. It's important for students to quickly recognise when they need help, and for them to take advantage of the many strategies available to respond to any problems.

↘ Thinking activity: Critical and reflective questions

1 Do I know where to get help at my tertiary institution so I can be successful in my studies? Specifically, do I know where to get help if I ever experience difficulties (e.g. with mental health, body health or student life generally)?

2 Have I explored the LMS before classes start to ensure I will not miss out on crucial information? Am I confident with my level of digital literacy? If not, have I checked where I can get help?

3 Am I confident with my academic English-language skills? If not, do I know where to get support for improving these skills?

↘ Useful weblinks

The University of Western Sydney has basic, introductory resources about navigating the web, discerning good from bad websites and developing and maintaining a digital identity. See the 'Digital literacy' link: **https://www.westernsydney.edu.au/studysmart/home/digital_literacy**.

The University of Adelaide has a 'Wellbeing Hub' with excellent information for tertiary level students including study tips, and information on mental health and making a successful transition to university. See **https://www.adelaide.edu.au/student/wellbeing**.

'The Good Universities Guide' is the official, up-to-date, government-funded website for everything you need to know about Australian higher education – from course selection to student support. See **https://www.gooduniversitiesguide.com.au**.

The University of Sydney has '10 Tips for First-Year Students' where they quote their students and confirm what we have said, but also add some extra ideas you may enjoy reading. See **https://sydney.edu.au/campus-life/student-news/2016/12/15/top-10-tips-for-first-year-students.html**.

Go to the 'New students' link in the sidebar of this University of Western Australia webpage, where you can learn about mentoring and find special information for your family and friends: **http://www.student.uwa.edu.au**.

Rachel Catherine's YouTube video entitled *Things I Wish I Knew before Starting University* has some practical tips from a young student's lived experience of surviving those early days on campus. See **https://www.youtube.com/watch?v=G23b1ITM7aM**.

Access helpful resources (some of them downloadable) from the 'Support and development' tab on the University of New South Wales's 'Current Students' webpage: **https://student.unsw.edu.au/support**.

For more ideas on how to set up a good study group, go to the 'Education Corner' website, an American resource for collating education website-based information: **https://www.educationcorner.com/study-groups.html**.

REFERENCES

Curtin University. 2020. 'Curtin Values.' **https://about.curtin.edu.au/who/vision-mission-values/curtin-values**.

Jahanian, Farnam. 2020. 'How Higher Education Can Adapt to the Future of Work.' **https://www.weforum.org/agenda/2020/01/how-can-higher-education-adapt-to-a-constantly-evolving-future-of-work**.

Kift, Sally. 2015. 'A Decade of Transition Pedagogy: A Quantum Leap in Conceptualising the First Year Experience.' *HERDSA Review of Higher Education* 2: 53.

Kinnear, Adrianne, Heather Sparrow, Mary Boyce and Sharon Middleton. 2008. 'Perceptions of Successful Students: Lessons for the First Year Experience.' Paper presented at 11th Pacific Rim First Year in Higher Education Conference. Hobart, Tasmania, 30 July.

CHAPTER 2

Online learning

CONTENTS

Being an online student

One of the biggest changes to education in recent times has been the development of online learning. The increasing accessibility of education has meant that more people are able to avail themselves of learning opportunities that were not so attainable in the past. Improvements to infrastructure, such as the National Broadband Network, and the decreasing costs of hardware and software have meant that education that was once out of reach for many people is becoming something that they can see as a viable possibility. This is to be celebrated!

The number of students choosing to study online has been rising for many years. Reasons for this, some of which might be familiar to you, include:

- Being located in a remote, rural or regional area where it is difficult to access a physical university campus.
- Prohibitive costs and excessive time needed to travel to campus for classes.
- Family obligations, such as caring for children or other family members.
- Work responsibilities and hours, which make attending on-campus classes difficult.
- Physical or mental health issues.
- Being able to enrol in a variety of units without initially having a degree in mind.
- Enjoying the flexibility of learning at your own pace and in your own space.

(Bailey et al. 2015)

The reasons for you choosing to study online will be important in determining the individual strategies you need to implement to succeed in this mode of learning. For example, if you are choosing online study because you are located in a remote or regional area, then you should ensure that you have reliable access to the Internet in your location; if you are studying in this way because you have family obligations that make being in a physical class during 'business hours' inconvenient, then you will need to ensure that you are still able to set aside time for study during the week. This might be at 'antisocial' hours, such as early in the morning or late at night. Later in the chapter you will find some tips from students who have successfully studied online.

Whatever the reason for choosing to study online, you have the same rights and responsibilities as an on-campus student. The specifics of these will be outlined to you in a Student Charter that is particular to your institution. This will include information about the way that you interact and communicate with your fellow classmates and teachers; the expectations surrounding the completion of examinations and the submission of assignments; the penalties that will be applied for late work; the processes for seeking extensions and appealing your marks and grades; and so on. It's important to understand that being an online student does not mean you have any fewer (or more) responsibilities than someone studying on a campus in person. When you begin studying online, you should familiarise yourself with the Student Charter of your institution. If you are studying through an institution such as Open Universities Australia, you may even find that you are actually taking units from a variety of physical universities – in this case, you'll need to look at the Student Charter from each one.

ACTIVITY 2.1 Before you begin . . .

Before going further in this chapter, complete this self-assessment. You might be surprised at some of the factors you should be considering before embarking upon online study. If you mark any of them as 'no', be sure to focus on them (there are chapters in this book to help you!) to ensure you are set up for success.

	Do I have ...	✓ or ☒
Resources	a quiet place to work where I won't be distracted?	
	a physical space for studying? (desk, chair and so on)	
	a computer I can access whenever I need it?	
	a reliable Internet connection?	
Time	at least 10 hours each week to devote to *each* unit I enrol in?	
	regular time outside of my work, family, social and personal commitments that can be devoted to study?	
Prior knowledge	an understanding of how to use a word processing program, email and web browsers without assistance?	
	strong academic English-language skills?	
Support networks	family/friends who know I'm studying and support my decision?	
	people to call on when I need reassurance or to 'talk things out'?	
Personal	motivation to study on my own, without being in a classroom?	
	confidence to ask for help when I need it?	
	self-discipline to manage my time effectively?	

Forms of online study

If you are a student who is returning to study after many years away, you might remember a time when 'correspondence courses' were commonly available. These courses involved enrolling in a course and being provided with hard-copy materials to be worked through, and assignments would be sent between you and your assessors through the post. These courses allowed students to access education where it would otherwise be unavailable to them, and to progress through their coursework at their own pace, often without set deadlines. While there are still some courses run in similar ways, such as some TAFE certificate courses, this method of study has largely given way to the modern delivery modes outlined in Table 2.1.

Table 2.1   **Delivery modes of online courses**

How will I…		Delivery mode		
		Asynchronous	Synchronous	Massive Open Online Courses (MOOCs)
	Learn content?	Lectures delivered live and recorded for those who cannot attend, or pre-recorded. May use study guides to deliver content rather than weekly lectures, or a combination of both.	Lectures delivered live at a specific time.	Lectures usually pre-recorded. May use study guides.
	Interact with tutors and peers?	Discussion boards, email.	'Chat rooms' or live collaborative sessions.	Discussion boards, email. There may not be regular interaction with a specific tutor.
	Attend?	Not required to be in a particular place at a specific time. Content will be worked through when it suits your schedule each week. Unit material will be scheduled over the study period or semester.	Students expected to be in their online classroom at a specific time, just as they would on campus.	Not required to be in a particular place at a specific time. Content will be worked through when it suits your schedule. Some MOOCs run for set study periods while others have material that can be accessed at any time.

Asynchronous study modes are sometimes known as 'learn at your own pace' courses. However, it's important to understand that this doesn't mean you are able to dip in and out as you please. Usually these units will still have specific deadlines and requirements to participate that you need to abide by. The 'at your own pace' label really means that you can be studying at any time of the day or night, at any time during the week, and that you can work through the materials as suits your schedule rather than having to be in a classroom at a specific time on a specific day.

It is common to find units that take a blended approach to delivery, with some of the lectures or workshops being synchronous and the rest of the work being done asynchronously. You should check your unit materials carefully to determine whether or not you are required to participate in any synchronous elements of your unit; if you have problems doing so, you need to contact your unit coordinator as soon as possible to discuss whether the unit will work with your study needs.

Massive Open Online Courses (MOOCs) are online courses that are open sourced (they are available to anyone, anywhere), largely free of charge and cater for enrolments of many thousands of students at a time. Some notable MOOCs are run through prestigious universities such as Stanford and Harvard. Many Australian universities offer MOOCs too. Due to the potentially large numbers of students participating in the units, assessments are generally carried out via online quizzes and examinations with automatic and peer grading systems. Some MOOCs offer their content free of charge, enabling anyone to participate, and only charge a fee when a student wishes to have their work assessed for the purposes of completing a recognised degree or program. They can be a good way to 'dip your toe in' to see if you have the time, motivation and resources to begin online study – if you don't, you won't have lost anything if you don't complete the course.

Common myths and misconceptions

Coming into online study, you may have heard some opinions from others about what you are getting yourself into. Whether you are doing academic research or getting advice from friends and family, it's always a good idea to evaluate your source! Are they speaking from experience? Is their advice biased by their own attitudes towards higher education in general? Is their guidance given with the aim of helping you or is it really about venting their own frustrations? In this section we will look at some common ideas and feelings that students have when beginning their online study journey.

Myth 1: I'm completely on my own

Many students find that the option to study their degree online makes education that would otherwise be unavailable to them suddenly a viable option. Our experience suggests that the population of online students is heavily weighted towards women, particularly those with children; people in full-time or part-time work; and those who live in regional, remote and rural areas. People who thought that higher education was out of their reach are now more easily able to access units and courses regardless of their circumstances and location. However, despite the benefits, online study can sometimes feel lonely and isolating. It is easy, and understandable, to sometimes feel like you are studying on your own with just your computer for company. The rich, vibrant community vibe of a physical campus is difficult to replicate online. But remember: *you are not alone*!

Your units will be managed by a coordinator, who will often run regular lectures and provide you with administrative assistance whenever you need it. Usually you will be allocated a tutor, whose job it will be to guide you and provide lots of feedback on your work and progress. You also may be placed into a tutorial group with other students to discuss unit content and ideas. It is important to make yourself known to all these people – they will be your biggest supporters and cheerleaders. You can do this through participating in online lectures and workshops when you can, by making posts to your tutorial or unit discussion boards regularly, and by contacting your tutor whenever you feel you are struggling or need guidance. Reaching out to all of these people will be key to feeling like you are part of a group in an online unit. You can choose to study on your own if you wish, but doing so will likely mean that you're missing out on important information, helpful feedback and, importantly, the parts of study that are not about the information, such as building friendships and networks with others studying the same units and courses as you.

You get out what you put in!

Your tutors are there to guide and assist you, but they are not mind readers! If you need help with a concept or skills, make sure you ask questions. Put up your (virtual) hand frequently and get involved right from the start. In our experience, students who are active participants on the group discussion boards are usually the ones who are able to achieve their potential. Remember that discussion boards are for interaction between students, too – if you know the answer to a classmate's question, go ahead and reply!

Challenge yourself to:

- be the first to make a post
- respond to at least three other people's posts each week
- share your response to an activity
- give another student feedback or advice, or answer their question.

Myth 2: Online study is completely flexible

One of the benefits to online study is the ability to take a flexible approach. Perhaps you work best very early in the morning or very late at night; perhaps you have medical requirements or other obligations that make travelling or being able to commit to a specific tutorial time difficult. Online study means that you are still able to participate in further education in a way that suits your situation. However, this doesn't mean that a relaxed or ad hoc approach will be possible. Online study often requires a greater level of commitment and motivation than an on-campus study mode would because you are having to be self-regulated in your approach. Some students find it difficult to motivate themselves to get started on their assignments or complete the unit work because they don't have to be anywhere in person at a particular time, and they may not have someone regularly checking up on them. Assignments will still need to be submitted on time and completed to a high standard, and there will be formal processes that you need to go through to be granted extensions. Planning your study carefully will be important – don't expect to be able to take time off to go on holidays or to be able to cram all the unit and assignment work into a couple of days or a week. Treat your study times like appointments and keep them, and ensure that you are making careful note of deadlines and important dates throughout the study period. Student reflection 2.1 offers some great advice on how to do well in online study.

🕮 Student reflection 2.1   How to succeed in online study

Online study is great, you work in your own schedule and time, not bound by the physical restrictions of campus 'open hours'. BUT… It does require your discipline. Set aside dedicated study time where this is the ONLY thing you do – no study while trying to cook dinner or do the washing. Allow more time to complete weekly activities than you think you will need and be guided by the weekly activities: each week builds on and expands on tasks from previous weeks and if you work on them out of order it won't make sense.

Christine Regan, Professional Writing student

Myth 3: Online study is easier than studying on campus

Online units are designed to be just as rigorous as on-campus units. When you complete a unit online you are achieving the same standard as someone studying in a traditional format. Your assignments will be marked to the same specifications and you will not be given any leniency for being an online student. Many tutors who teach online also teach on campus, often in the same units, so they are able to ensure that the standards for the work being produced by online students are applied just as rigorously as to those studying on campus. Your 'online degree' is worth the same as an on-campus one – there is no distinction made between them and you should be proud of your achievements in online study!

Myth 4: My tutors are available all the time

As an online student, you will have access to a vast range of formal and informal resources to help you with your studies. These include the unit materials provided on your Learning Management System (LMS), study skills and language assistance through your institution, and the unit coordinator and tutors allocated to you. Some of these things are available to you whenever you need them but others, particularly the 'human resources', are not necessarily as flexible.

The staff working with you in an online unit are generally very accommodating to the diverse needs of their students and often work in a much less formally timetabled way than those you would find on campus. It is not unusual for a tutor in an online unit to be responding to posts and emails in the evenings or on the weekends. However, they are not available to you 24 hours a day, seven days a week, or during public holidays. Tutors are allocated very limited hours of work each week and they must spread them out to be able to help many students who are all adhering to their own schedules. You may find that your tutor has a specific time of day that they are able to check emails and discussion board posts; you may find that they do not work at all on particular days. When you send an email or make a post, remember that you are not posting to social media – you are not going to get an immediate response or a 'like'. You will need to allow time (usually 24–48 hours) to receive a response. Ignore the urge to send follow up emails or posts before then as this is not considered appropriate etiquette. If you have waited for a day or more and have not received a reply, then it's acceptable to send a polite email or make a follow-up post, just in case your original communication was lost or overlooked. When doing so, think carefully about how you are wording this so as not to come across as pushy or impatient. Chapter 1 notes some things to consider when sending an email to people in your unit.

Your tools for success in online study

During your time studying online, you will develop a range of skills and knowledge that will lead to the achievement of your chosen degree. Your units will be designed to build this knowledge over the course of the degree program and you will receive lots of input to help you develop your understandings. To make the most of this input, you will need to arrive to your online studies with some skills and knowledge so that you are set up to succeed.

In their research into why students studying online withdraw from their courses, Greenland and Moore (2014) found that some of the most common reasons were difficulties faced in balancing work and study; the impact of personal situations such as family crises and health problems; having the required skills to use the necessary technology; being able to participate in the online space effectively; and time management issues. Being able to anticipate these challenges and plan for them will help you remain motivated and capable to complete your course in an online format.

The online space

Working in a virtual environment can be just as daunting for some students as walking into a face-to-face classroom. Even students who would be considered digital natives – those who have grown up surrounded by technology and use it as a completely natural and normalised part of their lives – can often struggle to feel completely comfortable when starting out in online study. Not being able to see the people you're talking to and therefore not being able to read their body language and facial expressions can lead to feelings that everyone is judging us or that others are smarter or more capable. When we are online, we can't see that almost everyone is just as nervous and overwhelmed as we are!

Some of those feelings of uncertainty will fade simply by becoming a more experienced student, just like they would if we were on campus. The best advice is to simply have a go. Your tutors are there to assist and advise you – they want to help! They are also there to monitor the interactions between students and they will not allow anyone to behave in ways that make others uncomfortable. If you are feeling uncertain or worried about anything, reach out to your tutor by email and let them know. They will be able to provide you with advice and strategies to help you find your feet in the online space.

Computer and IT literacy

It may sound obvious, but in order to effectively study online you will need a reasonable understanding of the technology you will be using. Before your unit begins, it is worth spending time making sure you have at least a basic understanding of:

- how to create and organise a folder on your computer desktop
- how to use word processing programs (Microsoft Word and Pages are the most commonly used) and how to save these documents to specific folders
- how to save your documents as PDF files
- how to access websites and other online content
- how to send and receive email.

Many local libraries and community centres run free or low-cost computer literacy courses, which can be very helpful for students who have limited IT skills. Don't wait until you start your studies to access these resources, though. As soon as you start thinking about becoming an online student, enrol in a course like this so that you are ready to go on day one.

You will also need reliable access to both a computer (either a desktop or a laptop) and the Internet. Some students like to use a tablet or other mobile device, though it is our experience that these are not as effective for online study as a desktop or laptop computer. Often the LMS used by your university will not perform well on a mobile device and it is also more difficult to produce the lengthy assignments you will be required to complete on them. If you do not have your own personal Internet connection or computer, you could investigate options for using the resources of your local library. Bear in mind, though, that public libraries often have restrictive content blockers or only allow limited booking times for their computers, which can make it difficult to complete your unit work. Find out what you can and cannot access and the limits on usage before you enrol.

Studying and communicating in the virtual environment

The interactions you will have with your unit coordinators, tutors and classmates will commonly take place on a discussion board. This is a form of asynchronous communication, which involves making contributions in a virtual space to which everyone in the group can read and respond. Often you will be instructed to make specific posts to this space so that your work can be checked and feedback can be given to you. While it can be nerve-wracking to post to these spaces, it's important that you do; if you are not communicating with your tutor, then they cannot help you. Keep reminding yourself that everyone is nervous and we are often our own harshest critics. In all likelihood, your posts will not only help you with your learning but will also be helpful to everyone else, too. Learning with and from each other is a core part of tertiary study.

The specific layout of a discussion board will be different depending on the LMS being used and the way the board has been set up for the unit itself. Below is the terminology you are likely to come across when using these boards.

- **Discussion board:** The 'top level' where you will find a list of forums to which you can post. This might be called something like *Humanities Group 1*. The discussion board is your online classroom, where you will meet with your class and discuss your ideas. People will come and go from this space in their own time.
- **Forum:** You could consider this a table or meeting space in your online classroom. This is a more specific area, where you will make

contributions about particular topics. For example, *Referencing*, *Reflective Writing* or *General Issues*. When making a post, you should think about where your question or contribution most logically fits. Your study materials might also tell you where you should put your post.

- **Post:** This is your contribution to the discussion in the forum. You could think of this as putting up your hand in your virtual classroom and saying something out loud. For example, in the *Referencing* forum, you might make a post that shows your tutor an attempt at referencing a scholarly journal article for them to comment on and let you know what you've done well and where there might be some errors to correct.
- **Thread:** This is like an online conversation, consisting of an initial post and its replies. A thread could be as short as a post and a single reply or it might be lengthy, with many replies going back and forth between people.

ACTIVITY 2.2   Make a post to your group discussion board

If you are already enrolled in an online unit, navigate to your group discussion board (or relevant collaborative area of the LMS) and make a post introducing yourself.

In your post, you might include:

- where in the world you are located
- why you have chosen to study online
- something that you are excited about or looking forward to
- something that you are nervous about.

These ideas have not been suggested arbitrarily: sharing this kind of information is beneficial for you and your classmates. Noting where you are broadly located (e.g. in regional Western Australia, Dubai or suburban Auckland) can help your tutor understand some of the issues you might face with time differences or connectivity; sharing something you're nervous about with your classmates can help to 'break the ice' and lead to making connections with others in your group. Of course, share only what you are comfortable with and beware of 'oversharing'. Think of this like small-talk at a party – a low-key way of getting to know others you'll be interacting with throughout the unit.

In a physical class, you would get most benefit from both listening and contributing – the same is true in the online environment. Make spending time on your discussion board a priority. Devote some time to 'listening' by reading other students' posts and the tutor's responses to them. Much can be learned by seeing how others have completed a task and noting what they have done well and what improvements have been suggested to them. They might have already had the same question as you and the answer will be right there waiting already. Give time over to contributing, too. Take the opportunity to have a go at a skill or task and receive feedback on it *before* you have to submit it in an assignment. All tutors want their students to do well and enjoy interacting with them. None of them want to see errors or issues in your assignments that they could have helped you with, had you only asked in the weeks prior to submission. Participating in the discussions happening in your virtual classroom is also very important in building a community of learners who are sharing experiences and developing their skills together.

A note about using social media in your studies

Many students who choose to study online are already familiar with the world of online communications, particularly social media platforms such as Facebook and Instagram. It is common for students to create groups on these platforms in order to chat to each other and share their fears, questions and support. Sometimes it's a place where students feel they can speak more freely about their concerns or frustrations. Creating networks of support such as these is a great thing and mirrors the sorts of social interactions you would have on campus. However, sometimes students become over-focused on the social media group and forget that the best place to ask questions about assignments and skills is in the dedicated tutorial group on the LMS. All too often, misinformation is spread on social media because someone has trusted the advice of a peer instead of asking their tutor directly. Use and enjoy social media for its informal, friendly and relaxed atmosphere, but direct the important questions about your tasks, skills and concepts to the people who can answer them most accurately: your tutors and unit coordinators.

Accessing resources and unit materials

If you are able to access the campus of a physical university, you may be able to enrol as a library member and borrow books and other resources in person. Online library membership and access to online material (including e-books, journals, newspaper articles and so on) is likely to be included as part of your enrolment. As noted in Chapter 1, as soon as you are enrolled, take a virtual tour of your institution's library and familiarise yourself with the services and resources offered. As a university student, regardless of your study mode, you'll be using them a lot over the duration of your studies.

Many online resources available through your university's online library will have restrictions on how many people can be viewing the text at the same time – just like borrowing a physical copy. If you have a unit textbook or other resource that you know many other students will need to access, make sure you leave yourself plenty of time to borrow the text before the deadline of an assignment; you may have to 'get in the queue' with lots of other students trying to view it.

As soon as your unit begins, take some time exploring your LMS and locating the study materials you will need, such as any weekly study guides, collaborative spaces, lecture recordings, any frequently asked questions (FAQs) or how to guides, the unit outline and so on. Chapter 1 has some useful advice about this. While all students should take time early on in the unit to familiarise themselves with the unit materials, it will be even more important for those studying online. It is likely that you will be working through these materials at your own pace (rather than being given all the relevant information in one session or lecture) and it can be easy to overlook important details. If you are struggling to find something or having problems downloading the material you need, ask your tutor or unit coordinator as soon as the problem arises; don't put it off believing that someone will think you foolish. It's better to ask the 'silly' question and get the answer you need than to struggle on alone. It can also be a great idea to visit bricks and mortar libraries, too, as suggested in Student reflection 2.2.

 Student reflection 2.2 **Advice on how to still have the 'university experience' while studying online**

Get creative with when and where you study. I highly recommend checking out your local library to get out of the house on study days to mix it up. Visiting your local university's library is a fantastic way of getting the university experience if you start feeling isolated in your journey – yes, you can do that as an online student!

Jason Robards, Construction Management student

Technology challenges

One of the most predictable situations in any online student's life is that technology will fail at some point. Being prepared for this will help you overcome the problem and avoid panic. Some things you can do to minimise the difficulty of these situations are:

- Make sure you always have a backup for your important files. Saving your assignment work, important unit documents and research into both a desktop folder and an external device such as a USB memory stick or a cloud storage service such as Google Docs will ensure that if your computer crashes you are not going to lose everything.

- Don't leave things to the last minute. Aim to upload your completed assignments some time before the due date – waiting until five minutes before the deadline is asking for trouble! There is very limited leeway (if any) allowed by most units for late submissions due to technology problems.

- Find out how to access IT assistance through your university. Your tutors will not always be able to help you with the technological problems you are facing; however, most university faculties have dedicated IT helpdesks, which you can email or phone. They will be able to talk you through your problem.

- Try a different browser. One of the most common solutions to problems students have when uploading assignments or accessing resources is to change browsers. For example, if you are using Google Chrome, try switching to Firefox; if you're using Firefox, try switching to Internet Explorer. It sounds simple, but it's our experience that this is very commonly a solution that works.

Managing your time and planning for the unexpected

Many students choose to study online because of the flexibility it affords them, and this is certainly one of online education's biggest advantages over face-to-face modes. However, it is vital that you don't allow this flexibility to become your undoing. It's preferable that you ask yourself – and honestly answer – the following questions *before* you enrol in online study. However, even if you're already enrolled, they are still important questions to reflect upon.

- **Why am I choosing to study online rather than on campus?** As noted in Chapter 1, studying online should not be seen as the easy option. Being an online student often requires *more* commitment, time and intrinsic motivation than on-campus study does.

- **Am I able to devote the required time to my studies? Can I fit study time into my current schedule?** A good rule of thumb is that every unit you undertake will need an average of 10 hours of dedicated time each week. This might be significantly more in the week or so leading up to an assignment submission.

- **What other commitments do I have that could interfere with my ability to complete my studies?** Does your job often require unexpected overtime? Are there restructures or projects coming up that could get in the way of your study plans? Do you have plans to go on a family holiday? Work commitments and pre-planned travel are rarely seen as legitimate reasons for extensions to assignments or special arrangements to be granted, so it's important to consider the likelihood of these sorts of situations arising. (A common exception to this is programs designed for elite athletes – if this is applicable to you, make sure you have looked into the arrangements that your institution has in place to accommodate your needs.)

- **Do I have some built-in time to account for unexpected problems such as being unwell, caring for family members, or just 'life getting in the way'?** Make sure you're not cramming study into an already jam-packed timetable. Studying should be enjoyable and fulfilling; it's unlikely to be so if you are squeezing it into the last available minutes of your week. Doing so also won't allow you to work through unforeseen situations that could rob you of your usual study time.

- **Do I have supportive networks of people around me who will be assets to my study plans?** Sometimes people who don't have experience with being an online student make assumptions such as 'it's only an online unit, it's not that important' or believe that you aren't a 'real' university student because you're not attending a physical campus. Make sure that the people around you know that you are committed to your studies and that they need to respect your decisions and your space when you tell them you can't join them for a coffee or babysit at particular times because you are studying.

Addressing these issues before you begin studying online will help you to understand what will be required to see your studies through and, importantly, to enjoy them. Be realistic with yourself and if now is not the best time to be studying then it's perfectly fine to withdraw from your unit and come back at a later date when the situation is more favourable to success. Be sure to do this officially through the institution you enrolled with before the census date to avoid financial or academic penalties. Student reflection 2.3 offers some good advice about why giving yourself enough time to get your work done always pays off.

Student reflection 2.3 — My advice? Give yourself time to do a good job

The flexibility of online study is great but it shouldn't be an excuse to procrastinate either; things happen, life happens, and you don't want to be rushing at the last second, or worse, miss a deadline. Plus, you can always go back and look over your work with the time you have left and adjust things if you feel that it just doesn't look or sound right. It's important to have that extra time, you might be tempted to submit that essay as soon as you've finished it, but give it a day and re-approach it with fresh eyes and make sure you're 100% happy with what you've written, and that your tired self hasn't missed anything, like spelling and punctuation. Those are easy marks that you don't want to miss out on because you're in a rush.

Crystal Beaini, Internet Communications student

REVISION TOOLS

↘ Revision activity: Revise these ideas

1 Online study is fantastic for making education accessible to many people. However, it is not for everyone. Studying as an online student requires technological competence, a supportive network of people around you and lots of intrinsic motivation to spur you on.

2 There are a number of modes of online study available. When you sign up to an online course or unit, make sure you investigate the requirements for assignment submissions, interaction with tutors and other students, and the use of a specific LMS.

3 Online study does not have to be an isolating experience. Get to know your tutors and peers. Interact with them as much as possible – it will benefit you and them!

4 Avoid falling into the trap of allowing flexibility to become complacency. Know your due dates and treat your study times like non-negotiable appointments.

5 Investigate the resources that are available to you as an online student, such as the university library, student services, IT assistance, and online modules and help for writing and other academic skills.

↘ Thinking activity: Critical and reflective questions

1 What skills do I currently possess that will help me succeed in online study and what are those on which I need to improve?

2 Who can I call on to assist me in my study success? Who are the people who are going to be important in my ability to devote the required time and enthusiasm to my studies, and who are those who are going to be helpful in the academic aspects of my study?

3 How can I become involved in the social aspects of online study and how can they be managed so that they do not become distractions?

4 Where does my study sit in my list of priorities? What am I willing to sacrifice to be able to succeed, and what am I not willing to compromise on? Does this fit with giving myself a realistic chance of success?

↘ Useful weblinks

Consult the following online resource for further information and tips for studying online:

Online Study Australia: 'How to Succeed in Online Courses' **https://onlinestudyaustralia.com/courses/how-succeed-tips**.

REFERENCES

Bailey, M., D. Ifenthaler, M. Gosper, M. Kretzschmar, and C. Ware. 2015. "The Changing Importance of Factors Influencing Students' Choice of Study Mode." *Technology, Knowledge and Learning* 2015 (20): 169–84. **https://doi.org/10.1007/s10758-015-9253-9**.

Greenland, S., and C. Moore. 2014. "Patterns of Student Enrolment and Attrition in Australian Open Access Online Education: A Preliminary Case Study." *Open Praxis* 6 (1): 45–54. **https://doi.org/10.5944/openpraxis.6.1.95**.

↘ PART TWO

RESEARCH SKILLS

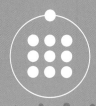

Research, one of the central aspects of university study, comprises a series of interconnected skills:

- identifying appropriate and useful texts
- evaluating these texts in terms of whether they are appropriate for academic study by first-year students
- reading and making meaning from scholarly texts
- referencing these texts.

In Part 2, you will find chapters devoted to these skills. In Chapter 3, you will learn the basics of research. You will focus on finding journal articles, books, websites and other resources on your topic, and you will learn that research involves much more than Google! You will then learn to distinguish scholarly texts from popular ones, so that you will be able to choose appropriate resources for your assignments. Chapter 4 will focus on how to read texts, both written and audio-visual, in order to make meaning from them so that you can incorporate the authors' ideas into your writing. In Chapter 5 we will explain how to reference your texts according to the referencing system required by your department. For now, just keep a careful record of the details. If you forget to write down these details now, you will waste a lot of time trying to trace them later.

→ **Chapter 3:** Identifying and evaluating appropriate resources

→ **Chapter 4:** Reading academic texts, both written and recorded

→ **Chapter 5:** Referencing and academic integrity

Identifying and evaluating appropriate resources

CONTENTS

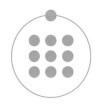

Choosing a topic

When you are given a research assignment, you will often be able to choose from several topics. The first step is to choose a topic, and you should, of course, select one that interests you; but before you make a final decision, you need to consider the amount and type of information available on the topic. If, after a few hours' searching, you find very little information, or the information you find is either too difficult to understand or too simple to challenge your thinking, then you may decide to change your topic. We explain the process of choosing and researching a topic in this chapter.

Before you start researching

Before you start your research, set up a file on your computer to store the bibliographic details of each text that is appropriate for your assignment (author's name, title, publisher, journal title and so on). How do you know what details to write down? If you're unsure, find out which referencing system your department requires and look briefly at your library's handout on this system, which will generally be available on the library website. Some of the details you will need might surprise you (some systems require that you add the date you accessed a particular website), but you will soon get used to what to look for. It's best to write down every detail you can think of at this stage. You will learn about referencing in Chapter 5.

Research is time-consuming and can be frustrating!

Be aware that research is likely to take much more time than you anticipate, and you may need to rethink your plans and directions several times as you proceed. Allow yourself enough time to complete research assignments.

Search tools

You may have developed sound strategies for identifying appropriate resources during your secondary schooling. However, it is likely that when you start tertiary study, you will need to refine your search strategies in several areas, such as:

- using library catalogues to find less familiar types of text, including trade publications, national or international standards, conference proceedings, reports and government legislation

- using electronic databases to find scholarly journal articles, as well as all the types of text listed in the previous bullet point
- efficient Web searching.

The first two of these areas will probably be new to you, since you may not have read these types of text in your previous education. You will almost certainly have done some Web searching, but may not have developed efficient techniques. We find that most of our students do little more than enter some keywords into a basic search engine such as Google, and then browse through the entries (sometimes millions of them!) they receive. Or, worse, they realise they can't look at all the listed entries, and so confine themselves to the first few, whatever they are. You will definitely need to develop more sophisticated Web-searching techniques than these if you are to use your time efficiently and find appropriate resources for academic study.

Let's start at the beginning of the research process.

A word on primary research

There are several ways to categorise scholarly research, and these differ across disciplines. In this text, we use the categories of primary research and secondary research.

Primary research involves information that you collect yourself: surveys, interviews, focus groups, observations, experimental results and so on. The key to primary research is that you design and analyse the research yourself. So, for example, if you conduct your own interview with a key person in your field we call it primary research, while the report of someone else's interview with the same person is secondary research (for you), because another person has shaped, analysed and reported on the interview.

Primary research is very important for tertiary studies – more important in some disciplines than in others – and can be very time-consuming. In most disciplines, you will do very little primary research in your first year. In your second and third years, though, you might devote entire units to learning how to conduct good primary research within your particular discipline. Such formal primary research can require special permission and sometimes an ethics clearance from a university committee. If primary research is required in your first year, it will be informal and will only be a 'taste' of what you could do in your future studies.

Here are some examples of the more informal primary research that you might conduct in your first year:

- You might interview a professional or academic in your field on a limited topic and then report on the main ideas from this interview in writing or in an oral presentation.
- You might conduct a small survey of responses of fellow students or community members to a specific issue and report on the results of your survey.

- You might conduct an observation of a particular site or action over a period of time (e.g. observe the entrance to a building, examining whether it is well designed for different people who might use the building).

Research of cultural artefacts

Another type of primary research – one that is common in the built environment disciplines, social sciences and cultural studies – is the study of cultural artefacts or objects made by particular groups of people in order to explore what these objects suggest about the groups that made them. In this type of primary research, you identify and select certain cultural artefacts and then analyse them. For example:

- Students of urban and regional planning might collect photographs and advertisements from a community newspaper in order to build a picture of the 'flavour' of a suburb or regional area.
- Students of project management might examine prospectuses, plans and artists' sketches of a new project to consider how that project will fit within a community.
- Students of cultural studies, history or anthropology might identify examples of music popular among a specific group in order to explore the group itself.

If you conduct this type of primary research, lecturers and tutors who are subject specialists in your discipline will teach you how to present your findings, since each discipline has its own rules about how you must write or speak about your primary-research conclusions. This advice is particularly true if you are researching the world's First Nations. For example, there are protocols about conducting research about Aboriginal and Torres Strait Islander peoples – and the artefacts that belong to them – so check with your lecturers before starting your research.

If you conduct primary research as part of a written or oral assignment, you must properly integrate your discussion into your assignment and reference it appropriately. See Chapter 5 and check your appropriate university referencing guide for information about how to do this at your institution.

ACTIVITY 3.1   Planning primary research and research into cultural artefacts

With another student or individually

Choose one topic that you plan to research. List some of the types of primary research that might be relevant for your research. If appropriate, also consider cultural artefacts.

_____

_____

In a group or class

Share and discuss your ideas for primary research.

Note: We recommend that you keep this list and add to it as you continue your research – your understanding of the possible areas of primary research will develop as you research the topic.

Secondary research

The rest of this chapter will deal with *secondary research*, which involves ideas and information you glean from other people's research – that is, second-hand information.

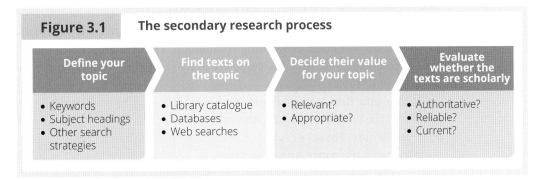

Figure 3.1	The secondary research process

Define your topic	Find texts on the topic	Decide their value for your topic	Evaluate whether the texts are scholarly
• Keywords • Subject headings • Other search strategies	• Library catalogue • Databases • Web searches	• Relevant? • Appropriate?	• Authoritative? • Reliable? • Current?

Start with the library

Some students have become so comfortable using the Internet and other electronic resources that they forget the most useful place to start looking for information on any assignment: the university library. As well as print, non-print and electronic resources, your library provides you with librarians who are trained not only to help you find the resources you need but also to use them efficiently. Even those of you who study online will find your librarians respond quickly to your questions, whether you ask them by email or a phone call.

Look for library guides and classes

All university libraries have excellent guides to help you research effectively. See some of the guides listed in the 'Useful weblinks' section at the end of this chapter, as well as the guide for your own institution. These guides will help you improve your skills in searching not only the library catalogue, but other resources like databases and the Internet. Even if your own library has not yet developed detailed

HINT

resources, most university libraries make their guides publicly available. You will quickly become familiar with those that you find most helpful.

You will also find schedules of regular face-to-face classes listed on your library's webpage.

Subject guides

Many tertiary libraries now provide subject guides (often called 'libguides') designed to introduce you to the main resources relevant to your discipline. Many also include referencing guides. These are a very useful way of becoming familiar with the vast range of resources that will be useful for your research.

Search the library catalogue

The library catalogue is the best place to start your research, whether you are in the library itself or working from home. This catalogue will direct you to books, journal articles, complete journals, videos and other media texts on your topic.

When you find a journal article you think will be useful for your research, the subject headings, abstract, introduction and conclusion will help you decide. For other types of text, look for equivalent sections, such as introductions, blurbs and summaries.

Use electronic databases

Until the last decade, library catalogues did not list individual journal articles. Before this, students had to use *electronic databases* – vast electronic catalogues of articles written throughout the world on almost every imaginable subject. Most library catalogues now provide direct links to items in these databases, which will make your initial searching easier.

It is still very useful to learn the traditional way of searching for journal articles through electronic databases – these are often more detailed and more reliable than library catalogues. In particular, you will often want to select the databases that will be most useful to your discipline, rather than allowing the single-search facility to control which databases you consult.

While you are an undergraduate student, you don't need to read all that has been published on a certain topic, so we recommend you begin your research with *full-text databases* – that is, databases that include complete articles, as well as their bibliographic details. Popular full-text electronic databases that are generally available to tertiary students through their library websites include:

- Scopus
- Emerald Insight

- Project MUSE
- Wiley Online Library
- MEDLINE and PsycINFO (for health sciences)
- Business Source Premier/Complete
- Informit (especially for Australian resources; choose your subject area(s) from the tags at the top of the homepage)
- ProQuest (especially for health and education).

If you do not have access to any databases through a university, you can use a free online database such as PMC (for health and life sciences; see **https://www.ncbi.nlm.nih.gov/pmc**) or AustLII (for Australasian legal information; see **http://www.austlii.edu.au**). These databases, which list articles from different journals, are all constructed slightly differently. Become familiar with the databases that are most useful for your discipline by browsing through them or by attending workshops offered by your library's staff members.

Databases aren't easy!

Databases represent the most difficult area of searching for first-year students, but you will find them useful as you continue your studies, and when you have mastered them, you will find them your most useful sources for academic research. Don't worry if you struggle with them at first – you'll get better at it with practice. Even experienced researchers sometimes have problems finding useful materials on a particular topic, and just have to keep trying alternative combinations of words until they find some suitable resources. For help with using databases, always talk to a librarian – they are the experts in this area.

Most libraries produce very useful guides and face-to-face classes to help you learn to use databases efficiently. These are excellent tools for growing your skills as your studies continue. These guides and classes will teach you how to develop search strategies shaped for particular topics.

Search the Web
Search engines

A *search engine* is a database that accesses millions (and sometimes billions) of websites. When you type in keywords, the search-engine robot (sometimes called a 'spider') will search instantly through its websites to give you a list of 'hits' – websites that contain those words – and allow you to open the websites that you want to read by clicking on their links. All search engines list websites in order from the most relevant to the least relevant to your search; however, the individual formulas (or algorithms) they use to decide on this relevance are trade secrets, so it is sometimes difficult to understand why a particular website is listed at the top of your list of hits.

Which search engines do you know about? To this question, many of you will reply, 'Google'. In fact, this name is so well known that it has become a verb. (People now use the phrase 'I'll just Google that now' to mean 'I'll look it up on the Google – or any other – search engine'.)

Google Scholar

Google Scholar (see **https://scholar.google.com.au**) works just like the basic search engine, but searches only scholarly sources. Most tertiary libraries offer access to Google Scholar. If your library does, we urge you to access it in this way, since you will be given free access to articles you would have to pay for through the standard Google Scholar access. For example:

- On the University of the Sunshine Coast website, go to **https://www. usc.edu.au/library/collections/databases**, then click on 'G'.
- Macquarie University has a direct link to Google Scholar under the search box on its library's homepage, found at **https://www.mq.edu. au/about/campus-services-and-facilities/library**.
- Curtin University students will find it useful to access Google Scholar via the library's 'Databases A–Z' link (under 'G').

Why evaluate a text?

In the first half of this chapter, we described how to find texts relating to your chosen topic. But you must do more than this; you must also examine these texts carefully to make sure they are both *relevant* for your purposes and *reliable*. This has always been important for students, but it has become essential in recent years with the huge growth of the Internet, which allows all writers to publish their ideas easily and cheaply, but without the controls on quality and reliability provided by most publishers of books and journals.

When they find a new text, academics make a very quick decision about whether it will serve their purposes; they do this intuitively, without needing to work through an evaluation process. In your first year of tertiary study, however, you will usually need to think through the following issues before deciding whether to use a particular text in your research.

Relevance

Finding a text on your topic is only the first step – you then need to decide whether it is relevant to your purposes, because if it isn't relevant, you can stop reading it immediately. Even if a certain text is on your topic, it will not be relevant for your purposes if its level of sophistication is inappropriate.

Level of sophistication

You need to find texts that are pitched at an appropriate level for you as a tertiary student, while challenging your thinking:

- Some texts will be too simplistic for your purposes. While it is fine to begin to research a topic by reading relevant sections in an encyclopedia (including Wikipedia) or by looking up terms in a dictionary, these texts will provide you with introductory ideas only, and must not form the foundation of your thinking. You must move on quickly to significant scholarly texts.
- On the other hand, some texts you discover (particularly articles from scholarly journals) will be aimed at a much more academic reader. In these cases, apply the 'five-finger rule' to your reading (see Chapter 4).

Reliability

When you find a text that is about your topic and is written at an appropriate level, you then need to decide if you can rely on the information and arguments you find in it. The following sections outline some considerations.

Reputable sources
Books

If the text is a book, does it appear to have been published by a reputable publisher? Look at the imprint page (on the back of the title page), where you will find the most comprehensive publication details. Have you heard of this publisher? Google the publisher to see what kinds of text they tend to publish. Look at other titles published by the publisher (which are often listed on an early page in the book, or on the back pages or back cover). Is the book self-published? (Occasionally, writers pay to publish books themselves, often because their intended audience is not large enough to warrant professional publication.)

ACTIVITY 3.2 Evaluation of publishers

As an individual or with another student

Following are five texts on the subject of interior architecture. Look up the publishers of each text on the Internet to get a sense of whether they are likely to be reputable, scholarly publishers. Place a tick in the box next to each text you would consider using to support your argument in a scholarly essay.

☐ Evans, Ian. 2004. *The Federation House: A Restoration Guide*. Mullumbimby, NSW: Flannel Flower Press.

☐ Leydecker, Sylvia. 2013. *Designing Interior Architecture: Concept, Typology, Material, Construction*. Basel: De Gruyter.

☐ Scott, Fred. 2008. *On Altering Architecture*. London: Routledge.

☐ Stapleton, Maisy. 1983. *Historic Interiors: A Collection of Papers*. Glebe, NSW: Sydney College of the Arts Press.

☐ Stine, Daniel John and Aaron R. Hansen. 2012. *Interior Design Using Autodesk Revit Architecture*. Mission, Kansas: Schroff Development Corp.

In a class or group

Discuss your answers, articulating the reasons for your decisions to include or exclude each publisher.

Journal articles

If the text is a journal article, is it from a *peer-reviewed* or *refereed* journal? These are journals that only publish articles evaluated by acknowledged experts in their field, rather than just by an editorial board. You can generally find out whether a particular journal is peer-reviewed or refereed by looking for a statement about this in its opening pages or, if you have found the article in an electronic database, in the database link that gives publishing information about journals. You can also look up the journal on your favourite search engine. Be careful, however – even if a journal is peer-reviewed, this doesn't mean that all articles in it are scholarly argumentative articles. Some are brief opinion pieces or editorials that do not include reference lists.

Note, on the other hand, that journal articles from non-refereed journals might still be considered scholarly journal articles if they are edited by academics in relevant disciplines.

Increasingly, journal articles are being published without having followed the traditional publishing route. They are not peer-reviewed, but are published by academic publishers. Many websites (for example, ResearchGate; see **https://www.researchgate.net**) publish articles written by recognised academics, but do not have traditional peer-review processes. Many universities also publish conference papers and articles written by their academics that have not been published elsewhere.

This increasing blurring of boundaries can make it difficult to make decisions about which texts are scholarly. We can only suggest you focus on the author of any text you are considering, and discuss with your lecturers any texts that you are in doubt about.

Newspaper articles

Newspaper articles (whether from print or online newspapers) are not valid academic sources because they are neither peer-reviewed nor scholarly. Journalists might have broad general knowledge about many topics, but are generally not recognised as scholarly authorities on any single topic. Newspaper articles can, however, give you valuable statistics, examples, anecdotes or understandings of community perspectives on particular issues, provided that you acknowledge their limitations and place them alongside academic sources to develop your analysis or argument. (See the first part of this chapter for more about primary research through media sources, which is particularly important in the humanities areas such as built environment and cultural studies.)

If you find it difficult to tell the difference between newspapers and academic journals by looking at their titles, then you need to look up the titles on the Internet to ensure that you have found scholarly sources. As you progress in your studies, you will become familiar with the main academic journals in your discipline.

ACTIVITY 3.3   Evaluation of newspapers

As an individual or with another student

Below is a list of academic journals and newspapers. Place a tick in the box next to each one you consider to be a scholarly journal.

☐ The Huffington Post	☐ Bulletin of the World Health Organization
☐ Science	☐ The Age
☐ Open Access Journal of Sports Medicine	☐ 3D World Magazine
☐ Textile World	☐ Insurance Business Weekly
☐ The Wall Street Journal	☐ Libraries: Culture, History and Society

In a class or group

Discuss your answers, considering how much you can rely on titles to help you decide whether publications are scholarly.

Our students' most common error in evaluating texts

Many of our students refer to newspaper articles as if they were scholarly texts. Remember that even if you find a newspaper article in a library catalogue or database, this does not mean it is scholarly. Many library catalogues and databases allow you to click on a box to limit yourself to scholarly articles – make sure you do this before you start browsing the list of texts you have found.

Websites

If the text is a website, can you identify its origin? Once you have determined the organisation or individual(s) responsible for the website, look up the organisation on the Internet to develop a sense of its focus and concerns. This will give you some clues as to how reputable the organisation is as a publisher.

ACTIVITY 3.4   Evaluation of websites

As an individual or with another student

Following are five webpages about crime prevention. Next to each one, make notes about whether you would use it to support your argument in a scholarly essay, explaining briefly why or why not.

Website 1

COUNCIL OF CAPITAL CITY LORD MAYORS	
ABOUT CITIES ▾ PUBLICATIONS MEDIA RELEASES CITIES MATTER SITE PROFILES	
Crime prevention through environmental design (CPTED)	Capital Cities
Crime prevention through environmental design (CPTED)	Adelaide
	Brisbane
	Canberra
	Darwin
	Hobart
	Melbourne
	Perth
	Sydney
	Media Releases
City of Perth Safer Design Guidelines	Council of Capital City Lord Mayors
The Safer Design of commercial and residential areas, is an important issue for local government. These guidelines for the City of Perth address the safer design issues for a high density environment, especially particularly for areas used after dark – entertainment precincts, public transport, public toilets and around vulnerable development such as licensed premises.	8 Geils Court, Deakin Canberra ACT 2600
	Phone: (02) 6285 1672 Fax: (02) 6282 4253 Skype: cclm01 Twitter: @cclm01 email: info@lordmayors.org

_____

_____

_____

_____

Source: Council of Capital City Lord Mayors

Website 2

Source: Australian Institute of Criminology CC BY-3.0

_____

_____

_____

_____

Website 3

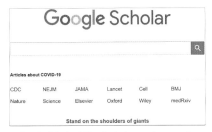

Source: Community Crime Prevention Unit, Department of Justice and Regulation, State of Victoria

_____

_____

_____

_____

Website 4

Source: Google Scholar; https://scholar.google.com.au/

_____

_____

_____

_____

Website 5

Source: The Design Partnership 2017

_____

_____

_____

_____

In a class or group

Discuss your answers, articulating the reasons for your decisions to include or exclude each website.

A reminder on bias

Of course, company websites will generally seek to support or sell the company's ideas or products, so you need to take care when using information from them. This doesn't mean, however, that companies' websites are the only 'biased' websites. Remember that *all* information is biased in some way – government bodies, educational institutions and non-profit associations, for example, may try to promote their projects and decisions, and will select and shape information in such a way as to persuade you to accept their ideas. In deciding the value of texts for your research, do not seek out texts that you think are 'the truth'; instead, seek to understand the points of view of the writers, and to gain balance by finding texts from a range of points of view. (For more information on this concept, see Chapter 6.)

Authority

Is the text written by someone who has an appropriate academic background? If this is not stated in the text itself, look up the author on the Internet to see if you can find any relevant information.

Accuracy

Based on what you have read so far, do you feel that the information in the text you are considering is accurate? Does it support other information you have discovered in your research? Does it present contradictory ideas? Does the writer ground his or her ideas in a study of previous academic research and include a list of references?

Currency

The balance you adopt between current and older texts will depend on your subject. For example, for nanotechnology topics such as nanomedicine or space elevators, or for research on the Square Kilometre Array in rural Western Australia and South Africa, most of your sources will need to be based on up-to-the-minute research. On the other hand, for many other topics in the sciences – as well as in the health sciences, humanities and so on – you will also need to understand earlier key research or ideas in the field, which is often called *seminal* research. Thus, if you were researching the topic of Australian suburbia, it would be valuable to consider Donald Horne's seminal book *The Lucky Country*, originally published in 1964, as well as recent journal articles by Australian urban transport expert Professor Peter Newman, such as his 2015 article 'Transport Infrastructure and Sustainability: A New Planning and Assessment Framework'.

Additional hints for evaluating a webpage

All of the above information also applies to evaluating a webpage. However, webpages require more detailed evaluation than other texts, for several reasons:

- Webpages may sit within larger and more complex websites, whose structure is not as readily visible as the structure of a book or journal.
- Websites can be posted easily and cheaply by any individual or group and have not been subjected to the publishing controls applied to books and journal articles.
- Information published on websites can be more ephemeral than that in traditional texts. For example, websites often list the names of organisations or officeholders from past years or discuss projects in their early stages. When the names change or the projects are completed, the original websites are neither updated nor deleted.

When you find a webpage that you think might be useful for your research, ask yourself these basic questions:

- If you came to this page through a search engine, is it clear 'where you are' in the broader website? Can you navigate back to the homepage?
- Can you tell who published this page? Can you find out anything about the organisation that may give you a clue as to its point of view on the issue concerned? (Hint: Google the organisation.)
- Does the page have a title? Does the title state clearly what the page is about?
- Are you told the author's name and anything about this person?
- Does the author of the page acknowledge the sources of her or his information?
- Is this webpage (or the website's homepage) dated? Is the date reasonably current? Do you think the information might have changed since the page was published?
- Are you given contact details (generally an email address) for the author or organisation?
- Is there a search box on the website's homepage so that you can find other relevant pages of the website?
- Can you navigate easily to other pages on the website through other links?
- Are there links to other websites? Do the links work? What type of websites are linked to, and do they contain useful information?

New types of text

The Internet has created a wide range of new types of text that you might want to consider as part of your secondary research. But, even if you choose to refer to new types of text, you still need to consider the authority of the authors and their purpose in presenting the text.

Here are some text types you might consult during your research:

- the YouTube video of an oral presentation by a recognised authority
- a blog or webpage created by a recognised authority
- the script or recording of an interview with a recognised authority.

The authors' purpose in presenting the texts is important in your decision making. Ask yourself whether they considered their comments carefully and made them in order to be part of an ongoing conversation on an issue before you decide to use them – even recognised authorities do not want to be quoted academically for the off-hand comments they might make.

Of course, you can always refer to these new text types in your primary research – they are a strong indication of the attitudes and perspectives of particular groups of people on a topic. (For more details on this use of primary research, see the section on cultural artefacts at the beginning of this chapter.)

ACTIVITY 3.5 Evaluation of a text

As an individual or with another student

Make notes evaluating the relevance and reliability of one text on your research topic that you consider is relevant for your purposes, using the headings given so far in this chapter.

In a class or a group

Bring to class your text and the notes that you have made on its relevance and reliability. Share your evaluation with other class or group members. As a group, choose the evaluation that you feel best demonstrates the principles of relevance and reliability, and then report to the class on your conclusions.

ACTIVITY 3.6 The results of your research

This class activity is the culmination of your research and evaluation activities. It is designed to give you an opportunity to develop your oral presentation skills, as well as to share some of the interesting ideas you have discovered on your chosen topic. (Your tutor will allocate you a week in which to make this presentation. Over the semester, you will hear information about a range of topics.) If you are reading this book alone rather than in a classroom situation, you can do this activity with a fellow student or a friend.

In a class or group

Prepare a brief, informal oral presentation for your class about one of the useful texts you have found on your topic and evaluated as scholarly. Explain the main ideas of the text and how these ideas have developed your thinking on the topic. (For example, you might have decided to explore a certain subtopic or subtheme that this text introduced to you.) Also explain briefly the techniques you used to find this particular text.

If you are still feeling lost about research …

If you are still having difficulties with research, go to your university library's homepage and find links to the various guides and training available. Complete any online tutorials or enrol in a hands-on session in your library. Always remember to ask a librarian if you need help.

REVISION TOOLS

↘ Revision activity: Revise these ideas

1 Research can be separated into *primary research* (i.e. research you conduct yourself through surveys, interviews, observation and so on) and *secondary research* (i.e. study of other people's arguments and ideas). First-year students conduct mainly secondary research; if they begin to be involved in primary research, they must learn the specific processes of their discipline.

2 Become familiar with the research guides of your university (or another university whose guides you find useful). They will teach you how to use catalogues, databases and search engines efficiently.

3 Databases are vast lists of journal articles on almost any topic. It takes a great deal of practice to learn to use them efficiently, but you can start by becoming familiar with full-text databases, which include many complete journal articles.

4 Experienced researchers are able to assess quickly whether a text is appropriate for scholarly research. In your early semesters of study, you need to think carefully through the qualities of each text before deciding to use it for your research.

5 Scholarly texts must have reputable authors. Books must be from reputable publishers, and journal articles from peer-reviewed journals. Newspaper articles cannot be viewed as scholarly because journalists are generalists, rather than scholars in specific fields. New text types, being introduced frequently into scholarly fields of research, are pushing the boundaries of what is considered scholarly.

6 Websites demand particular care when conducting scholarly research, since few of them have scholarly control and oversight.

↘ Thinking activity: Critical and reflective questions

1 What previous experience have I had in researching? How can I adapt my previous experience in order to be successful at university?

2 Research can be time-consuming and frustrating. How will I respond to these difficulties, and how can I better organise myself to cope with them?

3 In what areas of my life other than study do I think research skills will be useful to me, both now and in the future?

4 What would happen if people in universities decided to ignore traditional judgements about what makes a text academic and accept a wider range of texts as academic? Reflect on as many possible effects as you can, both positive and negative.

↘ Useful weblinks

Consult the following online resources for further information about research skills:

The University of Western Sydney Library's 'Successful Searching' tutorial: **http://library.westernsydney.edu.au/main/guides/online-tutorials/successful-searching.**

Curtin University Library's study and research guides: **https://libguides.library.curtin.edu.au/study-research#linkid=library-home-links-libguides.**

Most university libraries also publish subject guides (libguides) in which they list useful resources for each discipline taught at the university, for example:

Monash University's library guides: **http://guides.lib.monash.edu.**

University of Tasmania's library guides: **http://utas.libguides.com/home.**

Deakin University's library guides: **https://www.deakin.edu.au/library/help/resource-guides.**

Edith Cowan University's libguides: **http://ecu.au.libguides.com.**

The University of Adelaide's subject portals: **http://libguides.adelaide.edu.au/home.**

The University of Auckland's subject guides: **https://www.library.auckland.ac.nz/guides.**

Consult the following websites for more information about evaluating resources:

The University of Auckland Library: 'Academic and Popular Journals': **http://www.library.auckland.ac.nz/subject-guides/bus/topicguides/academic_popularjnls.htm.**

Online Writing Lab (OWL) at Purdue University, Indiana (US): 'Evaluating Sources': **https://owl.purdue.edu/owl/research_and_citation/conducting_research/evaluating_sources_of_information/general_guidelines.html.**

REFERENCES

Horne, Donald. 1971. *The Lucky Country*, 3rd rev. ed. Harmondsworth, Middlesex: Penguin.

Newman, Peter William. 2015. 'Transport Infrastructure and Sustainability: A New Planning and Assessment Framework.' *Smart and Sustainable Built Environment* 4 (2): 140–53. **https://doi.org/10.1108/SASBE-05-2015-0009.**

CHAPTER 4

Reading academic texts, both written and recorded

CONTENTS

Reading scholarly texts

In this chapter we explore approaches and techniques for reading and viewing scholarly texts. The ways you read written texts and view audio-visual ones are similar; we will start with the written texts, and then explore additional approaches and techniques that will help you with the audio-visual ones in the second half of the chapter.

When you have found a text on your subject and assessed that it is appropriate for your research, then you need to think about how you will read it. This may sound silly – you have been reading since primary school, and you know how to do that! However, the ways you will read at university are likely to be very different from the ways you have read in the past.

You are probably used to starting to read a text at the beginning and following it through sentence by sentence. You may skim-read a little (that is, leave out or skip through certain sections that you feel are less important for you), but you will generally read in a linear way, from beginning to end. At university, you can't afford to do that for several reasons:

- You will be expected to read many texts, and won't have time to read every word of them all.
- You will read texts in which only certain sections or ideas relate to the issue you are researching.
- You will be seeking key ideas from a text, and you may need to have an overview of that text before you start to read it more carefully, so you have a strong context for understanding those key ideas.

👓 Student reflection 4.1 Reading scholarly texts is different!

I've always loved reading and I thought this semester's reading would be easy – how wrong I was! I looked at the huge list of texts for this unit and thought, 'how can I do this?' Some of the articles are more than 20 pages long and I have to read five of them. And that's just for a start! Then I learned that you read scholarly texts differently from the texts I've been used to at school, and it all seems more manageable. Now I just have to practise this new way of reading – but I guess it'll take some time to learn.

Jasmine Lei, Nursing student

How to read a scholarly journal article

The most complex type of reading you are likely to do in your first year of studies is reading scholarly journal articles – that is, articles that are written to present a detailed argument, contention or perspective on a subject. (See Chapter 9 for more discussion about arguments.) Because this is the most complex type, we will focus on it for the rest of this section; however, you will be able to apply the approaches we discuss to many other types of text.

Reading is an active process

Reading any text is about making meaning from that text. It involves much more than passively absorbing ideas – you read best when you are constantly challenging your brain to make patterns and connections as you read. Here are some of the active approaches you might take:

- Predict what ideas you are likely to find in the text, based on the title and on what you already know about the subject, so that you're not reading 'in a vacuum'.
- Notice clues during your reading about how the text will be structured and developed.
- Look for your predicted ideas as you read, and notice ideas that you hadn't anticipated.
- Make mental connections with other texts as you read in order to deepen your thinking.

Reading for argument

As you approach a scholarly journal article, remember that the authors' purpose is to convince you of a particular argument or perspective. Your first aim, therefore, is to identify that argument and, related to that, the main ideas that the authors have used to make their argument convincing. (For more information on this, see the section 'The thesis statement' in Chapter 9.) Don't start to read the entire article, but approach it from this perspective. Here are the main sections that will help you identify the argument:

- the title
- the abstract at the beginning (which acts as a summary)
- the introduction
- the headings and subheadings
- the conclusion

When trying to identify the main ideas that build the argument, you will find them in the sections listed above, but also in the opening sentences of each paragraph.

ACTIVITY 4.1   Identifying the argument of an article

As an individual or with another student

Using the titles of the following journal articles to help you, choose one of them that might be appropriate for your studies. (If none of them is directly appropriate, choose the one that most interests you.) Through your library catalogue, find a copy of this text and download it to your own computer.

- A journal article by Tearlach Hutcheson called 'Australian Cinema: Searching for a National Identity'
- A journal article by Rachel H. Salk and Renee Engeln-Maddox called "'If You're Fat, Then I'm Humongous!": Frequency, Content, and Impact of Fat Talk Among College Women'
- A journal article by Kieran O'Doherty and Amanda Lecouteur called "'Asylum Seekers", "Boat People" and "Illegal Immigrants": Social Categorisation in the Media'
- A journal article by Jake Olivier, Sofiane Boufous and Raphael Grzebieta called 'The Impact of Bicycle Helmet Legislation on Cycling Fatalities in Australia'
- A journal article by Marilyn Charles called 'Caring for the Caregivers: Building Resilience'
- A journal article by Larissa Karklins and Derek Dalton called 'Social Networking Sites and the Dangers They Pose to Youth: Some Australian Findings'
- A journal article by Donna Weeks called 'An East Asian Security Community: Japan, Australia and Resources as "Security"'
- A journal article by S.M. Solaiman, Yusuke Yamauchi, Jung Ho Kim, Joseph Horvat, Shi Xue Dou, Gursel Alici, Lezanne Ooi, Boris Martinac, Muhammad J.A. Shiddiky, Vinod Gopalan and Md Shahriar A. Hossain called 'Nanotechnology and its Medical Applications: Revisiting Public Policies from a Regulatory Perspective in Australia'
- A journal article by Stephen Krashen and Fay Shin called 'Summer Reading and the Potential Contribution of the Public Library in Improving Reading for Children of Poverty'
- A journal article by Paul Cozens called 'Public Health and the Potential Benefits of Crime Prevention through Environmental Design'
- A journal article by Michael Bounds and Alan Morris called 'Second Wave Gentrification in Inner-City Sydney'

By reading just the sections that help you identify the argument (listed in the paragraphs before this activity), write down the argument of this article, in your own words. You will generally be able to do this in just one sentence, but occasionally will use two interlinked sentences. So that you can demonstrate your understandings clearly, make sure that you completely rewrite the authors' sentences – don't just replace some words with synonyms. (See Chapter 5 for a discussion of plagiarism.) Write this argument below.

_____

_____

_____

Use the word 'that' in your statement

Include the word 'that' in your statement of argument to ensure that you focus on its argument rather than just its subject. For example:

> The authors argue that online study demands particular skills and approaches from students, which develop slowly and with practice.

> **Not:** The authors write about the skills and approaches students need to develop for online study.

In a class or a group

Working with a group who have chosen the same text, share your thesis statements. Give each other feedback on whether:

- each statement is a clear argument
- it encapsulates the argument of the text effectively
- it is written in the student's own words.

ACTIVITY 4.2   Identifying the main ideas that build an argument

As an individual or with another student

Taking the article you chose and the argument you identified in Activity 4.1, identify the three or four main ideas the authors use to build that argument. Use the article sections you used for Activity 4.1; you might also read quickly through the first sentences of each paragraph. Do not include descriptions, background details and examples among your ideas – although the authors will have mentioned these in order to explain the context of their research, your focus must be solely on the ideas that help build this argument.

Write your three or four main ideas below. Once again, ensure you write in your own words and sentence structures – don't just take the authors' sentences and replace occasional words.

_____

_____

_____

_____

_____

_____

_____

_____

In a class or a group

Working in the same group as for Activity 4.1, share your main ideas. Give each other feedback on whether:

- these are ideas, rather than description or examples
- they work to build the argument
- they are written in the student's own words.

Two student examples

In the following examples, two students have combined Activities 4.1 and 4.2. In Example 4.1, the student has read an article about hostile architecture – that is, architecture designed to discourage people from loitering – in particular areas of the city of London.

Example 4.1 Reading for argument and ideas: article on hostile architecture

Petty, James. 2016. 'The London Spikes Controversy: Homelessness, Urban Securitisation and the Question of Hostile Architecture.' *International Journal for Crime, Justice, and Social Democracy* 5 (1): 67–81. **https://doi.org/10.5204/ijcjsd.v5i1.286**.

The main argument for this text is that the public outcry over the installation of spikes that target homeless people in London is a reaction to the sudden visibility of increased urban security systems.

The following related ideas support this argument:

- There has been a shift from punitive laws and policing of deviance towards influencing of norms and behaviour. Hostile architecture is a physical manifestation of this.
- Hostile architecture such as spikes, ultraviolet lighting, security cameras, automatic sprinkler systems and benches that prevent resting are social control mechanisms that regulate the order of the city by excluding deviance.
- The spikes provoke a negative reaction because they are a constant visible reminder of homelessness, without providing a solution to the actual problem.

James Gibson, Architecture student

In Example 4.2, the student has read an article assessing the value of caring for country programs for Aboriginal and Torres Strait Islander peoples.

Example 4.2 Reading for argument and ideas: article on caring for country programs for Aboriginal and Torres Strait Islander peoples

Jones, Roxanne, Katherine A. Thurber, Alyson Wright, Jan Chapman, Peter Donohoe, Vanessa Davis and Raymond Lovett. 2018. 'Associations between Participation in a Ranger Program and Health and Wellbeing Outcomes among Aboriginal and Torres Strait Islander People in Central Australia: A Proof of Concept Study.' *International Journal of Environmental Research and Public Health* 15 (1478): 1–13. **https://doi.org/10.3390/ijerph15071478**.

The main argument for this text is that participation in caring for country programs improves the health and wellbeing among Aboriginal and Torres Strait Islander peoples and improves a person's cultural connection.

The following three related ideas support this argument:

- Those who were non-participants in caring for country programs (Rangers) had much lower life satisfaction than those who participated in these programs.
- Participants in caring for country programs reported greater family wellbeing, higher financial status and higher employment rates than non-participants. These results are hypothesised to be linked with routine engagement in cultural activities through caring for country programs.
- Improved health and wellbeing from these programs are associated with increased cultural engagement across many age brackets, and enhanced knowledge transfer within communities.

Ashleigh Morris, Biology student

Reading for detail and example

Once you have identified the argument and the main ideas used to build it, you will be able to understand the rest of the article much more easily. For some articles, you will choose not to read any more than these sections already discussed; for others you will read or skim-read through other sections; and for some you will read the entire articles. This will depend on how the article fits with the rest of the research you are doing. For example, if a particular article covers only a side issue of the main subject you are researching, it might be enough to understand its authors' argument and main ideas; whereas if the article contains a detailed case study that is central to an argument you are building for an essay or report, you may choose to read the entire article.

To support your reading of each article, it will be helpful for you to understand how it is structured. Remember that journal articles tend to draw on the results of new research to create their argument, though this does not have to be what is traditionally viewed as research (e.g. scientific experiments, responses to surveys, interviews with key people, observations of the behaviour of groups, or surveys of previous writings).

HINT

What is data?

Even material that is not numerical is generally called 'data'. Data is divided into 'quantitative data' (that is, items that can be measured and expressed in numbers, graphs, statistics and so on) and 'qualitative data' (that is, words, ideas, images and other information that can be observed but not measured).

Recently, research in scholarly journal articles, particularly in the humanities, has begun to include more innovative data, such as personal stories, creative writings and reflections. Nevertheless, you are likely to read more traditional scholarly journal articles in your first year of studies, which generally contain standard sections, identifiable from the headings and subheadings. In addition to subheadings that are specific to the subject of the article, you will generally find general headings and subheadings that will help you make meaning from the articles:

- After the introduction, there may be a section called 'Background', which gives the context for the authors' research.
- You will often find a section called something like 'Research methods' or 'Methodology', which explains how the data was gathered and interpreted.
- There will often be sections called 'Analysis', 'Discussion' and 'Findings', where the data is analysed and ideas developed to build the authors' argument. In the first of these sections, you will sometimes find complex analysis of data that you do not currently understand, but

don't give up here – look for the authors' explanations in the discussion and findings sections to help you understand the gist of the ideas.

- In some articles, you will also find a short section called 'Limitations' or 'Scope', which outlines the focuses the authors were able to pursue within their study or the impediments to their research.
- These sections will then take you to the 'Conclusions' section, which you have already browsed through in your first reading, and where you will find the main argument and findings restated clearly.

If you have decided you want to read a section from the body of the article (or indeed the whole article), two techniques will help you do this efficiently.

Technique 1: Skimming

The skimming technique is most suitable for texts that outline a procedure, present an argument or explain a concept or idea in a straightforward, logically structured way. It is excellent if your purpose is to gain an overview, and if the material is relatively simple or familiar to you. If you are finding the article complex, then work with one section at a time.

When you skim, you read only the main ideas in a text by going through the following procedure:

- Notice any headings and subheadings in the section, as well as graphs and diagrams, all of which will give you additional perspectives on the words written.
- Read the opening paragraph of the section you are focusing on, in order to establish the context of the section.
- Read the opening sentence of each following paragraph, where you will generally find the main idea of that paragraph.
- Read the final paragraph.
- If some ideas are not clear, go back to the relevant sections and read them in more detail.
- Depending on your purpose in reading, and on the complexity and relevance of the text, make notes as you go or after you have skimmed the entire text. (See the section on making notes later in this chapter.)

Technique 2: Scanning

The scanning technique is appropriate for all articles that present ideas or concepts, however complex, especially if your purpose is to find specific information, definitions, formulas or ideas, or to answer a particular question.

When you scan, you look for certain keywords or phrases you have identified as important to the information you seek, by moving your eyes quickly over complete pages. You should pay particular attention to headings and to graphics. Keywords in these areas are likely to indicate the presence of significant information that will be relevant to you. If you are reading an electronic text, use your device's 'Find' tool to search for all the places where the word or phrase is used. You can then read just the sections containing these words and phrases.

As with the skimming technique, you will need to adapt the amount and frequency of your note making to your purpose and to the complexity of the text.

ACTIVITY 4.3   Reading a scholarly text

As an individual or with another student

Using the article you have already worked with in Activities 4.1 and 4.2, identify a section from the article that you will read in more detail. Depending on your purpose in reading this section, choose to either skim the section to identify key details that will support your overall argument and ideas, or to scan the text for certain words or phrases that are crucial to the argument. Write three or four details or ideas you have learned from this activity in the space below. (Write the ideas in your own words – do not copy and paste from the text.)

_____

_____

_____

_____

In a class or a group

Compare your choice of strategy with the rest of the group, along with the answers you have written above. Discuss the merits of skimming and scanning, and which technique was better suited for different types of information you found in your reading.

Strategies for reading complex texts

Sometimes, you will come across a text you find difficult to understand, and even after employing the approaches outlined above, you may still find it difficult to make meaning from what you read. First, realise that scholarly texts are some of the more difficult and complex texts that we come across in our lives – it is appropriate and to be expected that you will struggle to understand some of them. The following sections give our suggestions for strategies to deal with such a text.

Strategy 1: Avoid it or put it off until later

No, this is not a joke! Some of the texts you discover in your research may be too difficult for you. For example, they may be written by academics for their colleagues or for postgraduate students.

It is counterproductive to struggle with a text that is too difficult in the early stages of your research in a topic. But this may not mean that you should discard it completely. If you are intrigued by a difficult text, note its bibliographic details (author, title and so on) or bookmark it, and come back to it later in the research process.

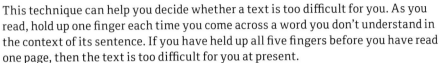

The five-finger rule

This technique can help you decide whether a text is too difficult for you. As you read, hold up one finger each time you come across a word you don't understand in the context of its sentence. If you have held up all five fingers before you have read one page, then the text is too difficult for you at present.

Of course, if a lecturer has set a particular text as compulsory, you will have to read it. You may find some of the following strategies useful to help you make meaning from it.

Strategy 2: Look up the essential words

You need to learn to distinguish between words that are essential to the meaning of a passage and words that are peripheral to it. As you read, you should thus look up in a dictionary only essential words you do not understand that are specific to your discipline. Write down these dictionary definitions and keep them next to you while you continue to read the text.

However, you may find that a dictionary definition does not help you to understand a word immediately. In this case, write down all the phrases in the text that contain this word. Develop a cumulative list of phrases containing the word, and look back over this as you find each new use of the word.

Learners' dictionaries are also useful to give you a sense of how words might be used in context. (See Chapter 5 for a discussion of these.)

The language of your discipline

The essential words you encounter in your set readings are likely to be core terms in the language of your discipline. It will be very useful for you to start building a list of these terms, along with examples of ways in which they are used.

Strategy 3: 'Google' the essential words

It is often useful to read how other writers have used the same key terms. Enter them into your favourite search engine and browse some of the websites you find there. You might add some of the uses of the words to your growing list.

Strategy 4: Pay particular attention to any graphics in the text

Graphics (tables, graphs, figures, diagrams, maps, photos and so on) often present clear overviews of large sections of text. If you are a visual learner, you will find them a particularly useful tool for making meaning from the text.

Strategy 5: Draw a mind map of the information

Try to draw a mind map or other graphic organiser that shows the relationships among ideas in the text. This is another example of active reading – in working to create the graphic, you are shaping your understanding of the text. There are many helpful websites on mind-mapping, all with examples you can use as models. (See the 'Useful websites' list at the end of Chapter 6 for some useful resources on mind-mapping, including free software that enables you to mind-map electronically.) Figure 4.1 (following) shows a mind map made from a lecture, but you can also make such a map from a written text.

Strategy 6: Make notes as you go

Write the information in your own words as you read, working paragraph by paragraph for very difficult material, or section by section for less complex texts. If you have a photocopy or download, you might annotate in the margins. This process will also help you make meaning from the text, and the notes or annotations will be useful to you later for review purposes.

Viewing audio-visual scholarly texts

This section includes advice on how to make meaning from videos and podcasts. In recent years, many universities have begun to replace live lectures with recorded versions (iLectures), making the recordings available through their learning management systems. While you lose the immediate impact of a live presentation, you benefit by having a recording that you can watch in your own time. You can also replay significant sections as often as you like, particularly if you are making notes on complex ideas. Many of our students for whom English is an additional language, in particular, appreciate this option very much.

Audio-visual items are called 'texts' too!

Remember that we use the word 'texts' to refer to all items of communication, whether they are written or audio-visual. This includes every item from shopping lists to full-length feature films.

The other audio-visual texts you are likely to view or listen to in your studies include TED talks, YouTube videos and podcasts of radio broadcasts (such as ABC programs).

Many of the approaches and techniques we explored above for reading scholarly texts are also relevant to viewing audio-visual ones. In particular, the audio-visual texts you will view will most often seek to present an argument and a series of main ideas that will build that argument. Even if there is no one argument, there will be a series of ideas that present a perspective on or analysis of a subject. You should therefore use these approaches when you view the text:

- Begin by anticipating what the text is likely to present to you, and considering what you already know about this subject.
- Look for hints in the early moments of the presentation about the likely argument and/or ideas you will be presented with. These hints might include the following:
  - the title
  - the introduction (for an iLecture, there will probably be a PowerPoint, which might include a slide giving an overview of the session)
  - early phrases about what will be included and how the presentation will be structured
  - early graphics and headings, for visual texts.
- As you continue to view the presentation, stay engaged in your viewing and listening by adopting the active reading techniques for a written text (listed in the previous section).
- Make notes as you listen. (See below for advice on this.)
- When you have finished viewing the text, deepen your understanding by creating a mind map or other graphic representation. This will also have the benefit of helping you retain the ideas much longer, since you have engaged with them deeply. Figure 4.1 is an example of a mind map made from an iLecture on language learning.

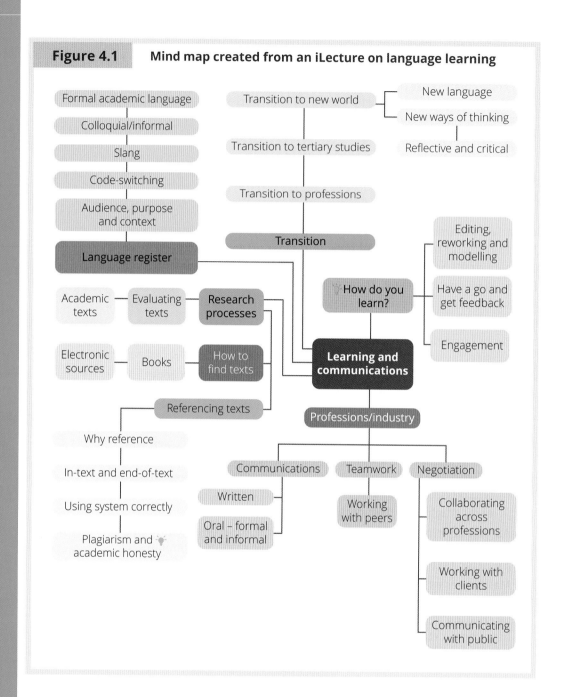

Figure 4.1   Mind map created from an iLecture on language learning

Formal academic language

Colloquial/informal

Slang

Code-switching

Audience, purpose and context

Language register

Transition to new world
— New language
— New ways of thinking

Transition to tertiary studies
Reflective and critical

Transition to professions

Transition

Academic texts — Evaluating texts — **Research processes**

Electronic sources — Books — How to find texts

Referencing texts

Why reference

In-text and end-of-text

Using system correctly

Plagiarism and academic honesty

How do you learn?

Learning and communications

Editing, reworking and modelling

Have a go and get feedback

Engagement

Professions/industry

Communications

Teamwork

Negotiation

Written

Oral – formal and informal

Working with peers

Collaborating across professions

Working with clients

Communicating with public

ACTIVITY 4.4 Viewing the beginning of a scholarly text

As an individual or with another student

Using a TED talk or YouTube video chosen by you or provided by your teacher, watch the first section, then write what you believe will be the main argument and/or ideas presented in the audio-visual text. Make notes on a separate piece of paper so that you have enough space for this activity.

In a class or a group

Compare your answers to this activity. Discuss what strategies you used and clues you noticed that led you to reach these answers.

ACTIVITY 4.5 Viewing the entire scholarly text

As an individual or with another student

Now view the rest of the text you started in Activity 4.4., using the active listening techniques designed to keep you engaged in the viewing. Make notes below on the ideas you had anticipated, but also on ideas you had not anticipated. What extra ideas and details surprised you?

_____

_____

_____

_____

In a class or a group

Compare your answers with the rest of the group, noticing similarities and differences. What active listening techniques most helped you make meaning from this audio-visual text?

Making notes from your reading or viewing

When you read or view a scholarly text, you will often need to make notes on it. For a printed text, you might also highlight or annotate the text. Many iLecture systems also allow you to make notes on side screens as you view.

How to make notes

- Write down all the bibliographic details of the text (e.g. author, title, URL) so that you won't waste time later trying to find the text again.
- For written texts, go through the process of reading for the argument and ideas, then skimming or scanning, as explained earlier.

- For audio-visual texts, use early visual and verbal clues to anticipate what arguments and ideas the text will present.
- Never write in full sentences. Write only as many words as you need to make sense of your notes when you read over them later in the year. You will develop this skill as the academic year progresses, and will probably find that you write fewer words as you improve your note-making skills.
- Develop your own abbreviations of common words. You are the only one who needs to understand your notes, so you can invent any abbreviations you like; however, you may find it easier to use some of the generally accepted abbreviations you are already familiar with (such as 'e.g.', 'εt', 'i.e.', '≠' and '∴').

Practice will make it automatic

At first, you may feel this note-making process is time-consuming, but if you continue to use it you will find that it will become automatic for you. It will both save you time and develop your thinking more deeply.

ACTIVITY 4.6   Making notes from a printed or audio-visual text

As an individual or with another student

Read or view a text chosen by you or given to you by your teacher. Make notes below on this text.

_____

_____

_____

_____

_____

_____

_____

_____

_____

_____

_____

In a class or a group

Compare your notes with the rest of your group, noticing similarities and differences. What techniques do you feel worked best for you in making meaning from this text?

When you photocopy from books and journals and download from the Internet, you can highlight and annotate rather than make traditional notes. However, there will be times when you cannot photocopy a book or a journal article, and so you will have to make notes from it. It will therefore be very useful for you to develop your note-making skills, as explained so far.

When you make photocopies or print downloads, you will use different skills, of emphasising and commenting on particular ideas – the skills of highlighting and annotating.

Highlighting

By *highlighting*, we mean the process of marking particular sections of your copy of a text, either with a coloured highlighter or by underlining them. Our suggestions for highlighting in a productive way include the following:

- Don't mark too much of the text; look for the main ideas only. There is little value in a page that has more highlighted than unhighlighted text because when you come to review the text you will need to re-read almost the entire page.

- Be very careful when you incorporate the ideas from highlighted sections in an assignment. Because you're working with the author's own words, the dangers of plagiarism are very high. (If you're unsure about plagiarism, see Chapter 5.) Most importantly, always put aside your photocopy of an author's text after you have reviewed it and before you start writing. Do not write an assignment with the text in front of you. (We will discuss paraphrasing and quoting in much more detail in Chapter 5.)

Annotating

By *annotating*, we mean the process of writing notes, arrows and other symbols in the margins of your copy of a text. You can equally do this on a PDF or Word version of an electronic text. This is a very productive way of responding actively to a text. Here are some ways in which you can make annotations work for you:

- Annotations are your response to, and shaping of, the ideas in a text. Annotate as often as you can – the more you annotate, the more active you are being as a reader.

- In as few words as possible, make notes on your responses to particular ideas. (For example, do you agree? Do you find the idea convincing? Interesting? Challenging? Laughable? Does it link with something else you have read?)

- Also make notes on how the ideas relate to both the content and the structure of your assignment. (For example, will they form the basis of a certain section? Will they provide you with a valuable concessive argument [see Chapter 9]? Will they answer a specific question?)

- Note page numbers of other sections (in the same text or a different one) that relate to this idea. Use a symbol such as an asterisk to mark these related ideas.

Many published sets of annotations will give you ideas on how you might do this. Here are a few interesting examples:

- In 2017, James Comey, the ex-Director of the FBI, appeared before the US Select Committee on Intelligence. Here is the annotation of his testimony by Josh Marshall, editor of Talking Points Memo: **https://talkingpointsmemo.com/edblog/my-annotated-notes-on-the-comey-statement**.

- Medical and other science students frequently annotate diagrams. See this example of an annotated diagram of the human heart: **https://bmcmededuc.biomedcentral.com/articles/10.1186/s12909-019-1529-7/figures/3**.

- This amazing annotation by a Chinese student published in the British Mirror newspaper is a work of art: **https://www.mirror.co.uk/news/uk-news/how-students-unrecognisable-work-art-11895659**.

ACTIVITY 4.7 Annotating a text

As an individual or with another student

Annotate a one-page printed text on a subject you are currently studying. Use marginal notes, highlighting, coloured symbols, cross references and any other techniques to deepen your thinking.

In a class or a group

Pin up the annotated pages and discuss. Within your discussion include questions like what you think the annotations mean, and what different ways people represent ideas (e.g. in words, as symbols, using colours).

REVISION TOOLS

↘ Revision activity: Revise these ideas

1 Scholarly reading and viewing at university are often very different from the reading and viewing you have done in your previous education.

2 You need to read and view actively – that is, engage your mind in making patterns and asking questions before, during and after your reading and viewing.

3 The most complex types of text you are likely to read as a first-year student are scholarly journal articles. They have their own common conventions, and understanding these will help you make meaning from the texts.

4 Your viewing is likely to include iLectures, TED talks and YouTube videos; for all of these, your approaches and strategies for making meaning will be similar to the approaches and strategies you learned for printed texts.

5 Some scholarly texts are very complex and, as a first-year student, you need specific strategies to help you make meaning from them.

6 Mind-mapping is a valuable active technique for reading and viewing; you may find it particularly useful throughout the rest of your studies.

↘ Thinking activity: Critical and reflective questions

1 What reading and viewing approaches and techniques have worked well for me in the past? How do I need to adapt them so that they will suit university study?

2 How do I make judgements about what is appropriate and relevant to read and view for my studies each semester?

3 Am I often overwhelmed by the amount of reading and viewing I am faced with in my studies? What approaches and attitudes will help me learn to work with these texts most efficiently?

4 Why is the amount of reading and viewing I need to do increasing dramatically in my university studies? How might this relate to my future studies and professional life?

↘ Useful weblinks

Consult the following online resources for further information about reading and viewing scholarly texts, including making notes from these texts:

Kishwaukee College Library, *How to Read a Scholarly Journal Article*: **https://www.youtube.com/watch?v=EEVftUdfKtQ**.

Professor Pete Carr, University of Minnesota, *How to Read a Paper Efficiently*: **https://www.youtube.com/watch?v=IeaD0ZaUJ3Y** (focuses on reading science articles).

Ross Avilla, *How to Read a Psychology Article*: **https://www.youtube.com/watch?v=w9xc6AnAACk**.

Healey Library, University of Massachusetts, Boston, 'Reading Research Articles': **https://umb.libguides.com/c.php?g=351041&p=2368716**.

University of Maryland Libraries, '"How Do I Even Read That?" Understanding Scholarly Articles': **https://umd.instructure.com/courses/1082806/pages/how-do-i-even-read-that-understanding-scholarly-articles**.

University of New South Wales, 'Listening Note Taking Strategies': **https://student.unsw.edu.au/note-taking-skills**.

College of Saint Benedict and Saint John's University, Minnesota, 'Lecture Note Taking': **https://www.csbsju.edu/academic-advising/study-skills-guide/lecture-note-taking** (useful section on signals to look for in lectures).

Referencing and academic integrity

CONTENTS

Getting started on referencing

Once you have found some reliable and relevant texts on your topic, as we outlined in Chapter 3, you need to understand how to reference them correctly.

Even if you are not yet ready to start writing a formal assignment, it is good to learn about referencing now because it will affect the way you make notes on your reading and the bibliographic details (author's name, title, publisher, journal title and so on) you keep about the texts you find. Most students make the mistake at least once of forgetting to keep a note of where they found particular texts, and then having to retrace their steps later to find the full details they need for their referencing. Avoid the hassle and the huge waste of time by collecting the information as you go! As soon as you start to research, set up a document on your computer in which you keep full details of all the texts you find. Even if you don't end up needing all of them, it's helpful to have a repository of all the texts you looked at in your research in case you need to go back to them for a future assignment.

Learn how to reference

This chapter is about referencing in general, not about how to reference according to a specific system. Your school, department or library will have guides for particular systems, and you must always follow those guides. There are often subtle differences in the way the systems are applied in a particular institution, so always use your guide – even when you think you know what you're doing!

Why reference?

When you write any formal assignment at university, you are required to acknowledge where you found the ideas that you include in the assignment. You must identify the source of *every* idea, quotation, graphic or statistic that you find in your research, and you have to do it according to the system required by your department. This is called *referencing*.

There are several reasons for referencing:

- Ideas are like works of art – their creators have the right to be recognised for them.
- You need to develop your thinking by critically reading other people's ideas, agreeing with some, disagreeing with others and adapting still others to new shapes. This requires the ability to *synthesise information* (see Chapter 9), a high-level thinking skill appropriate at university level. In your written work you will therefore present (and acknowledge) a wide range of other people's ideas, which you will analyse and synthesise to answer your research question.

- By acknowledging your sources, you take your place in the world of academic scholarship. Think of scholarship as an ongoing conversation conducted by researchers all around the world. By reading and responding to other people's ideas – including acknowledging where you found these ideas – you are taking part in the ongoing conversations in your discipline.
- Referencing helps others to locate the texts you used to come to your conclusions. Your reader can check that the assertion you're making is logical or that it applies the information accurately, or they may simply be interested to read more about the topic!

Students often find themselves feeling somewhat resentful about having to use what can seem like an extraordinary number of citations in their work. A common complaint is, 'but these are *my* ideas. Why do I need to cite them?'. It's understandable that early in your tertiary studies you might feel this way too. However, citing your research is not about giving away your ideas or looking for someone who has said the same thing already. Instead, it's about marshalling an army of scholars behind your work to support your ideas. Your citations not only acknowledge the source of your ideas and quotes, they also provide strength and weight to your assertions; they are like holding up a sign that says, 'this expert supports what I'm writing – you should believe me too!'.

Just 'knowing' something is not enough in academic writing; you need to be able to show that there is a basis in research for the conclusions you're drawing. We all like to think that our own experiences are important (they are!) but they are not enough evidence from which to generalise. Just because you have personally experienced something doesn't mean that this is a widespread occurrence or an inarguable fact. Citations in your writing demonstrate that someone who is expert and well-versed in the field supports what you are suggesting. Remember, using citations in your work is not about 'ticking a box'; rather, it is about looking for and acknowledging research that strengthens your ideas and conclusions.

 Student reflection 5.1   **Academic integrity**

I wouldn't like to pay for an espresso that was made using instant coffee. Even worse is imagining that espresso coffee should be expected to taste like instant coffee! Whatever your opinion of instant coffee is, it's not accurate to say it's the same as an espresso. Academic integrity is a bit like that: a university education is only as esteemed as the authenticity and validity of the research behind it.

Christine Polowyj, Humanities student

HINT

Learn to be more than a doer

Some of our students state that they have come to university to learn how to be better designers, photographers, teachers, physiotherapists, accountants and so on. They're not interested in taking part in conversations about their discipline – they just want to learn to *do* it better.

If this is how you feel, consider how much you are limiting yourself to the opinions of your teachers and fellow students. If you are to be the best professional you can be and play a productive role among your future colleagues, you must be aware of new trends and ideas in your discipline – you must understand them, think about them critically and apply them to your own work.

If you're not convinced about this, think about how you would feel to have your children taught by teachers who were unaware of new approaches to education, or to have your spine cared for by physiotherapists who had not read recent research in their field. This could apply equally to designers, construction managers, photographers, accountants and so on. We rely on all professionals to keep up to date with the scholarly conversations in their disciplines.

How to reference

Referencing is something that many people find daunting and finicky. We often hear students complain that 'surely a full stop doesn't matter that much!' or 'it's just a capital letter!'. Referencing is time-consuming and requires attention to detail but it is something that you *can* get completely correct! The following section will help demystify the process and rules of referencing.

Know the system required by your department

When you reference, you acknowledge, or *cite*, the source of each idea that you mention, giving enough details of this source so that your reader can find it. Systems have been developed over the past decades to cite these sources in a consistent way, so that there can be no confusion over what each reference or citation means. Commonly used referencing systems in Australian universities include the following:

- The *Chicago referencing system*, developed by the University of Chicago, and the *Harvard referencing system*, developed by Harvard University, are both used in a wide range of disciplines, including most science, engineering and business disciplines, and some health, humanities and social science disciplines.

- The *APA system*, developed by the American Psychological Association, is most common in psychology, social work, education and media studies.

- The *MLA system*, developed by the US Modern Languages Association, is preferred in some humanities disciplines, particularly literature and cultural studies.

Other general referencing systems used in some departments include the Vancouver and Toronto systems. Some disciplines have their own systems; for example, Exploration Geophysics students adopt the guidelines of the Society of Exploration Geophysics (SEG), Law students often use the Australian Guide to Legal Citation (AGLC) and Physiotherapy students need to learn the *Australian Journal of Physiotherapy* (AJP) system.

We are not going to explain in detail any of these systems in this book. Instead, we will just give you some ideas about how *all* of these systems are structured.

HINT

Guides to your referencing systems

Your department or school may publish a guide to the referencing system that you must use, or it may specify the system and require that you find an appropriate guide. Check your university library's information desk or some of the excellent online guides available from Australian universities. (We list some of these at the end of this chapter.) For example, Health Sciences students at Curtin University must refer to the helpful and detailed *Curtin Health Academic and Study Guide* (see **http://healthsciences.curtin.edu.au/wp-content/uploads/sites/6/2015/11/CHAS_BOOKLET_2014-16112015.pdf**), which explains in detail several relevant referencing systems and moves beyond referencing into formatting and language use.

Understand the basic structure of referencing

All referencing systems adopt the same approach, but the details differ. Each of them will have a specific way of acknowledging the source of the idea briefly in the text, as well as in full at a later point.

The in-text citation

All referencing systems require that you place a label next to each idea, quote, statistic or graphic that you have found in another source. This label's purpose is to represent a particular text *as briefly as possible*, so that your readers can understand which text you are citing without having the flow of their reading seriously interrupted. The label might be a footnote number, but could as easily be a picture, word or any other symbol connected in some way to the particular citation. This label is generally called an *in-text reference* or *in-text citation*. The two most common types of labels or citations are:

- numerical citations (as in the MLA and Vancouver systems), where a number is placed directly after the citation

- author–date citations (as in, for example, the Chicago and APA systems), where the author's family name and the year of publication are placed in parentheses directly after the citation. (If there is no author, you use the title instead.)

Comma or no comma?

The punctuation and formatting within a reference or a citation may seem incidental but in fact the placement of it is crucial. Becoming adept at referencing is about being pedantic and having great attention to detail. Many students are initially surprised by the amount of time it takes to reference well. Don't leave your referencing to the last minute! Plan to spend several hours on constructing and checking your reference list and citations. Having a completely correct list is possible and expected in tertiary level writing. It shows your reader that you have taken care in your work and that you respect the conventions of the institution.

Consider the differences in punctuation for a book written by three authors when constructing a Chicago citation, an APA citation and a Harvard one:
- Chicago: (Grellier, Goerke and Fielding 2021, 67)
- APA: (Grellier et al., 2021, p. 67)
- Harvard: (Grellier, Goerke & Fielding 2021, p. 67)

Can you spot the differences? They may seem insignificant but in fact they are a key part of correctly using these systems.

Author–date systems are popular because they provide instant basic information about your citation – your readers will quickly become familiar with the details of each text you cite, and will not need to check the full publishing details each time you refer to this text. On the other hand, a numerical label represents a text but does not speak for itself – your readers need to check which text each number refers to. This means that their eyes will be drawn regularly to the foot of the page or the back of your document to check your sources. Those who support numerical systems, however, claim that the numbers do not interrupt the reader's flow of concentration as much as author–date citations do.

URLs are not in-text citations

A common mistake among our students is to use a website's URL as an in-text citation. You should cite a webpage the same way you would cite any other text: by its author (or title, if there is no author) and year of publication. (Note that there is a situation in which you might cite the URL directly; namely, when you are referring to a complete website, generally of an organisation. For example: 'The Responsible Cafes website (**http://www.responsiblecafes.org**) provides practical advice for reducing the waste we generate when enjoying takeaway coffee.') You should always check your referencing guide carefully for information about how to cite a whole website or an individual webpage in the particular system you are using.

The end-of-text reference

The label described above must refer to a complete reference placed elsewhere in your writing – on a separate page at the end of the complete text or a section of the text; as a footnote on the relevant page; or, in the case of a website, sometimes on a separate page or in a drop-down box hyperlinked to the label. This reference is called an *end-of-text reference*.

The list of references and the bibliography

The *list of references* (called a 'Works cited' list in the MLA system) is the complete list of all the texts you have cited in your piece of writing. To make it easy for your reader to find the work that corresponds with a particular label, you must arrange this list in alphabetical order by the author (or by title, if there is no author). In most systems you must indent the second and subsequent lines of each entry (called a *hanging indent*), so that the authors' names stand out.

The *bibliography* is the list of all relevant texts that you have consulted in your research on this topic, not just those you have cited. The list of references is therefore a subset of the bibliography. Check with your lecturers whether they want you to add a bibliography or require only a list of references. See Figure 5.1 for an overview of the differences

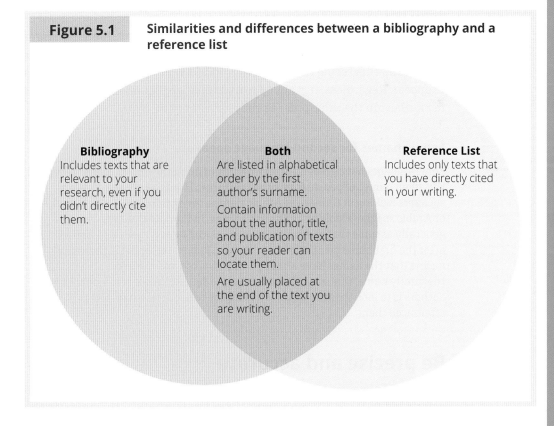

Figure 5.1 **Similarities and differences between a bibliography and a reference list**

Bibliography
Includes texts that are relevant to your research, even if you didn't directly cite them.

Both
Are listed in alphabetical order by the first author's surname.

Contain information about the author, title, and publication of texts so your reader can locate them.

Are usually placed at the end of the text you are writing.

Reference List
Includes only texts that you have directly cited in your writing.

and similarities between these two types of end-of-text referencing conventions.

For an example of correct setting out of both lists of references and bibliographies in the Chicago system, look at the references at the end of some of the chapters in this book.

Alphabetical order

End-of-text references usually need to be listed in alphabetical order based on the surname of the first listed author (or the title, in the absence of an author) of the text. However, it's important to realise that the authors' names on a text might not be themselves listed alphabetically. You must *never* rearrange the authors' names as they are listed on the text you're referencing. For example, this book is written by Jane Grellier, Veronica Goerke and Katie Fielding. The reference, in APA 7th edition style, would look like this: Grellier, J., Goerke, V., & Fielding, K. (2021). *Communications toolkit* (5th ed.). Cengage.

Even though alphabetically Fielding comes before Goerke, which comes before Grellier, you must not change the name order as it was presented on the book. In academia and publishing, there are strict hierarchies that govern the order that people's names appear on their work. Sometimes this has to do with their credentials (e.g. a Professor's name would appear before a research assistant's name); other times it might be indicative of the division of labour (e.g. one person might have contributed a larger proportion of the writing of the text); sometimes it might simply be a matter of the authors agreeing that this is the order in which they wish their names to appear. Regardless, it is not up to us to change that name order – always list authors in the same order as they appear on the text.

Family names for second-language speakers

Some students have great difficulty distinguishing the family names from the given names of people from other cultures. This is as true for English speakers looking at Chinese or Arabic names, for example, as it is for Chinese or Arabic speakers looking at English names. In European names, you can generally assume that the family name is placed last. If there is a comma after the first name mentioned (e.g. 'Brown, James Alexander'), then this means that the names have already been inverted and the first name listed is the family name. One way to find out how to set out the names of published authors is to look them up on a search engine to see how others have referenced them.

Be precise and accurate

Referencing is a very precise skill, but not a difficult one to develop. You don't need to learn a large number of rules; just follow the guide to the system required by your department – keep this with you when you make notes and write academic texts. Even experienced academic writers follow referencing guides, rather than learn small details of multiple referencing systems.

 Student reflection 5.2   **A student's guide to referencing success**

Below is an example of the process a student follows to make sure she paraphrases and references well in her assignments. Developing a system that works for you will help you study efficiently and achieve success in your assignments.

- When I start a new reading, I write the article name, author/s and year at the top of my page.
- When I write a note, I always put the page number in the left column so I can refer back to it.
- If I think it's an important point, or relevant to an assignment, I put a star in the left column.
- I have a mixture of direct quotes and paraphrasing in my notes but always put direct quotes in quotation marks so I know I need to paraphrase if I use that part in an assignment.
- I have a Word document open and put the reference in straight away so I can't misplace it.
- If there is a salient point from someone else in the article I'm looking at, I will find the source, have a read, and reference from that.
- I have a copy of the referencing guide I need to use on my desk and refer to it when needed.
- In my notes, I highlight themes and ideas in different colours, making it easier to connect ideas across the readings.

Sarah Lazzaro, Education student

ACTIVITY 5.1   End-of-text referencing

With another student or individually

Consult the appropriate referencing guide and create correct end-of-text references for the following texts according to the referencing system required by your department. If you are working in a class group, your tutor may assign you a selection of the items. (Take care with capital letters in the titles – we have capitalised only the first word of each title, so you will need to check how to capitalise different types of titles in your system.)

1 Ian Colquhoun wrote a book entitled Design out crime, published by Taylor & Francis in Hoboken, New Jersey in 2012.

_____

_____

2 A book with the title User Participation and the subtitle A new approach to school design in Korea was written by Sun-Young Rieh, Jin-Wook Kim and Woong-Sang Yu and published in Paris in 2011 by OECD Publishing.

_____

_____

3 In March 2011, Kathryn Shultz presented a Ted Talk called 'On Being Wrong', which can be viewed on the Ted Talks website at **https://www.ted.com/talks/kathryn_schulz_on_being_wrong?language=en.**

_____

_____

4 Peter Newman published a chapter in a book with the title More than luck and the subtitle Ideas Australia needs now. The book's cover page reads 'Edited by Mark Davis & Miriam Lyons'. It was published by the Centre for Policy Development in Sydney in 2010. Newman's chapter in the book is called Sustainable cities, and runs from pages 149 to 158.

_____

_____

5 Linked with the previous publication, Peter Newman also published a chapter in a different book in 2010. The book's title is Resilience and transformation, and its subtitle is Preparing Australia for uncertain futures. It was published by CSIRO in Collingwood, Victoria, and the title page reads 'Edited by Steven Cork'. Newman's article in this book is entitled Resilient cities, and runs from pages 81 to 98. Supposing you cited from both of Newman's chapters (Question 4 and this one) in your essay, write the citations you would use so that your reader could distinguish between them.

_____

_____

6 A video with the title Respect and the subtitle Dignity, autonomy and relationships was published by Medcom in Cypress, California in 2006. No author is named.

_____

_____

7 Raymond J Cole and Richard Lorch edited a collection of essays entitled Buildings, culture and environment and subtitled Informing local and global practices, which was published by Blackwell Publishers in Oxford, England in 2003.

_____

_____

8 Volume 18, issue 2 of a journal called Qualitative inquiry, published in February 2012, contains an article written by Arthur P Bochner. The article is called Bird on the wire, and its subtitle is Freeing the father within me. It runs from pages 163 to 173 of this issue of the journal. Its doi is 10.1177/1077800411429094.

_____

_____

9 A Twitter user called LucyF tweeted 'can't get this song out of my head! #babysharkdoodoo #earworm' on Monday 4th May 2020. The URL for the tweet is **https://twitter.com/LucyF/status/826435920.**

_____

_____

10 An article was retrieved from the PubMed database on 8 July 2017. Its title is Considering the definition of addiction, and its authors are Steve Sussman and Alan N Sussman. It was published in volume 8, issue 10 of the International journal of environmental research and public health, appearing on pages 4025 to 4038. Its doi is 10.3390/ijerph8104025.

_____

_____

11 An article from The Australian newspaper, with no author, is entitled It's a miracle and subtitled Mice regrow hearts, and was published on 29 August 2005 on page 53.

_____

_____

12 The joint conference of the 47th Croatian and 7th International Symposium on Agriculture was held in Opatija, Croatia, from 13 to 17 February 2012. The proceedings were edited by M Pospisil, and published by the University of Zagreb Press, Zagreb, Croatia.

_____

_____

13 A website entitled Collection and preservation of blood evidence from crime scenes, written by George Schiro, is available online at **http://www.crime-scene-investigator.net/blood.html**. There is no date on the website, and it was accessed on 3 May 2017.

_____

_____

14 A website created by an organisation called time-warp is entitled 'Welcome to time-warp' and subtitled Archiving technology through the decades. It is dated 2012, and was consulted on 3 May 2017 at **http://www.time-warp.org**.

_____

_____

In a group or a class

Share your answers around the group to ensure you understand how to reference according to the style you're expected to use in your course.

EndNote

EndNote is a useful software package that is available free of charge to students in some universities. (If you don't have free access to it, you can buy it commercially.) When you enter into EndNote the information about your texts, it does the referencing work for you according to the system you specify, as well as helping you keep track of everything you read during your course.

EndNote:

- stores bibliographic information about texts in your own electronic 'library' – you can store many thousands of references in one library

- allows you to search for and sort texts by author or keyword in any field that you have set up
- automatically enters your citations and list of references in a Word document correctly formatted in your required referencing system and allows you to change the styles easily.

We encourage you to explore what EndNote can do for you. Some students are put off by the fact that they need to spend time initially learning to use it, but once you have learned, it will help you reference your assignments. If you're thinking about doing further study, consider the value of having a store of information about all the texts you've ever read that you can access using simple search terms.

EndNote does not replace your referencing system

Even if you use EndNote, you still need to learn your referencing system because EndNote does not make all referencing decisions for you. Occasionally, the references EndNote generates are not completely without error, and you need to be able to correct these. EndNote is just a computer program and does not make decisions or judgements like a human being does. As a past student once noted: *Rubbish in, rubbish out!* Make sure you check the references generated by EndNote using your referencing guide with the same attention to detail you would if you had constructed them yourself.

Paraphrasing and quoting

When you *paraphrase*, you write the ideas of an author in your own words; when you *quote*, you write them in the author's original words. First-year students often find it difficult to find an appropriate balance between paraphrasing and quoting – they generally quote too much. Disciplines vary in their citation practices, including the number and length of quotations included in texts. You will gradually become familiar with the practices of your discipline as you continue to read and write.

When you paraphrase, you must be sure that you understand what you are reading. This is so that you do not lose the meaning or intent of what the author originally wrote. This is a skill that takes work to develop! Don't just look for synonyms – you should not be simply replacing a few words here and there. Instead, you need to fundamentally change the 'shape' of the sentence. A helpful approach can be:

- Read the section you need to paraphrase a few times.
- Cover the text up or close the book and think about what the author is trying to say.
- Write out the main point you have read about without looking at the original. Re-read what you have written: does it convey the same meaning?

- Check the original again, making sure that you haven't inadvertently used the same phrasing or structure.

This will take time – like all aspects of academic writing, this isn't something that you're going to be able to do well if you rush it. Make sure you are budgeting your time carefully so that you don't end up scrambling to complete an assignment and unintentionally plagiarising your research.

Don't over-quote

Contrary to what you might assume, quotations are not necessarily better than paraphrasing. When you paraphrase into your own words, you demonstrate that you understand the text and that you can shape the information to suit the context of your own writing. Often, quotes don't really help you convey your ideas because they are too specific to the text they come from. Look to *understand* the point the author is making and then put it into your own words so that it works within the structure and grammar of your own text. Show your reader that you are developing your own position and ideas, using your research to support you rather than replicating what someone else wrote.

Frequently asked questions: paraphrasing and quoting

Below you will find a series of questions on paraphrasing and quoting that we have been asked by our students over many years – often by panicked email the evening before an assignment is due! Most of the information is general information you can apply to most systems (we have based specific examples on the Chicago 17th edition author–date system). Make the appropriate adjustments if you are using a different system.

What about an idea that is common knowledge?

'Common knowledge' refers to knowledge that you would expect people in your discipline to have, and you do not need to acknowledge it in your academic assignments. For example, the statement that a large part of Australia's export income derives from minerals is common knowledge, so you do not need to acknowledge your sources for it in an essay. However, if you were to go on to list the annual incomes gained for various mineral exports, then you would need to cite the source(s) in which you found these statistics.

If you're unsure whether certain ideas or information are common knowledge in your discipline, ask your lecturer. You may need to work within a discipline for some years before you can be confident about which ideas can be considered common knowledge in that discipline.

How do I reference a figure (i.e. a graphic)? And what do I do if I've modified the figure?

Write Figure 1, 2, 3 and so on under your figure, followed by a colon and the title of the figure (you may have to create this yourself, if the figure you are using does not have a title). Add the in-text citation in parentheses, setting out the citation in exactly the same way as you would a quotation – with the author's family name, the year of publication and the page number (except for websites, where you can omit the page number).

If you have modified a figure or created a graphic from information or statistics, add the phrase 'adapted from' to your in-text citation. For example, place the following under your figures:

Figure 2: Mineral exports from Australia, 2000–2010 (adapted from Peterson, Galbally, and Wright 2012, 36)

How do I punctuate an in-text citation within my own sentence?

Place the full-stop *after* the citation. If the last words of your sentence are part of a quotation and that quotation ends in a full stop, leave out that full stop. Then close the quotation marks, write the in-text citation and add the full-stop – the full-stop of your own sentence. For example:

The value of using online spaces isn't black and white: They 'can be time-consuming, dull, and harmful. They can also be empowering, creative, and community-forming' (Douglas 2019, para. 29).

How do I set out a long quotation?

If you need to quote a large section from someone else's work, write a complete sentence in your own words, add a colon, set out the quotation as a separate block and indent it, but do not add quotation marks. For example:

The value of using online spaces isn't black and white:

Engagements with social media can be time-consuming, dull, and harmful. They can also be empowering, creative, and community-forming. And they might be everything in between. Either/or debates are not useful here: we need to develop much more nuanced discussions on this fast-shifting cultural terrain. And these discussions are best driven by young cultural consumers and producers (Douglas 2019, para. 29–30).

Before you use a long quotation, ask yourself if it is necessary. Generally, it is better to paraphrase ideas than to include large quotations (except in the case of some humanities disciplines when you need to analyse the language used in a text rather than just present the ideas).

How do I set out a quotation if I want to include it as part of my own sentence?

First, you need to make sure that the phrases you quote flow within your sentence; that is, with the quoted phrases included, your entire sentence is grammatically correct. Then you need to alter the punctuation and capital letters of the quoted phrases to suit their position in your sentence. (See below on how to punctuate these changes.) Remember that your sentence controls the structure, not the words you quote. For example:

> Douglas (2019, para. 29) suggests that 'engagements with social media can be time-consuming, dull, and harmful', but that they can also have positive impacts for users.

What do I do if I want to leave some words or phrases out of the middle of a section I am quoting?

As with the previous answer, you must first make sure that the parts you quote flow grammatically without the omitted sections. Then you can replace the phrases you leave out with three dots – no more than three, since this is a particular punctuation mark (known as an *ellipsis*), just like a full-stop or semicolon. For example:

> The value of using online spaces isn't black and white:
>
> Engagements with social media can be time-consuming, dull, and harmful. They can also be empowering, creative, and community-forming ... we need to develop much more nuanced discussions on this fast-shifting cultural terrain (Douglas 2019, para. 29–30).

What do I do if I need to add or change words in a quote in order to make it flow in my own sentence?

Use square brackets for any additions or changes to words and letters within your quotes. For example:

> Douglas (2019, para. 29) suggests that 'engag[ing] with social media can be time-consuming, dull, and harmful' but can also lead to 'empower[ment], creativ[ity], and community-form[ation].'

Ways to introduce paraphrases and quotations

When you are using author–date systems or MLA, there are two basic ways in which to introduce paraphrases or quotations into your own writing.

Method 1: In your own sentence

This method is most useful when the author of a particular idea is an important figure in an academic conversation, or when the text represented a crucial step in the conversation. In these cases, you can use a phrase to refer to the author (and sometimes the date) within your own sentence. (See Table 5.1 for a range of possible phrases.) The first time you refer to this author, state the author's full name and explain the basis of this person's authority to write on the issue (generally, his or her position or academic background), if relevant. Within your own sentence you might also describe the text that you are citing.

Table 5.1	Useful verbs and other phrases
The author/writer/text:	
... states	... writes
... explores	... introduces
... examines	... articulates
... studies	... discusses
... purports	... debates
... argues	... describes
... says	... tells
... expresses	... raises the idea/point
... declares	... focuses
... believes	... concentrates
... explains	... derides
... highlights	... criticises
... contends	... supports
... claims	... praises
... acclaims	... endorses
... proclaims	... illustrates
... implies	... draws on the idea/concept/theme of [X] to do [Y]
... suggests	
Other useful phrases	
In the author's view/opinion ...	
According to the author ...	
In the words of ...	

So, your sentence might read something like:

According to Susan Wright, Professor of Geology at Townsville University, in her ground-breaking 2004 article on the possibilities of geosequestration in Australia …

Or:

Michael James, a widely published writer in the field of astrophysics, claims in his 2009 article that …

For all the subsequent references to this author, only use the author's family name (*never* only the given name).

Note that this way of including an author in your writing can make your writing seem somewhat conversational in tone – the sort of writing you might find in a magazine article, for example. You should use this sort of phrasing sparingly; it should only be used when you really need to demonstrate the importance of the author or the text to your discussion. In the vast majority of cases, you should simply use the author's surname (see Method 2).

Researching an author's authority

How do you know about an author's authority if this is not stated in the text you are reading? Look up the person on the Internet – you will almost certainly find all the details you will need about a person's position and publications.

This method of referring to the author within your own sentence affects the way you set out the in-text citation. Whether you refer to the author's full name or just the family name, your in-text citation in most systems will show only the year of the publication. For example:

Wright (2003) endorses the idea that …

Or:

This attitude can be compared to the suggestions of James (2009), who contends …

Note that in MLA, however, since you do not include the year within an in-text citation, you do not need to include a citation at all if you mention the author's name when you paraphrase.

In author–date systems, such as Chicago and APA, when you refer in your own sentence to both the author's name and the date of the text you are citing, you need no in-text citation at all, unless you are referring to an idea on a particular page of the text, in which case you will need to add the page number.

HINT

Use your own voice

Notice how each of the examples above describes what an author does? That is, you're telling the reader what the author suggests, claims or argues. This can be useful sometimes but be careful that your writing does not just become a long summary of what other people have said and done (unless, of course, your task is to present a summary of your readings!). Your reader expects to hear your voice – paraphrasing an idea into your own words and acknowledging it through a citation at the end (see Method 2, next) is usually a stronger and more sophisticated way of presenting your points.

Method 2: In an in-text citation

This method is more common than Method 1, particularly in the sciences and engineering, where ideas are generally considered more important than the researchers who present them. In this method you paraphrase an idea, make a quotation or insert a graphic or statistic in your own sentence, then add the author and date (or just the author in the MLA system) in parentheses afterwards.

When you quote, reproduce a graphic or cite a statistic, you *must* add the page number to the in-text citation. When you paraphrase, you will also often add a page number according to the following rules:

- You generally add the page number to a paraphrase if the idea occurs on only one specific page of your source. (However, some departments rule that page numbers must be used only for direct quotes – check with your lecturer.)
- You omit the page number if the idea you are paraphrasing is a general contention or commonly recurring idea in the source, and therefore isn't located on only one page.
- You cannot include a page number when you cite an online text, even for quotations, graphics and statistics. (If the online text is a PDF file, of course, you can include the page number.) In this case, many departments require that you include the paragraph number by counting through the paragraphs in the site – once again, check with your lecturer.

Your in-text citations would therefore look like the following in the Chicago system.

A direct quotation

'Sustainable architecture is not only a sensible concept. If we are to protect the environment in Australia, it is essential for the preservation of the environment as we know it' (Brown 2003, 236).

(Note that this quote is not from a real publication.)

A paraphrase of a contention that you found on a specific page of a text

The uptake of broadband will increase markedly in Australia over the next ten years (Jones 2005, 26).

A paraphrase of a claim put forward throughout a text, so it is not possible to add a page number

Geosequestration provides strong possibilities for safe, long-term storage of nuclear wastes (Wright 2003).

A paraphrase of an idea you found on a website, meaning it is not possible to add a page number

Jargon and bureaucratic language are increasing in Australian university documents, which makes these less accessible to first-year students (James 2016, para. 14).

Language for introducing quotes and paraphrases

Your writing will be more interesting if you use a range of verbs to introduce your quotes and paraphrases – don't just repeat a phrase such as 'the author says that …'. In Table 5.1 we offered you an extensive list of useful verbs and other phrases so that you can vary the words you use. But be sure of the exact connotation of those that you want to use – they are all slightly different.

Learner's dictionaries

So how can you be sure that you are using a word or phrase appropriately? The best tool to help you is a *learner's dictionary*, which gives you not just the definitions of a word but also phrases in which the word is used correctly. We recommend the *Oxford Advanced Learner's Dictionary*, which is available free online (see **http://www.oup.com/elt/catalogue/teachersites/oald7/?cc=global**). For other online dictionaries and thesauruses, see the 'Useful weblinks' list at the end of Chapter 12.

ACTIVITY 5.2   Introducing an author's ideas

With another student or individually

Below are 10 sentences. For each one, replace the bold-face verb with an alternative from the list given in **Table 5.1** without changing the meaning of the sentence. Use a different alternative for each sentence. The first has been done for you.

1   Wilkinson and Smart (2016) **say** that it is appropriate in most situations for Australian pharmacists to issue certificates for sick leave.

Wilkinson and Smart (2016) contend that it is appropriate in most situations for Australian pharmacists to issue certificates for sick leave.

---

2 Rogers (2015, 26) **believes** that artists are as valuable to Australian society as accountants.

_____

_____

3 In her article on geosequestration, Rogers (2017) **says** that techniques have not yet developed for safe levels for storage of nuclear waste.

_____

_____

4 Jenkins (2013) **says** that comedy and the arts are the best ways to promote multicultural understandings.

_____

_____

5 Robinson, Telfer and Barton (2012) **write about** the issue of sustainability in the building industry.

_____

_____

6 This article **suggests** that the United Nations has lost significant authority in the Middle East in the past decade.

_____

_____

7 Clarke and Richardson (2016) **blame** the rise of the Internet for young people's poor literacy skills.

_____

_____

8 The authors **describe why** it is valuable for students to learn about paraphrasing (Jones et al. 2015, 356).

_____

_____

9 In his article on Indigenous sporting stars, Walker (2017) **says** that success in sport allows young Indigenous people to enter successfully into other areas of Australian life.

_____

_____

10 Engineers Australia (2015b, 35) **says** that driverless cars will be safe to drive on Australian roads within the next 10 years.

_____

_____

In a group or a class

Share your sentences, with the understanding that there is no one correct answer. Discuss whether each answer maintains the meaning of the original sentence.

Summarising

One useful way to practise paraphrasing is to write short summaries in your own words of ideas you encounter in your reading. These summaries will generally be only one or two sentences long, but make sure you write in full sentences for your own practice. They will help you learn to paraphrase, and may also be useful in future assignments. See Chapter 10 for more information on writing a summary.

Academic paragraphs

Now you need to put together everything we have presented to you in this chapter about referencing, paraphrasing and quoting in order to understand what an academic paragraph may look like. Example 9.7 in Chapter 9 gives a particularly useful example. Analyse how the author makes citations, and notice the number of different texts they cite in a single paragraph.

Relevant sections on academic paragraphs in this text

For more on academic paragraphs, see:

- the section on paragraphing in Chapter 6
- Chapter 8 on report writing
- Chapter 9 on essay writing
- Chapter 10 on writing summaries and annotated bibliographies.

'Bookending' references

If you occasionally need to paraphrase a long passage from one text, you should use a combination of Methods 1 and 2 (described above) to 'bookend' your paraphrase with two references. When you first mention the text, include the author's name in your own sentence, as in Method 1, then use regular phrases to show that you are still referring to the ideas of the same author (phrases such as 'he goes on to say' or 'in her opinion'), then conclude with a complete in-text citation according to Method 2. Think of this like a pair of bookends – you are indicating that all the ideas between your first mention of the author's name and the final in-text citation come from the same text. This then allows you to precede or follow this passage with your own sentences without confusing your reader as to which ideas are your own and which come from another writer. Example 5.1, from a student of Urban and Regional Planning, demonstrates a 'bookended' passage.

Example 5.1 A 'bookended' passage

Unplanned land reclamation through the dredging process raises major environmental concerns for marine habitats and the ecosystem. Zainal et al. (2012) suggest that, as time progresses, the world begins to suffer from land limitation relative to the increasing population density and economic development, which leads to dramatic needs for additional space. They contend that unplanned land reclamation seems to be the only immediate 'solution' to these problems, creating extra land to accommodate these demands. However, it cannot be a long-term conclusive approach as the process causes cumulative and permanent losses of major habitats and seabed, also indirectly eliminating key species of native and commercial marine ecology, and further threatening the already endangered environment (Zainal et al. 2012). Therefore, thorough scientific research must be undertaken prior to the commencement of reclamation to identify and avoid possible threats in order to protect our natural landscape.

Alex (Ping Hei) Chan, Urban and Regional Planning student

You'll notice that the first and last sentences of the paragraph are his own sentences developing the argument of his essay, while the middle part is a series of ideas from Zainal et al. (2012), bookended correctly.

While this method gives you the ability to paraphrase an idea over a series of sentences, try to avoid falling into the trap of writing whole paragraphs that do little more than summarise a single text. Academic paragraphs require you to synthesise ideas and information from a range of research. Bookending should be done in *conjunction with* synthesis, not instead of (see Chapter 9 for more detail about constructing a synthesis).

Your originality

We often find that first-year students resent the idea that they must base their thinking on the work of others. But remember that your originality lies in the way you develop your thinking in light of what you have read; in the way you respond critically to other people's ideas; and in the way you structure and synthesise your argument – that is, the way you are part of the ongoing scholarly conversation. If you can demonstrate sophisticated critical thinking and synthesising skills, you will succeed in university studies.

ACTIVITY 5.3   Quoting and paraphrasing

With another student or individually

Collect three brief texts (of 200 to 300 words each) that relate to one idea from your discipline. Go through the following process:

1   Write a direct quote from each text. Punctuate them all correctly and add in-text citations as needed.

2 Write a paraphrase from each text. Ensure that you write in your own words, using as few of the exact words of the authors as possible in order to avoid plagiarising. (You will learn more about plagiarising later in this chapter; for now, just do the best you can by using your own words.) Use a combination of Method 1 and Method 2, described above.

In a group or a class

Use the same three texts so that you can share around the group your quotes, paraphrases and syntheses in order to develop your understandings of these academic processes.

Inadvertent plagiarism

Most tertiary institutions now use Turnitin or similar software to check paraphrasing. We understand that many of you are very nervous about being reported for inadvertent plagiarism, fearing that your Turnitin report might match phrases that you have written yourself with the same phrases written by other authors. We talk about Turnitin in more detail below, but our first message is that *the best way to avoid plagiarism is to practise good paraphrasing and quoting techniques*. These are the bases of academic honesty.

Academic honesty

Academic honesty is frequently a contentious issue in the media; you will have seen news reports about academic fraud and plagiarism among scholars and students in many countries. Your lecturers will outline what constitutes academic honesty in your discipline – a much broader topic than can be covered completely here. Our main concern is to help students acknowledge their sources properly, so that their work will follow the requirements of academic scholarship.

What is academic integrity?

Academic integrity is a cornerstone of academic institutions like universities. Without it, we would not see new research or ideas being published, and we wouldn't be able to build on the work of others to find new approaches or solutions to problems. This is because academic integrity is about a shared understanding of the importance of acknowledging the work of others. It is also about the way we conduct ourselves when it comes to creating and disseminating our work. When we talk about having academic integrity, we are thinking about:

- **Respect:** we respect the work, time and effort that people put into their research. We take the time to learn how to appropriately acknowledge them, and we ensure we do so every time we use someone else's research.

- **Trust:** we trust that others will use our work appropriately and that it will be acknowledged. We send our work out into the world to be discussed and built upon, believing in this shared understanding.
- **Honesty:** we conduct ourselves with integrity, even when results might not suit our agenda or when doing so might be harder than not. We don't manipulate results or ideas to suit how we want to use them. We use the work of others in the spirit in which it was intended, and we adhere to rules about the use of it.

Everyone who conducts or uses research needs to be conducting themselves with academic integrity. This applies to students who are submitting assignments for a class just as much as it does to a professor who is conducting a research project or a group of scientists developing a new medication. Adhering to principles of academic integrity is something that the vast majority of students do. Sadly though, sometimes there are situations where we see the wrong thing being done. Often this is due to desperation (forgetting a due date, or finding the content too hard); sometimes it comes down to laziness (not wanting the bother of writing an assignment); other times it's simply a matter of not understanding the rules. It is this last reason that we see in the vast majority of cases.

It is important to understand from the outset though, that your intent makes little difference when it comes to issues of academic integrity. Ignorance of the rules (outside of some very narrow circumstances that *might* apply, such as being in your first semester or study period) or not meaning to cheat will not be seen as acceptable excuses if you are found to be plagiarising or colluding during your studies. Alongside the information here, be sure to become familiar with the rules and expectations of your particular tertiary institution. If there is anything you don't understand, ask your lecturer to explain so that you can submit your assignments with confidence.

Collusion

Collusion occurs when two students submit two identical assignments, or sections of an assignment, as their own individual work. It is an act of cheating. It is a very serious offence, and can result in you being expelled from your course.

Occasionally, one person involved in an incident of collusion has not cheated deliberately – this person has lent an assignment to another student who has asked to read it in order to get ideas or inspiration. This second person then copies the first student's work without their knowledge. Sometimes the first student even provides an electronic copy of the assignment, and the second student copies the layout as well as the content of the original. Although it may seem unfair, the penalties for *both* students in this situation are likely to be high as it will be deemed that one student provided the other with the opportunity to cheat, even if they didn't intend to or know about it. Therefore, we strongly advise you *not* to provide a completed assignment to another student. Work together discussing ideas, but never pass over your assignment to another student.

Collaboration versus collusion

Some students are confused when they are invited by a lecturer to work with other students in preparing an assignment but are then required to submit separate versions of it. If lecturers give you these instructions, they generally intend you to share ideas and perhaps some resources. However, they would penalise you for any of the following:

- an identical list of references
- an identical structure (e.g. the paragraphs of two essays have the same set of main ideas in the same order, or the decimal notation of two reports is identical)
- conclusions that are expressed in the same or very similar language
- identical paragraphs or sections of an assignment.

If you are in any doubt about how closely you may work with others on an assignment, ask your lecturer before you start writing. Chapter 15 explores the idea of teamwork in more detail.

Plagiarism

Plagiarism occurs when you copy other people's words or ideas without acknowledging them correctly. We believe that, in contrast to collusion, most first-year students do not deliberately plagiarise, but instead may do so as a result of poor note making (see Chapter 4) or paraphrasing skills (see the section on paraphrasing earlier in this chapter), or a misunderstanding about what constitutes plagiarism.

Your university's policy on plagiarism

Find your university's policy on plagiarism (it will be on the institution's website) and read it carefully. Become aware of how seriously your university treats the issue, and note the penalties for plagiarism. However, don't be overawed by this information; instead, take this year to become very clear about what plagiarism is, how to avoid it and how to build good academic scholarship practices.

What is plagiarism?

Most students are surprised to learn what constitutes plagiarism. You are plagiarising even if you use only a phrase from another writer without placing it in quotation marks, *even if* you acknowledge where you found that phrase. Don't adopt the common student habit of copying and pasting sections from the Internet, then changing just a few words in each sentence or reversing the order of clauses in a sentence – you will be plagiarising! Your sentence needs to have its own structure, not someone else's.

Here is a paragraph from an essay about online confessions by Kate Douglas, published online in 2019:

> While confessions on reality TV programs, on certain current affairs shows, and from YouTubers who thrive on controversy are now quite formulaic, new spaces are constantly opening up for confessional narratives. Anonymous social media spaces such as 'Reddit' have shown that there is something potentially liberating about sending an anonymous (or semi-anonymous) confession out into the world. While these do have the potential to cause harm, they show just how strong the confessional impulse can be.

Consider Example 5.2, which a student might write in an essay or report.

Example 5.2 Plagiarism

Confessions on reality television programs, on certain current affairs shows, and from YouTubers are now quite formulaic. Anonymous social media spaces have also shown that there is something potentially liberating about sending an anonymous confession out into the world.

You will certainly recognise this version as plagiarism – it is very close to Douglas's original, and the direct quotes are not placed in quotation marks. It doesn't acknowledge the author in any way.

Now consider Example 5.3.

Example 5.3 Is using an in-text citation enough?

Confessions on reality television programs, on certain current affairs shows, and from YouTubers are now quite formulaic but other online forums are now becoming available. Anonymous social media spaces have also shown that there is something potentially liberating about sending an anonymous confession out into the world (Douglas 2019).

This version is also an example of plagiarism (even though an in-text citation is included), because it is very like the original. You also can't write an in-text citation at the end of the paragraph and expect it to hold all the ideas of the paragraph – your reader can't tell here which are Douglas's ideas and which belong to someone else. For example, is the first sentence of this paragraph Douglas's idea, yours or someone else's?

Finally, consider Example 5.4.

Example 5.4 Whose ideas and words are these?

> Confessions shown on reality tv shows, as part of some current affairs programs, and from online users have become quite standard. However, other online arenas are now becoming available for this purpose. Anonymous online spaces like Reddit have also shown that there is something freeing about sending an anonymous confession out into cyberspace (Douglas 2019).

Are you surprised that this version, too, is plagiarised? It is still too close to the original, using the author's phrasing and sentence structure. You can't just replace every third word with a synonym and call it your own phrasing.

But remember: the solution to all of your plagiarism problems is *not* to simply place all your borrowed phrases in quotation marks. This results in an awkward mess of phrases 'glued together' to create something that does not flow, and certainly does not show your own voice.

ACTIVITY 5.4   More paraphrasing practice

With another student or individually

After reviewing the examples of plagiarism above, paraphrase Douglas's paragraph into your own words.

In a group or a class

Share your work with the class and discuss who has been able to capture the essence of the text effectively. Reflect on what it takes to ensure you're not plagiarising the original, and what strategies you can use to make this process easier.

The best approach

HINT

It is worth repeating here that you are most likely to create original, strong and personal sentences if you focus on developing your own argument and on *having this argument drive the structure of your writing*.

 Student reflection 5.3   **Making academic integrity work for you**

Plagiarism, what an awful sounding word! My first look into what all this academic integrity fuss was about left me with some serious doubts about not being suited to university level study. That said, I also had an inkling that I was not alone, and this was likely a common reaction. I also felt some frustration from a lot of it not making any practical sense such as using your own work from something you did previously being considered plagiarism. The way to combat these emotions and feelings is by first accepting that these are the rules and you can't change them. Instead of harboring these dark clouds of doubt and frustration, turn the tables and use that energy productively by accepting these rules and mastering them. Referencing, citations, paraphrasing and quoting can sound daunting and technical, not something I ever imagined myself having a grasp of, that's for sure. As it turns out, you just have to be open enough to give it a go.

Jason Robards, Construction Management student

ACTIVITY 5.5   Even more paraphrasing practice

With another student or individually

For this activity, use either the three texts you found for Activity 5.3 or three new texts.

1 Write a general sentence that presents one main idea from one of these texts. This sentence will be the first sentence (i.e. topic sentence) of a paragraph you might write in an essay. Write in your own words, then follow with one or two sentences in which you paraphrase an idea from the text as an example. Include the correct citation.

2 Repeat this activity for the other two texts.

3 In your own words, create one sentence that presents an idea based on two or three of these texts (i.e. a topic sentence). Follow this sentence with additional sentences in which you paraphrase ideas from the two or three relevant texts, as examples of your own first sentence. Include citations at the end of each sentence you have paraphrased. (This one is more difficult, so don't worry if you struggle with it at this stage – you will learn how to do this in future chapters, but this is a good way to start your practice.)

In a group or a class

Share and discuss your paraphrases. For each one, discuss the following issues:

- Is the wording too close to the original wording in the article?
- Is each example an accurate representation of the idea in the text?

How to avoid plagiarism

Strong study techniques such as the following are essential in developing good academic scholarship:

- Understand the referencing system you are required to use, and the rules of how and when to make in-text citations.
- Collect all the bibliographic details (author, publisher and so on) of each text you read. Be particularly careful when you photocopy a text or download a text from the Internet; it's very easy to forget to note all the required details on your copy.
- When making notes, use three different formats (e.g. pens of three different colours): one for when you copy a quote exactly; one for when you note an idea from the text in your own words (making sure these words are very different from the original words); and one for when you add your own comments or annotations. Then, when you base your assignment on these notes, you will be able to distinguish between your own words and those of authors you have read.

- Number every note you make, and add the page number of the original text so that you can write in-text citations easily.
- When working with photocopies of texts or with pages downloaded from the Internet, highlight or underline relevant sections and make notes in the margins about your own responses to the ideas.
- Use your notes and photocopies to create mind maps of, and plans for, assignments. Ensure your own ideas drive the structure of the assignment, rather than the ideas within particular sources.
- Do not keep your notes and photocopies in front of you while you write each paragraph – have only your plans or mind maps. If your assignment is flowing easily, you might choose to check back over your notes at the end of each section, or even at the end of your first draft, to make sure you have included all the relevant ideas. If you are struggling with complex ideas, however, you might check back over your notes more regularly. Nevertheless, resist the temptation to have these notes open as you write, since it is very difficult to avoid using other authors' phrasing and structure when you are incorporating their ideas into your own writing.
- As you write, acknowledge every idea, graphic and statistic that you found in another text with an appropriate in-text citation. Never leave out the citations with the intention of adding them after you have written the first draft; it is easy to overlook ideas that need citations or to forget which text an idea came from originally.

Notice how much of this advice is based on having a process in your research that you stick to. Taking a disciplined and thoughtful approach will help you to avoid some of the pitfalls of plagiarism as well as having to do extra work to find texts again without all the required details. When you are doing your research and reading, have all the things you need ready to go: your coloured pens, your pages ruled up with margins in which to note page numbers, and so on. Avoid just 'diving in' and reading a text without these tools ready to go.

Turnitin

If you are required to submit assignments via Turnitin or any similar text-matching website, treat this experience as a learning opportunity. Never assume that an arbitrary similarity score is 'too high' or 'ok'. The score itself is irrelevant and your marker will always check the report regardless of the Turnitin score you receive. You could have a similarity score of 80% and not be plagiarising (because the matches are references, quotes and cover pages); you could have a similarity score of 2% and find yourself in hot water for plagiarism because despite the number being low, it could represent a section of text that is not in your own words. Always take the opportunity to generate a Turnitin report, and always check it carefully before submitting your assignment for marking.

Student reflection 5.4   The benefits of Turnitin

As I had previous experience in online study, I was well aware of the implications of plagiarism. When I did the compulsory course for academic integrity, I must say I got a little scared for a second time! However, I made sure I read through my chosen articles to try to understand the content and avoid plagiarising. The Turnitin program was a good resource. In some units, you can resubmit as many times as you want so that you can check your Turnitin report, so don't leave submission too late in case you need to change anything.

Niamh O'Sullivan, Fine Art student

HINT

Note-making skills

If you find yourself saying, 'I don't know where I read this idea – it was in a lot of the texts I read,' or 'I didn't read this anywhere; I just knew it,' then your note-making skills are possibly ineffective. Read back over the section on note-making in Chapter 4, and start to make notes as soon as you begin your research. If you are sure that a certain idea is common knowledge, you can make a decision not to add a citation.

Self-plagiarism

This is one of the most common plagiarism mistakes our students make – you cannot submit any assignment, even part of an assignment, that you have previously submitted. If you do this, it is called *self-plagiarism*. There are two situations in which this is most likely to happen:

- You repeat a unit you have previously failed or not been able to complete, and resubmit part of an assignment you submitted for that unit in the previous semester.
- You feel that a section of an assignment that you complete for one unit is also relevant to another unit you are studying or have studied in the past, and so add it to your new assignment.

The advice in both of these instances is the same: do not resubmit any part of any assignment you submitted before.

Many students find this particular academic integrity rule the hardest to understand. They ask, 'but why can't I submit something that is clearly my own work?' To answer this, it can help to think of the following analogy.

In 2008, Usain Bolt broke the world record for the 200-metre sprint by running it in 19.30 seconds. In 2009, he won again and broke his own record by finishing the race in 19.19 seconds. To achieve this, he had to run the race *both times*. He could not simply sit in the stands in 2009 and tell the race officials, 'just use my time from last year, thanks!' He had to run the race again to prove that he was still the fastest. He could not just keep using his 2008 result again and again.

This is akin to the rules about self-plagiarism. You need to demonstrate that you have the skills and understandings, and can apply them, in the context of the piece you are currently writing, and not simply that you've done it before. Remember, there are no quick tricks to succeeding in your academic studies. Enjoy the process rather than looking for short cuts.

REVISION TOOLS

↘ Revision activity: Revise these ideas

1 When you write academically, you must acknowledge the source of every idea, graphic, statistic and so on – that is, everything you have read from another author. These acknowledgements are called citations in many referencing systems.

2 Making many citations in an essay is not a weakness. Instead of suggesting you have no original ideas, citations indicate you are taking part in a worldwide academic conversation and demonstrate the scholarly support for your points.

3 All referencing systems follow a basic format to allow you to acknowledge the sources of your ideas without getting in the way of your meaning. Follow the system chosen by your university or department, but remember that it is easy to move among systems when you follow a guide meticulously.

4 Paraphrasing and quoting are your methods of incorporating your reading in your essay. Both require practice, and you will gradually improve in these areas over the course of your studies.

5 Tertiary institutions value academic honesty, and many use software text-matching systems such as Turnitin to identify students who paraphrase incorrectly.

6 Many beginning students plagiarise inadvertently because they have not yet learned to make effective notes and to paraphrase. They might also have misunderstood the issue of self-plagiarism. Treat your early studies as a time to learn sound academic practices.

↘ Thinking activity: Critical and reflective questions

1 What do I find easy about referencing, and what do I find difficult about it? How could I work in these areas to improve my referencing?

2 How much care do I take to get referencing correct? How does this relate to my attention to detail in other parts of my studies and in my broader life? In what parts of my life do I focus on close detail?

3 Why do academic communities emphasise academic acknowledgment and honesty? How would things change (for better and worse) if this emphasis was not so strong?

4 How do I feel about the word 'plagiarism'? What emotions does it bring to the surface? Where do these feelings come from?

↘ Useful weblinks

Many Australian and New Zealand universities have websites that cover several different referencing systems. These discuss issues of referencing in general, and then take you to guides for a range of specific systems, including Chicago, APA, Harvard, MLA, Vancouver and others.

Different universities may have slightly different versions of the various systems, and you will need to become familiar with your own university's version. In addition to your own university's information, you may find the following resources useful.

University of Auckland (New Zealand) Library: **http://www.cite.auckland.ac.nz/index. php?p=useful_links** (see also the useful 'Referen©ite' website at **http://www.cite. auckland.ac.nz**).

Curtin University Library: **http://libguides.library.curtin.edu.au/home**.

Murdoch University Library: **http://library.murdoch.edu.au/Getting-help/Referencing**.

University of Queensland Library: **https://guides.library.uq.edu.au/referencing**.

James Cook University Library: **http://libguides.jcu.edu.au/referencing**.

University of Canterbury (New Zealand) Library: **http://library.canterbury.ac.nz/services/ref/ style.shtml**.

REFERENCES

Douglas, Kate. 2019. 'YouTube Apologies and Reality TV Revelations – The Rise of the Public Confession.' *The Conversation*, May 24, 2019. **https://theconversation.com/friday-essay-youtube-apologies-and-reality-tv-revelations-the-rise-of-the-public-confession-114970**.

↘ **PART THREE**

ACADEMIC WRITING

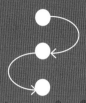

A great deal of your university life will be spent writing, as it was in primary and high school, but the writing you do will be different because you will write in the genres, or types of writing, appropriate to your discipline. During your time as a writer at university, you will also be starting to prepare yourself for the kinds of audiences, purposes and contexts that are more appropriate for your future professional life.

While your professional audiences and contexts will become more varied as you study, the range of genres in which you write will be more limited, and you will need to develop them more deeply to meet the needs of your discipline. Depending on your discipline, you may no longer write in some of the genres you wrote in at school – for example, poems, recounts of particular experiences or lab reports – and will need to master new genres.

In Part 3, you will find some general advice for improving your writing skills (Chapter 6), followed by separate chapters on reflective writing (Chapter 7), report writing (Chapter 8) and essay writing at tertiary level (Chapter 9). Chapter 10 deals more briefly with some other tertiary genres: summaries, annotated bibliographies and case studies, as well as some online genres such as blogs. We have included models from our students' assignments throughout these chapters to guide your own writing.

→ **Chapter 6:** Approaches to writing

→ **Chapter 7:** Reflective writing

→ **Chapter 8:** Report writing

→ **Chapter 9:** Academic essay writing

→ **Chapter 10:** Some other tertiary genres

Approaches to writing

CONTENTS

Assumptions and biases

Before you start any research or writing, try to identify your own assumptions and biases about the relevant topic. Be aware of any generalisations you bring to a subject; for example, some people believe without question that women are natural caregivers, that unions are bad for the economy or that moving to renewable energies is a practical way of protecting the environment.

One role of university education is to challenge students to question all the beliefs they have inherited from their families, their schooling and the media, so that they can approach their studies with an open mind. This is not to suggest that everything you have learned or believed up until now is wrong! However, if you don't question your preconceptions before you begin your research, you will find that they skew your thinking and limit your final writing.

Think about what is meant by the concept of *bias*. It is easy to identify bias in a highly emotive piece of communication; but you need to realise that *all communications are biased*. Having a bias is not something of which you should be ashamed or defensive. It is something that we *all* have simply because we are human and have existed in a particular time, place and set of circumstances.

Here are some ideas to think about and discuss:

- All people have assumptions and biases, even those who hide them through an overtly detached tone. When you communicate in writing or orally, it is preferable to acknowledge your biases so that they are 'on the table'.

- All communication requires you to select details and information to support your case. Your bias influences what you select and what you choose to leave out. Even when you present a concessive argument (i.e. one that acknowledges some of the opposing arguments – see Chapter 9), you choose details that make your own argument stronger than that of the opposition.

- Groups that you might feel are unbiased (such as educational and research institutions, and government bodies) are influenced by their own assumptions, policies, support groups, power bases and so on. Their biases might not be obvious, but they are significant.

- When you focus on communicating in a detached, scientific way, you are working from the Western bias that a detached reliance on facts is the most valid and authoritative approach to communication. This is only one, culturally biased, view of communication.

Bias is, therefore, not a negative thing, and it will not be possible for you to find reading material that is not biased. You should instead try to identify the biases in the texts you find and seek to balance them. Our best advice here is to research as widely as you can so that you are likely to come across a wide range of assumptions and biases.

> **Balancing your reading – an example**   ⟨HINT⟩
>
> If you read material on, for example, global warming from the Greenpeace organisation, you should balance it with material from government organisations (preferably governments from developing countries as well as the developed world), educational groups and scientific research organisations. As you do, consider what information is the same and what differs between the texts, how information has been presented, the language used in each, and so on. Ask yourself why this is – what are the reasons that there might be differences and similarities?

Improving your writing

Even if you are not allowed to redraft an assignment in response to teacher feedback, there are some practical things you can do to make sure the assignment you hand in is as good as possible:

- Think about what you already know about the characteristics of the genre in which you are working (e.g. essay, analytical report) before you begin to write.
- When you complete your first draft, carefully edit the content and proofread the grammar of your writing. (We discuss editing and proofreading later in this chapter.)
- Keep next to your computer a list of your common errors and weaknesses, as identified by those who comment on your writing (i.e. teachers and peers). Add to this list as you receive feedback. If necessary, read over your writing several times, focusing on only one significant weakness each time (e.g. sentence structure).
- Set up an informal network with fellow students. (Chapter 1 has more detailed comments on the value of peer networks and study groups.) Arrange to meet together several days before an assignment is due in order to respond to each other's drafts. Use guidelines or checklists to help you focus on various aspects (see Table 6.2 and Table 8.2). Then make a final copy in time for the submission date.
- Add a range of useful online writing resources to your 'Favourites' toolbar in your Internet browser so that you can access them easily.

Developing your writing muscles

Writing is like physical or artistic activities such as football, dancing or playing the piano: you need to perfect your skills, but you also need to develop the appropriate 'muscles' for the activity – and the only way to develop those muscles is to do hours of exercise. Those who want to be top footballers spend a large proportion of their time running, lifting weights and practising kicking; those who want to be dancers repeat set exercises over and over again; those who aspire to be concert pianists train by playing scales and set pieces for hours a day. They do these activities unsupervised, without a coach or teacher correcting their style. This is their muscle-building time.

So it is with writing – you should not expect that the only writing you do will be the final version of an assignment you hand in for marking by your lecturer. You need to develop your writing muscles by doing lots of writing in lots of different genres.

Writing in the professions

You may think that your future profession is not one in which writing will be important, and that this chapter's advice does not apply to you. However, professions have changed rapidly in recent decades, and now all of them require members to have strong written and oral communication skills. If you glance through advertisements for positions in your profession on websites such as Seek (**http://www.seek.com.au**), you will realise the truth of this.

If you want to pursue further studies in your profession, you will need to undertake postgraduate studies, and if you want to work in an academic field, you will need to publish books and articles in scholarly journals. All of these require strong writing skills in a range of genres.

Online reading and writing

There are many different ways in which you can improve your writing skills, including through reading and writing online. Experts in writing say that good language users 'read like a writer, and write like a reader', so absorbing yourself in both reading and writing online will be very beneficial for you. We suggest you read a range of online texts, from formal journals and newspapers to more informal blogs. As well as reading about your discipline, look for texts on your hobbies and interests. You can search for journals and newspapers through your favourite search engine, and a specialised website like Blog Search Engine (**http://www.blogsearchengine.com**) can help you find blogs on any country, or on hobbies and interests as diverse as Indy cars and hamster breeding.

For the same reason, write as much as you can. Write a blog, or write on your Facebook page, write a letter to the editor of a newspaper, or write reviews on Trip Advisor, or do all of these. As you write, notice the different levels of language you are using in different contexts – this conscious writing will develop your writing skills in all areas.

Writing for thinking – study journals and reading/viewing journals

One way you can build writing muscles is to develop a habit of using writing as a thinking tool. First, you can begin writing a *study journal*. When you are given an assignment, spend some time at the beginning writing reflectively about your ideas on the topic: what you already know about it, what questions you can ask yourself about it, what areas you might find interesting and so on. You can do this as often as you like during the assignment.

Don't write this as a formal essay; think of it as a journal entry written for your own purposes. Imagine you're talking to yourself. You can write in full sentences if you like, but you will probably not do this throughout. Remember that your writing is more than a series of brainstorms – you are using your writing to think through your ideas on the topic and your approach to the assignment.

Another excellent way to build your writing muscles, as well as to develop your thinking for an assignment, is to keep a *reading or viewing journal*. Use a notebook or a section of your study journal file, and start a new page for each text. At the top of each page, write out the full reference for the written text or video you will discuss (a useful way of practising your referencing skills!). Under this, write a paragraph in which you explain briefly, in your own words, the main argument and supporting ideas of the text, keeping it as simple as you can. Then add several paragraphs about your response to the text; for example:

- What aspects of the argument and ideas do you agree with, and which do you dispute?
- Which of the ideas do you find thought-provoking? Appalling? Laughable? Sensible? Why do you feel this way?
- What biases underpin the argument and ideas presented?
- From what you know and are currently learning as a writer, how well do you feel the text works? What made it clear or difficult to understand?
- What aspects of its crafting do you notice? In the case of videos, how do the visual elements develop the argument and ideas, and have an impact on your responses?
- How do the ideas link with other ideas you have read or thought about?
- What ideas for designs, projects, assignments and so on do you have after reading this text?

ACTIVITY 6.1   Reading or viewing reflection

This activity is an opportunity to challenge your thinking, as well as to develop your writing muscles. The writing may be an example of reflection (see Chapter 7); however, its main purpose is to encourage you to write more fully and regularly.

As an individual or with another student

Choose a text (written or visual) that is relevant to your studies, or use one provided by your tutor. Referring to the questions in the above list, write a reflection on this text in which you challenge the argument and ideas presented in it. Write in continuous sentences and paragraphs, rather than answering each question separately.

In a class or a group

Share your reflections and discuss. Compare and contrast the ideas of the whole group. Where relevant, consider how each student has challenged the thinking of the text being considered. (Note that this is not a requirement of the activity, but a bonus.)

Students for whom English is an additional language

If you speak English as an additional language and do not yet feel completely confident in it, then you, in particular, need to immerse yourself in reading, writing, speaking and listening to the language. All the suggestions listed above for improving your writing are as relevant to you as they are to more experienced English speakers. Here are some specific suggestions we make to our students who want to develop their English:

- If you live with people with whom you share another language, try to speak English as much as possible. Look for opportunities to mix with other students who don't speak your first language(s) – it is even useful to spend time with overseas students from other countries because you will speak English as your common language. Join an organisation or club, get involved in your student guild or council, or look for a job or voluntary work in which you are required to speak English.

- If you are studying online, try to find a 'study buddy' in your online group to share English writing and ideas with. You can then write to each other by email, in addition to working on the unit's formal assignments.

- Enrol in any free classes to improve your English offered at your university.

- As well as reading newspapers in your own language, develop a habit of reading newspapers in English (e.g. *The Australian*, *The Age*, *The Sydney Morning Herald*). See whether you can locate an international English-language newspaper that includes news from your own country or region (e.g. *Asia Times Online*, at **http://www.asiatimes.com**, or *The Guardian Weekly* – see **https://www.theguardian.com/weekly**).

- Read good academic texts in English beyond those set for your course, such as journal articles in your discipline. Explore the Internet to see which journals are available online, and visit the library to locate the journals relevant to your discipline. Don't be put off if you initially have problems understanding them – many undergraduate students who speak only English also have difficulties understanding academic journal articles. Keep looking until you find some journals whose articles are reasonably accessible to you.

- Watch television programs in which English is used formally (e.g. news, current affairs and documentaries associated with your discipline). Even if you find these difficult, keep watching – you'll begin to make more sense of them little by little. Don't expect to be able to make meaning out of reality-TV programs or soap operas in English, which use mainly informal and slang English.

- Keep a list of the grammatical errors you make most frequently (see Chapter 12 for typical errors) and focus on these when you check your final drafts.

- Look up the grammatical areas in which you have problems on some of the online writing labs developed for students seeking help with English (see the 'Useful weblinks' list at the end of Chapter 12). Read the explanations, work through the exercises and check your answers.

- Contact support services at your university to find out what supports exist for your writing; for example, Curtin University's Learning Centre (see **http://studyskills.curtin.edu.au**) or the University of Western Sydney's The College: Learning Support (see **https://www.westernsydney.edu.au/thecollegestudents/westerncentral/learning_support**).

- Look for university writing websites that you can access even if you are not a student at those universities. For example:
  - Griffith University's English Help (**https://www.griffith.edu.au/international/englishhelp**)
  - Monash University's Research and Learning Online (**http://www.monash.edu/rlo**)
  - RMIT's Learning Lab (**https://emedia.rmit.edu.au/learninglab/welcome**)
  - University of Wollongong's UniLearning (**http://unilearning.uow.edu.au**).

- Most importantly, resist the temptation to say that you have no time to work on your English because you are busy with assignments in your discipline. You will need to be able to communicate well in English in order to succeed in your course, so be prepared to devote time to developing your English skills.

In Student reflection 6.1, a student comments on some of the issues she has faced as a student for whom English is not her first language.

 Student reflection 6.1   **Some challenges when English is not a first language**

A problem I found when writing academically (and in everyday writing as well) was remembering the correct rules of writing in English. For example, when to use 'is' and 'are', and the different parts of a sentence. I tend to use 'and' a lot and struggled with being more concise. Don't even get me started on paraphrasing!

Don't be afraid of asking your tutor for help. Do not be afraid of being an annoyance because you are not the only one with these questions. Don't be afraid of embarrassing yourself. If you don't understand the answer provided by the tutor, ask it again and explain what exactly you are not understanding. If you are using a discussion board, read what other students have posted as it will help you to see an example. Use all the tools available to you, such as Studiosity and Smart Thinking before submitting anything, and go through all their suggestions. Remember that you are not the first EASL student and you won't be the last, and all of us have the same questions and concerns.

Carol Rusch, Education student

The writing process

Good writing is *not* a one-step process. For example, you may be writing new paragraphs while you are editing those you have already written, or developing ideas in more detail while you are correcting your grammar. Rather than being a linear process, writing is more like a spiral, as shown in Figure 6.1.

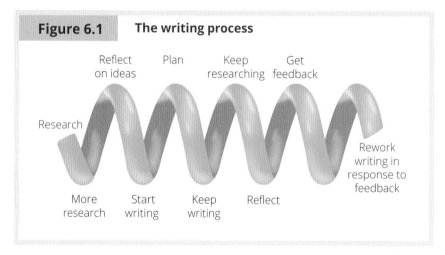

Figure 6.1   **The writing process**

Reflect on ideas   Plan   Keep researching   Get feedback

Research

More research   Start writing   Keep writing   Reflect

Rework writing in response to feedback

Planning

When you feel that you have researched enough to start structuring your writing, it's time to create a *plan*.

Are you a student who has always ignored your teachers' instructions to create a plan before starting to write? If so, you're certainly not alone; but you will have to change your habits now – university assignments are generally too long and too complex to be written 'off the cuff'. So you will need to start practising different ways of planning to see which one suits you the best. Following are some possibilities.

The writing process is very valuable!

Research shows that the following process is one of the best ways to improve your writing and your grades: Planning → Drafting → Editing → Proofreading → Making a good final copy.

The list

This is the simplest form of plan – as the name suggests, it's just a list of ideas. You write the ideas in any order you like, as they occur to you, and then number them in the order you will discuss them in your essay. You can use decimal notation (2.1, 2.2 and so on) to link connected ideas, and to show main and secondary ideas. As your thinking develops, you are likely to change the numbering several times.

The table

This is an extension of the list, but you set up a second column for the evidence that supports or illustrates each item on the list. For example, you might write the first few words of a quote or paraphrase with its citation, or the title of a figure, also with its citation (e.g. 'Map of current nuclear plants, Jones 2004, 26'), or a note about an idea from an interviewee (e.g. 'Stephenson's comment nuclear waste in Aust.').

The mind map

You've probably seen mind maps before, but may not have used them for your own planning. Their advantage is that they allow you to add new ideas anywhere on the mind map as you think of them, and link them to each other visually with arrows and circles. You can also add evidence to each idea, and number ideas in the order you will discuss them in your essay. Use a large piece of paper for your mind map so that you can expand it as you go. The Internet contains many websites on mind-mapping, all with examples. (See the list at the end of this chapter for a range of websites that will get you started in developing your mind-mapping skills.) If you would like to create your mind map electronically, download the free software FreeMind at **http://freemind.sourceforge.net/wiki/index.php/Download** or use one of any number of free online mind-mapping tools such as Bubbl.us (**http://bubbl.us**).

Figure 6.2 is an example of a mind map produced by a student as part of a research assignment. Notice the way that they have colour coded ideas and included citations so that they can easily find the source of their information.

Figure 6.2   A mind map developed by Amado Mendoza, an Education student, in preparation for a research assignment

Microplastics are made as pellets and:
- Used in cosmetics
- In the plastic industry
- End up in sewage
- Microplastics can also come from larger plastics through degradation of the material.
(Chagnon et. al., 2018, p . 127)

- Most marine based plastic comes from fishing industries
- They contribute 640 000 tons of plastic every year
(LI et al., 2016, p. 335)

80% of plastics comes from land based materials. (LI et al., 2016, p. 335)

In a study there are an estimated:
- 5.25 trillion plastic particles.
- Weigh around 269 000 tonnes.
- Float on the surface of the sea.
(Eriksen et al., in Romeo et. al., 2015, p. 358)

Studies found a large amount of man made materials in:
- The ocean
- The marine food web.
Via Ingestion of marine organisms
(Eriksen et al., in Romeo et. al., 2015, p. 358)

17% in Eastern Mediterranean Sea. Bluefin Tuna (Karakulak et al., 2009, p. 758)

14.3% North Atlantic Ocean Yellowfin Tuna in 2006 only (Rudershausen et al., 2010, p. 1355).

Bluefin Tuna 32.4% Mediterranean Sea (Romeo et al., 2015, p. 359)

Albacore Tuna 12.9% Mediterranean Sea (Romeo et al., 2015, p. 359)

32% Samoa, Yellowfin Tuna (Markic et al., 2018, p. 551)

10% Rapa Nui, Yellowfin Tuna (Chagnon et al., 2018, p. 130)

Plastic ingestion based on geographical location.

How does plastic get into the ocean?

Introduce legislation to limit plastic debris and additives (LI et al., 2016, p. 333)

Have more accountability from plastic industries (LI et al., 2016, p. 333)

Governments should play an active role (LI et al., 2016, p. 333)

Plastic end of life recycling or upgrading of programmes (LI et al., 2016, p. 333)

- Trophic interactions are non linear
- They can alter migratory behaviour
- They can modify the stability of the fish community
(Mariani et al., 2017, p. 1552)

How does Tuna affect the marine ecosystem?

Tuna (Thunnus)

Can have major impacts on local marine ecosystems because:
- They can reduce prey population
- They can lead to trophic cascades that affect the whole marine ecosystem
(Mariani et al., 2017, p. 1552)

What can be done to reduce the impact of plastics?

The potential for Tuna to starve to death if they ingest too much plastic. (Perera et al., 2015, p. 7)

Health issues for Tuna related to plastics.

ACSSU073 (ACARA, nd.). An altered population of Tuna could affect other marine species ina negative way. (Marian et al., 2017, p. 1552)

Plastics may have a detrimental effect to Tuna. Some chemicals that leach from plastics are toxic and may cause negative health effects to the species.

Plastics are easily ingested by marine life; they may act as a way for chemicals to transfer pollutants in the food chain. (LI et al., 2016, p. 334)

The reason for plastic ingestion is mostly due to the fact that Tuna are opportunistic and non discriminatory regarding their food. (Romeo et. al., 2015, p. 359)

Year 4 ACSS Science Understanding

Curriculum links

Science inquiry skill

Year 4 ACSS Science as a Human Endeavour

ACSHE062 (ACARA, nd.). Understanding issues with plastic pollution in the ocean will make us more aware of the effects and how to avoid adding to that problem. (LI et al., 2016, p. 333)
Identify questions that can be investigated. ACSIS064 (ACARA, nd.).
- How do plastics get into the ocean?
- What health effects does plastic have on Tuna?
- What effect does Tuna have on it's ecosystem?
- How to reduce the impact of plastics on oceans.

ACSHE062 (ACARA, nd.). Through research of this topic The author realised how much plastic waste comes from the fishing industry. (LI et al., 2016, p. 335)

ACSSU073 (ACARA, nd.). An altered population of Tuna could affect other marine species in a negative way. (Marian et al., 2017, p. 1552)

Amado Mendoza, Education student

ACTIVITY 6.2   Mind-mapping

It is important that you compile a list of the arguments you have read in your research before beginning to write, and consider how you will incorporate these arguments.

As an individual or with another student

Create a mind map for your preferred topic. (You will be adding to this mind map as you research, so leave plenty of space on the page.)

In a class or a group

With a scribe or tutor writing on the whiteboard, create a class or group mind map of one chosen topic.

Drafting

At the *drafting* stage, you need to get your ideas down in words. Most students today write directly onto their computers, but if you find this impossible, write on paper and type it later. Have two documents in front of you as you type:

1 your plan or mind map, which should be clearly visible as you work
2 your notes, which should be covered over so that you don't copy them word for word, but close at hand so that you can consult them for detail.

Some people find that they can write fluently when they're writing their first draft, without worrying excessively about their written expression. Other people prefer to read back as they go, editing and perfecting their language before moving on. Do whatever feels comfortable to you at this stage – there is no value in trying to change your approach to writing completely, provided it works well for you. But realise that, if you tend to draft quickly without worrying about your written expression, you will need to focus more on your expression at the editing stage.

In-text citations and drafting

Even if you choose not to worry greatly about your written expression at the drafting stage, never allow yourself to forget about in-text citations, thinking you'll go back later and insert them. It's very easy to forget which ideas you have taken from other texts or to forget where you found them. For more information about in-text citations, see Chapter 5.

You will have developed many of your ideas for a piece of writing while you were researching and planning your assignment. But don't be surprised if new ideas pop into your head as you're writing your first draft, editing or proofreading your work (or, frustratingly, after you've submitted the assignment!). All writing – even assignment writing – is a creative process so be prepared for flashes of inspiration at any time in the writing process.

Your first draft is only half your task

Develop the habit of finishing the first draft of an assignment at least several days before the assignment is due. Then put away the draft for a day, so that you can read it with fresh eyes. Make time to get together with other students to look at each other's drafts, then edit and proofread your own draft yourself and make a final good copy for submission.

Throughout this book, we often suggest getting together with other students to look over each other's work. This can be daunting! Allowing others to read your work and inviting them to critique it can be difficult. Try to avoid becoming overly attached to your writing and getting defensive when people make suggestions. Learning to detach yourself from what you have produced will be an important step in improving your writing because it will allow you to judge it more objectively.

The paragraph

The building blocks of any piece of formal writing (essay, report and so on) are your paragraphs. The body of an essay is no more than a series of interconnected paragraphs that develop your analysis or argue for the thesis statement you have presented in your introduction; the body of a report is a series of paragraphs (organised under headings) that develop your analysis and lead to your recommendations. You might feel confident with writing paragraphs but others may not have written one for a long time, so we will briefly review them here. Even if you have been writing paragraphs recently, for example if you have recently completed secondary school, it is worth reminding yourself of how they are structured before you begin your first academic assignment.

Elements of a paragraph

Each paragraph in a piece of academic writing contains a range of elements:

- *one idea* that connects to your overall argument or analysis (i.e. the topic sentence), which is sometimes your own idea and sometimes a paraphrase or quote from someone else (with a citation)
- an *explanation, elaboration, development or challenge* to that idea, arising from your reading and including citations
- *evidence* of your idea, with examples from your primary or secondary research, including an explanation of how these examples link with the idea of the paragraph (correctly referenced)
- a link to the following paragraph, or back to the overall argument.

Each of these elements may require several sentences or you may be able to cover them in one sentence each. Therefore, your academic paragraphs will be much longer than your informal paragraphs in reflective writing.

Look at the examples throughout this chapter and in Chapters 8, 9 and 10 to gain a sense of how paragraphs might work. Following are some successful paragraphs from first-year students.

Paraphrasing and quoting

Look back at Chapter 5 to remind yourself about how to integrate paraphrases and quotes into your own paragraphs. Then notice how the students have paraphrased and quoted in the student samples throughout this chapter and in Chapters 8, 9 and 10.

Standard paragraph shape

Annotated example 6.1 is a standard paragraph shape from a report on the Australian construction industry and the environment by a Construction Management student. This paragraph is from the introduction to his report. He starts with his main idea, then elaborates on this by giving examples and statistics. His final sentence links to his next paragraph.

Annotated example 6.1   Strong paragraph from an analytical report

Topic sentence – main idea of paragraph

> The construction industry is Australia's worst industry with regards to recycling. The industry throws out a third of Australia's potentially reusable waste (Schultmann and Wang 2011). The Australian Bureau of Statistics released figures in December 2011 indicating that the industry is the fifth largest consumer of energy, consuming over 5% of Australia's energy. The industry also consumes large amounts of scarce resources (ABS 2011). The Australian Government in 2010 released statistics that show 43 777 000 tonnes of waste were generated in Australia in 2006–07, of which 52% was recycled and 48% was landfilled. Of the 43% of waste that the construction industry contributes, more than 75% went straight to landfill (Australian Government 2010). These statistics demonstrate the impact that the construction industry has on the environment, an impact that is beginning to attract attention from the industry and the government.
>
> *Jonathon Borrello, Construction Management student*

Development of the idea

Next four sentences give statistical background and include two separate examples of bookending

Shows how examples apply to the idea of the paragraph and links with next paragraph

Other paragraph shapes

Once you have mastered the standard paragraph shape, you can then vary the order of the sentences in some of your paragraphs. For example, in Annotated example 6.2, this student begins this paragraph with an example that she has already introduced into her previous paragraph, then applies this example to her topic sentence, which she then develops and elaborates on with reference to her research.

Annotated example 6.2 Paragraph in which the topic sentence is in the middle

Example, which was introduced in previous paragraph and is now applied to a new topic sentence (following)

Elaborations on the main idea, with citations

> The fear of having their children taken away, and the wish to protect them from experiencing the discrimination that comes with being an Aboriginal in Australia, compelled Morgan's mother and grandmother to hide the truth about their family's cultural identity. This example demonstrates why Indigenous Australians from the Stolen Generations fear that sharing their stories of assimilation could cause it to happen again. The descendants of the Stolen Generations have not experienced the same level of discrimination as their ancestors, which allow them to have less fear of speaking out about the unfair treatment their family has endured. This is a contributing reason for the slight increase in Aboriginal life histories being written since the late eighties. As Mckemmish, Faulkhead and Russell (2011, 218) assert, the current climate of reconciliation and the decreased risk of the removal of children has led to the growth of public testimony from Indigenous Australians. The reduced danger of discriminatory actions being taken against them has given Indigenous writers more freedom of expression than they had in the past. Despite this, there are still issues that keep Indigenous voices from being heard.

Freyja Taverner, Professional Writing and Publishing student

Topic sentence – i.e the main idea of the paragraph – which links from the previous paragraph

Link with next paragraph, where Taverner will discuss more issues

Annotated example 6.3 is from an essay by a first-year student in Urban and Regional Planning, on urban planners' responses to climate change. He starts with his example and leaves his topic sentence to the end.

Annotated example 6.3 Paragraph that finishes with a topic sentence

Starts with an example, including citations throughout

In London, the Thames Barrier has been constructed, another 'hard defence' model that crosses the River Thames, protecting 125 square kilometres of central London from flooding (Greenwich Council 2011). The barrier, operational since 1982, is comprised of ten gates that rise as high as a five-storey building (Environment Agency 2011). This is just one of many coastal defence mechanisms in place across England, in conjunction with more natural, 'soft defences', such as saltmarshes. The Environment Agency (2011) states they are effective in reducing the impact of a wave by up to 95%, while also being easy to maintain and less expensive. Globally, it is evident that governments have already started preparing methods to defend their coasts from flooding. The Australian Government needs to use coastal defences, in conjunction with setting back future developments to ensure safety of infrastructure.

Applies example to global situation

Topic sentence, summing up the examples discussed earlier in the paragraph

Ryan Quinn, Urban and Regional Planning student

Paragraphs in which the topic sentence comes in the middle or at the end are more difficult to write than those with the more common structure, where the topic sentence is at the beginning. They are difficult because you need to hold the threads of your examples until you can present your argument at the end of the paragraph. If you struggle to write logical, well-constructed essays or reports, it is fine to use just a series of paragraphs that start with topic sentences; but if you would like to challenge yourself to write with more variety, try occasional changes of structure.

ACTIVITY 6.3 Successful paragraphs

As an individual or with another student

Read through the three examples of paragraphs above and consider:

- Which one presents their point most clearly? What makes it more successful than the others?
- What aspects of these paragraphs would you like to be able to emulate more successfully in your own paragraphs?

Share your ideas with the class. Does everyone have the same opinion about which is the most effective paragraph?

ACTIVITY 6.4 Writing an academic paragraph

If you can master the academic paragraph, you will have made a large step towards successful essay and report writing.

As an individual or with another student

Find an accessible academic text (or several texts) on a topic you are researching for an assignment, then follow these steps:

1 First, write one sentence in which you incorporate a direct quote from the text you have chosen. Remember that you must use the quote to support the idea or argument of your sentence.

2 Next, write another sentence in which you paraphrase an idea from the text to support your own idea.

3 Make sure you include correct in-text citations in both sentences.

4 Finally, write a whole paragraph incorporating one quotation and at least one paraphrase, all correctly cited. Start the paragraph with your own topic sentence that will drive the whole paragraph – the other sentences will be elaborations, developments or explanations of the opening sentence. Then give examples and discussions of those examples.

5 When you have finished the paragraph, look back over the citations. If all your ideas come from just one text, you should bookend the referencing in order to make the paragraph elegant and streamlined. (See Chapter 5 for information on bookending.) If your ideas come from several different texts, you should include all citations within the paragraph.

(If you find this activity difficult, look back at the student examples included above for ideas.)

In a class or a group

Do the above activity with texts provided by your tutor or by classmates. Share paragraphs and give each other feedback.

Linking paragraphs

By now, you have created a series of paragraphs that present good ideas that are well developed and supported from your research. You now need to link these paragraphs to your introduction (especially to your thesis statement in an argumentative essay) and to each other, so that each paragraph:

- supports the analysis or thesis statement
- follows on logically from the previous paragraph
- leads logically into the following paragraph.

Figure 6.3 shows this visually. To do this well, you use a range of synonyms and connectives.

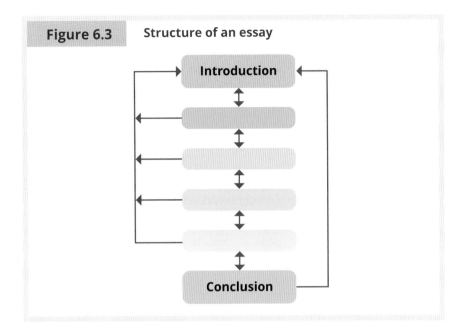

Figure 6.3 Structure of an essay

Synonyms

Synonyms are words or phrases that mean the same as, or are similar to, other words or phrases. They're very useful to help you link in a subtle way. First, identify the key ideas in your analysis or thesis statement. Then write a list of synonyms for each of these key ideas. To help you do this, use an online thesaurus, dictionary or synonym website (e.g. **http://www.synonym.com**) or the 'Synonyms' tool in Microsoft Word (place your cursor on the original word in your document, right-click and then go down to 'Synonyms' near the bottom of the pop-up menu).

For example, if your thesis statement was 'A rise in sea levels is the most dangerous result of global warming because it will flood many low-lying developing countries', then your list of synonyms might look something like Table 6.1.

Table 6.1 Sample list of synonyms for key ideas

Key idea	Synonyms
Rise in sea levels	• Higher sea levels • Increased sea levels • Rising sea levels
Dangerous result	• Harmful effect/impact • Destructive effect/impact • Damaging effect/impact

Key idea	Synonyms
Global warming	• Greenhouse effect • Greenhouse gases • Depletion of the ozone layer • Thinning ozone layer • Climate change
To flood	• To submerge • To swamp
Low-lying developing countries	• Countries that are close to sea level • Non-industrialised countries • Economically disadvantaged countries • (*Note:* While 'third-world countries' is a synonym of 'developing countries', it is generally considered to be an offensive term – see Chapter 14 for information about inclusive language.)

ACTIVITY 6.5   Creating synonyms

As an individual or with another student

Working alone or with someone else who is preparing to write on a similar topic, go through the following process:

1   First, identify all keywords and phrases of your topic. Write them in the left-hand column of a chart like the one in Table 6.1.
2   Then, using the synonym resources listed above, write as many synonyms as you can for each of these words and phrases in the right-hand column.

In a class or a group

Share the synonyms. If all students are preparing to write on the same topic, prepare a class chart of synonyms. If individuals will write on different topics, make suggestions to each other for additional words and phrases.

Keep the list of synonyms in front of you as you write your first draft, and make sure you include at least one of them in each paragraph. This technique has two advantages:

- It reminds you of your argument or ideas, and stops you wandering off track.
- It also helps your readers stay on track as they read your essay.

A word of warning: synonyms often have subtle differences in meaning so it is not always appropriate to replace key words or those which have specific scientific or conceptual links. For example, the word *exponential* is often inserted to replace 'large' or 'increased'. However, exponential describes a very particular pattern of mathematical growth and so should be used with caution, particularly if your audience is likely to be mathematicians or scientists!

Connectives

Connectives are words and phrases that show the progress of your analysis or argument. You use them to connect each paragraph to the preceding and following ones, and to link ideas within a paragraph. Annotated example 6.4, a paragraph from a report on urban regeneration by a Construction Management student, demonstrates sound linking techniques.

Annotated example 6.4   Paragraph with strong links

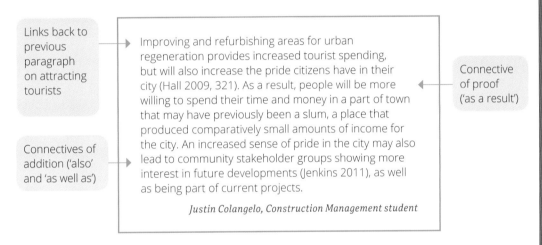

Links back to previous paragraph on attracting tourists

Connectives of addition ('also' and 'as well as')

Improving and refurbishing areas for urban regeneration provides increased tourist spending, but will also increase the pride citizens have in their city (Hall 2009, 321). As a result, people will be more willing to spend their time and money in a part of town that may have previously been a slum, a place that produced comparatively small amounts of income for the city. An increased sense of pride in the city may also lead to community stakeholder groups showing more interest in future developments (Jenkins 2011), as well as being part of current projects.

Connective of proof ('as a result')

Justin Colangelo, Construction Management student

When you start to use connectives consciously, you may tend to overuse them. They should not jar the reader or make your writing seem 'heavy'. Keep practising using them, and pay particular attention to them when you are redrafting. Think about where it is necessary to include them, and where they are just becoming unnecessary 'fluff'. It's easy to use connectives if you think of them as falling within several groups:

- for additions to previous ideas; for example, 'in addition', 'moreover', 'furthermore', 'and', 'as well as', 'along with'
- for contrasts with previous ideas; for example, 'on the other hand', 'however', 'not only … but also'
- for comparisons; for example, 'while', 'whereas', 'although', 'though', 'despite'
- for demonstrations or proofs of previous ideas; for example, 'therefore', 'as a result of', 'it is evident/clear that'
- for cause and effect; for example, 'because', 'since'
- for lists; for example, 'first … second … third', 'another'
- for summaries; for example, 'thus', 'so', 'in summary'.

(You can find many useful examples of connectives – also called *transition words* – on the Internet.)

Editing

Editing is not about improving written expression or correcting grammatical errors. When you edit your first draft, you re-read your work for its *content* and *structure*. Once you have written the whole draft, look back over it and question how successful you have been. Table 6.2 can be used to critique your own work, or it can be used when providing feedback for another student. Some of the sections might not be relevant to all the texts you produce – replace them with the relevant components of the text you are writing.

Table 6.2	An editing checklist	
Essay author: **Topic of essay:** **Reviewer:**		**Rating scale**
Introduction	The introduction is engaging and gives a clear sense of the main points that will be raised in the essay.	|--------------- |----------------- |
	The thesis statement included in the introduction expresses a clear and debatable viewpoint.	|--------------- |----------------- |
Body	The argument is structured in a clear and logical way.	|--------------- |----------------- |
	The main ideas are convincing and easy to understand.	|--------------- |----------------- |
	All paragraphs have a clear topic sentence that relates to, and helps demonstrate, the thesis statement.	|--------------- |----------------- |
	Examples are appropriate and illustrate the topic sentences.	|--------------- |----------------- |
Conclusion	The conclusion sums up the argument and makes the essay feel 'complete'.	|--------------- |----------------- |

Essay author: Topic of essay: Reviewer:	Rating scale
Referencing and in-text citations — All in-text citations are included and correct according to the referencing system used.	|--------------- |----------------- |
The reference list and in-text citations match, and each reference is constructed correctly according to the system used.	|--------------- |----------------- |
Writing — The English expression is clear, correct and pleasing.	|--------------- |----------------- |
Connectives are used appropriately to show the links between each paragraph and the introduction, and between sentences within the paragraphs.	|--------------- |----------------- |
The register (i.e. level of formality) is appropriate throughout.	|--------------- |----------------- |
Research — The topic has been researched thoroughly and uses appropriate academic resources.	|--------------- |----------------- |

General comments:

In addition to Table 6.2, use the guidelines for report writing in Table 8.2 (see Chapter 8) to help you edit. Make any necessary changes in response to these questions/items before you move to the proofreading stage.

Proofreading

Proofreading your draft means re-reading the edited draft for its written expression – is it clear, concise, correct and pleasing? To proofread your essay effectively, follow the steps outlined in this section.

Please edit and proofread your assignments!

Some first-year students very quickly get into the habit of writing one draft of an assignment, finishing it at the last moment (often after a long night of writing) and handing it in without even proofreading it. It is disrespectful to the reader to submit a piece of writing that is filled with errors that would have been picked up easily had the assignment been re-read even once before being submitted. This also shows a lack of respect for yourself as a student and a future professional.

First, read your work aloud

This will force you to read more slowly than if you were reading silently, meaning you will be more likely to notice errors and clumsiness in your writing. Try to pause a little longer than you would normally for the full stops and commas, which can help you identify problems in sentence structure.

Then proofread again, to pick up any further errors

Here are some guiding questions that you might ask yourself as you proofread your writing:

- Is my sentence structure correct? Is it simple enough to be easily understood? Is the structure appropriately varied to be interesting? Do I start sentences with a range of different words and phrases? Have I avoided run-on sentences and sentence fragments? (See Chapter 12 for information on different sentence structures.)
- Are my grammar and punctuation correct? For example, do the subjects agree with their verbs? Have I made the mistake of separating any subjects from their verbs with commas? Are apostrophes used correctly? (See Chapter 12 for information on grammar and punctuation.)
- Have I checked all the homophones, particularly those that I often confuse (e.g. there/their/they're; were/we're/where; whether/weather)?
- Is the spelling correct? (Use the spelling-check feature of your word-processing program, but don't rely on it – it will only identify words that do not exist.) Become familiar with the words that you commonly misspell. (See Chapter 12 for more advice on spelling.)

Making a final copy

When you have completed these steps, you are ready to make a *final copy*. You demonstrate your respect for your readers by giving them a neat, legible copy with enough space in the margins and between each line in which to make comments and corrections.

A reminder

Writing is a complex, many-stepped process. Until you are comfortable as a writer, you need to think consciously about each step in the process, though you will adapt this to suit each task. But, above all, remember that the process is not linear, but spiral – revisit Figure 6.1 to refresh your memory of this concept.

The discourse of your discipline

Each discipline has its own discourse or language (including vocabulary, genres and structures, referencing conventions, and preoccupations and ways of thinking). As you continue to study in your discipline, you will become familiar with its discourse. Here are some things you can do to help you develop this familiarity more quickly.

First and third person

The *first-person* point of view involves using 'I'/'me'/'my' and 'we'/'us'/'our' in your writing. In contrast, the *third-person* point of view avoids these words, using a range of alternatives, which include 'the author', 'they', 'one' and 'people'. The first-person point of view is generally seen as more personal than the third-person; the third-person has traditionally been used in scholarly texts by academics who seek to detach themselves from their research.

Academic research in all fields, but particularly in the humanities and social sciences, has entered a period of huge change and challenge in the past several decades. Many researchers are questioning their authority to speak with certainty on any topic, and particularly their right to maintain an objective position in regard to their subjects. They believe that their own contexts shape their research, not only affecting what meanings they make from the research but also influencing their subjects themselves by their engagement in this research. These changes in attitudes are now affecting areas that used to be seen as 'objective', such as health sciences, commerce, the sciences and engineering.

You will hear more about these developments as your course proceeds, but in the meantime, you will need to think about how they are shaping language use in your discipline. In particular, the issue of first and third person will be important. In some humanities and social science disciplines many lecturers will expect you to write some sections of your assignments in the first-person singular (i.e. using 'I', 'me', 'my' and so on) in order to acknowledge your own perspective and contexts on the issues you are researching. You may find some of your lecturers in other disciplines will also allow or even require you to use the first person. This may not happen in all assignments – lecturers may set some assignments that they see as less 'formal' in which they want you to acknowledge your position, while in essays or academic reports they may want you to demonstrate that you can adopt a more 'formal' tone, which they will see as one that avoids the first person. (See Example 9.6 in Chapter 9 for an example of a text that relies on the first person.)

The best advice we can give you in responding to this issue is to always ask a lecturer which voice is preferred when they set an assignment if this is not clear from the assignment instructions. Don't assume that, if one lecturer in a discipline sets out particular requirements, all other lecturers in the same discipline will have the same expectations.

Vocabulary

Keep a list of discipline-specific words and phrases that you come across in your reading and in listening to lectures. Although these may be unfamiliar to you at the moment, they will become the basis of your communications in your future study and professional life.

Discipline-specific vocabulary is called *jargon*; some people use this word in a critical way (e.g. they may call a piece of writing 'jargon-filled', meaning that it is unnecessarily heavy and difficult to understand). Professional people in any field, however, must understand a shared jargon and use it with each other, since it simplifies and speeds up communication.

Genres and structures

Professional people use a variety of genres to communicate among themselves; for example, the mathematical theorem, critical reading, lab report, poster presentation and case study. Even within the same genre, different structures have developed to suit the needs of different disciplines. For example, a first-year Physics student's ideal lab report will contain significant measurement-uncertainty calculations using partial derivative methods, while first-year Chemistry students will be expected to treat their uncertainties with simpler fractional methods, or to ignore them altogether. Your lecturers will explain how to structure the various genres you need to master for your discipline, and show you models of successful examples. You can enhance your understanding of these genres by noticing their conventions as you read different examples of them.

Referencing conventions

As we have noted, it is important that you are aware of the specific referencing conventions of your department or institution, and that you follow these. Consult Chapter 5 for details on how to reference and information on useful referencing websites.

Preoccupations and ways of thinking

The various preoccupations and ways of thinking of different professions have shaped their discourse. The most obvious example is the traditional 'scientific method', whereby scientists seek to prove facts that can be verified as true in all situations. When scientific researchers employ traditional methods, they start with a hypothesis that has resulted from an observation they have made; they then observe and collect data, which they analyse in order to verify their hypothesis. If the data fail to verify their hypothesis for all observed instances, they then modify their hypothesis and repeat the process. Traditional scientific language is therefore the language of demonstrating, proving and defining.

Cultural studies researchers, on the other hand, are concerned less with what things 'are' than with how they relate to each other. Their language is the language of exploring, comparing and connecting. Cultural studies academics – like academics in many of the humanities disciplines – often write in the first person, since they believe that their own position on an issue shapes their research, and therefore needs to be acknowledged. (In contrast, scientific researchers see their findings as independent of the individual researchers, and almost always present them in the third person.)

Be aware, and read and talk with professionals

As noted above, your understanding of the discourse of your discipline will develop as you progress in your studies; however, you can accelerate it by being aware of the above information, by seeking out a range of written texts in your discipline that you can then read with awareness of their conventions, and by taking every opportunity to talk with professionals about how they use language in their discipline.

REVISION TOOLS

↘ Revision activity: Revise these ideas

1 All writing arises from the author's assumptions and biases, including writing that appears to be detached and scientific.

2 A range of writing strategies can help you become a more effective writer. These strategies enhance your writing processes before you start, during your writing, and when you edit and proofread your first draft.

3 You need to develop your writing 'muscles', just as you would develop those necessary for artistic or sporting pursuits. Only writing when an assignment is due won't be enough to develop these muscles.

4 For students for whom English is an additional language, other strategies can enhance writing skills. Don't be afraid to ask for help or to have something explained in another way.

5 Writing is a spiral rather than a linear, one-step process. It involves intersecting stages of researching, planning, writing a first draft, editing and proofreading.

6 The paragraph is the building block of the essay. It includes several elements that can be combined in many different ways, but the most common and easiest is to start with the main idea.

7 Connectives and synonyms help writers establish relationships among ideas, and help readers appreciate these relationships. They can be overused though, so be aware of them as you write.

8 All disciplines have their own languages and ways of seeing the world. As students progress in their studies, they become familiar with these, and do not need to focus on many of these aspects as consciously as they did in their early days of study.

↘ Thinking activity: Critical and reflective questions

1 How did I approach major writing assignments at school? What was successful about these approaches, and what was not? What did I learn from my school writing experiences?

2 How have my writing approaches been different at university so far? In what ways have my approaches to writing worked, and in what ways have they let me down? What adjustments do I need to make to my previous approaches in order to be more successful now?

3 What have I learned about the subject discipline I have entered at university? What expectations about writing does my university or discipline have? Where can I go or who can I ask to learn more about this?

4 What biases and assumptions do I have about my discipline, the writing I will need to do, and about university study in general? How have some of these biases been challenged by my experiences so far?

5 What is the value of having strict conventions of formal writing in university and in my discipline? How might these conventions be valuable, necessary or unavoidable, and in what ways might they be overly restrictive or stifling?

↘ Useful weblinks

The following online resources, which contain dozens of examples of mind maps, will improve your mind-mapping skills:

James Cook University: The Learning Centre: 'Mind Mapping': **https://www.jcu.edu.au/__data/assets/pdf_file/0005/115394/Mind-Mapping.pdf**.

Monash University Research and Learning Online: 'Brainstorming and Mind Mapping': **https://www.monash.edu/rlo/research-writing-assignments/understanding-the-assignment/brainstorming**.

RMIT Study and Learning Centre: 'Mind Mapping and Brainstorming': **http://www.dlsweb.rmit.edu.au/lsu/content/1_StudySkills/study_pdf/mindmap.pdf**.

Reflective writing

CONTENTS

Thinking at university

One of the major differences between secondary school or technical college and university is the depth at which students are required to think through issues. Most universities list 'critical and reflective thinking' among the attributes they expect of their graduates.

There are many definitions of both critical and reflective thinking – we suggest you look up both terms in your favourite subject dictionary or online dictionary. (A list of these is provided in the final section of Chapter 12.) Despite the variations, all commentators agree about one aspect: critical and reflective thinking are *high-order thinking*. They are much more complex than the linear, logical thinking that would have been typical of much of your previous education: they involve processes such as questioning assumptions and challenging, deconstructing and examining the contexts in which we reach understandings.

What is reflective thinking?

In this book we describe *reflective thinking* as questioning the assumptions that underlie particular actions and issues, then following through a series of thoughts in order to develop your thinking deeply. When you think reflectively:

- You don't look for easy, quick answers.
- You may not solve some of your problems or questions in one semester – indeed, you may not reach definite answers about some of them during your whole course (or even your whole life!).
- Even when you have an answer that satisfies you at the moment, you might change your mind significantly about this in the future.
- The way you work through your thinking is more important than your answer.

Reflection and critical reflection

You can view reflection in two different ways, both of which are valid. First, there is the conventional understanding of reflecting as letting your thoughts range deeply and in a sustained way about a particular subject. Synonyms for this connotation of the verb 'to reflect' include:

- 'to ponder'
- 'to cogitate'
- 'to explore'
- 'to wonder about'
- 'to brood over'
- 'to consider'
- 'to ruminate'.

A second, and deeper, understanding of reflection is what we call *critical reflection*. It involves identifying the assumptions that underlie particular beliefs, and questioning those assumptions. These assumptions could be our own or they could belong to other people. Critical reflection may occasionally lead us to change our entire worldview. This second version of reflection is common among academic researchers and professionals, who often choose to turn a reflective light on themselves, examining their own underlying assumptions, expectations and positions in their research communities.

Figure 7.1 is a mind map created by student Samia Scott from an iLecture on reflection. See Chapter 6 for a discussion of mind maps.

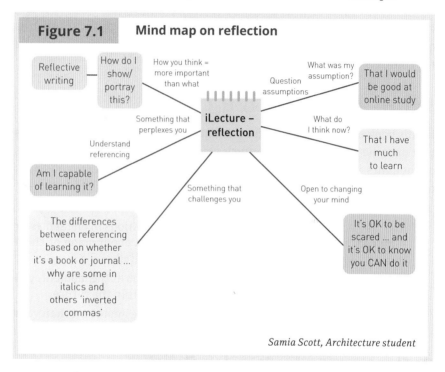

Figure 7.1 Mind map on reflection

Reflective writing

How do I show/ portray this?

How you think = more important than what

Question assumptions

What was my assumption?

That I would be good at online study

Something that perplexes you

iLecture – reflection

What do I think now?

That I have much to learn

Understand referencing

Am I capable of learning it?

Something that challenges you

Open to changing your mind

It's OK to be scared ... and it's OK to know you CAN do it

The differences between referencing based on whether it's a book or journal ... why are some in italics and others 'inverted commas'

Samia Scott, Architecture student

A word on the importance of writing

Some of our students tell us that they think reflectively without having to write down their thoughts. However active you are as a thinker, though, the process of writing generally deepens and extends this thinking. You may start by questioning, but by writing down your questions and pursuing them as far as you can, you will deepen these thoughts much more than if you had limited yourself just to thinking them. Most professional researchers value reflective writing, and many keep reflective journals during their research projects.

Documenting your thoughts also provides you with a permanent record of your thinking that you can revisit later. Sometimes you will be amazed at how much your thinking has developed; at other times, you will be equally amazed at how perceptive you were at an earlier time. In addition, writing supports your learning processes because it allows your teachers to 'eavesdrop' on your thinking in order to offer guidance.

How can you learn to write reflectively?

Reflective thinking can be difficult to learn because there are no formulas or recipes that work for everyone. However, here are some things we know are helpful:

- You need to write and keep writing – the more regularly you do this, the more you will develop.
- Regular feedback from your teachers and fellow students about your reflective thinking can help you develop this form of writing.
- It will also be helpful for you to read as many examples of other people's reflective writing as possible.

In this chapter we will include more examples of our students' writing than in other chapters as a way of giving you guidance. These examples all demonstrate a high level of reflective thinking, although they are all very different from each other. As you become a more experienced reflective writer, you will start to find your own voice, but in your first year you will probably need to try a range of different approaches, and some of the examples in this chapter may provide you with valuable models.

Start with where you are

Start by considering your own life experience, beliefs and perspectives. Often, we take these for granted so much that we think everyone shares them – that they're 'truths' rather than just personal positions. Only by understanding this concept can we start to question and challenge our own thinking. In Student reflection 7.1, a student starts reflecting on rural development in Australia by considering her own life experience, what she understands and what she is currently unsure about.

Student reflection 7.1

Reflection that starts with personal experience

Having grown up on a station in remote NSW, I hold a special place in my heart for rural Australia. While it is a beautiful place to live, the harsh reality is that there is significant development needed to ensure the survival of those living in the country is maintained. I think some of the most urgent areas for regional development include access to healthcare and education facilities. I understand that rural Australia is a vast land, and that populations can be spread out, making it difficult to supply adequate resources whilst still remaining cost effective. I think that issues surrounding healthcare can be improved with a more mobile network of medical professionals, however I am still unsure which type of regional development will be the most effective in solving inferior access to education and aged care in a viable way. I admit I do not yet know a lot about Indigenous Land Ownership rights, and the issues surrounding government development on Indigenous land.

Olivia Hamblin, Construction Management student

ACTIVITY 7.1 Your own perspectives

With another student or as an individual

Consider one issue on which you have some experience and opinions. On a separate piece of paper, write about how your life experience has influenced your perspectives on this issue. Describe your current knowledge and beliefs about this issue, and what you are aware of not yet knowing.

In a group or a class

Share your writing with other students considering the same issue. Compare the differences in your perspectives, considering how they may have been influenced by your different backgrounds. Compile lists of things you already know as a group, and things that you do not yet know.

Focus on asking questions

The most useful technique for practising reflective writing is to focus on asking questions, and then pondering on possible responses.

John Dewey, an educational philosopher, described the act of reflection as having two subprocesses: '(a) a state of perplexity, hesitation, doubt; and (b) an act of search or investigation directed toward bringing to light further facts which serve to corroborate or to nullify the suggested belief' (1910, 9). We suggest you think of the reflective thinking process as pondering a chain of questions – each question requires you to think more deeply, which generates other questions, without seeking definite, permanent answers.

Student reflection 7.2 is a good example of a student using questions to push her thinking more deeply. The student is reflecting on a TED Talk by renowned Danish urban design expert Professor Jan Gehl.

 Student reflection 7.2 | **Reflection that asks questions in order to deepen thinking**

If I am going to question the assumptions of others, I probably should continue to question my own as well. One that I made after first listening to Jan Gehl was that this was the best way to design cities and I thought anyone would want to do this in their own city. Does Jan Gehl assume that the Copenhagen style of urban planning is best for all cities? I have heard the term 'Copenhagenise' used both positively and negatively. Some people believe that it is the way for all cities and some cannot see it as viable in other places (particularly with regard to biking as a key mode of transport). Given that I am only a first-year student, with no experience in urban design and planning at all, maybe I was easily influenced by his way of thinking? Perhaps this is because these cities seemed more like my idea of a nice place to live.

But is a person's experience of a space subjective or can we conclude that one style of building, street or overall urban plan is better than another? My own experiences have definitely played a part in my assumptions about what makes a city a good and sustainable place to live. But will everyone experience these places in the same way I do? As an able-bodied person, how is my experience different to that of someone in a wheelchair or a child? Will a disabled person appreciate the quaintness and history of European cobblestone streets? What about autistic people? Do they find the empty, open spaces of 'bird-shit architecture' more calming than jostling through crowded village streets? Do deaf and blind people experience cities in the same way I do? Perhaps social and economic statuses also influence how a person experiences a city; some areas might be a nice place to eat and socialise but are they accessible only to people with money? Do people without it feel comfortable in these areas?

Anneliese Hunt, Architecture student

Ponder possibilities

In conjunction with asking questions, it is important to ponder on ideas that arise during your questioning. In doing this, you are seeking to keep an issue open. Avoid coming to quick and definite answers, which will cause you to 'draw a line' under your thinking. The more you can keep an issue open in your mind, the more you will create chances to deepen, elaborate on and alter your ideas as you ponder. Notice how the student in Student Reflection 7.3 uses phrases such as 'I wonder' and 'perhaps' in her reflection on the impacts of reflective thinking.

Reflection that ponders possibilities

I never previously understood how pliable language is and how easily words can be adapted to create a perception or an illusion of what is desired. For example, I never considered the word 'sustainable' to be so flexible, or to represent ideas opposing my perception of sustainable. This flexibility of language has opened my eyes to different perspectives and understandings; also learning from these different points of view because they are just as valid, but I do pause to wonder how I did not notice these extremes in language before. Perhaps we bulldoze our intentions through life and assume everyone is on the same page or maybe we surround ourselves with subcultures who share the same point of view. This new understanding will help in the future to clarify communication, and articulate intentions and perspectives, so when ideas are being developed and compromised in the design process, perhaps I can work towards a better understanding of someone's needs ... Officially 'learning' for the first time in over 15 years has been challenging and liberating. Not only have I had to change my lifestyle, my whole family has had to adapt.

Naomi Fisher, Architecture student

ACTIVITY 7.2 Questions and pondering

With another student or as an individual

Choose one issue that has arisen for you in your studies this week. This might concern your own study skills, your sense of what it means to you to be a student, a professional practice experience, or a video or lecture you have encountered. Write down as many questions as you can about this issue without seeking answers at the moment. Let each question lead on to another, deeper question. Try to write between six and 10 linked questions. Then add a series of thoughts between each question – these must be open-ended possibilities rather than definitive answers to the questions.

In a group or a class

Listen to volunteers reading their questions and ponderings. Challenge each other to develop your thinking more deeply by suggesting additional questions and thoughts.

Choose ideas you respond to strongly

Intense responses to ideas can make a good starting point for reflection. Student reflection 7.4 is an example of a student reflecting on ideas she has found inspirational, and then linking them to her own communities in Perth. The student writes about a TED Talk from Dutch community art group Haas&Hahn, which has used art to transform poor communities around the world, including in Rio de Janeiro and Philadelphia.

Student reflection 7.4 **Reflection can apply inspiring ideas to local contexts**

Inspiring does not begin to describe how this TEDx talk made me feel. Haas&Hahn certainly know how to raise the spirit within downtrodden villages. I wonder if when they decided to undertake the project they realised it would take off like it has.

Although this has worked well within the communities of Brazil and Philadelphia, could this be an initiative that all communities could be a part of? Thinking of the community I live in, I wonder if something like this would bring us together. Could we work together to give life to the community? Although we are already a close-knit community, one of the suburbs has been identified as having one of the highest increases in crime in Western Australia. Would this work against creating a vibrant town? Could it be a draw card to even more graffiti in the town centre with people wanting to ruin all the hard work people have worked so hard to achieve?

I also think about how multicultural Perth is. How you could incorporate this into the artwork or patterns that you display on some of the beautiful buildings we have. What about some Indigenous artwork displayed throughout the city centre? What a great inspiration this could be for the younger generation to see this generation's Elders' take on the dreamtime in larger than life pictures. How amazing would the cultural centre in Northbridge look with paintings from Japan, China, Italy, Brazil, South Africa and all other nationalities that make Perth the city we are? Would this bring more awareness and understanding into these nationalities' history, culture and beliefs? Would this bring more people together, working together, talking together, laughing together?

Sally Potsch, Library Studies student

Write informally

When you are writing reflectively, there are fewer restrictions on your writing style than there are for academic writing. The most valuable approach is to seek your own voice, so that your writing will be authentic. Throughout this chapter you will find that students write in different styles; however, you can draw some general conclusions from the pieces included:

- Write in an informal register (see Chapter 11) – perhaps imagine you are having a conversation with yourself.
- Write in first person.
- Write as correctly as you can, but focus predominantly on your thinking rather than on your grammar. In order to advance your thinking, it's fine to use incomplete sentences, individual words, dashes, exclamation marks and so on. However, write mainly in complete sentences – a series of brief dot points will not deepen your thinking as much as a continuous paragraph will.

Chapter 7: Reflective writing **145**

Reflection for first-year students

Reflective thinking is very challenging for most first-year students. In 1994, Patricia King and Karen Strohm Kitchener published a ground-breaking study into how students and adults learn to think reflectively. They analysed examples of reflective writing from thousands of students in the US, and created a seven-level hierarchy of reflective thinking, of which only Levels 6 and 7 were truly reflective; Levels 1 to 5 were presented as necessary preparation for the top two levels. They found that when first-year students arrived at university they were generally thinking at Level 3 or 4, and that they became more critically reflective throughout their undergraduate years, reaching Levels 6 and 7 only in postgraduate studies.

This does not mean the researchers recommended ignoring reflective thinking during the first years of study; in fact, they insisted that becoming reflective is an incremental process, and that students must give it attention throughout their undergraduate studies in order to develop their reflective thinking (King and Kitchener 1994).

What can you reflect about?

If you are given an open choice about the subject of your reflection, you may find it difficult to choose an issue. Most importantly, look for an issue that you feel strongly about – there is no value for you in reflecting on something you don't care about, and the resulting reflection is likely to lack energy and insight.

There are two broad areas on which you will most often reflect as a university student:

- You can reflect on your own work as a student and an apprentice professional to consider how and why you did something, and how you might improve it next time. This will make you a better learner, and more creative and adaptable in your future profession. If your course includes a practical component, you can reflect on your approaches and performance during your practical units.
- You can reflect on other people's work – ideas you read or hear in lectures, podcasts, research and so on. This promotes deeper learning because it encourages you to think actively and widely about the ideas, and to tie them to other things you already know about.

Both of these types of reflective writing will improve your performance in your profession and, ultimately, improve the professions themselves because members of the professions will question why they are doing things in particular ways, how they can perform better and how they fit into the particular communities in which they work.

ACTIVITY 7.3 What can you reflect about?

With another student or individually

Write a list of issues you could currently reflect about in the space provided below. They might be about yourself as a student or about ideas you have heard or read about in your studies. Remember that you must care about the issue in order to be able to write valuable reflections on it. Choose three or four issues.

_____

_____

_____

In a group or a class

Share and discuss these issues.

Reflections on being a student

When reflecting on yourself as a student, there are many different issues that might concern you. The following advice might help you develop a focus for your writing.

Reflect on a fundamental study decision

Fundamental issues (e.g. why you have begun or are continuing to study, or why you have chosen a particular course) might be important to you. Reflecting on these issues can help you deepen your thinking about them. In Student reflection 7.5, a student reflects, during the first semester of her studies, on the fundamental issue of whether she should have given up work in order to come to university. In this valuable reflection, she asks herself questions and ponders possible responses. She has not made a decision about this question, but has opened herself to continuing to think through this fundamental issue that underpins her decision to study.

 Student reflection 7.5 **Reflection that asks fundamental questions about one's study**

I have made a decision to sacrifice my time and pay a substantial amount of money to enter into a commitment of three years of learning. I feel a tremendous amount of pressure to succeed in my chosen discipline and to make this time at university a worthwhile and valuable investment of both time and money. Will this investment be valuable to me? What value will be added to my life? Am I not capable of learning professional skills outside of a university environment? Should I just learn the practical skills from online tutorials and Adobe classroom in a book? My inner critic and sceptic emerged and I was questioning the value of attending university at all. I thought more about this and why I was being sceptical. Do I feel something is deficient in myself or do I feel adequately capable of doing the job I wish to have already?

I feel as though I may inherently possess some good attributes and perhaps my time at university will help me to build on these skills so I can be received well in the context of my discipline. Does simply passing a series of units guarantee my success? At this point in time I believe that ultimately, my success is my responsibility and my choices and my efforts will reflect how well I demonstrate these attributes. But this is only the beginning and, for now, all I may do is ponder these thoughts and hope I have made the right decision to further my education.

Jessica Matthews, Creative Advertising and Graphic Design student

Reflect on particular learning processes

There are many learning processes you might want to reflect about, but the two our students most commonly choose are time management and teamwork. Both of these are particularly crucial issues for our Open Universities Australia (OUA) students, most of whom begin their online studies concerned about whether they will be able to manage their workload and to communicate with others online.

In Student reflection 7.6, a student acknowledges her feelings of discomfort about teamwork and then asks herself a series of questions that help her reflect deeply on her responses.

Student reflection 7.6   **Reflection that uses questions to think about an uncomfortable learning situation**

My experience with group work this semester was a learning curve. I wouldn't say that I was entirely comfortable with the process and I am still trying to understand why that is. It was something I really struggled with this semester … and I was a little surprised by it. Could it be something as simple as feeling inadequate to openly discuss ideas within a group? Or something more complex? It's hard to admit to a weakness, but I feel as though it is something I need to address in order to enhance my chances of success with the many years of study that lay ahead.

What I wanted to do during the group project was focus solely on my own contribution and put my head down to work. It felt like added pressure having to include myself in discussions and contributing ideas felt overwhelming at times, which I understand is something I will be required to work on. I feel as though I am beginning to uncover multiple layers about myself in relation to my study style these past couple of months. I found that what worked best for me to remain calm was by chipping away at my work slowly each day and by focusing solely on my work load. But is this learning style productive? How can I adjust my learning style so that it's more flexible? My approach to the group project was to contribute what was necessary and take what information was vital. I have always been fiercely independent and it's not a natural mechanism for me to rely on others, so with group work I felt uncertain how to utilise the ideas and contributions of others and I am left wondering if this [is] a skill I can build on or hope to improve?

Tammy Beven, Professional Writing student

Reflect on your professional practice

If you are enrolled in a course whose major focus is to prepare you for a specific profession, you can reflect on how your understandings of your profession are developing. In particular, your course may include a professional practice component – such as in education and many of the health sciences – and you can benefit greatly by reflecting on your experiences in these practical situations. In Student reflection 7.7, Samantha Petri reflects on her clinical practice in medical imaging sciences.

 Student reflection 7.7 **Reflective writing on professional clinical practice**

A benefit of having the coordinator was that professional relationships between colleagues were more peaceful and respectful. This was because it was within the coordinator's role to help with conflict resolution. A clear example of this was when two radiographers disagreed on the type of exam that should be performed for a patient with a cervical spine trauma. The argument became very tense and if there was no coordinator I believe it would have ended with one radiographer walking out of the department. However, because there was a coordinator, she ensured each person felt understood and came to a solution that both viewed as fair. This ensured that the relationship between the two was maintained. Also, it meant that the patient received a high level of care, as many opinions were considered for their imaging choice, to ensure they could have an optimum health outcome.

By critically reflecting on this incident between the two radiographers, I have realized the key attributes that assisted with the situation were the coordinator's patience and empathy. She ensured that neither of them felt rushed to explain their opinions and that each of them felt like their concerns were valued. Personally, if someone makes me feel understood and valued, it makes me feel like they genuinely care about me. This makes me respect and trust them, and so more likely to take their advice and be accepting of their criticism. Therefore, being patient and empathetic are not only characteristics that are suitable for the coordinator, but also leaders in general. I could also emulate this in the future when associating with students or radiographers. This will ensure students take on my advice to gain the most from their learning opportunities and also help maintain professional relationships, in order to make the work environment more enjoyable.

Samantha Petri, Medical Imaging Sciences student

ACTIVITY 7.4   Reflective writing on yourself as a student

As an individual
Write an in-depth reflection on one issue in as much detail as you can (at least 300 words). Resist the temptation to write a diary entry (e.g. 'Yesterday I went to [X] lecture and the lecturer told us about [Y]; then I went to [Z] tutorial and the tutor asked us to do an experiment').

In a group or a class
Listen to volunteers read their reflections, and then discuss the characteristics of each one. What makes each piece reflective? How might it be valuable to developing the student's understanding?

Reflections on ideas you are encountering

In Chapter 4 we talked about the importance of engaging actively with your lectures, reading and viewing in order to develop a deep understanding of the ideas presented. Here are some questions you can ask yourself in reflecting on your lectures, reading or viewing:

- Which ideas did I find most interesting, challenging or inspiring?
- What new ideas did I learn?
- How does an idea (or a group of ideas) link with what I know already about my discipline?
- What connections can I see between this text (lecture, podcast, website, book and so on) and other texts I know?
- How did the ideas develop or change my understandings of my discipline?

Reflect with other students in order to deepen your thinking

All the strategies for reflective writing offered in this chapter are relevant to reflection on the ideas you are encountering in your studies. In addition, by reflecting in conjunction with other people, whether you are learning in classrooms or online, you will have the best opportunities to practise and refine these strategies. When you understand that others have different perspectives from yours, this will help you to challenge yourself. While our on-campus students share their reflections in groups, online students use discussion boards to explore their reflective thinking. The examples in this section are from these discussion boards.

Annotated example 7.1 shows a reflective conversation that was sparked among online built environment students by a YouTube video on recycling in Colombia. We have annotated it to highlight some of the techniques already discussed in this chapter.

Annotated example 7.1   A reflective conversation sparked by YouTube video *How Recycled Plastic Bottles Are Building Homes*

> **YouTube, uploaded by Great Big Story, October 22, 2018.**
> **https://www.youtube.com/watch?v=5BMOL4VwIII**
> I came across a great video that demonstrates how Colombia is utilising plastic bottles as a building material. Reusing plastic and adapting it for use as something holding food or drink into a durable building material. I was drawn to this text as it shows how a country which had a specific problem could utilise this as a commodity and found a sustainable use for an otherwise throwaway waste product.

When I (and others I imagine) think of building products it tends to be the traditional materials of wood, stone, steel etc., not something that usually holds something we drink. It really got me thinking and opened my mind to see things not based on how they appear but to approach them from different angles and realise that there are multiple uses for most products that we use and that there are ways to utilise 'waste' products, not just sending everything to landfill. It forced me to challenge my assumptions that single-use plastic is maybe not just single-use and can be adapted to create a building material that will provide shelter that will last 500–600 years for those really needing housing and educate them on sustainability at the same time.

Has this video made anyone else challenge different assumptions? How could we adapt this in Australia? I see this as maybe being a good material to apply to public buildings such as public amenities, sports buildings to start with perhaps as a trial run. It made me consider what else would need to change to implement such a unique building material … it was successful in Colombia I imagine partly as there are many living in poverty and needing housing so this offered a solution for that cheaply. I wonder if it's something our government would embrace or would regulations and politics get in the way.

Sarah

....

Hi Sarah,

Thanks for sharing this video. I love this idea!

I think it's so important to try and reduce our use of plastic and recycle where we can. It also made me wonder if this could be replicated in Australia, especially after reading all the articles where affordable housing is such a huge issue! I wonder how much plastic waste we send to landfill in comparison to Colombia and how our recycling system compares?

It also made me wonder how the residents feel about these homes? Are they comfortable to live in? The framework is made of the recycled plastic but I wonder what that does for insulation? Are these homes solar powered too to make them even more sustainable?

Ellie

....

Thanks for your thought, Ellie. I wonder that too … how would or could this model be used in Australia? I have seen this concept of creating building materials being used in Africa and India in other texts also so it is already in use in a few other countries but as Australia is known as a more 'developed' country I wonder if people would accept this sort of thing to be used and if the demand warrants this being produced.

I like how you brought up the question as to how would the residents feel – this is so important! I got so excited seeing the possibilities sustainability-wise and hadn't factored in as much the end user and the material performance which is obviously important and a key aspect in the product's success. It would be interesting to see

Starts with own experience and assumptions, so differences provoke reflection.

Asks questions, then ponders possibilities, using words and phrases such as 'maybe', 'I imagine' and 'I wonder'.

Relates example to Australia, particularly issue of affordable housing in Australia.

Asks series of questions about residents' responses.

Relates discussion to her previous reading.

Pulls together previous ideas by pondering possibilities.

how the end product could be reviewed and also how this would affect product pricing compared to similar products on the market and if it is more affordable than conventional materials I wonder if people would be more inclined to use it?

Sarah

....

Hi Sarah,

What an incredible transformation from waste to reuse! I think your thought of trialling a product like this in public amenities and sports buildings is a great idea, but I wonder if it was successful and was to then become more mainstream – as Ellie suggested, possibly affordable housing – could its use be hampered by its association to public amenities, etc.? Could it possibly differentiate affordable/public housing too distinctly? As you mentioned, Australia is a developed country (where you would think technology like this would be encouraged), but I wonder if there may be an unconscious assumption that we don't need to utilise materials like this because of our access to more 'sophisticated' and mainstream building materials?

Either way, the concept and technology is an incredible example of what more developed countries should perhaps be investing in also.

Sigrid

....

Hi Sarah,

Great video!

I think reusing plastics into a building material is commendable. After watching the video and process, my first response was to question the amount of emissions and carbon footprint created to reuse this material. The additives, the heating and so forth appears to also create pollution. It would seem counter-productive to produce more chemical by-product and more emissions when trying to create a sustainable building product from single use plastic.

While I whole heartedly believe in recycling rather than mass consumption, Australia's stringent building standards would require any new building product to have a compliant fire rating, measurable off gassing, and pretty demanding insulative qualities. It would be interesting to see what standards Colombia has measured the product against and how it performed.

I personally do not find the building product aesthetically pleasing and I wonder if this would impact a consumer's decision to use it to build a home, even with its green credentials. Is there opportunity with research and development to create a product that would aesthetically cater to a wide range of tastes?

Lisa

Sarah N. Falzon, Ellie Willoughby, Sigrid Kautzner and Lisa Podbereski,
students of Built Environment

Links back to two previous postings, then adds new perspectives on affordable housing in Australia.

Acts as devil's advocate in conversation: challenges sustainability of Colombian processes, then legal issues, and finally aesthetics of design.

How to foster group support

In this conversation, you will also notice phrases designed to foster the group collaboration and positive feelings: members thank Sarah for her original post and approve of her text; Sarah herself asks the others what they think of it, and draws them in with the phrase 'When I (and others I imagine) think of building products …'; everyone refers back to ideas opened by previous speakers, and then elaborates on them, or takes them in different directions. These kinds of friendly pleasantries are very important to support any group collaboration, but most of all for online groups, where people are likely to start off feeling a little insecure and awkward. Don't underestimate how important such pleasantries are to help your groups function, whether face to face or online.

Over to you ... applying what you have learned

Now you have a chance to pull together everything you have learned in this chapter, by considering two reflective conversations conducted online by our students. As you read them, notice how they use the techniques we have discussed throughout the chapter, and how they work together to enhance each other's reflective thinking.

Example 7.2 is a conversation about the value of TAFE and university studies among a group of humanities students.

Example 7.2   Reflective conversation on the value of TAFE and university studies

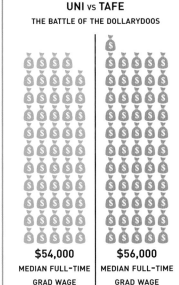

UNI vs TAFE

THE BATTLE OF THE DOLLARYDOOS

$54,000
MEDIAN FULL-TIME
GRAD WAGE

$56,000
MEDIAN FULL-TIME
GRAD WAGE

Hey everyone,

I found this advert interesting. On the surface it looks like you would be better off completing your education at TAFE compared to uni. I wonder if this is an accurate depiction, I always thought that a university degree gave you a greater earning potential despite your graduate salary. It makes me question, why do we place so much emphasis on our future earnings compared to our education. This appears to be targeted at a generation that is about to leave school and who have to make the decision to either study at uni or alternatively complete a certificate. Is this how we should be informing young adults about the value of their future? And if not, how should we be advertising it?

Daniel

Skilling Australia Foundation. 2020. 'Where You Have to Graduate from to Earn the Most $$$ (Comparison Graph).' https://saf.org.au/graduate-earn-cosmopolitan-online/

Hi Daniel,

I like your question "why do we place so much emphasis on our future earnings compared to our education?" How would you judge a person's success? I personally would do so by their earnings rather than their education. Perhaps this is a factor when students are deciding which provider to gain further education through. Another aspect is the percentage of jobs available for university students in comparison to TAFE students. Australia is a rapidly developing country with constant construction and development underway in every major town and city. All trades require a TAFE certificate to be employed, as a result a lot of students studying at TAFE potentially are already employed or in an apprenticeship. In comparison to university students who may struggle to find employment with no real experience yet, rather, just a qualification.

I would be interested to see where they got their statistics from as well. Do they include online universities? I would argue that on-campus university students are often unemployed or work part-time compared to online students who are either parents or working full-time already and looking for a career change/progression. This would definitely impact these results.

Alex

....

I also like your question Daniel but I am going a different avenue to Alex.

I think while we do have to earn a wage to live and be comfortable, what success means for each of us may be different. Society places an economic value on success because we live in a capitalist society. But what if we taught our children success was a sense of accomplishment? Someone who has gone to TAFE, a carpenter, for example, may feel a sense of achievement when he completes a beautiful cabinet for a client or an artist may feel successful when they regularly sell their paintings. Maybe we put too much emphasis on success being equivalent to dollars? What if we told our children a different story about what success could mean for them?

As a side note, there are TAFE courses where you do not even earn half as much as what a University qualified professional does. If you look at childcare as an example, before they brought in qualified teachers a group leader was earning an average of about $41,000 which is a lot less than a teacher who has been working in education who can earn up to $110,000 a year as a principal.

Fiona

....

Fiona

Definitely agree with you, it's hard to define success. It does seem that society places a fair amount of emphasis on dollars when talking about success as seems to be the case in this advert. Your examples are definitely suitable alternatives to what success can be portrayed as. It makes me wonder what success would look like in a world without money.

Daniel

....

Spoiler alert, the owner of this advert is highly biased towards TAFE and I would be surprised if this was the result of a university study (that would be too ironic). I have to admit, I have never thought of the demographics that make up uni and TAFE grads or the role it plays in future earning potentials, giving me much to think about.

Daniel

Daniel Flynn, Alex Ogilvie and Fiona Harvey, students of Humanities

The second conversation, Example 7.3, developed among Built Environment students from an article on rubbish recycling during the COVID-19 pandemic.

Example 7.3 Reflective conversation sparked by an article on rubbish recycling during the COVID-19 pandemic

Reflection on the article: 'Rubbish is piling up and recycling has stalled: Waste systems must adapt.' https://theconversation.com/rubbish-is-piling-up-and-recycling-has-stalled-waste-systems-must-adapt-137100.

This article challenged my assumption that Covid 19 wouldn't affect reuse and recycling. I believe I had assumed this partly because I was oblivious to the effect that this pandemic has had on this industry. Although at present this is not an insurmountable problem, I think that now is a good time to address waste and recycling issues and start moving from a linear economy to a circular one. This is because if it doesn't start happening now and Covid becomes a long-term issue, it may be extremely difficult to correct later on. After reading this article I have realised that despite countries being able to continue on the path of a linear economy in the short term, the turning point from moving from a linear economy to a circular one may need to be sooner than we think.

Lars

Thanks for posting this interesting article Lars. It is a very concerning issue, especially when I believe Australia's economy is almost purely based on a linear model, with an unusually high amount of natural resource extraction for a 1st world country, and with few value adding industries. On a similar note, I have noticed a lot of articles in the media about the way the change in people's lifestyles due to the COVID epidemic might be impacting climate change, but this piece brings up a lot of points which make me question the optimism about this, and wonder about what other unanticipated complications will come up in the future.

James

Hi James,

I would like to do some more investigation into how linear the Australian economy is to get a broader understanding of it. With the reduction of commercial and industrial waste and increase of household waste, less reusable waste is becoming available and more waste needs to go to landfill or be recycled. So many recycling centres have shut down due to Covid too, so this may be a big problem. I think now may be a good time to move towards a circular economy.

Lars

Hi Lars,

Great article! This was really something that I hadn't anticipated – perhaps this is because waste disposal is the dirt we brush under the rug, most people are oblivious to the waste process beyond pushing their bins onto the street.

Unfortunately the thought of a circular economy is perhaps a pipe dream for the foreseeable future as the western countries have created consumer markets that rely on exploiting foreign countries for manufacturing. The circular economy would have to be a global effort and require all countries to participate.

Thanks

Seamus

....

Hi Lars

This is a great article to show the effect on just one industry in regards to Covid-19. I know where I live in Brisbane, the local recycling plant has closed down for over a month.

It should make people aware of how important recycling is, and how wasteful society is. Especially the building industry.

Projects always allow extras and this is quite evident in the amount of building waste of residential projects alone.

Zeik

....

Hi Zeik,

I am glad you enjoyed the article. We are truly a throw-away society, I agree. This appears to be a perpetual problem which can only get worse if a change isn't implemented. The onset of Covid resulting in the shutting down of waste recycling plants is a big problem. I am wondering this will be a wake up call to start addressing waste recycling and reuse more effectively. Could this be a good time to overhaul the industry and start thinking more long term?

Lars

....

Hi Lars

Great article! It also challenged my assumption that COVID wouldn't affect our recycling and re purposing services. And also made me question how linear my family and I are with personal and household items. The idea of a circular economy sounds great and would be amazing, but I worry that it would be hard to implement. Would companies do so if it not as profitable as a linear one? Would governments support it?

Kristy

....

Hi Kristy

One of the texts I chose for our first assignment was on urban mining and the circular economy. Urban mining is the reuse of building components like window assemblies, doors etc. in new buildings. The case study in the text was based on urban mining components in Singapore to build affordable house for disadvantaged communities. The case study found this practice to be very successful economically and environmentally. I think that urban mining is a great way to use building components that would otherwise be discarded in large quantities. Could developed countries possibly give or sell (at a low cost) their building waste to developing countries so they can build affordable housing? Which ever way you look at it, urban mining to what ever degree possible is a good thing. I am thinking of finding a text on it for this assignment possibly.

Lars

....

Lars Nielsen, James Gibson, Seamus Dobbs, Zeik Rafferty and Kristy Taylor, students of Built Environment

ACTIVITY 7.5   Analysis of reflective conversations

As an individual

Choose one of the two previous conversations (Example 7.2 or 7.3) and annotate it to show the reflective techniques the students are using, as we have done in Annotated example 7.1.

In a group or a class

Share your annotations with others who have chosen the same conversation as you. Discuss the similarities and differences in your annotations, and what you have learned about reflective writing by participating in this exercise.

ACTIVITY 7.6   Reflective writing on ideas you are encountering in your studies

As an individual

Write a 300-word reflection about an idea you have encountered in your studies (e.g. in a lecture, in your reading or in a YouTube or TED recording), applying the strategies explored in this chapter.

In a group or a class

Discuss your reflections with others who have chosen the same text as you, focusing on the different perspectives being raised in each, and on the reflective strategies each writer is using. Remember that there is no one 'correct' direction to take your writing – the range of perspectives enriches the reflective thinking of the group.

Final words from a student

Earlier in this chapter we commented that reflection at first-year level is a preparation for deeper critical and reflective thinking in future years. To emphasise this crucial point, we include a reflection from a student (see Student reflection 7.8), reflecting on an issue he has been challenged to consider throughout his first-semester studies: 'the Great Australian Dream'.

 Student reflection 7.8   **Reflective writing can begin your thinking processes**

Many issues attracted my attention in this lecture about suburbia and the Great Australian Dream. Perth suburbia to me is ideal when you consider the lifestyles available. This made me begin to wonder what the ideal lifestyle is to the average person. Does a backyard that is big enough to fit another family home really satisfy our lifestyle needs? I considered my own lifestyle where we as a family rarely use the considerably large yard, with the exception of family events such as birthday parties, barbeques and other social gatherings. Lifestyle rarely requires the use of such space, but nevertheless

I would never wish to lose it. The lecture made me realise that the majority of Australians share my attitude and drew my attention to what I believe is a misconception that people who think this way are selfish.

While Perth's suburbia is extremely extensive, so is our available geographical area. So why is it that more and more planners are pushing for higher density residential development in the close perimeter areas around the city? This question troubled me at first as I could not think why it is that people would choose to live in such places. It then occurred to me that not everyone opts for the lifestyle that I value.

Chris Lodge, Urban and Regional Planning student

When we contacted Chris the following year for permission to include his reflection in this book, he agreed, but added that he was embarrassed on re-reading this reflection because he felt his ideas had developed significantly since he had written it. This doesn't discount the value of this piece of writing. In trying to penetrate deeply into his thinking on the topic as a then first-year student, Chris was setting the foundations for his strong future studies. The most perceptive thinkers are those who continue to try out ideas, shaping, discarding, developing and contradicting them as they go. We are more concerned about our students who have no questions about what they are hearing than we are about those who try out half-developed ideas and change them frequently. Learning is about engagement!

REVISION TOOLS

↘ Revision activity: Revise these ideas

1 Reflection is high-order thinking and it is highly valued in all universities. Critical reflection involves identifying and challenging the assumptions that underlie our own ideas and the ideas of other people.

2 Writing down our thoughts usually helps us to think more deeply, as well as creating a record of our thinking that we can refer back to. For students, it's also beneficial because it allows teachers to 'eavesdrop' on the thinking processes and to offer guidance.

3 The best way to start learning to reflect critically is to ask many questions, and to ponder possible responses without 'drawing a line' under a final answer.

4 Reflective writing is generally written personally, in an informal register.

5 Reflective thinking develops gradually, with continued practice, guidance and models of good student reflections. Research suggests that critical reflection develops with maturity, and that when first-year students arrive at university most of them have not yet developed their critical and reflective thinking capacities.

6 Students can reflect on their own learning processes, on their professional practice and on ideas they encounter in lectures, iLectures, podcasts and tutorials.

↘ Thinking activity: Critical and reflective questions

1 What are some of my 'already knowns' or 'truths' that I have assumed belong to everyone? How are these being challenged by my studies or professional work so far?

2 How have my life experiences positioned me to look at the world in a particular way? What are some of the perspectives I hold that might help or hinder me in achieving my goals?

3 How will critical and reflective thinking be important for my professional life?

4 How do societies benefit from people challenging their own assumptions and the assumptions of others?

↘ Useful weblinks

The following resources will help you delve deeper into the concept of reflective writing:

University of Hull, UK: *Reflective Writing*: **https://www.youtube.com/watch?v=b1eEPp5VSIY**.

University of New South Wales Learning Centre: 'Reflective Writing': **https://student.unsw.edu.au/reflective-writing**.

Massey University (NZ): 'Reflective Writing': **http://owll.massey.ac.nz/assignment-types/reflective-writing.php**.

Queensland University of Technology: 'Reflective Writing': **http://www.citewrite.qut.edu.au/write/reflectivewriting.jsp**.

REFERENCES

Dewey, John. 1910. *How We Think*. Boston: D.C. Heath and Company.

King, Patricia M., and Karen Strohm Kitchener. 1994. *Developing Reflective Judgment: Understanding and Promoting Intellectual Growth and Critical Thinking in Adolescents and Adults.* San Francisco: Jossey-Bass.

Report writing

CONTENTS

What is a report?

A *report* is a clearly structured document describing what has happened, or what should happen, in a given situation, based on sound research by the report's author(s). Though there are many types of reports, they fall broadly into two categories:

- descriptive reports
- analytical reports.

In a *descriptive report*, you do what the name suggests: describe a subject or incident. This type of report is written in a concise, factual manner, without opinions or analysis. Any analyses or judgements are made by those who commissioned the report. Descriptive reports are usually written for workplace environments and we will briefly refer to them later in this chapter. As you are more likely to be asked to write some form of an *analytical report*, these are the report types that we will focus on in the following pages.

Analytical report types

Analytical reports can be classified with a variety of labels, and in this chapter we will discuss three types of these reports. Your assignment instructions may label the report differently, but they are likely to resemble one of our examples. Table 8.1 shows the sections you are likely to have in each of the three report types we have chosen.

Table 8.1	Three report types and their characteristics		
Section	**Major analytical report**	**Laboratory (lab) and project report**	**Site visit report**
Report title page	✓	✓	✓
Abstract/executive summary	Abstract of 100–300 words	✗	Executive summary of 100–300 words
Contents page	✓	✗	✓
List of figures	✓	✗	✓
Introduction	✓	Introduction and background	Introduction and background
Body of report	Description and analysis	Description	Description and (comparative) analysis
Conclusion	✓	✓	✓

Section	Major analytical report	Laboratory (lab) and project report	Site visit report
Recommendations	✓	Occasionally	✓
List of references	✓	If required	✓
Bibliography	Optional	✗	✗
Glossary	If required	✗	If required
Appendices	Optional	Occasionally	✗

Major analytical reports

Major analytical reports are the most detailed of the three types of reports. The main focus in this type of report is the analysis of a situation, and you are likely to be asked to suggest solutions to a problem. In many disciplines you will be asked to imagine that an individual or organisation has commissioned you to write the report; in these hypothetical situations, the people who have commissioned you to complete the report will have asked you to address specific questions or investigate a particular problem. You will be expected to conduct research and then interpret your findings. Your interpretation will lead you to make conclusions and, most importantly, to then develop recommendations. Also note that even if you decide to argue in favour of particular recommendations, you will usually be expected to appear to be as impartial as possible and show that you are basing your recommendations on the evidence only, rather than your personal opinion.

In such a report, state your objective clearly at the beginning. You should have one overriding objective that may also include a few smaller, associated objectives. Remember, for an analytical report, you must investigate the given situation in order to answer particular question(s) or to solve the particular problem(s). (Thus you cannot have an objective that is to 'inform' or 'educate' the audience about a given topic – this is an appropriate objective for a *descriptive* report only.)

Unclear about the objective for your report?

When you start your analytical report, you may not be able to articulate a specific objective until *after* you have done some preliminary research. As soon as you can after doing this early research, write down a clear objective before you conduct significant further research.

Laboratory (lab) reports and project reports

Laboratory (or lab) reports and *project reports* are examples of what we call *simple analytical reports*. Because these two types of reports have similar aspects, we will discuss them together.

The main purpose of simple analytical reports is to record and analyse what has happened in a test or experiment (a lab report), or a given task (a project report). In some lab and project reports you will be required to develop appropriate tasks to test a given hypothesis.

In your lab and project reports you will usually include information about the following:

- equipment
- procedure
- relevant variables
- final results.

You may be expected to give a presentation about the status of the project – perhaps you will need to share progress, discoveries or decisions. This can sometimes be labelled as giving a *progress report.*

Site visit reports

In some courses, such as surveying or engineering, your major analytical report could be based on issues arising out of one or more site visits. A *site visit report* is also a major analytical report because you will do more than describe the site – you will also need to do some or all of the following:

- Analyse how well the site works to achieve its objectives.
- If you visit more than one site, conduct a comparative analysis of the sites.
- Examine what you have learned about your discipline through the site visit(s).
- Identify some general issues related to your discipline that are appropriate to the site(s), and conduct secondary academic research about these issues, applying your research to the site(s).
- Make recommendations about the sites to a particular audience.

See Table 8.1 at the start of this chapter for the main characteristics of your report; however, where this differs from instructions you have been given, always follow your specific assignment instructions.

The Engineers Without Borders (EWB) Challenge

In many Australasian tertiary institutions, engineering students participate in the Engineers Without Borders (EWB) Challenge (see **http://www.ewbchallenge.org**). According to the organisation's website, EWB

(2020) has an overall aim of 'working toward the goal of a transformed engineering sector where every engineer has the skills, knowledge, experience, and attitude to contribute to sustainable community development and poverty alleviation'. The EWB Challenge program 'aims to contribute to this broader goal' (EWB 2020). Students who enter this competition are required to produce a group report.

The EWB report is a major analytical report with a specific format. (See the submission requirements on the EWB website.) The EWB website contains several examples of successful reports; it is worth studying these carefully before you start your EWB report. Consult Chapter 15 for general information about working in teams, and Chapter 16 if you are required to present your report.

Compiling the report

A report must be a readable, well-structured document. Unless you have been given other instructions, use the formatting instructions suggested here, ensuring you start each section on a new page. You may decide to use a template to help shape the report (beginning with the contents page) as long as you check that you have addressed any specific instructions for your assignment.

Even though a report has a clearly defined structure and a more definable 'skeleton' (see this chapter's section on decimal notation) than many other writing genres, you still need to plan, draft, edit and proofread it thoroughly to achieve a successful outcome. (See Chapter 6 for a reminder about the writing process.) Before you start to write, gather your research, note your report's objective and audience, and create a plan. Even if you have not completely clarified your objective, you need to build a plan so you can then structure your report according to the decimal notation system. The best advice we can give you on writing your report is to *start early* – don't assume you can write such a major assignment in a few days. This is especially important for group reports, such as the report that is part of the EWB Challenge.

Decimal notation

Reports are organised according to a range of different systems, including:

- paragraphs
- paragraphs with headings
- simple numbers
- the alphanumeric system (1a, 1b and so on)
- the decimal notation system (1.0, 1.1, 1.2, 2.0, 2.1, 2.1.1 and so on).

Decimal notation is the most commonly used system to help structure reports written for academic and professional settings. This system is simple, logical and helps you organise information in an attractive format. Remember that a report's structure must make it easy for readers to find the sections that interest them. Templates available in software such as Microsoft Word, which feature tools such as the 'Heading' function (under 'Styles'), make organising documents much easier. Explore available software packages, and get help from your institution's online tutorials and academic support services.

Using the multi-level decimal notation system is very helpful for ease of reading and for being able to refer to sections of a report, but it is not essential – especially for short reports. Example 8.1, following, is an excerpt from a short information systems report. Only part of Section 1 and all of Section 3 are included in this example. Note that, apart from simple numbering for the main heading, no further numbering is used; however, bullet points and font differentiation help organise the content. Also, since this is a descriptive report, one part (Section 3) was completed using a diagram with labels but without any accompanying sentences.

Example 8.1   Excerpt from a descriptive report using simple numbers, bullet points, headings and subheadings

---

1. General description

Title
Transaction processing system (TPS)

Overall function
The function of a TPS is to collect, modify and store any data involved in a transaction for a firm. A transaction is any business event where data are generated that have value (i.e. pass the ACID test). TPSs allow firms to process data quickly and efficiently. Transactions are usually processed in a batch or in real time. A batch is where transactions are collected, then processed later. Real time is when data is processed immediately (Gray et al. 2015, 17).

Users and uses
Workers at checkout areas of stores.

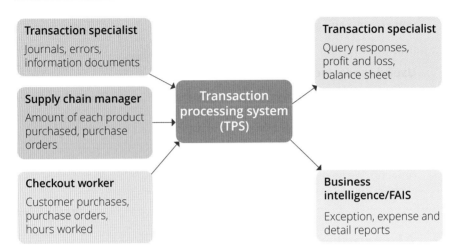

2. External view of TPS

Transaction specialist
Journals, errors, information documents

Supply chain manager
Amount of each product purchased, purchase orders

Checkout worker
Customer purchases, purchase orders, hours worked

Transaction processing system (TPS)

Transaction specialist
Query responses, profit and loss, balance sheet

Business intelligence/FAIS
Exception, expense and detail reports

3. Internal description

Information processors
Transaction specialist (non-computerised information processor), which:

- identifies errors in the previous transaction processes and develops responses to resolve these issues.
- ......

List of references
Gray, Heather, Tomayess Issa, Graeme Pye, Indrit Troshani, R. Kelly Rainer, Brad Prince and Hugh Watson. 2015. *Management Information Systems*. Milton, QLD: John Wiley & Sons.

'Information systems descriptive report': Aden Dielesen, Commerce student

Title page

The report's *title page* should look inviting, so (if you are not using a template) use a variety of fonts and visuals to make it look attractive and balanced. Information usually required on this page includes:

- report title
- audience (if required)
- name and position of author
- submission date
- place where the report was written.

In most reports the first two items are the most important, and should therefore be the most visible. Your report's title should be an appropriate and succinct rewording of the objective. You may choose to create a short, general title followed by a subtitle that contains more detail; the subtitle is usually printed on a new line and in smaller print. Again, there are report templates that you may use – or be instructed to use – and these will help you create a suitable title page.

Useful report websites

There are many good report writing websites listed at the end of this chapter. Some address aspects of report writing not covered in this chapter, such as the University of Southern Queensland website, which includes instructions on writing a letter of transmittal (see **https://www.usq.edu.au/library/ study-support/assignments/assignment-structure-and-writing/ reports**). We have not included information on this component in this chapter, since it is rarely required in an academic report.

Abstract or executive summary

The words *abstract* and *executive summary* are terms that are sometimes used interchangeably. Often abstract is used for shorter reports, whereas the term executive summary is generally used in long professional reports. Check Table 8.1 and your assignment instructions for the term you are required to use.

The abstract or executive summary section varies in length from about a few hundred words (e.g. for a site visit report) to several pages. It is a significant section of the report, and you should check and edit it carefully. Some points to consider when creating this section include the following:

- Tell yourself that this section is often read by those who either have no time to read the whole report or who are questioning whether they should bother to read the report at all.
- Create the abstract or executive summary only *after* you've completed the report. (Although note that it is generally positioned at the beginning, before the contents page.)
- Write in complete sentences and paragraphs rather than in point form, though aim to be as concise as possible.
- In some reports you may be required to copy and paste all of the recommendations (i.e. those that are in the recommendations section) into the end of this section.
- The executive summary of a *standard analytical report* will include:
  - a clear statement of the objective of your report and, where relevant, the audience
  - a brief statement naming the main subjects covered
  - a comment about the report's scope and any limitations of your research
  - information about the research methods you used

- the main conclusions
- the main recommendations.

- The executive summary of a site visit report should include:
    - a brief mention and analysis of the site(s) you visited (comparative, if required)
    - information about the professional issues that you saw arising from the site(s)
    - a comment about the scope and any limitations of your research
    - information about the research methods you used
    - the main conclusions
    - the main recommendations, if relevant.

Example 8.2 is the executive summary from a standard major analytical report by Construction Management student Paul Britton on the project management issues of a major teaching hospital built in Perth, the Fiona Stanley Hospital. His audience is the hospital's project management team. An executive summary for a site visit report could be similar to this sample.

Example 8.2   Executive summary from a standard major analytical report

This report has been created to identify important characteristics that are required by the project manager for the Fiona Stanley Hospital site to ensure efficiency and effectiveness in planning, organising, leading and controlling. These characteristics were applied to the management overseeing construction of the hospital. Specific methods of control are outlined and operational problems are predicted. Based on these predictions, solutions are applied to the project.

Research was limited due to construction of the hospital still taking place, although foundations of management were studied and applied to the hospital scenario. Scholarly journals were used to highlight difficulties in applying management principles, and websites were used for images and relevant background information to the Fiona Stanley Hospital.

Ensuring control in the project begins in the initial project plan and continues throughout the execution. Problems arise in a plan if it does not encompass all stages and contingency factors. Collecting and processing data is essential to provide feedback, and necessary to correct any actions if deviations from the original plan occur.

The report makes the following recommendations:

- Organise a project team, ensuring that each manager possesses sound technical, interpersonal and conceptual skills. The result of having these skills and combining them with the planning, organising, leading and controlling functions will ensure that work is done efficiently and to a high standard.
- Implement numerous operational plans while focusing on the main strategy. Diversion off the original plan can often be unavoidable; it is important to plan excessively to ensure contingency factors do not halt team's output.
- Set standards by which control can be measured. Key performance indicators can measure the output of the management team and be used to give feedback to the appropriate stakeholders at regular intervals.

- Ensure data is collected and presented in a meaningful way, as staff require it to be unambiguous, and key stakeholders will require it to be relevant. Proper documentation of information can be beneficial for use in future projects.
- Allow for variations in the original project plan, as unforeseen changes may require accounting for. Taking corrective action can often be time consuming and a waste of resources; excessive control processes should be placed on the project to ensure early detection.

Paul Britton, Construction Management student

Contents page

In all types of reports the purpose of the *contents page* is to show the reader the report's content and structure. To make this page easy to read, and to make your report look formal and organised, we suggest you use the 'Heading' function in your software package – this will format your contents page for you. If you are creating a contents page manually, the following information might help:

- Format the page using decimal notation (described earlier in this chapter).
- Justify the headings and subheadings to the left of the page, and the corresponding page numbers to the right. (Use the right-justification function on your word-processing program to do this neatly and easily.)
- Include decimal notation for all heading levels.
- Show the hierarchy of each heading through the font and indentation used.
- Check that each heading and subheading is informative and relevant to the subject.
- Check that the structure is logical.
- Use parallel construction in headings and subheadings. (See Chapter 12 for information on parallel construction.)

Example 8.3 is taken from the section of a report contents page from a standard major analytical report by Ashley Hunt on the shortage of engineers in Australia.

Example 8.3   Sample section from a report's contents page

Contents

...

Ashley Hunt, Engineering student

Headings and subheadings for various types of reports   HINT

If you want to check the similarities and differences in the sections – and thus the headings/subheadings for reports you may have to write for your assessments, go to the Royal Melbourne Institute of Technology (RMIT) website at **https://emedia.rmit.edu.au/learninglab/content/example**.

ACTIVITY 8.1   Exploring decimal notation   ☑

Example 8.3 is a sample from a contents page. Notice the way this student has linked, divided and subdivided his ideas. Create a detailed contents page for a report on the following topic and audience.

1   Topic/objective: From the perspective of a new tertiary student, assess the enrolment process at the place where you are studying. Was it an easy process? What should be changed, if anything?

2   Audience: The head of student services or faculty.

Share this contents page with a peer.

List of figures

A *list of figures* is a contents page for visuals only. It differs from a contents page in that it also includes citation details for each graphic. Example 8.4 shows a small section from a sample list of figures from an EWB Challenge report by Engineering students Ryan Pinto, Ben Caracciolo, Grant Perkins, Paul Buckley and Aidan Ashwin. This list consisted of 35 figures because the report included a large number of graphics from the students themselves. If you are writing a different type of report, your list of figures will be shorter than this one, but will follow the same conventions. Each entry in a list of figures includes:

- figure title (generally, you create this)
- citation details for the graphic
- the page where you have placed the graphic.

Example 8.4 Excerpt from a sample list of figures

List of figures

Source: 'EWB design project: Water meter': Ryan Pinto, Ben Caracciolo, Grant Perkins, Paul Buckley and Aidan Ashwin, Engineering students

---

Introduction

Introductions in reports are different from those in essays, in that they are designed to introduce the report, *not* the topic. While you will mention very briefly the background to the topic, your main background discussion will not take place until Section 2.0. The simplest way to achieve a successful report introduction is to state the report's objective in the first sentence. This is not essential, but it will help keep you on track throughout the report. The following elements are usually required in the introduction to analytical reports (but refer to your assignment instructions for any other specific requirements):

- statement of your objective (including the reasons why the report exists)
- name of the main audience for whom you have written the report (if required)
- statement outlining the problem you will address or the question(s) you will answer
- information about the research methods used to acquire the report data
- statement about the report's scope and limitations
- historical background relevant to the subject of the report*
- brief review of recent research by other people that relates directly to the aims of the report*
- brief outline of the make-up of the whole report.

* Introduction or body?

If you prefer, you could include the two items marked with an asterisk in the above list in the first section of the report body, rather than in the introduction.

Be careful to include in your introduction only the background necessary to the audience's understanding of your report – reports do not need long-winded introductory statements.

Example 8.5, taken from a marketing report by Lavinia Wehr, Emily Webb, Stephanie Walker and Stephanie Huynh, is an example of a short introduction where the background is not included as it is in the report body. These students are writing from their perspective as members of a company, Green PR.

Example 8.5   Sample short introduction for marketing report

This report explains both the analysis and recommendations by Green PR in regard to the issue of the global oversupply of milk in the dairy industry. All strategies and material are intended to be used by the company, WA Farmers, in order to not only raise awareness but also create a change in Australian attitudes and behaviour to support the people who are most adversely affected by this oversupply. The report includes extensive research into the issue as well as providing an insight into WA Farmers as a whole and the relevant stakeholders. The conclusion of this report will outline the key strategies and tactics as well as provide sample material to be used in the campaign in order to achieve the aforementioned goal.

Lavinia Wehr, Emily Webb, Stephanie Walker and Stephanie Huynh, Marketing students

Here is another example by Kathleen Nelly (Example 8.6), where after giving some historical background, she has strongly indicated her position in the last sentences of the introduction as a lead-in to the rest of the paper.

Example 8.6   Sample last sentences of an introduction

Mr Ward committed a minor offence and was refused bail by Laverton Police, and his transport to Kalgoorlie was arranged by G4S. The Police investigation into Mr Ward's death indicated that Laverton Police and the G4S transporting officers displayed unethical behaviour and collusion amongst all parties involved in the death (ALSWA 2010). Mr Ward was directly discriminated against because of his cultural background and treated less favourably because of this, which ultimately resulted in his death.

Kathleen Nelly, Commerce student

Example 8.7 is the introduction to an EWB Challenge report by John Aldridge, Samuel Hammond, Fiona Jones, Tim Kenworthy and Shaun Sullivan on their design of a water-dripper meter for Kandal Province, Cambodia.

Example 8.7   Sample report introduction (Engineers Without Borders report)

The purpose of this report is to offer Engineers Without Borders a viable, effective and sustainable solution to the problem of water metering, to be implemented through partner organisations in communities in Kandal Province, Cambodia. It achieves this by describing in technical detail the simplest, most affordable and most effective water meter possible, while also appropriately addressing the cultural, social and economic context in which it will be implemented. This report refers to economic, social, cultural, political and historical information on Cambodia inasmuch as it relates to a water meter design solution and its implications. Hence it shows not only the broader context into which the water meter will be introduced, but also the myriad possible implications that this will have for Kandal's way of life, economy and social fabric.

Where data is unattainable, assumptions based on similar situations elsewhere in the world have been made. While the body of the report contains only the designs for one water meter, appendices have been included for a range of different considered designs that chronicle the process with which the final design was created and justify choices made. The Dripper Water Meter's performance prediction is based wholly on equations that realistically describe the behaviour of fluids within pipes. Construction, maintenance and community training in relation to the water meter are addressed pragmatically and in detail. This report speculates over the water meter's broader economic benefits to communities, but makes no attempt to predict all of them with any certainty.

The current available meter is designed for a pressurised water system and costs US$50, a price that rural Cambodian families on US$2 or less per day cannot afford. The Dripper Water Meter overcomes the obstacle of measuring usage cheaply, sustainably and in a way that will be accepted by the people of Kandal, and has played its small part in the broader solution to supplying communities in need with a safe water source. The underlying problem that this water meter solves is the reluctance of organisations or companies to invest in a water supply system for a community whose usage cannot be recorded without the subsidising of water meters. If one company or organisation can read this document and decide that they are now able to install a water supply system because they know consumption can be monitored at low cost to all, then this report has achieved its goal.

John Aldridge, Samuel Hammond, Fiona Jones, Tim Kenworthy and Shaun Sullivan

Body of the report

In a report you should always link your information back to the report's objective (just as in an argumentative essay you must always link back to a thesis statement). In the body of the report, you should:

- name, discuss and analyse only data relevant to the report's objective
- support any theories and ideas with examples and illustrations. You may choose to include and analyse a case study. Deconstruct each topic logically so the content is easy to read
- use secondary evidence from credible, relevant sources only:
  - use this evidence to support or complement your primary research
- use visuals to help communicate your ideas
- check that the headings and subheadings match those listed on the contents page
- maintain logical decimal notation throughout:
  - divide the body into as many sections and subsections as you believe will help make the report more readable. In the body of all types of analytical reports you must describe and analyse your issue based on a relevant combination of primary and secondary research (see Chapter 3 for a discussion of these two types of research). Your analysis will lead directly to your conclusions and, where relevant, to your recommendations.

Connect recommendations to discussion in body

In many current published reports, recommendations are inserted into the body of the report wherever they may arise from the analysis and conclusions, usually in a box or in bold-face type to set them apart from the paragraphs of analysis. These recommendations are then copied and pasted into the recommendations section (and sometimes also into the end of the abstract or executive summary). We urge you to follow this practice, as it encourages you to ensure your recommendations arise logically from your analysis.

Example 8.8 is from a report by an Urban and Regional Planning student, Alexander VanderPlas. It illustrates a sound combination of primary and secondary research in his analysis of his own Perth suburb, Kelmscott.

Example 8.8 Section of the body of a report

> **4.0: Protection of local bushland**
>
> The issue of bushland protection in suburbs is very prominent today, especially with organisations such as the Urban Bushland Council of WA (Jennings 2006). According to Cunningham, an Associate Professor of Human and Environmental Studies at the University of New England, little importance was given to bushfire prevention and fire protection in the early days of the development of suburbs, towns and cities in Australia (Cunningham 2003, 28). This is especially true for Kelmscott, where the suburb was forged out of bushland and scrub. As a result of the increase of infrastructure located closer to bushland, the risk factor is now higher. When fires do occur, they have massive after effects because of the location of this infrastructure. Another feature of suburban development near bushland throughout Australia is highlighted by Humphreys (1989). He mentions that the location of vegetation is driven by the demands and needs of human beings. We get to preserve or conserve as we wish. Since Kelmscott was developed in a time before heavy environmental focus, little attention was paid to the preservation of natural environments. The only parts that were conserved were in areas that were too inaccessible.
>
> *Alexander VanderPlas, Urban and Regional Planning student*

Conclusion

You must include in your conclusion:

- a brief summary of the whole report (similar to what you have done in the abstract)
- major findings, based on your research and discussion in each section of the body.

Cover all the main issues

If you have discussed three issues in the body of your report, then you state at least three findings or conclusions about those issues in the report's conclusion section.

Example 8.9 is an example of a conclusion by Mariko Collins, an Engineering student. Mariko has done a tidy summary of what she did for the report and then clearly states her key findings, which have, in turn, led to her conclusion.

Example 8.9 Strong conclusion

The aim of this report was to explore an engineering role and the concept of a life-cycle assessment to assist in choosing a preferred engineering design. The report focused on chilled water systems, specifically 'Above Ground Insulated Steel Tanks' and 'Underground Uninsulated Concrete Tanks'.

Firstly, the report introduced chilled water systems and provided an overview of the two tank designs describing their structure, dimensions and energy usage. Secondly, a life cycle assessment was given for both tank designs which outlined the following stages:

- Raw Material Acquisition and Processing
- Manufacturing
- Use/Reuse/Maintenance; and
- Recycle/Waste Management.

The assessment focused on sustainability and after analysing the two tank designs it was concluded that the 'Above Ground Insulated Steel Tank' was a more sustainable option for the client. Factors contributing to this decision were the following:

1   At the end of both tank's lifespan (20 years), all concrete would be disposed of. Therefore, for the underground design the output of energy required to produce the tank – a minimum of 4.59×10^8 kWh – is not counterbalanced.

2   All steel would be recycled and used as scrap in producing more steel, therefore the waste management of the above ground tank would outweigh the environmental impacts it produces during production.

3   Soil excavation, maintenance and energy required to run the concrete tank is much greater than the steel tank.

Lastly, the report included an overview of various engineering roles involved in conducting the life cycle assessment. This section covered six different disciplines and outlined their role in society as well as their role in the life cycle assessment.

Mariko Collins, Bachelor of Engineering student

Recommendations

The *recommendations* section is the most significant part of many analytical reports, since it is here that you finally clarify answers to the questions from your audience that were captured in the report's objective. You suggest solutions to the relevant problems. This means that, on the basis of your recommendations, the audience can make decisions and take actions. Therefore, you should check that the report body only contains information directly connected to one or more of your recommendations. Recommendations may also include suggestions for further research or advice on future strategies. In the recommendations section, do the following:

- First, make a brief, persuasive statement. (See Example 8.10, which consists of the opening sentences from Khush Dodhia-Shah's report recommendations). Khush had done a report for Synergy investigating the implications of different Electric Vehicle (EV) uptake scenarios in Western Australia.

Example 8.10   Strong opening sentences in the recommendations section

WA should learn from more developed EV markets such as California and the UK. As demonstrated by the scenarios which assumed coordinated charging, even with large EV-associated demand, there is significant upside to incentivising and planning how EVs are going to integrate with the grid. The benefits include a greater overall consumption of electricity, with a load curve that is smoother, hence more stable and reliable. This would consume more free renewable energy, and reduce costs on the grid associated with ramping rates.

Khush Dodhia-Shah, Bachelor of Commerce graduate

- Follow this with recommendations that are clearly listed (with numbers or bullet points). Generate at least one recommendation for each issue analysed in the report's body.
- Also check that each recommendation flows from the report's conclusions. You may have several recommendations arising from one conclusion, so check there is a clear link between them and the relevant point in the conclusion. In this section you are directly responding to the report's objective by answering a question or solving a problem. Therefore, check that you have included 'words of action' (i.e. verbs) in every recommendation. Some extra advice about phrasing: although this is not the only method, it may be easier if you start each recommendation with a verb, as has been done in Example 8.11, an excerpt of some report recommendations written by Alan Ng, a Computer Systems and Networking student, on the subject of how to increase enrolments for information systems courses.

Example 8.11   Sample from the recommendations section of a report

6.1: Scholarship support

Offer a scholarship or introduce subsidies (e.g. textbook rebates) for new students enrolling into any one of the five computing courses. Many students have seen the engineering merit scholarship as a good incentive to study engineering at Curtin. With the relatively high cost of tertiary studies compared to high school, interested students could be encouraged to study computing at Curtin if given the incentive.

6.2: Raising awareness

Increase awareness of possible career opportunities in the IT industry. For example, more IT companies could be invited to attend Curtin's annual careers fair. Coupled with other possible actions such as promoting graduate employment programs from local companies, students can gain an idea of where they can go in the IT industry.

6.3: Industry consultation

Consult with industry when making changes to any of the computing courses so that the skills and knowledge taught to students stay relevant to what the IT industry wants.

▶

6.4: Include work experience

Incorporate work experience into the computing degrees. The inclusion of some form of work experience into the degree can help students underpin the skills they are learning and can also make sure that the material that is being taught is still applicable in the workplace.

Alan Ng, Computer Systems and Networking student

List of references

For detailed instructions on how to create an accurate *list of references*, use your library's online guides, consider utilising citation software (e.g. EndNote) and read Chapter 5 of this book.

Bibliography

As we outlined in Chapter 5, a *bibliography* includes all the sources you consulted in researching your report, not just those you cited. Though a list of references is essential, a bibliography is often optional.

Glossary

It may be helpful to define any jargon or complex terms included in a report by compiling and defining them in a *glossary* – an alphabetical list of words or terms deemed essential to understanding the report discussion. Include only words you think the audience may not understand.

Appendices

A report's *appendices* consist of information that supplements information in the body of the report. Here, include information that may deepen your audience's understanding of an aspect of the report's subject. If you do attach appendix material, refer to it directly at least once within the report's text. Note the three ways Khush Dodhia-Shah refers to the appendices in the excerpt of a business report given in Example 8.12.

Example 8.12   How to refer to appendices in a report

GNC Holdings, Inc. (GNC) is a specialty retailer of health and wellness products, including vitamins, minerals and herbal supplement products (VMHS category), as well as sports nutrition products and diet products. *For a brief background on the company, refer to Appendix 2.*

In the predicament that GNC has found itself in, it has introduced some strategies to change and take the company forward. *Refer to Appendix 4 for an overview* of the relevant new strategies. In terms of *marketing objectives (see Appendix 4)*, it is key that GNC both retains current loyal customers through its transitional period and further gains new customers, with their added benefits.

Khush Dodhia-Shah, Commerce student

Researching the report

Consult Chapter 3 for details about how to conduct your research. The one aspect we highlight here is that, since most reports will include both primary and secondary research, you should consult that chapter's sections on these topics. For more help on choosing the type of primary research to best suit your report context, see also the article 'What is Primary Research and How Do I Get Started?' at Purdue University's Online Writing Lab (OWL); see **https://owl.purdue.edu/owl/research_and_citation/ conducting_research/conducting_primary_research/index.html**.

Writing the report

Tone

Analytical reports should always appear impartial and balanced. As you write, provide all the relevant evidence so your audience can make a good judgement or decision about the subject. Even if the evidence is problematic and there may not be a clear answer, acknowledge this, but still argue for what you consider the best course of action. Remember, you are not simply describing your data; you are providing the audience with your reasoned analysis of it. Refer to the section on writing a concessive argument in Chapter 9 for help with this.

Language

Use Chapter 11 – and any specific assignment instructions you are given – to guide you as you write. Note, too, the following additional comments about language use in reports:

- Aim to be concise and to avoid expressions that could be ambiguous in their meaning. Check that your spelling is correct to improve clarity and to create a good impression.
- Check the assignment instructions about the use of the third-person passive voice versus the first-person active voice. See Chapter 11 for more on the active versus the passive voice.
- If you need to include personal pronouns, limit their use to the recommendations section.
- Avoid using jargon and abbreviations. If you include terms that are specific to your discipline, consider explaining them in a glossary.
- Verb tenses in reports usually follow the following protocol:
  - Use the past tense for tasks that are completed.
  - Use the present tense for ongoing work.
  - If relevant, use the future tense for work yet to be done.
  - The future-conditional tense is often used in the recommendation section.

Remember to use connectives

With decimal notation, you create visible links and divisions within the report. This doesn't mean, however, that you can be untidy in the way you link ideas within paragraphs, and between paragraphs. Remember to use connectives such as 'however', 'on the other hand' and 'furthermore'. Look at the section on linking paragraphs in Chapter 6 for more information on how to use connectives.

Visuals

The saying 'A picture is worth a thousand words' is particularly true for reports. For most reports, visuals can strengthen and clarify words and numbers. The inclusion of visuals may even be a report assignment requirement. Depending on your discipline, you may be required to include several visuals in your report. These might include charts, graphs, diagrams, photos and drawings, all of which you should refer to as 'figures'. Follow these guidelines for including visuals in a report:

- Ensure your visuals complement the text, yet have enough detail to stand alone.
- Ensure they are clear and large enough to read without difficulty.
- Give each visual an informative title.
- Make your visuals concise and accurate – the details must be easily understood.
- For most short reports, it will be acceptable to label the visuals 'Figure 1', 'Figure 2', 'Figure 3' and so on, in order throughout the report. However, you may be required to number them according to the section of the report they appear in; for example, if a visual is the second visual in Section 3, you might label it 'Figure 3.2'.
- Refer to figures specifically, by number and title, at the relevant places in your report – for example, 'Figure 6, Map of existing mine sites, shows … '; ' … as evidenced in Figure 3, Population distributions, 1950–2000'. Include each visual in the report immediately after you refer to it in the report's text.
- Place visuals in the appendices section if they present material that is additional rather than essential for the development of your argument.
- *Always* reference visuals according to your discipline's referencing guidelines. (See Chapter 5 for further details.)

Table or figure – what's the difference?

Tables are another way to present report data in an easy-to-read format. The key difference between a table and the other visuals referred to in this chapter are that tables are usually composed of numbers organised by vertical and horizontal lines. Word-processing software packages contain various table options. Rules about how to present tables are the same as those for other visuals.

Editing

Based on the advice above, and once you have completed a first draft of your report, use the report-writing guidelines in Table 8.2 to help you edit the report. Before starting this process, look back at Chapter 6 for general help with editing and proofreading.

Note that the following are only guidelines, and that you must check any specific instructions for your unit or course. For a site visit report, EWB Challenge report or any other report, follow carefully any particular guidelines and use the following table only where relevant. In the table, each report component is named in order of its appearance in the report.

Student reflection 8.1   Learning while report writing

Throughout this project I developed frustration, but from that I developed patience. The frustration came from me not understanding the assignment and the impact of circumstances caused by COVID–19. The forced online learning situation led to conversations that would've taken a couple minutes in person, to ones that stretched out over a couple of days. This led me to be patient towards my approach to the assignment. This capability will be important for future communications online for other projects or clients and co-workers within the workforce.

Mariko Collins, Bachelor of Engineering student

Table 8.2 Report-writing guidelines (or checklist) for major analytical reports

	Report component	Purpose	Explanation
1	**Unit cover page or assignment submission sheet**	Identify your details and assignment information.	This page will be provided for you, and its contents will be determined by your department or faculty. It may include such details as your student number, the assignment due date, your tutor's name and an assessment rubric.
2	**Report title page**	Identify the report's subject. (This page must look good.)	Include: • report title (with explanatory subtitle if needed) • audience (if required) • submission date • name and role of author • place where the report was written.
3	**Abstract or executive summary**	Summarise the whole report. (This is aimed at those who have little time to read the whole report, or who need to be convinced to read the whole report.)	• Be brief. • Position it before the contents page. • Write a few brief paragraphs. • Summarise the report's purpose, main discussion and findings. • If recommendations are required, also summarise these (unless you are required to include a copy of them at the end of the abstract/executive summary).
4	**Contents page**	Show the report's outline. Indicate where topics are addressed in the document.	• Create the contents page using software such as Microsoft Word; otherwise, format the page manually using decimal notation. – Left-align the headings and subheadings and right-align the corresponding page numbers. – Make the hierarchy of headings evident through format, font and decimal notation level. – Make each heading and subheading informative and relevant to the subject. • Express headings and subheadings in parallel phrases.

	Report component	Purpose	Explanation
5	**List of figures**	Provide details of any visuals used in the report.	• Give every visual a title. • Insert correct in-text referencing. • List each visual in correct sequence, adding the page number where it is placed in the report.
6	**Introduction**	Introduce the reader to the report's subject and objective.	• Give details about the report's objective(s). • Name the audience for whom the report has been written (if required). • Outline the problem to be addressed or the question(s) to be answered (including the reasons why the report exists). • Give information about the research methods used to research the report data. • Explain the scope and limitations of the report. • Give historical background relevant to the subject of the report.* • Give a brief review of any recent research that is specifically relevant to the aims of the report.* • Outline the structure of the whole report. *If preferred, you may include this information in the first section of the report body.
7	**Body**	Name, discuss and analyse information and data relevant to the report's purpose. Support your theories and ideas with examples.	• Only include information that is useful to the report's objective. • Structure each topic in a logical way using decimal notation. • Maintain decimal notation throughout. (You are likely to be using software to do this automatically.) • Include examples and illustrations from credible, relevant sources. • Include visuals. • Make sure the headings and subheadings match those in the contents page.

	Report component	Purpose	Explanation
8	**Conclusion**	State the main findings, based on research and discussion in the report's body. Give a brief summary of the discussion.	• Include a closing statement for each of the key issues analysed in the report's body.
9	**Recommendations**	Suggest actions that your audience can take to address the issues you have raised in the report. Give opinions and advice.	• Start with a brief, persuasive statement. • Follow this with recommendations clearly listed in numbered or bullet points. • Have at least one recommendation for each main section of the report's body. • Ensure the recommendations flow from the conclusions. • Give clear, direct advice to the report's audience.
10	**List of references (see notes at the end of this table)**	Acknowledge all the sources cited (either quoted or paraphrased) in the report.	• This is most easily created using software (e.g. EndNote). Or create the list manually following the required referencing style guide. • Format it correctly.
11	**Bibliography (optional)**	Name sources relevant to the report (e.g. background reading) but not used in report.	• Carefully follow the required referencing style guide.
12	**Appendices (optional)**	Provide supplementary information.	• Include material to help the audience understand the subject more fully. • Label each appendix with letters, not numbers (e.g. Appendix A). • Direct the reader to read the appendix material at relevant points within the report's body.
13	**Glossary (optional)**	Define any jargon or complex terms essential to the report.	• Define words or terms that are essential for understanding the report. • Include only words that are likely to be unfamiliar to your audience.

REVISION TOOLS

⬊ Revision activity: Revise these ideas

1 Reports are highly structured documents either describing or/and analysing an issue or event. They are the most common form of writing done in a workplace environment.

2 There are many types of reports, though they fall mainly into two broad categories: descriptive and analytical reports.

3 Report format requirements are very prescriptive, so follow the instructions for the particular report you have been asked to write; otherwise, use the guidelines summarised in Table 8.2.

⬊ Thinking activity: Critical and reflective questions

1 Have I checked what *type* of report I have to write?

2 Remembering that my audience is unlikely to read all my report, what way should I structure it to make it easy to read and find sections?

3 Am I confident that I can create a well-structured, readable report that is acceptable not only to my lecturer but also to a potential employer? If not, keep this chapter as a ready reference and create a 'Favourites' folder for website resources most suited to your subject area.

⬊ Useful weblinks

There are numerous websites on report writing – you may even find one at your institution. The following resources could be useful as you work on reports:

Information about the Engineers Without Borders Challenge and how to write the EWB report can be found on the following webpage: **http://www.ewbchallenge.org/content/about-program**.

The University of New South Wales has several excellent resources at the 'Academic study skills' tab at the following URL: **https://student.unsw.edu.au/report-writing-support**. (If you are a business student, especially note this link: **https://www.business.unsw.edu.au/students/resources/learning-support/resources/writing-editing**.)

The University of New South Wales also has a resource called 'iWrite', created by the Faculty of Engineering and Information Technologies for students and staff members. It covers various types of writing used in engineering and science: **http://iwrite.unsw.edu.au/iwrite.html**.

Deakin University describes how to write reports under three categories: 'Business', 'Experimental/laboratory' and 'Technical design'; see **http://www.deakin.edu.au/students/studying/study-support/academic-skills/report-writing**. For more academic skills support, go to the 'Academic Skills' page for current students: **http://www.deakin.edu.au/students/studying/study-support/academic-skills**.

Library Study Smart at the University of Western Sydney contains downloadable resources for various types of academic assignments, including report writing; see the 'Reports' link from the 'How-to assessment guides' link at **https://www.westernsydney.edu.au/studysmart/home/assignment_help/writing**.

See the formatting suggestions for reports at Monash University at **http://www.monash.edu.au/lls/llonline/writing/science/process/2.xml**.

The 'Assignment skills' section of the University of South Australia's study support website contains a link to a succinct YouTube video summarising how to write a report; see **https://www.youtube.com/watch?v=GV4yMF8vx6o**.

The Learning Lab website at the Royal Melbourne Institute of Technology has a simple video giving instructions for report writing; you can listen as you check your draft: **https://emedia.rmit.edu.au/learninglab/node/804**.

The University of Technology Sydney has a concise, practical page entitled 'Report Writing', which contains links to other report-writing websites; see **https://www.uts.edu.au/current-students/support/helps/self-help-resources/academic-writing/report-writing**.

REFERENCES

Engineers Without Borders Australia (EWB). 2017. 'Aims & Objectives.' **https://ewbchallenge.org**.

CHAPTER 9

Academic essay writing

CONTENTS

The academic essay

While the academic essay is viewed by some people as the pinnacle of student writing, it is just one of the many genres in which you will be required to write during your studies; it is no more prestigious than any other genre. But you do need to learn how to write academic essays in order to succeed in most university courses. We believe that, as a student, you can improve your essay writing by learning about the conventions of the academic essay; you can then learn to follow these conventions, and to adapt them to suit your purposes and your existing language skills. Your learning is further enhanced, we believe, by examining models of how other students have adapted the conventions in their essay assignments.

Several different types of academic essay are common in universities, but we will focus for most of this chapter on the argumentative essay. First, though, we will make some comments on another type of academic essay, the analytical essay.

The analytical essay

An *analytical essay*, as the name suggests, focuses on analysis. You generally need to begin this type of essay by describing *things* – situations, theories, works of art, problems, techniques and so on. Then you analyse them – that is, examine them carefully, pulling them apart and looking at their components – in order to understand them better. While you might hold a particular stance or position on the subject, and this stance might be identifiable throughout your analysis, you are generally not required to argue for one position strongly, as you would in an argumentative essay (which we will discuss below). So, for example:

- Literature or Cultural Studies students might examine how a particular image is presented in several different types of text
- Planning students might investigate various approaches to providing inner-city housing for older people, Indigenous Australians or young people
- Psychology students might explore various theories about how children develop language
- Geology students might consider several different methods for storing nuclear waste safely underground.

The endpoint in an analytical essay is the analysis itself. You must explore your subject fully, examining all aspects; noting strengths and weaknesses, possibilities and difficulties, and theories and disagreements about the subject; and perhaps making some evaluation about which ideas or approaches are more soundly based, innovative, appropriate to the particular contexts you are discussing and so on. Your analysis goes far beyond description – it involves comparison, contrast, synthesis and evaluation of ideas. But you do not need to reach a solution or conclusion in which you argue for one thing over another.

Much of what we will say in the rest of this chapter will be relevant to analytical essays, particularly our comments on paragraphing and academic language. But we will now turn our focus to the argumentative essay.

The argumentative essay

Unlike the analytical essay, the *argumentative essay* does require you to reach a conclusion – your conclusion is a coherent proposition that you will present, develop and support throughout the essay.

You must:

- present a clear argument that is supported by appropriate evidence
- consider your audience (generally your tutor or lecturer)
- write in a formal register (see Chapter 11) and use:
  - formal vocabulary, as clearly and simply as you can, while still expressing your ideas fully (Chapter 11 contains advice on clear, simple language)
  - correct, complete sentences
  - clear, correct and concise written expression
- write an introduction that introduces the subject, presents your argument and outlines your main ideas
- write a conclusion that reiterates the argument and the main ideas, and announces to your reader that you are finishing.

Early research

Chapter 3 will remind you how to do early research. For both the types of essay described in this chapter, you will probably start with secondary research, reading a range of material from different writers. As you research, you will discover many different aspects of the topic, some that may be familiar to you and others that are new. You might think of the topic as a pie, with different aspects being different-sized slices of the pie.

While you research, you will be making notes (see Chapter 4), and you might also do some writing. Many students who are successful writers have developed habits of writing beyond their formal tasks – they use writing to help them think through their ideas. This writing doesn't have to be in full sentences – it can be phrases, words or lists – but at this stage it is not an essay plan. Its main value is to help formulate ideas, questions and ways to approach the topic.

Research has three purposes in an academic context:

- It allows you to develop your own ideas.

- It provides the evidence that you will need to support the analysis or argument in your essay, and to demonstrate that you are not just writing 'off the top of your head'.
- It helps you understand other people's perspectives on your topic, so that you are able to see the contexts or frame in which you are developing your own ideas, and allows you to participate in the academic conversation around your topic.

Don't stop researching. As we have said several times in this book, academic writing is a spiral process rather than a linear one – each step in the process overlaps, feeds back on and develops all the others. (For a visual representation of this process, see Figure 6.1 in Chapter 6.) Even after you have chosen one thesis statement over others, and started planning and writing your essay, you may discover new ideas in your research that will cause you to alter your thesis statement, add another concessive argument or change the order of your main ideas. You will probably not decide to argue the opposite of your original thesis statement, but this has happened before. So continue your research, making notes as you go, and jotting down arguments for and against your thesis statement.

Primary research

While most of your research will be secondary research, you may be required (or you may choose) to also conduct some primary research – for example, an analysis of cultural artefacts, interviews, surveys, focus groups, observation, reflection on personal experience and so on. (Look back at Chapter 3 for more discussion of primary research.) You must integrate this research into your essay just as you would integrate secondary research: by using it as the application of your ideas.

You must reference most primary research in a slightly different way from secondary research. In the case of cultural artefacts, such as local newspaper articles or published photographs, you can often reference them in the same way you would reference secondary resources. However, you can't include personal surveys, observations, interviews or email conversations in your list of references because these are unpublished sources and so your readers can't follow them up. Because of this, **you must embed full details of the research in your own sentence**. For the correct in-text citation formats for these, check your department's referencing guide. You might add as an appendix to your essay a transcript of an interview, the list of survey questions or similar evidence.

Look at Annotated example 9.1 and notice the way that this student has integrated and referenced an interview with a farmer living and working on the urban/rural fringe. Notice how he has included a phrase within his own sentence – 'in a conversation at his home in West Swan' – as well as the in-text citation, to explain the context of his primary research.

Annotated example 9.1   How to incorporate primary research into an academic essay

Farmers have to change the practices they have used all their lives on the land; and now that housing is being built right up to the farming precincts, numerous complaints are surfacing from home owners recently moved into the areas on rural fringes (Turkich 2012). Con Bosanich (personal communication 2 April, 2012), in a conversation at his home in West Swan, says that over the last three to four years, ever since the new housing developments have occurred near his farm, he has experienced a handful of anonymous complaints from the public in regard to his usual farming practices such as using a tractor and spray units, which can be very noisy, whereas for years there were no complaints at all. All of this comes at a cost because if farmers' practices are affected by urban sprawl, this impacts on the production of goods.

Jonathan Lendich, Urban and Regional Planning student

ACTIVITY 9.1   Incorporating primary research into your writing

As an individual or with another student

Example 9.6 (later in this chapter) gives an example of a text written in first-person point of view. Using extracts from that text, or from your own experiences, write a few sentences that incorporate some of this primary research. Use Annotated example 9.1 as a model for how you might do this.

HINT

Don't let research get in the way of writing

Be careful if you're someone who overloads on research so much that you can't get down to writing. The amount of research you do needs to be proportionate to the size of your assignment task. Some people suggest you should spend about one-third of the time you have allotted to an assignment on research, and the remaining two-thirds on writing, editing and proofreading your work.

Developing your argument

This section refers specifically to argumentative essays. The most important thing to remember about an argumentative essay is that it must *present an argument*. If your essay is just descriptive or explanatory, it will be unsophisticated and will likely receive a very low mark. You should state your argument in your introduction, demonstrate it step by step through the body of your essay and then reiterate it in the conclusion. Your argument is generally known as your *thesis statement* (or, less commonly, your *proposition*).

The thesis statement

The *thesis statement* is generally written as one complete sentence, but occasionally might be two consecutive sentences. It plays a central role in an argumentative essay:

- It expresses your viewpoint or 'stand' on a subject (it must be debatable, not just a fact or self-evident statement).
- It introduces and anchors your whole argument.
- You must state it explicitly in your introduction and again – in different words – in your conclusion.
- You must validate it by the evidence you provide in the body of your essay.

Appropriate thesis statements

Example 9.2 shows some examples of successful thesis statements typical of the essays of our first-year students. Notice that each presents a strong, clear position that is not self-evident – that is, someone could mount a reasonable argument against it.

Example 9.2   Appropriate thesis statements

- Nanotechnology will revolutionise medicine more than any other discovery or breakthrough in history, by providing diagnostic tools that have no harmful impact on the human body.
- The major argument against nuclear power in any country is not the danger of catastrophic accidents but the problems of safely disposing of the wastes created by power plants.
- While professionals in the field have argued for sustainable design for many decades in Western countries, governments and industry have not supported it adequately. They need to invest much more money into research if sustainable design is to reach its full potential for both domestic and industrial building.

Inappropriate thesis statements

Example 9.3 illustrates some attempted thesis statements that do not meet the requirements. They either do not present a viewpoint at all, or are so limited, self-evident or extreme that there is no value in arguing them.

Example 9.3   Inappropriate thesis statements

- Some people argue that nanotechnology will revolutionise medicine in the twenty-first century, while other people claim that it is only one of many powerful breakthroughs.
- The first nuclear reaction happened in the US in 1942.
- Sustainable design is the only way to save the environment.

Students who write sentences such as these last three find that their essays are unsuccessful because they have not established a strong, debatable argument from the outset.

Preliminary thesis statements

When you have read and written enough to have developed particular viewpoints on several aspects of the issue, you can create *preliminary thesis statements* on some of these aspects. These statements will probably be quite simple, and you will expand and deepen one of them as you continue your research. Even if you later change these thesis statements considerably, at the moment, they will give you a useful focus for your reading. For example, for the topic of global warming, these statements might be:

- Global warming will harm developing countries more than it harms developed countries.
- A rise in sea levels is the most dangerous impact of global warming.
- Higher temperatures caused by global warming will increase the incidence of fatal diseases.
- Developed countries must reduce their use of fossil fuels in order to limit global warming.
- Governments need to give much more money to research global warming.
- The melting polar ice caps will pose the greatest threat of this century.

 HINT

Including words such as 'must' in your thesis statement can be helpful in ensuring you have a strong stance. Phrasing your thesis to imply a comparison can also make your position clear.

For example: The project manager is the most important person in protecting health and safety on the worksite.

(This statement implies that there are other people who are less important in this regard than the project manager.)

Another way of thinking about your thesis statement is to ask yourself what you want to convince your reader to do, believe or change. Doing this can remind you that your statement needs to be a perspective on an issue rather than a statement of fact or a description.

The concessive argument

The verb 'to concede' means 'to allow or accept'. At its most extreme, it means 'to give in' (as in conceding defeat to someone). In the context of an argumentative essay, a *concessive argument* is one in which you argue a particular point of view strongly, but also allow that opponents could present some reasonable counterarguments. You outline each counterargument briefly, but then go on to explain why that argument falls down or is weaker than yours. This last step is often called the *rebuttal*. Here are some typical approaches to rebuttal. You might:

- acknowledge the counterargument but show why it is not relevant in the social, geographical or historical context you are discussing
- suggest that the author has not taken into account a particular circumstance in her or his analysis
- describe how discoveries or theories that have been published since the author's article have changed disciplinary understandings
- align yourself with another researcher's work that contradicts the counterargument you are rebutting.

Rather than conceding defeat, the concessive argument actually strengthens your case because it shows that, while you have taken into account the arguments of the opposition, you still hold your position.

Some teachers suggest that you devote one paragraph to the counterargument (some recommend placing this paragraph as the first one in the body of your essay, some making it the last one before your conclusion), and some even suggest a whole paragraph of rebuttal. We recommend that you discuss and rebut each counterargument briefly at the appropriate time in your essay – that is, when you introduce the idea to which the counterargument relates. So some paragraphs of your essay will include a counterargument in perhaps one or two sentences, or even in just a phrase; other paragraphs will contain no counterargument at all. There is no set rule. The number of counterarguments you include depends on your topic.

Here are some key words and phrases that will help you introduce a concessive argument:

- However ...
- On the other hand ...
- While ...*
- Whereas ...*
- Although/though ...*
- Despite ...*

---

*A note on sentence structure

The four words in the above list that are marked with an asterisk do not introduce complete sentences – you need to include a main clause in order to make a complete sentence. (See Chapter 12 for a discussion of different sentence structures.)

HINT

Look at the concessive thesis statement in Annotated example 9.4. Notice that the first clause – 'Although fairy tales facilitate essential childhood development' – is not a complete sentence. You need the second part of the sentence – the main clause, including the main subject ('Disney's animated Princess films') and the main verb ('continue to perpetuate') – to complete the sentence. So, you will see that your concessive arguments do not even need complete sentences – they might be half-sentences, or even short phrases.

Annotated example 9.4   Concessive thesis statement

Although fairy tales facilitate essential childhood development, Disney's animated Princess films, with the Disney Princess marketing image, continue to perpetuate traditional gender roles and promote increasingly sexualised body aspirations to young girls, which may lead to negative body image and low self-esteem.

Jennifer Zeven, Humanities student

Zeven has strengthened her argument by accepting in the first half of her thesis statement the counterargument that fairy tales have a powerful influence on childhood development, but claiming in the second half of this sentence that such positive influence does not override the destructive impact of Disney Princess films on young girls' sexualisation.

Next, look at the example in Example 9.5 of a concessive paragraph. This thesis statement contends that scientists who take a role in public debate have the potential to make major scientific and cultural contributions to our society. The student presents one counterargument in the first two sentences of the paragraph. In the rest of the paragraph he goes on to rebut the counterargument by referring to the ideas of an expert in his disciplinary area (and strengthens his position by acknowledging her academic position).

Example 9.5   Concessive paragraph

Scientists, past and present, who have taken a public stand on a particular issue have often been attacked by members of the public who disagree with their point of view. Ultimately, some people also tend to question the motives of the scientist, citing the fact that some scientists may be outspoken in order to receive the government research grants that are so desperately required. But, as Mark Floyd (1999) notes in a story about Professor Mary Jo Nye, Horning Professor of Humanities at Oregon State University, 'if scientists do not become involved in public policy debates, the result can be a decision-making process involving complex, critical issues that are not fully understood'. Ultimately, it was, and currently is, with the assistance of scientists that humanity, as a species, is able to unlock the secrets of the physical and the natural universe. A historical overview of scientific philosophy will result in an acceptance by the reader that without the intervention of men and women of science in controversial public issues, breakthroughs that have the potential to erase common ideologies will become scarce.

Daniel Frewer, Engineering student

ACTIVITY 9.2 Aspects of a topic and thesis statements

As an individual or with another student

1   Create a pie chart, mind map (see Chapter 6), or other graphic organiser identifying the aspects of the topic you have discovered from your research.

2   For each aspect, write at least one preliminary thesis statement of one or two sentences that presents a debatable viewpoint on the topic. Make at least one of them a concessive thesis statement.

In a class or a group

Form a group of students who are researching similar topics and work through the individual part of this activity together. Remember that you might have two contradictory thesis statements on any one aspect. (For example, while one group member could argue that more research needs to be undertaken into the treatment of waste products, another might argue that enough research has already been done for governments to enact legislation.)

Report to the class on these thesis statements – what they are, which ones you find most interesting and which you think you will be able to argue most convincingly.

Writing your essay

This section is relevant to writing both analytical and argumentative essays. It's important to start writing your essay well before it is due – remember that you will start with a first draft, and that you should not expect your work to be complete when you type the last word of your conclusion. Make sure you leave yourself enough time to edit and proofread it after you have finished this draft – see Chapter 6 for more information about this.

ACTIVITY 9.3 Clarifying your ideas

A good way of preparing to write your essay is to explain your ideas to someone else, especially to someone who is younger or less knowledgeable about the subject than you. Notice, while you are writing or speaking, how the informal language you use for an unprepared explanation to a friend or family member differs from the formal language you will use for a polished essay.

As an individual or with another student

Write a brief (about 200 words) explanation of your ideas aimed at a 15-year-old friend or family member. Your register should be informal. Read it over carefully to make sure that this person would understand your ideas or argument and your vocabulary.

In a class or a group

Explain your ideas (or argument, if you are preparing an argumentative essay) orally (in about two minutes) to another student in your class who has not researched your topic. Answer questions from this person about anything that was not clear or needed further detail.

First or third person?

One of the first questions our students ask is whether they should write in the first-person ('I', 'me' and so on) or the third-person ('she', 'he', 'the author', 'they' and so on) point of view. This depends on the discipline in which you are studying. First person is often considered more informal than third person (though this is not always true) and for this reason may not be appropriate for the purpose for which you are writing. Check with each lecturer about their expectations before you write your first essay. For more discussion about this important issue, see Chapter 6.

Example 9.6 is a extract from an essay written in a relatively conversational style using the first-person point of view. It was written to be published in a local newspaper in a section called 'Think'. Its purpose was to prompt reflection and discussion.

Example 9.6 Paragraph from an essay that uses the first person

We need to recognise racial difference. Acknowledging that difference doesn't reduce individuals to their racial group; it acknowledges the context in which individuals and their families have occurred. It recognises how racism of the past and present makes up that context.

I sometimes visit my refugee cousin in Mirrabooka. The world around me gets browner and poorer then. When I return to my progressive part of town it gets whiter. I wonder about the meaning of that.

I brought this up with a friend recently and she responded that people like being around their communities. I suppose that's true, but why is poverty colour coded? Are we ignoring the fact that brown people were banned from migrating to Australia until the 70s?

To fight racism we need to consider differences for a while longer. Being colourblind is ignorant.

Khin Myint, Humanities graduate

Language and approaches to writing

The principles of academic writing – which are discussed in detail in Chapter 11 – apply to all types of academic essays. For further information on the points listed below, we suggest you read through that chapter, focusing particularly on ideas that are new to you. Some of the language issues that are particularly relevant to the academic essay include:

- *Formal language:* You need to write in a formal register.
- *Clear, concise language:* Use clear, concise language rather than an overly complex, flowery style.
- *Active and passive voice:* Where possible, use the active voice to help develop a strong voice and a clear, concise style.

- *Headings and subheadings:* Traditionally, academic essays were written without headings – this was one of the things that distinguished them from reports. In recent years, however, some people have encouraged students to use headings and subheadings in their essays as a way of indicating the structure of their ideas. Check with your lecturers about whether to use headings and subheadings in your essay. Even if you do use headings, however, you should not use self-evident ones such as 'Introduction' and 'Conclusion'.

The introduction

Some teachers recommend that you do not write the introduction until after you have written an essay, especially when you are writing an exam or an in-class essay, so that you already know your conclusions before you write the introduction.

However, we don't recommend this for essay assignments. You will have spent many hours researching, discussing and planning this essay, and so will be clear by now about your ideas. You need to write your introduction at the beginning so that your directions in the essay are clear to you and can act as anchors and a series of signposts for the rest of your essay.

In an analytical essay introduction:

- Introduce the topic in an engaging way.
- Briefly mention the contexts of your subject (e.g. relevant background information, theoretical positions, why the subject is considered important).
- Signal your main points.

In an argumentative essay introduction:

- Introduce the topic in an interesting way.
- Provide any definitions of equivocal or subject-specific terminology that are required. (These should be your own definitions as you intend to use them in your essay, not ones taken directly from a dictionary.)
- Signal your main points.
- Include your thesis statement (generally, but not always, as the last sentence).

If you feel you need to use in your introduction an unsubtle phrase like 'In this essay I will be writing about …', write it, finish writing your sentence and then go back and delete this phrase. Then see if your sentence makes sense without it – often, it does still make sense, or you may be able to alter it slightly to make it grammatically correct.

Annotated example 9.7 is an introduction to an essay on the role of architects in designing smart houses. Notice that, unlike in the majority of academic essay introductions, the thesis statement is the second-last sentence of the paragraph; in this case, this works well because it allows the student to introduce the figure of the architect before he signposts the main ideas he will cover in the essay.

Annotated example 9.7 Introduction of an essay

Starts with an interesting statement to start readers thinking about possibilities.

Concessive phrase

Imagine home owners being able to control all features of their homes with a remote control or voice commands. It is very possible, and although it is usually only available for the wealthy, it is already available in some homes across the world. Houses with that accessibility are usually referred to either as 'smart houses' or 'home automation' as Jackie Craven (2012) mentions in her blog. A smart house, as David Bregman (2010, 35) explains, is an intelligent home with an automatic system that is highly advanced for controlling features around the house. These features include the temperature, lighting, alarms, curtains and many more. According to Davin Heckman (2008, 126), the purpose of the smart house technology is not only to make living easier, but also to make the home react to the owner's presence. Heckman (2008, 135) also states that modern smart houses are used as an entertainment facility more than anything else; however, smart houses should not only simply be used for wealthy people who want to own an automotive home for their own purposes.

Explains subject by referring to a range of published texts (both formal, such as journal articles, and informal, such as blogs) to be discussed in more detail in the body of the essay.

Thesis statement

It is the role of the architect to take special care when designing smart houses to make them sustainable and safe for people who require assistance to carry out required activities. Smart houses should mostly be available for the elderly, people with disabilities, parents with young children; they also help the whole community in lowering greenhouse gases.

Signposts main ideas he will cover in the essay.

Sanan al Abbasi, Architecture student

ACTIVITY 9.4 Writing your introduction

As an individual or with another student

Write the introduction to your essay, following the instructions and model described above. (If working with another student, discuss how you will approach your writing and write each introduction together, if desired; but be careful not to finish with similar introductions for your two essays.)

In a class or group

Pin up introductions and critique them for each other. Consider how each critique might apply to your own introduction, and make changes as necessary.

The paragraph

The building blocks of your essay are your paragraphs, and the body is no more than a series of interconnected paragraphs that develop your analysis or argue for the thesis statement you have presented in your introduction. Refer to the section on paragraphing in Chapter 6 for a detailed discussion of how to write effective academic paragraphs. In that section, you were introduced to the structure of a paragraph and several approaches as to how you can order the information within it. The structure given there is applicable to any form of writing in which you are aiming to lay out your discussion in a clear and methodical way. The following section on synthesis details how you will draw on your research to present an argument or position in an argumentative essay.

Synthesis

The word 'synthesis' comes from Ancient Greek – *syn* means 'with' or 'together', and *thesis* comes from the verb 'to set down'. It suggests the idea of structuring two or more elements together to create something new. You can synthesise many different kinds of things. For example, creators of animated film synthesise art and computer graphics to create their products; and nylon is a synthetic in which coal, water and air are synthesised to create something unlike any of them individually.

When we refer to synthesis in the context of tertiary communication skills, we mean the pulling together of ideas from several sources into one coherent argument. The new product is your own argument. The most important thing about synthesising is that *you* must create the shape of your argument and use other people's ideas just to expand and illustrate this argument.

Synthesising therefore involves a sophisticated level of thinking that is essential for tertiary studies. You are required to see connections and comparisons among ideas, and to use these to create your own argument, rather than just repeating other people's ideas.

Writing a synthesis

To begin synthesising your ideas, follow this basic formula:

- For each text, identify the thesis, the main ideas and the necessary supporting ideas.
- Write each main idea in your own words without looking at the text. (Check the original text later to make sure your version is accurate.)
- Create your own argument from these main ideas, using them to support each other, to develop each other's argument or to contrast with each other.

Structure of a synthesis

The following examples will help clarify the differences between synthesising and simply repeating the ideas of one or more other people. Example 9.8 shows what your writing would look like if you focused on the ideas you found in just one text (a fictional text written by a writer named North and published in 2018).

Example 9.8 A weak passage of academic writing relying entirely on one source

[_____] (North 2018). [_____

_____

_____

_____] (North 2018).

[_____] (North 2018).

[_____] (North 2018). [_____

_____

_____

_____] (North 2018).

[_____] (North 2018).

Example 9.9 represents what your argument would look like if you allowed your sources to dictate the shape of your argument. The first paragraph is based on the ideas of North from her 2018 publication; the second paragraph relies on a text by South published in 2010; and the ideas in the third paragraph come from a text by West published in 2011. This is a collection of ideas, not a synthesis, because you are not creating something new from the ideas.

Example 9.9 A poorly synthesised passage – the sources are driving the shape of the content

[_____] (North 2018). [_____

_____

_____

_____] (North 2018).

[_____] (North 2018).

[_____] (South 2010). [_____

_____

_____] (South 2010).

[_____] (South 2010).

[_____] (West 2011). [_____

_____

_____] (West 2011).

[_____] (West 2011).

When you have synthesised well, your writing will look more like Example 9.10. Notice that in each paragraph the ideas are drawn from more than one text to develop and illustrate the argument. In the second paragraph, ideas from a fourth author, East, published in 2012, have also been added.

Example 9.10 A well synthesised passage – the sources are used extensively for support, but the content is driven by the author of the passage

[_____] (North 2018). [_____

_____

_____] (North 2018).

[_____] (West 2011).

[_____](South 2010; West 2011).

[_____

_____] (East 2012).

[_____

_____] (South 2010).

[_____] (North 2018).

If you occasionally need to present an argument for which you have only one supporting text, then you must 'bookend' your references, as shown in Chapter 5.

Example 9.11 shows how the writer's own argument can drive the synthesis. A variety of sources are used to support the points the student is making. As you read this paragraph, pay close attention to where the citations appear. Notice that these nods to research *support* the ideas rather than replace them. The student is writing in their own voice, not simply telling us what other authors have said or done.

Example 9.11 Sample synthesis

The risk that psychological performance strategies pose to the stability of an actor's sense of identity is another reason for why they must be used carefully. Lee Strasberg's Method is a highly controversial acting tool, developed as an extension of Stanislavski's affective memory technique (McAllister, 2018). Many film actors have been known to build their repertoire of work upon the foundation of method acting as their primary character development technique. Heath Ledger's performance as The Joker in *The Dark Knight* (2008) is perhaps the most infamous example of the dangers of method acting. Prior to filming, Ledger locked himself inside a hotel room for over a month, constructing a scrapbook full of imagery and quotations relating to matters of violence, psychopathy and severe mental illness, all in an effort to fully epitomize the character (New York Film Academy, 2015). Ledger died of a drug overdose six months before the film's release, and although it is unable to be confirmed, many fans and critics believe that Ledger's use of method acting may have contributed to the drug misuses that led to his death (Kampa, 2019). Various studies have provided evidence to suggest that actors who use method acting – and other similarly extreme character development techniques – will have a higher likelihood of unconsciously adopting the personality traits of their characters, as well as beginning to experience dissociation from self. Actors who are already vulnerable in the sense of having high self-doubt, low self-esteem and experience struggles with identity are most at risk (Panero, 2019). Given Ledger's performance in *The Dark Knight* is recognized as the primary reason for the overwhelming commercial success of the film (Sternagel, 2012), and his method acting choices were arguably the reason for this terrifyingly compelling performance, it can be understood that perhaps method acting is a somewhat useful strategy actors can use to elevate their characterization capabilities. However, psychological performance strategies such as this can destabilise the actor's sense of self, removing their ability to exercise control over both their life and work, leading to potentially tragic outcomes.

Ella Wakeman, Humanities student

ACTIVITY 9.5   Writing a synthesis

As an individual or with another student

Collect three passages of about 300 words each from three different sources you want to use for an upcoming written assignment. Applying the advice from this chapter, write a 300-word synthesis that includes the ideas in these passages. Ensure that your argument shapes the synthesis, and include all necessary in-text citations (see Chapter 5). When you are finished, you should be able to add the synthesised passage to your assignment.

The conclusion

Your conclusion tells your readers that you are winding up the essay and prepares them for the finish. It provides your reader with a strong summary of the key points you raised and how they support the overall argument. In your conclusion you must do several things:

- Restate your thesis statement in different words (for argumentative essays).
- Restate your main ideas.
- Use connective words that signal a conclusion.

Example 9.12 is a conclusion to a student's essay on the influence of the Heidelberg School on contemporary Australian art. Notice that they sum up the main points in the essay, mentioning some key researchers without needing to include in-text citations because this was already done this in the body of the essay. The student finishes by restating the thesis statement. Notice that the student doesn't use any of the traditional phrases that signal a conclusion (such as 'In conclusion … ' or 'to sum up … '). These are not needed because the clear summary of the key points and thesis statement provide the signal that the essay is coming to an end. To the reader, it is a satisfying conclusion because the author reiterates her main ideas strongly.

Example 9.12   Conclusion of an essay

The Heidelberg School has created a solid base, point of reference and influence for contemporary art in Australia and holds a strong, central position in the Australian art history. A key point in this transformation and its influence today was the historical climate in the post-war and interwar periods that embraced the romanticised, positive idyll of Australian life. The school's easy application to contemporary issues such as feminism and the modernist movement in art have encouraged further interest in the movement. The Heidelberg School created the basis for a national style that no longer relied solely on English taste and convention. The School's lasting appeal and strongest point of influence is arguably its glorification of Australian folklore and legend – it immortalised the critical and difficult pioneer period in Australia's history that has gained more and more importance as it moves further and further into the past. Exploration of the Australian landscape unfettered by a preference for English light and aesthetic arguably helped create an authentic and definable Australian style that appealed to Australians' sense of nationalism and pride. The Heidelberg School can be seen as a building block for much Australian art, and the artists of the Heidelberg School cannot be discounted as models for young artists today.

Esther Adeney, Fine Art student

ACTIVITY 9.6 Identifying the key points in a conclusion

As an individual or with another student

Read the conclusion in Example 9.12 and note down the thesis statement and the key points the author has raised to support it.

Reflect on:

- the location(s) of the restated thesis statement
- the amount of detail given for each key point.

A sound conclusion should provide you with a clear overview of the author's argument and supporting points. How well do you think this author has achieved this goal?

Editing and proofreading your essay

Once you have written your first draft, you are only part of the way through the process – you still need to edit this draft until you are satisfied with it, and to proofread your final version so that it will be as correct, clear and pleasing as possible. If you find redrafting a difficult or negative process, you might take heart from Student reflection 9.1, a piece of reflective writing from a mature-age student of interior architecture who explores her changing attitudes to writing. Even if you do not yet share Shaughnessy's positive attitudes to writing, you can appreciate that a positive approach is possible.

Student reflection 9.1 Redrafting

I feel as though my thoughts may have changed. I am finding essay writing to be more enjoyable than I remembered. Perhaps I have unlearned some troubling habits, rushing being one of them, instead enjoying the process of putting thoughts, ideas, facts and research onto paper. The process of editing, scrutinising and amending is enjoyable because I am affording it the time I feel it needs. Altering and improving my approach to study, in particular essay writing and exam preparation, has made it a more enjoyable experience.

Kelley Shaughnessy, Interior Architecture student

See Chapter 6 for ideas about how to edit and proofread your essay, and a list of guiding questions that you might ask yourself. Remember, your essay is not finished when you write the final word of your conclusion! Taking the time to carefully proofread and edit your work ensures that you avoid errors that detract from the professional polish of your writing.

REVISION TOOLS

↘ Revision activity: Revise these ideas

1 An argumentative essay presents a strong argument, supported by ongoing reference to scholarly reading and primary research; an analytical essay applies scholarly reading and primary research processes to analysing a topic, without arguing for one position.

2 An argumentative essay starts with a thesis statement – a clear statement of the author's position or contention on the subject. This thesis statement can be concessive (i.e. it can acknowledge contradictory views on the subject), but it must state the argued position very clearly.

3 Research is an ongoing spiral process; initially, it helps you develop your thesis statement and main ideas, but it is likely that you will continue to research after you have begun writing your essay. This ongoing research will add depth to your argument; it may also require you to adjust your thesis statement after you have started writing the essay – this is normal!

4 Essays must be written in formal, clear and concise language. In some disciplines you are encouraged to write some sections in the first-person point of view, while in other disciplines you are not permitted to do this. You should check this with your lecturer.

5 In your essay introduction you signal the ideas you will discuss in the essay and state your thesis statement; in your essay body you develop your ideas one after another, linking them all back to the thesis statement; and in your conclusion you reiterate your argument and the main ideas that built this argument.

6 Drawing on research to support your ideas requires you to synthesise from a variety of sources. Using citations in your writing demonstrates that your ideas have a basis in evidence and research, and provides strength to your position. Keep your writing in your own voice, though; avoid simply describing what others have written.

↘ Thinking activity: Critical and reflective questions

1 How do I feel about essay writing, both in a general sense as well as in the context of my discipline? How might essay writing be relevant or useful in my field of study?

2 How does the essay writing I am required to do at university differ from school essay writing? Have I understood and adapted to the differences?

3 What parts of essay writing are my strengths, and what areas do I need to work on? What attitudes about academic writing do I hold that might be holding me back from achieving my best, or that may push me to improve?

4 What qualities of good essay writing are important in society in general? (*Hint:* Think about ways in which different groups of people communicate with and understand – or fail to understand – each other.)

↘ Useful weblinks

The following online resources provide further useful information about essay writing:

Australian National University Academic Skills and Learning Centre: 'Essay Writing': **http://www.anu.edu.au/students/learning-development/writing-assessment/ essay-writing**.

University of Sydney Learning Centre: 'Planning and Structuring an Essay': **https://www. sydney.edu.au/content/dam/students/documents/learning-resources/learning- centre/writing/planning-and-structuring-an-essay.pdf**.

University of New South Wales Learning Centre: 'Essay and Assignment Writing': **https://student.unsw.edu.au/essay-and-assignment-writing**.

Purdue University (US) Online Writing Lab (OWL): 'Academic Writing': **https://owl.purdue.edu/ owl/general_writing/academic_writing/index.html**.

REFERENCES

Myint, Khin. 2020. 'Feeling Aussie.' *Fremantle Herald Interactive*, June 12, 2020. **https://heraldonlinejournal.com/2020/06/12/feeling-aussie/**.

CHAPTER 10

Some other tertiary genres

CONTENTS

Introduction to tertiary genres

This text contains chapters with detailed explanations about most common written communication genres in higher education such as essays, reflective writing and reports. In this chapter we include other writing genres you may be asked to use in your studies. We note especially that it is becoming more common for students to be asked to present their assignments in 'non-traditional' formats. This reflects the modern workplace, in which we are expected to interact with stakeholders in a variety of ways, including on social media platforms, visual presentations with infographics, blogs and so on. Each of these text types has their own rules and audience expectations, and their own requirements for formality and style. While this chapter outlines some of these texts and styles, it is by no means an exhaustive discussion and you should always check with your tutor for the specific requirements of the assignment you're working on.

The summary

A *summary* is a shortened version of a text that focuses on just its main ideas. You are most likely to write it as part of an assignment (e.g. the abstract or executive summary in a report is a summary of the whole report; see Chapter 8), and your lecturer may specify the word count for the summary. Summarising is a useful academic skill as it teaches you to identify the main ideas of a text, and to write clearly and concisely. It also provides you with small, manageable chunks of information that can be useful for exam revision.

Unlike lecture or research notes, which you write 'on the spot', summaries are formal and structured – you need to plan, write and redraft them until you have expressed the main ideas of each text as succinctly as you can.

Writing a summary

Here are some helpful steps to take when you're writing a summary:

- Read all of the original text.
- Re-read the text and underline its thesis or proposition (see Chapter 4).
- Find and highlight the main points. (*Hint:* Try looking at the headings, topic sentences and repeated ideas.)
- Highlight the essential words in these points.
- Hide the original text and rewrite the ideas in your own words.
- Compare your version to the original and ask yourself if you have captured its 'essence'. Do this by checking that you have written the thesis statement in the first sentence, and that you have included the key ideas to support this thesis.
- Re-read and edit your summary, by checking you have:

- created complete sentences and paragraphs
- included only ideas from the original (no other sources)
- excluded examples and peripheral discussion
- not included your own opinion.

When summarising a text, you do *not* need to include in-text references, provided you have referenced the text at the beginning of your summary.

Sample summaries

The sample we give in Example 10.1 is very brief. This example demonstrates the importance of identifying a text's thesis or proposition, and shows how you can adapt a summary to fulfil particular word count requirements. You will probably be required to summarise a much longer passage than this one. Your summaries will, therefore, be longer, and you will be allowed to use more words to identify main ideas that support the thesis. This student sample comes from an assignment written by a group of students for their Behavioural Science course.

Example 10.1   Examples of text summaries

Original text: 218 words

Analysis of the demographic data of youth-engagement service provision for culturally and linguistically diverse (CALD) youth in the City of Armadale, with particular focus on the areas of Harrisdale, Piara Waters and Forrestdale, indicates that when working with young people, a strengths-based approach is more successful than other approaches.

The experiences and challenges that CALD youth can face in negotiating competing cultural identities is explained in this report through theoretical understandings of acculturation, sense of community and a multi-level wellbeing model. This enables a deeper appreciation of why CALD youth may be disengaged; how to build better relationships among different cultural groups in society; and the importance of understanding how interactions among individuals, as well as their relationships and broader societal structures, affect wellbeing.

After exploring a variety of government resources and reports and academic literature, and drawing from key findings presented by service providers at a community forum in Armadale, it is clear that adopting a strengths-based approach to improve the understanding of youth-services providers, policymakers and community developers is the means by which to facilitate transformational change for youth-engagement strategies. The provision of a broad, holistic framework enables the self-determination and empowerment of young people, and gives them the voice and the tools needed to reengage in matters that affect them, their families and their communities.

Megan Goerke, Lewis Stewart and Tashia Abeyasinghe, Behavioural Science students

33-word summary

The use of strengths-based framework by all community services in Armadale will empower culturally and linguistically diverse (CALD) youth, and enable them to engage with issues affecting them, their families and their communities.

15-word summary

The use of a strengths-based approach by community services results in youth feeling more empowered.

Now look at Example 10.2, a sample summary, presented as a short abstract, by a Health Sciences student. It is written in formal, passive language and captures the key information in their research study, which was entitled 'The Influence of Neuroscience on Satisfaction'. This abstract was included before the introduction to the report on the study.

Example 10.2 Example of an abstract

This study was dedicated to the influence of neuroscience explanations on satisfactory ratings in second-year undergraduate university students who were enrolled in a statistics unit titled 'Psychological Science Experimental Methods' at Curtin University. A total of 367 students (293 females, 73 males, one other) were included in this study, and responded to an 18-item questionnaire containing good and bad descriptions paired with, and without, neuroscientific explanations. The hypothesis that descriptions with neuroscience would be rated with higher satisfaction was supported. It was concluded that students found items with neuroscience more satisfying.

Ebony Clare Chang, Health Sciences student

Example 10.3 is an example of a text summary, written by an Interior Design student, which was constructed for a specific assignment. In this example, the student is identifying a journal article's main argument (i.e. the thesis) and the key ideas that support that perspective.

Example 10.3 A journal article summary

Read, Dustin C., and Drew Sanderford. 2017. "Making Places and Making Tradeoffs: Mixed-Income Housing Development in Practice." *Journal of Place Management and Development* 10 (5): 461–78. https://doi.org/10.1108/JPMD-12-2016-0074.

The main argument for this text is that the needs of low-income residents often give way to the wants of private investors in mixed-income housing developments, negatively impacting upon the outcome.

The following three related ideas support this argument:

- In order to invigorate disadvantaged neighborhoods, governments often seek to build more affordable housing. As a way to help finance these projects they often form a partnership with profit driven developers in the private sector.
- Early stage planning meetings are used to serve political interests and do not always hear the views of the development's neighboring residents.
- Economic constraints leave local governments with few options to fight for the needs of low-income residents, such as thoughtfully integrating public units into the development.

Ellie Willoughby, Interior Design student

The annotated bibliography

As we explained in Chapter 5, a *bibliography* is a list of resources or texts (books, articles, audio-visual materials, websites and so on) on a topic, formatted according to the rules of a particular referencing system. It is usually organised in alphabetical order so that it will be easy to find items on the list. In an *annotated bibliography*, a brief comment – or *annotation* – is added after each item. This comment generally describes the content of the item and may include an evaluation of its worth for certain readers.

You can best understand how an annotated bibliography works by thinking about the familiar concepts of *audience* and *purpose*. An annotated bibliography is written for particular readers on a topic that relates specifically to them. It generally has several purposes:

- to inform readers about resources relevant to the topic, and the content covered in each
- to suggest the most appropriate resources for different subgroups within the audience (e.g. experts on the topic, students of the topic, beginners in the area)
- to recommend which resources are most valuable to particular readers, and to explain why.

In previous decades, annotated bibliographies were usually written by academics; however, now many people write and share annotated bibliographies for various purposes. In a tertiary course, an annotated bibliography assignment will probably require you to prove that you have good research skills and have thus evaluated a variety of texts on a given subject (see Chapter 3). You may also be required to lay the groundwork for another assignment by including texts you plan to use. Some of these may be unreliable or inappropriate, and you will be expected to explain your concerns in the relevant annotations. As we have stated, always check the assignment instructions carefully for what will be assessed for that particular course.

Annotations versus summaries: the key difference

In writing an annotation, you take a step back from a text and describe what it is about, what it deals with, what it concerns, what subject it covers and so on. You also comment on its reliability, relevance and quality as a text. In an annotation, therefore, you are examining the text as a construction.

This is different from writing a summary where you remain 'inside' the text or group of texts and rewrite their key ideas in your own words. In a summary, you are thus engaging with the ideas of a text, not looking at the text from the outside.

The annotation

Traditionally, an annotation is any note you add to a text, often in the margins, making a comment or adding a question or explanation. In the context of an annotated bibliography, however, an *annotation* is a separate paragraph added after each end-of-text reference.

The length of an annotation varies enormously from one bibliography to another – each one can be as short as one sentence or as long as several hundred words. Short annotations generally focus on just the *content* of each text; in longer ones, the writer might consider a range of questions, such as:

- What main subject areas are covered in the text?
- What arguments or contentions does the author present? What are the author's attitudes to or perspectives on the issue?
- What types of material are included (e.g. statistics, graphics, case studies, bibliography)?
- Who is the text written for (e.g. what age, educational background, experience on the subject)? How useful is this information for this audience?
- How reliable do you feel the information is? Is the author an authority on the subject?
- What research methodologies has the author used? Do you feel that these are valid and appropriate?
- What is the writer's response to the text (ideas, language, format and so on)?

Writing an annotated bibliography

Start by browsing some published annotated bibliographies. You will find these in your library by typing 'annotated bibliography' and a general subject into a keyword search in your library's catalogue. Experiment with search terms until you find successful ones – for example, 'annotated bibliography' and 'environment' is likely to give you results, while 'annotated bibliography' and 'global warming' may be too specific. On the Internet, you will find them by typing 'annotated bibliography' and any subject into a search engine. You will also find some resources containing examples of annotated bibliographies listed at the end of this chapter.

Skim-read a range of these texts, both printed and online. Think about the audience, purpose and context of each one, and about how these aspects affect the final product. As you read, take notice of the:

- vocabulary
- types of ideas included
- content and amount of detail in the annotations

- format of the complete text
- way the bibliographic references and annotations are set out.

As mentioned, annotations can range from a single sentence to several hundred words. Note any set word limit for annotations; this will control the amount of detail you include. If you are writing a short annotation, you might limit yourself to including:

- a brief description of the content
- a comment on the expertise or role of this author
- a statement about the intended audience
- words to indicate your response to the text, incorporated within what you have written in the above three points.

A 50-word annotation might look something like Example 10.4.

Example 10.4   A short annotation

This well-researched article explains how attitudes to sustainable architecture developed in the second half of the twentieth century in Australia. It was written by an academic who has been working in the area for more than 20 years, and for undergraduate students. It presents ideas that are both accessible and challenging.

Example 10.5 is a more detailed 160-word annotation, followed by its bibliographic reference.

Example 10.5   A more detailed annotation

This journal article argues that Internet users should better prepare and protect themselves (and their computers) so that they can enjoy a safer online experience. Online security fraud, for example, is not uncommon, and is merely one of the risks involved with using the Internet. That is why 'The great American privacy makeover' also argues that Internet users need to be aware of the dangers they face online.

The article supports its arguments by informing the reader of the different ways that fraud and other security breaches are carried out. It provides real-life examples of people who were in different situations, and broadly examines what happened, and what could have been done. Various methods of protection are recommended, and links to helpful Internet sites and software are presented.

Of particular relevance is that the article suggests improvements in how computer users protect themselves. An outcome of my research topic is to make similar recommendations, and so this article will be of great assistance in composing my written assignment and achieving that outcome.

Kandra, Anne, and Andrew Brandt. 2003. 'The Great American Privacy Makeover.' *PC World* 21 (4): 144–60.

Damien Lay, Computer Science student

Notice, in the last paragraph, that Lay refers to his 'written assignment'. This annotation is from an annotated bibliography he wrote in preparation for a major report on the same subject, in which he was asked to consider the relevance of each text for this upcoming assignment. If you are asked to write an annotated bibliography to prepare for another assignment, it is important to shape your annotations to the specific purposes of the second assignment.

The language of an annotated bibliography

Lay's annotation is a very useful model because, while his language is formal, it is also succinct. He does not fall into the trap of using flowery, convoluted language in order to try to sound more academic. Read Chapter 11, where we offer tips for writing in clear, concise but formal language.

Use formal language

Be careful when you examine the language of annotated bibliographies published on websites – remember that these may be written in a much more informal register than is acceptable in academic assignments. Take note of those written in a formal register (generally those written by academics for their colleagues or students) and use these as models for your own register.

Our students generally pitch their vocabulary at an appropriately formal level in annotated bibliographies but sometimes make the mistake of writing in incomplete sentences. *Don't* write phrases like these ones, which are informal and incomplete sentences:

- 'An entertaining article written by an authority on the subject.'
- 'A really good read.'

Remember that you are not writing a *review* of the text – you are *evaluating* it for a specific purpose. Avoid subjective statements about the enjoyment one might get out of reading the text, or whether it was interesting or boring.

To help you write annotations in clear, concise and appropriately formal language, Table 10.1 lists some words and phrases to describe the content of a text.

Table 10.1 Possible words and phrases to describe the contents of a text

This text ...	
argues that ...	focuses on ...
examines ...	treats the topic of ...
explores ...	concentrates on ...
discusses ...	is an introduction to ...
considers ...	begins with ...
covers the issue of ...	concludes with ...

You will find a much longer list in Table 5.1 in Chapter 5. But a word of warning: make sure you understand what each word or phrase suggests before you use it. The words listed in Table 5.1 have different nuances of meaning that will affect the way you use them in your sentences.

Table 10.2 lists some words and phrases for describing your response to a text.

Table 10.2 Possible words and phrases to describe your response to a text

Positive comments	Negative comments
Thorough	Limited
Authoritative	Of little value
Influential	Difficult to read
Extensive research	Incoherent
Well-documented	Unsubstantiated claims
Detailed	Repetitive
Informative	Superficial
A concise introduction to ...	Lacking in evidence
Comprehensive	Emotive
Of particular interest to ...	Biased
Readable	Over-complicated
Well-written	
An original work	
An important work	

The case study

Providing a single explanation for a case study is a little difficult as this is dependent on the context in which it is being used. In this instance, we have chosen to define a *case study* as an account of a situation chosen because it contains information and issues that provide learning opportunities. The account could be of a real experience, including real details; or of a real experience in which some elements are changed to prevent identification; or of a completely hypothetical situation. Most importantly, a case study provides students with opportunities to explore and apply skills and theories they have learned in a related field of study. In occupational therapy, for example, you may have to think from the perspective of an occupational therapist who needs to research and apply relevant theories to devise a treatment plan for a hypothetical client.

In the early years of studying a course you are more likely to be asked to analyse or study a case rather than actually create your own case study. In some fields of study, such as business and health, you may be required to describe and analyse cases using methods and sources specific to that discipline. This section offers general instructions about how you could perform an analysis of a case.

A case study analysis

A *case study analysis* is about your response to the case. Your audience – probably your lecturer or clinical supervisor – wants to know what you think should be done in the given situation. You may be given a template or list of questions to help you structure how you approach a given case, otherwise, we suggest the following steps:

- First, skim-read the case so you get a sense of the whole story.
- Then, read over the case more carefully, making notes as you go.
- Read critically, looking for positive findings and outcomes, as well as identifying problems or potential problems.
- As you identify the problems, make notes about potential solutions and research relevant theories (that are likely to have been already covered in the unit/subject you are currently studying). As you do your research, look for evidence of similar cases to help you resolve or critique your particular case. Depending on the complexity of the case and your assignment requirements, you may decide to work on solutions to a few problems rather than try to find solutions to all of them.

Writing a case study analysis

You are likely to be asked to write your case study analysis in a report format, with an outline, and therefore a contents page, like the simple, clear example in Example 10.6, created by a Speech Pathology student. Use Chapter 8 – along with any assignment instructions – to guide you. However, since this format varies among disciplines, you may find Chapter 9 and its instructions about essay writing helpful as well.

Example 10.6   Contents page of a case study analysis

Abbey Prentice, Speech Pathology student

The writing style remains formal and conclusions or advice is clear. Example 10.7 is an example of one paragraph from a case study analysis report written by another Speech Pathology student. This case involved the interpretation and application of relevant theories to analyse the cognitive processes of a child who has traumatic brain injury. Notice the succinct analysis of one cognitive process relevant to the case (consciousness), the formal register used and the smooth synthesis of the case description with the relevant theories that apply to the analysis of this case.

Example 10.7   A paragraph from a case study analysis

Consciousness: Impairment to the basic cognitive process of consciousness would affect all other processes and consequently all levels of Levelt's Speaking Model (Levelt 1989). Adrienne is suffering from seizures and it is known that mild seizure activity can cause intermittent disturbance of consciousness (Parker 1990). Without consciousness, she would not be able to operate the many processes needed in communication. However, the case information states that the medication she is taking for her seizures is working, and, therefore, this factor may have moved from being impaired to spared.

Alannah Goerke, Speech Pathology student

Finally, Example 10.8 gives another example, from a Nursing student. We have two sections from the opening paragraph of the case study analysis. You can see the clear opening sentences followed closely by a coherent synthesis of published research into treatment of the disease as is relevant to the case being critiqued for this assignment. The last part of the example is from the end of the case study analysis; it gives the recommendations for treatment and links back to those introductory statements.

Example 10.8   Three sections from a case study analysis

Opening sentences: Pneumonia is an infection that develops in the lungs, most commonly occurring in children and the elderly, with patients being over 65 the most likely to be hospitalised (Welte 2007). This study of pneumonia will focus on a 69-year-old lady named Amelia who has presented with the following signs and symptoms.

....

Explaining what the research states about treatment in similar cases: Assessment and diagnosis of pneumonia is done through several tests, and together they form the diagnosis. If pneumonia is suspected from the signs and symptoms that present in a person, the tests that are generally performed are a white blood cell count, chest X-ray, stains and cultures of respiratory secretions and blood cultures (Craft et al. 2011). One of the most important diagnostic tools for pneumonia is the chest X-ray. This shows how much infiltrate is in the lungs (Butt & Swiatlo 2011), and is represented on the X-ray as a white area spread across the thoracic region, or patchy spots of white spread over the same area (Craft et al. 2011).

....

Last paragraph: Amelia came down with pneumonia after an overseas holiday, which is an illness of the respiratory system, affecting the ability of the lungs to oxygenate the blood, as fluid builds up in the alveoli. This illness' symptoms include fever, shortness of breath, difficulty breathing and productive cough, all of which Amelia experienced. Amelia should be treated with antibiotics as well as non-pharmacological treatments. Amelia should try to reduce or quit smoking, reduce her alcohol intake and exercise to reduce her weight. This will hopefully reduce the likelihood of pneumonia occurring again and complications developing, and keep her healthier for as long as possible.

Sarah Edmiston, Nursing student

Other common genres

During your studies you may be asked to write assignments that are less formal in style. Along with formal texts such as essays and case studies, students are often asked to write text types they are likely to come across throughout their professional careers. Below we have outlined just a few of the ones commonly included in tertiary courses.

Blogs

Blogs (shortened from 'weblogs') are a commonly used text type and many university units incorporate them for student collaboration and assessments. While they are usually associated with more informal writing, their inclusion in tertiary studies speaks to graduate attributes that are common for many universities, such as being able to communicate effectively and use technologies appropriately.

Writing a blog

The first things to think about when writing a blog are:

- who is your audience?
- what is the purpose?

Determining this before you begin will ensure that the 'pitch' of your blog is appropriate. For example, a blog for a group of your peers for the purpose of sharing classroom activity ideas learned while you were on your teaching placement might be quite informal in its language and could include uploaded documents or activity sheets you want to share. In contrast, a blog to document your research process for your tutor may be more formally written and include photos of you conducting experiments, or include bibliographies or reference lists.

One of the benefits of blogging is that the creator has a great deal of control over the look and 'feel' of the space. There are many WYSIWYG ('what you see is what you get') website builders that allow you to choose your backgrounds, colours, fonts, layout and so on, enabling you to customise the space to your personal taste. This can be lots of fun, but remember the two guiding questions above and always ask whether the combination of style and language is appropriate to your audience and purpose.

ACTIVITY 10.1 The audience and purpose of blogs

Below are a variety of blogs that focus on different topics. Choose two or three to view and consider how they appeal to their audience and suit their purpose. Which do you find most appealing to view, and why?

- Lisa Nielsen, The Innovative Educator: **https://theinnovativeeducator.blogspot.com**
- Notes on Becoming a Famous Architect: **http://famousarchitect.blogspot.com**
- Nurse Click (Australian College of Nursing): **https://www.acn.edu.au/blog**
- Art Gallery of Western Australia: **https://artgallerywablog.wordpress.com**
- Questacon: The National Science and Technology Centre: **https://www.questacon.edu.au/visiting/galleries/the-shed/blogs**
- Tim Blair Blog (*The Daily Telegraph*): **https://www.dailytelegraph.com.au/blogs/tim-blair**
- Geography Directions (Royal Geographical Society UK): **https://blog.geographydirections.com**

Wikis

Put simply, a wiki is an online document that has been developed collaboratively by its users. The most famous wiki is Wikipedia, so named because it is an encyclopedia that has been constructed in this way. Entries can be created and edited by anyone, building a huge database of knowledge much larger than could ever have been created by a single person or team. A system in which all users have the power to edit can be dangerous – either by design or accidentally, anyone can change the content. Wikis such as Wikipedia often have processes where information may need to be confirmed before the edit is accepted, as well as general rules and accepted protocols for contributing. Others have 'moderators', people tasked with checking information and changes before they are published. In your studies, you may use wikis for many purposes: sharing content with your peers and tutors, contributing to discussions or activities in class, working on group assignments and so on. When using a wiki, always be mindful of:

- changing other people's contributions – as a general rule, if you didn't write it, think very carefully before you change it! (Some wikis will have a 'history' function, which allows accidental or inappropriate changes to be reverted to their previous state, but don't rely on this!)
- your audience – is this content going to be read by a group of like-minded friends, or is this something that your tutor will be reading and possibly assessing?
- the purpose – is this a casual 'working document' or is it something more formal? Is it for planning or is it the final product?

The final two points will guide the language and register you use when contributing, as well as the content you create and include.

Infographics

Infographics combine information and imagery to communicate through visual language. That is, they don't rely on text to convey the information. They will often include text, but the visual language is the predominant communicator.

Infographics are useful as they convey a lot of detail in a concise and visually appealing manner. Generally, they will cover a variety of key points or particularly interesting details related to a topic rather than trying to say everything about it. In other words, this text type is not going to *replace* a 3000-word essay, but it could condense the key points into a visual summary.

When constructing an infographic, you should aim to limit the writing and focus on the visual language. Think about how you can convey the information through imagery, colours or graphical representations. A very simple example of this is demonstrated in Figure 10.1.

| Figure 10.1 | Simple demonstration of communicating information visually |

Three out of five students in Australian public schools have reported being the target of bullying

Performing a Google image search for 'infographic' and any topic will result in myriad examples of infographics. Take some time to view some that you find and reflect on how they communicate information by focusing on the visual language over the written. Free web-tools such as Canva (**http://www.canva.com**) and Piktochart (**http://www.piktochart.com**) provide templates and stock images that you can use to construct your own infographics.

Social media

Given the ever-changing nature of the field, it's difficult to get a really up-to-date snapshot of how many of us are regular social media users. However, it's clear that it is a communication tool that continues to grow, albeit at a somewhat slower pace than in the past. Social media encompasses a wide variety of platforms. Some of these will seem obvious, such as Facebook and Instagram; others, such as YouTube and LinkedIn may not come to mind so quickly. Each enables us to share ideas and interactions with others quickly and in a highly dynamic way.

Social media tends to be something we think of as personal and outside of our studies or work. However, more and more, social media is becoming a part of our professional and academic interactions. Conferences will often adopt a hashtag (#) so that delegates can use Twitter or Instagram to share their thoughts and experiences of what they are learning; professional colleagues might use platforms such as Yammer to interact with each other within and outside the workplace. While these provide convenient ways to communicate with others in our areas of interest, they can also lead to inappropriate or inadvertent interactions.

Who we are online is not always the same as who we are in person. This online persona is known as our 'digital identity'. We present a version of ourselves online that is often highly curated – our 'best self'. However, in other circumstances, we post our thoughts quickly and unfiltered. This can lead to misunderstandings or offence being taken in situations where we would likely have been much more careful with what we said or did in person. The profiles we create of ourselves, both in setting up a social media account and in interacting with it, can be found easily by others. Increasingly, employers are accessing prospective employees' social media accounts to make determinations about whether they are suitable candidates for the position. What we post online cannot be considered private or fully erasable.

When using social media, particularly in an academic or professional context, remember:

- what is posted to a social media platform may be easily discovered by people for whom it was never intended
- the context of what is posted is unlikely to be known by everyone who sees it
- what is said in the 'heat of the moment' may be seen by many people before we've had the chance to rethink it and delete
- when we invite someone into our online space (such as when participating in a conference by using a hashtag) they may have access to our entire history of posts, some of which may be inappropriate in their new context.

With these points in mind, it's worth auditing your social media presence. Consider whether you would be comfortable with a colleague or someone in your wider network seeing *everything* that is there. If not, take steps to limit your 'digital footprint' by:

- having separate personal and professional accounts
- setting profiles to 'private' or 'by invitation only'
- being discerning about who you 'friend' or allow into your online space
- deleting inappropriate or offensive material.

Additionally, and perhaps most importantly: Consider your digital actions as carefully as you would your real-world ones. Think before you post!

REVISION TOOLS

↘ Revision activity: Revise these ideas

1 Learning to write a summary is a very useful professional writing skill. Writing a summary (probably in the form of an abstract or executive summary) usually happens at the end of a project and takes time, as you often need to complete several drafts.

2 The process of compiling a case study can be very specific to the discipline area, and case studies are often written in a report format.

3 In a case study analysis, you demonstrate to your lecturer how you have understood a given situation, considering both its positive and problematic aspects.

4 A case study analysis provides an objective critique of the case based on sound research evidence.

5 Blogs, wikis and infographics are examples of text types that are becoming increasingly common in academic assessments. Always remember the key questions of 'who is my audience?' and 'what is my purpose?'.

6 Communicating via social media is something many of us now take for granted. In an academic or professional context, always be mindful of respectful and appropriately formal language and protocols.

↘ Thinking activity: Critical and reflective questions

1 What are the key ideas of this chapter? How can they be summarised into three or four points?

2 What are the pros and cons of leaving summary sections, such as the executive summary or the abstract, until the end of a writing task?

3 Which writing genre will I be required to use most often throughout my course? How familiar am I with that particular text type and what do I still need to learn?

4 What does my digital footprint look like? Would I be comfortable with my colleagues or academic network seeing everything I have posted on social media?

↘ Useful weblinks

All universities have websites with writing resources, so first check out what your institution has to offer because you may have access to internal feedback and support while you complete assignments. Here are some other websites that might be helpful:

Academic writing

The University of New South Wales website 'Academic Writing Links' has links to excellent international (English-language) websites about writing for various disciplines; see **https://student.unsw.edu.au/writing**.

The regularly updated 'Language and Learning Online' website, from Monash University, provides a useful search tool, instructions and downloadable resources, plus annotated student examples from various disciplines of writing and speaking, as well as other academic skills-related information: **http://www.monash.edu.au/lls/llonline**.

The University of Melbourne has some excellent downloadable documents at the 'All resources' link on its 'Academic Skills' website; see **http://services.unimelb.edu.au/academicskills**.

Queensland University of Technology's 'cite|write' website provides clear instructions on various written assignment formats, including annotated bibliographies and case studies: **http://www.citewrite.qut.edu.au**.

Annotated bibliographies

The following websites are especially helpful in outlining and providing examples about how to construct an annotated bibliography:

The University of Newcastle libguide 'Creating an Annotated Bibliography': **https://libguides.newcastle.edu.au/annotated-bibliography/creating-an-annotated-bibliography**.

Academic Skills Office, The University of New England. 2020. 'Writing an Annotated Bibliography.' **https://aso-resources.une.edu.au/assignment-types/writing-an-annotated-bibliography**.

Deakin University 'Annotated Bibliography' webpage: **https://www.deakin.edu.au/students/studying/study-support/academic-skills/annotated-bibliography**.

↘ PART FOUR

REFINING YOUR WRITING

We have two main purposes in this part. The first is to help you redraft your writing so that you can express your ideas as clearly, correctly and strongly as you can. We want to remind you that you write not only to communicate with your readers but also to give them pleasure in the reading.

Our second purpose is larger: to enlist you in the fight against the muddy, tortuous English that is taking over much of professional communication. We want you to be horrified by this language, and not to feel that you have to imitate it in order to succeed at university. Don Watson, who was once a speechwriter for Australian Prime Minister Paul Keating, and so was actively engaged in shaping and responding to language, has for some time been leading the fight against poor language use in Australian public life. In his seminal book *Death Sentence: The Decay of Public Language* (2004, 12–14), Watson writes:

> In the information age the public language is coming down to an ugly, subliterate universal form with a fraction of the richness that living English has. Relative to the potential of the language, the new form approximates a parrot's usage. It is cliché-ridden and lacks meaning, energy, imagery and rhythm. It also lacks words. It struggles to express the human. Buzz words abound in it. Platitudes iron it flat. The language is hostile to communion, which is the purpose of language … Our public language is becoming a non-language … Military leaders while actually conducting wars sound like marketing gurus, and politicians sound like both of them.

Part 4 contains two chapters. The first gives you practical suggestions for writing clearly and concisely while retaining the formal register needed for academic writing. The second deals with some of the grammatical 'nuts and bolts' that have helped our students to write correctly. We hope that they help you to write with 'meaning, energy, imagery and rhythm'.

→ **Chapter 11:**   Two principles of good academic writing

→ **Chapter 12:**   Grammar, punctuation and spelling

↘ CHAPTER 11

Two principles of good academic writing

CONTENTS

Principles of successful academic writing

Here are the two principles we suggest you adopt in order to be successful writers at university:

- *Principle 1:* The KISS principle – keep it simple, students!
- *Principle 2:* Make it formal, where appropriate.

Principle 1: The KISS principle – keep it simple, students!

One of the most valuable ways you can develop your academic writing (and indeed your writing in general) is to focus on writing in a clear and straightforward style. This helps you to communicate well with your audience – your teachers and fellow students, as well as your future employers, colleagues and clients.

Writing develops thinking

When we write, we generally start with a basic idea, then develop the idea more fully as we write. This is why it is vital to write clearly – muddled writing is more than a sign of muddled thinking; it can actually *cause* muddled thinking!

The first focus for your writing at university should therefore be on developing *clear* and *concise* English. Each year, some of our students fall into the trap of trying to sound complex and academic because they believe university students should write like this. Their style becomes heavy and rambling. If you find yourself doing this, you need to focus on keeping your English as simple as you can.

A convoluted style is made worse when you are engaging with new and complex ideas. Most people in our society believe that if primary-school students are taught properly about sentence structure, then they will always be able to write in correct sentences, no matter what they are writing about. This is one of the biggest fallacies about learning to write. As university students, the first thing that will fail you when you embark on a new discipline, or when you try to explain unfamiliar and complex ideas, will be your sentence structure.

If you receive feedback that your sentences in one particular section of an assignment are incorrect, this is an indication that you do not understand the ideas you are trying to express in that section. Don't despair when this happens to you – just review the ideas, make sure you understand them as well as you can, and then try to express them in shorter, clearer sentences.

The simplest way to explore this concept is to look at statements of argument for an essay – thesis statements (see Chapter 9). Such statements are key to writing clearly – if you can hone your thesis statement into a clear, strong sentence that encapsulates your thinking, then you are well on the way to writing a thoughtful, well-developed essay. Look at the following examples, which are typical of the way our students' thinking develops as they prepare to write an essay.

✂ How to spot and how to fix flowery language

How to spot a flowery thesis statement	How to fix it with a clearer, stronger verb-based sentence
There is a role for technology to continue to be adopted, developed and embraced by teachers in primary school classrooms in the pursuit of allowing teaching and learning to experience enhancement, excitement and being relevant to students.	▶ Primary school teachers must continue to use technology in their teaching in order to enhance their students' learning, excitement and sense of relevance in their studies.
It is an indisputable fact that a part in the development, maintenance and promotion of safety on their construction sites should always be played by construction managers. But nowadays, in this day and age, importance and fundamental emphasis is also placed by them on the daily and perpetual promotion of healthy habits, emotional attitudes, good gender relationships, beneficial interpersonal interactions with other workers, good society benefits, etc.	▶ While construction managers have always promoted safety on construction sites, in the 21st century these construction managers must now focus on the mental and physical wellbeing of their workers, which will in turn help create a healthy and equitable society.
Monetary wealth playing a role in the assurance, maintenance and sustainment of the mental, emotional and physical well-being, and improving the satisfaction of the populace, as well as their power, credibility and being happy since the dawn of time.	▶ Monetary wealth influences people's mental, emotional and physical wellbeing, making them more satisfied, powerful and happy in their lives.

The strong sentences in the right-hand column above have several things in common:

- Their verbs are stronger than their nouns to drive their thinking.
- Their verbs are active rather than passive.
- They are shorter and more concise than their more flowery alternatives.
- They replace complex words (e.g. 'populace') with more straightforward ones (e.g. 'people').

- They avoid empty and clichéd phrases such as 'it is an indisputable fact' and 'in this day and age'.

In this chapter you will find these and some additional hints that our students find useful in redrafting their writing. The KISS principle consists of the following eight hints:

1 Make your verbs do the heavy lifting.
2 Write in the active rather than the passive voice.
3 Use simple, direct language.
4 Avoid redundant phrases.
5 Avoid clichés.
6 Avoid ugly English.
7 Take care with pronouns such as 'it', 'this' and 'they'.
8 Avoid unnecessary use of expletives.

KISS hint 1: Make your verbs do the heavy lifting

The most valuable tools to help you write clearly and concisely are your *verbs*. You'll remember from your primary schooling that verbs are the doing or action words of your sentence. When you focus on making your verbs hold the significance of your idea, you will advance your thinking much more clearly, both for your reader and in your own mind.

The opposite of focusing on your verbs is to place the importance on nouns to shape your thinking. This is called *nominalisation* and leads to heavy, weak and 'flowery' sentences. Unfortunately, many writers in the past have seen excessive nominalisation as a marker of good academic writing. This is gradually changing, and you will now find that most of your disciplinary teachers value clear, strong and straightforward writing over a heavy and flowery style. This is important in your early years of tertiary study, particularly for those of you for whom English is an additional language, since it is very easy to lose control of your sentence structure (and therefore your thinking) when writing very convoluted sentences.

Look back at the thesis statements in the table above, and notice that the writers have strengthened them by placing more importance on the verbs than the nouns.

What is a noun?

A *noun* is a word that represents a person, place, thing or idea. You were probably taught at school that nouns can be:

- *proper nouns:* names of people and places, such as 'Joshua', 'Princess Mary' and 'Australia' – they always start with capital letters
- *common nouns:* names of things, such as 'table', 'water' and 'flock of pelicans'

- *abstract nouns:* names of qualities, ideas or emotions, such as 'happiness', 'honesty' and 'gravity'.

We have also included in Chapter 12 a brief discussion of count and non-count nouns for people who are learning English as an additional language.

The following list of common noun endings in English may help you understand the range of nouns in the language, as well as start to recognise the nouns in the sentences you read and write:

- *-tion/-sion* (e.g. implementation, creation, segmentation, nominalisation, tension, obsession)
- *-ment* (e.g. commitment, procurement)
- *-ness* (e.g. laziness, carelessness)
- *-ity* (e.g. futility, impermeability)
- *-y* (e.g. fury, sympathy)
- *-ance/-ence* (e.g. abundance, pretence, experience)
- *-or* (e.g. competitor, investigator)
- *-al* (e.g. dismissal, committal)
- *-age* (e.g. leverage, courage)
- *-our* (e.g. candour, favour)
- *-ing* (e.g. understanding, writing).

Note: Some of these endings are also found in other parts of speech. For example, the -ing ending can also indicate the part of a verb called a *participle* – 'she was being', 'he is writing', 'the children will be sleeping'.

The following 'How to spot and how to fix' box shows some examples of nominalised sentences followed by their clearer, more concise alternatives. We have italicised the unnecessary nouns and their replacement verbs and adjectives, and marked whether the alternatives are adjectives or verbs in brackets.

✂ How to spot and how to fix nominalised sentences

How to spot a nominalised sentence	How to fix it with a clearer, stronger, verb-based sentence
The student experienced a great deal of *tension* at the *approach* of her examination.	▶ The student felt very *tense (adjective)* as her examination *approached (verb)*.
The *commitment* of the woman to the project was clear.	▶ The woman was clearly *committed (verb)* to the project.
Young people in Western societies have a *tendency* to *laziness*.	▶ Young people in Western societies *tend (verb)* to be *lazy (adjective)*.

ACTIVITY 11.1   Making your verbs do the work in your sentences

As you rewrite the following sentences, we hope you will appreciate that simple, clear English driven by verbs rather than nouns is always more powerful and easier to understand than flowery and unnecessarily complex English. If you are working in a classroom, your tutor may allocate you some of these items and ask you to then report to the rest of the class.

The language in the following 10 sentences is unnecessarily complex and heavy, and some of the sentences are grammatically incorrect. Rewrite them in clear, correct English, avoiding nominalisation but retaining all the ideas included in them.

1   The two companies reached an agreement to undertake a collaboration on the project.

2   Melissa experienced a sense of devastation at her dismissal from her position with the company.

3   The overseas visitors felt excitement at the wildflowers because of their abundance and their intense colouration.

4   The mountaineer felt an enormous terror as her awareness grew of the dislodgement of the boulders on the summit above her.

5   Feeling a desire to create a good impression on his supervisor, the young architecture student rushed his drawings and forgot to provide an indication of the depth of insulation required in the ceiling.

6   She reached an appreciation of the value of simple, clear English as she followed a slow progression through the activity.

7   So great was the young girl's fury at her father's refusal to buy her some chocolate that there was no hesitation in throwing herself on the ground and emitting a scream.

8   Because of his strong commitment to the concept of sustainable architecture, the new graduate experienced a great deal of difficulty in exhibiting patience with some of the other architects in his office.

9   The IT executive turned the blame onto his young assistant, feeling a disturbance at the complexity of the problem.

10 After providing an agreement to be an investigator on this project, the development of my understanding grew rapidly.

KISS hint 2: Write in the active rather than the passive voice

Active and passive voice

The terms *active voice* and *passive voice* refer to the verbs of your sentences. Active verbs emphasise the *agent*, or the person or thing doing the action of the sentence, while passive verbs focus on the action itself. For example:

- *Active verbs:*
  - The students *conducted* many experiments to demonstrate the truth of the hypothesis.
  - The author *suggests* that the Internet was the most significant invention of the twentieth century.

- *Passive verbs:*
  - Many experiments were *conducted* by the students as a demonstration of the truth of the hypothesis.
  - The Internet is *suggested* to have been the most significant invention of the 20th century.

The two active sentences above focus on the subjects of the sentences – that is, the students and the author. The passive sentences focus on the experiments and the suggestion, rather than on the people responsible for them.

Here are some tips to help you recognise passive sentences:

- Look for the word 'by' to indicate a passive sentence. Some passive sentences mention the agent, usually in a phrase beginning with 'by' ('by the students'), while in others the agent is not mentioned at all, as in the second passive sentence above.
- Look for one of the forms of the verb 'to be', as this verb is always part of a passive verb; for example:
  - he *is* considered; they *are* prevented (present tense of 'to be')
  - Ella *was* given; the girls *were* awarded (past tense of 'to be')
  - the students *will be* presented (future tense of 'to be')
  - the websites *have been* downloaded (present perfect tense of 'to be')
  - the writers *would be* honoured (conditional tense of 'to be').

Active or passive?

Many teachers of writing recommend that you avoid the passive voice as much as possible. The active voice promotes simple, clear and direct language. There are, however, some situations in university writing in which you are forced to use the passive, or might prefer to use it. To understand why, let's consider what the passive voice does. (We do not recommend all of the uses included in Table 11.1, but it's valuable to explore them.)

Table 11.1   The passive voice

Qualities of the passive voice	Example(s)
The passive emphasises not the agent but the action.	• You will be awarded a medal if you win this annual event. • The students were punished severely for colluding on the assignment.
The passive often focuses on a process.	• The experiment was conducted. • The equipment was installed.
The passive is useful when you don't know the agent, when the agent is obvious or when the agent is unimportant.	• Her assignment was stolen from her bag before she could submit it. • The solution was heated to evaporate the gas. • The exam was cancelled because the hall was flooded after the water main burst.
The passive can also hide responsibility or blame for an action (common in business and politics).	• Your protest has been noted, and your letter will be kept on file. • Thousands of people were prevented from voting because of irregularities in the electoral rolls.
In some persuasive writing, the passive is used to create an impression of being 'objective' and therefore reliable. Because the emphasis is not on the subject of a passive sentence, the sense is created that all people would agree with the statement made.	Compare these two sentences, then consider which one you would be more likely to find in a company brochure advertising a new product: • Passive: This discovery is considered to have been the most significant breakthrough of the decade. • Active: The company considers this discovery to have been the most significant breakthrough of the decade.
The passive allows the writer to postpone mentioning the subject of the sentence until the end, in order to create suspense.	• And the right to hold the Olympic Games for 2000 has been awarded by the committee to the city of Sydney.
The passive is generally wordier than the active voice.	• The student was reminded of the need to be very careful of the security of her assignments by her experience of having been robbed and having her major assignment stolen.

The passive used to be preferred in all academic writing, but the active is becoming more acceptable in some humanities and social sciences disciplines, where the emphasis is placed on the individual's viewpoint rather than on an objective process or 'truth'. (Notice the passive verbs throughout the previous sentence!)

ACTIVITY 11.2   Active and passive voice

When you do this activity, notice the different emphases created by the original sentences and your alternative versions of them. This will help you make your own decisions about when to use the active and the passive voice.

Complete the following for each of the 10 sentences below. (If you are working in a class, your tutor may assign you particular questions and ask you to report back to the class on your answers.)

· Identify whether the sentence is written in the active or the passive voice.
· Rewrite it in the opposite voice. (In some cases, you will need to supply some information that is not present in the original sentence.)
· Describe the different emphases of the original sentence and your alternative.

1   The assignments were submitted on time.

2   James Watson and Francis Crick announced the discovery of the double helix of DNA in 1953.

3   A crowd of students watched the candy-pink Monaro as it rolled into the campus car park.

4   The ornate and beautiful church of the Sagrada Família in Barcelona was designed by architect Antoni Gaudí.

5   'The medium is the message' is a phrase created by Marshall McLuhan in *Understanding Media* (1964).

6   The students used straws and sticky tape to build bridges spanning the space between the desks.

7   A bizarre planet, which is said to orbit our sun in the opposite direction to the other planets in our solar system, has been discovered far beyond Pluto.

8   'And this year's First-Year Design Prize has been won by a student whose approach to the set problem showed both elegance and creativity: James Donaldson.'

9   It is thought between 70 and 90 per cent of all species became extinct in the Permian–
    Triassic period, 250 million years ago, as a result of massive volcanic eruptions over
    thousands of years.

10 Many people who saw the movie *Shrek* claimed that it was just a children's movie, but it
    was still voted the best movie of the year in a radio poll. *(Hint: Be careful with this one –
    notice the two different verbs in the sentence!)*

KISS hint 3: Use simple, direct language

Many English writers have argued during the past century that writers
must write in simple, clear language. George Orwell, in his key essay
'Politics and the English Language', published in 1946, recommended the
following rules for writing:

> - Never use a metaphor, simile or other figure of speech which you are
>   used to seeing in print.
> - Never use a long word where a short one will do.
> - If it is possible to cut a word out, always cut it out.
> - Never use the passive where you can use the active.
> - Never use a foreign phrase, a scientific word or a jargon word if you
>   can think of an everyday English equivalent.
> - Break any of these rules sooner than say anything outright barbarous
>   (Orwell 1946).

Henry Watson Fowler, a famous English grammarian who was writing
in the early 20th century, wrote a very similar list in his guide, *The King's
English*:

> - Prefer the familiar word to the far-fetched.
> - Prefer the concrete word to the abstract.
> - Prefer the single word to the circumlocution.
> - Prefer the short word to the long (Fowler and Fowler 1973, 11).

You begin on the path to good, clear writing when you choose to use
simple vocabulary. Avoid the temptation to try to sound more educated
than you feel by using long words – instead choose shorter, more powerful
alternatives. Verbs, in particular, are very important elements of sentences.
If you can use strong, clear verbs, you will give your sentences solid cores.
Look at the verbs and their alternatives shown in Table 11.2, for example.
The complex versions in the left-hand column will encourage you to write
in rambling, pompous English, while the simpler alternatives in the right-
hand column will give your writing clarity and power.

Table 11.2 Some verbs and their alternatives

Complex version	Simpler version
To acquiesce	To agree
To ascertain	To discover
To cease or to desist	To finish, to end or to stop
To expedite	To hasten
To facilitate	To make easy or to simplify
To initiate	To begin or to introduce
To necessitate	To require or to demand
To utilise	To use

KISS hint 4: Avoid redundant phrases

Redundant phrases make your language heavy and add nothing to the meaning of what you are saying. There are many examples of these, but the following 'How to spot and how to fix' table shows some of the common ones we find in our students' writing.

🔧 How to spot and how to fix common redundant phrases

Redundant phrase	Example of a redundant phrase	How to fix it
because of the fact that; due to the fact that …	Because of the fact that inner-city developments are now common in Australian cities, the urban sprawl is being reduced.	▶ Because inner-city developments are now common in Australian cities, the urban sprawl is being reduced. Or: ▶ The increased popularity of inner-city developments is helping reduce urban sprawl in Australia. *(This is even better than the first concise version because it's in the active voice – see KISS hint 2.)*
basically, precisely, definitely, actually, generally, kind of, etc.	These actions basically suggest to the viewer of the film that it is the man who holds the power in this relationship.	▶ These actions suggest to the viewer of the film that the man holds the power in this relationship.

it is essential/ important/significant/ interesting that ...	It is interesting to note that the author has been writing on this subject over a period of the past 10 years.	▶	The author has been writing on this subject for the past 10 years. *(You wouldn't be writing this if it was not interesting to you, so you don't need to say that it was!)*
each and every	It is essential to ensure that each and every underground nuclear waste storage facility is placed in a geologically stable region.	▶	Every underground nuclear waste storage facility must be placed in a geologically stable region.
the end result/the final outcome	The end result of this research is to show that space exploration provides many benefits for man.	▶	This research shows that space exploration provides many benefits. *(This is also better because it avoids sexist language – see Chapter 14.)*

KISS hint 5: Avoid clichés

A *cliché* is a phrase that has been used so frequently that is has become empty of meaning. It holds no power or interest. In fact, if you state the first few words of a cliché, most people can finish it for you without thinking. You might occasionally use clichés in your informal writing (e.g. in reflective journals), since this tends to be more free-flowing and less exact than formal writing. However, you must never use them in formal essays and reports. Here are some of the common clichés we see in students' formal assignments:

- for days/weeks on end
- at this point in time
- each and every
- everyday life
- this day and age.

KISS hint 6: Avoid ugly English

Every day we hear and read in the media many examples of ugly English – written or spoken English that is unnecessarily complex, using complex phrases often borrowed from current business or political jargon. This language both confuses the reader, and lacks power and energy. The ugly English is often deliberate – that is, someone is trying to give an impression that they are well educated (in fact, they usually create the opposite impression) or to disguise their own or someone else's responsibility for an action.

The best-known Australian critic of such ugly English is Don Watson (whom we mentioned in the introduction to Part 4 of this book). He uses phrases such as 'weasel words' and 'worst words' in his seminal book *Watson's Dictionary of Weasel Words, Contemporary Clichés, Cant and Management Jargon*, and his 2015 book co-authored with Helen Smith, and in many recorded speeches and interviews (details at the end of this chapter). In a YouTube presentation entitled *The Invasion of Management Speak*, he gives the following example of what he calls 'piffle' from a brochure written by the director of an unnamed Australian Government department:

> 66 For the past three months we have been focusing heavily on strategic planning. I am excited by our new vision and I want you to be excited too, to be a catalyst for continuous improvement in the accountability and performance of the public sector supported by our values: integrity, personal accountability, teamwork, learning and being outcome focused. I look forward to working together over the next five years towards achieving our vision through the implementation of our key priorities. 99

He finishes by describing the style of the brochure as "to language what dead sheep round a dried-up bore is to pastoralism" (Watson 2010). Our goal in our teaching and in writing this book is to encourage more people to use language like rich pastoralists, rather than creators of 'piffle' and 'dead sheep'.

KISS hint 7: Take care with pronouns such as 'it', 'this' and 'they'

Pronouns are words that stand for nouns (*pro* is Latin for 'for'). You use them to replace particular nouns that you have just used and don't want to repeat. The most common pronouns in academic writing are 'it', 'this', 'which', 'that', 'he' (or 'him'), 'she' (or 'her') and 'they' (or 'them'). For example:

- The lecturer was very patient with the students. *She* explained the problem a second time when *she* realised *they* didn't understand.
- Global warming will affect tropical countries very badly, causing *them* to heat up and providing rich breeding grounds for disease-carrying mosquitoes.
- The students conducted their experiments very competently, didn't they? *Which* do you think was most successful?
- The one that *they* completed on Monday was the best, I think. *It* showed *them* as capable of solving complex problems.

Be very careful when you use pronouns – you need to make clear what the pronouns refer to. Don't make your reader do the work for you. The following 'How to spot and how to fix' box shows examples of the confusing use of pronouns in the kinds of sentences some of our students write.

How to spot and how to fix confusing pronoun use

How to spot a confusing pronoun	How to fix it with a clearer phrase
This article provides a different perspective on the subject of literary frauds and hoaxes because the author considers it to be an act of literary criticism. (What does the pronoun 'it' refer to – the article, a perspective, the subject of literary frauds or the fraud itself?)	This article provides a different perspective on the subject of literary frauds and hoaxes because the author considers literary fraud to be an act of literary criticism.
In this interesting article taken from the *New York Times*, it contradicts most beliefs held in society today. (And what about the pronoun 'it' here – does it refer to the article? If so, the sentence isn't grammatically correct and could be written much more concisely.)	The author of this interesting article taken from the *New York Times* contradicts most beliefs held in society today.
With the increasing popularity of forensic science novels and TV shows, many more students each year are choosing to study forensic science at university. This is making entry into Australian forensic science courses more competitive. (The pronoun 'this' is too vague to hold the complex ideas of increasing popularity and thus increasing numbers of students.)	With the increasing popularity of forensic science novels and TV shows, many more students each year are choosing to study forensic science at university. This trend is making entry into Australian forensic science courses more competitive.
The earth has experienced five major extinction events in the past 500 million years, and in each event most of the species alive in that era were destroyed, which has led scientists to question what might have caused such extreme destruction. (This is like the previous example – the word 'which' is far too weak to hold the ideas of the extinction events and the destruction of the species. You'll need a much more informative subject for this clause, and would be better off starting a new sentence.)	The earth has experienced five major extinction events in the past 500 million years, and in each event most of the species alive in that era were destroyed. The size of extinction events and the number of species destroyed have led scientists to question what might have caused such extreme destruction.

 HINT

Be clear

You need to take the same care with the possessive pronouns 'its' and 'their'. For example, look at this sentence: 'The purpose of building safety regulations in Australia is to create safe working conditions for building workers, and their development is protected in legislation.' What does the possessive pronoun 'their' refer to – the regulations, the working conditions or the building workers? In a clear, concise sentence, you would need to specify this more carefully.

KISS hint 8: Avoid unnecessary use of expletives

You might think an expletive is a swear word – and you'd be right! But in grammatical terminology the word *expletive* means a phrase that is unnecessary to the meaning of a sentence – it just takes up space. The most common expletive phrases are 'it is', 'there is', 'this is' and 'there are'. Notice how you could make your writing more concise by leaving out the expletives in sentences such as those in the following 'How to spot and how to fix' table.

✂ How to spot and how to fix expletives

How to spot an expletive	How to fix it with a more concise sentence
There are many ways in which nuclear waste can be safely stored.	Nuclear waste can be safely stored in many ways.
There are two questions the author asks in this article.	The author asks two questions in this article.
It is the insurance industry that spends more money on climate modelling in Australia than any scientific body.	The insurance industry spends more money on climate modelling in Australia than any scientific body.
This is a provocative study of global warming that focuses on rising sea levels.	This provocative study of global warming focuses on rising sea levels.

Good writing shows consideration for your reader

You write to communicate with a reader. If your writing is clear, correct and pleasing, if it is punctuated to show the progression of your ideas and if it uses lively and varied vocabulary and sentence structure, you demonstrate your consideration for your reader's task in making meaning from what you write. If it is muddy and convoluted, if mistakes in grammar hide your meaning and if your vocabulary and sentence structure are repetitive and bland, you demonstrate your lack of respect for your reader's task.

Principle 2: Make it formal, where appropriate

Formal and informal registers

All acts of communication, whether written or spoken, can be placed on a scale that runs from the formal register, through informal (or colloquial), to slang (see Figure 11.1). The position of each communication varies according to its:

- audience
- purpose
- context.

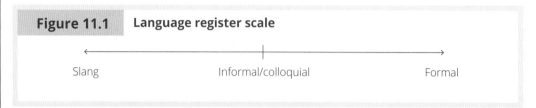

Figure 11.1   Language register scale

Slang   Informal/colloquial   Formal

Most of the writing you do for university assignments will be at the formal end of the scale. The exceptions are some reflective writing and other writing you do to develop your own thinking.

ACTIVITY 11.3   Recognising register

Consider the following eight situations, and then discuss with a partner or group of other students how the audience, purpose and context of each of the following communications would affect its register. Place the number representing each item on its appropriate position on the language register scale shown in Figure 11.1.

1   You discuss ideas with your tutor in a group of 20 students. It is the middle of the semester, and you are comfortable with your tutor and fellow students.
2   You ask a question of a lecturer after a lecture she has given to 200 students. You have not spoken to her before, although she has given several lectures in the unit.
3   You visit your tutor in his office to request an extension for an assignment; it is overdue, and you have been told you must always request extensions before the due date.
4   You send an email to the same tutor two days before an assignment is due, requesting an extension because you have been sick; you have a doctor's certificate.
5   You give a prepared oral presentation in the same tutorial group as in Item 1. The oral presentation is to be assessed.
6   You have been accused of collusion, and are required to write a letter to the head of department explaining why you should not be expelled from your course.
7   Your tutor has invited a group of students to attend an evening presentation in a series called 'Pubtalk', in which academics and postgraduate students present informal talks related to your discipline. You are in a group of five students who sit with the tutor at the pub and discuss your response to the talk.
8   You write a 1500-word argumentative essay for your communication skills unit, based on thorough research and correctly referenced.

Code-switching

Most of you will have had little difficulty completing Activity 11.3. If so, then you have the understandings you need to be a successful *code-switcher*, able to adjust your register effortlessly to suit your audiences, your purposes and the contexts or situations in which you find yourself.

However, you may be finding that you are having some trouble adjusting to the formal register required of university assignments. We find each year that some of our students pitch their register too close to the informal end of the scale. This is generally because, although they understand that reports and essays must be written in formal register, they have not yet fully developed their sense of the differences between formal and informal register. If you have problems writing in the formal register, we suggest you work through this section of the book carefully, and examine some texts that you know are formal (e.g. your course textbooks), looking at how they use language, and reading sections aloud to try to improve your sense of the structures of formal language. This will be a gradual process, but will be valuable to you as a student and as a professional in your discipline.

A comment on writing in first person

As noted in Chapter 6, first person is the 'I' person of the verb (including 'we', 'my', 'our' and so on.). It is difficult to give you a consistent rule for using first person in all academic writing because professionals and academics disagree as to whether they should use it in their own writing, and therefore on whether students should be encouraged to use it. Humanities students are increasingly expected to write in the first person, which emphasises their ownership of the ideas they are presenting. On the other hand, students in most science disciplines must write in the third person, placing their focus on scientific processes rather than on the role of the particular writer or scientist. Here are some common responses you will hear among academics:

- 'All academic writing must be written in the formal register, and there is no place in the formal register for the intrusion of the individual, as indicated by words like "I".'
- 'First person is fine in some genres of writing, such as reflective writing, and in introductions and conclusions to assignments, where students are most likely to be presenting their views on an issue. In fact, I value students using first person in these situations. In all other situations, I believe they should avoid it.'
- 'I want my students to use first person throughout their academic work. My discipline is based on students developing their points of view on issues, and being very clear that their points of view are just some of many. I don't want to read the "disembodied writer" without a personal voice.'

So how do you deal with such contradictions? First, you should ask your lecturers about their positions on this issue, and make sure you comply with these positions in assignments you submit to each of them. Then, become familiar with the typical texts of your discipline (especially the most current journal articles and books), and notice whether the academics writing these texts choose to use the first person in their writing and how they do it (e.g. how formal their language is; how they express personal responses and so on).

Principle 2 (make it formal, where appropriate) consists of the following eight hints:

1 Use clear, concise, discipline-specific vocabulary.
2 Avoid strongly emotive language.
3 Avoid slang and colloquial language.
4 Avoid phrasal verbs.
5 Avoid using 'you' and 'we'.
6 Avoid abbreviations.
7 Avoid contractions.
8 Use informative adjectives.

Formal hint 1: Use clear, concise, discipline-specific vocabulary

Formal writing involves very careful, precise language use. You must choose your vocabulary carefully, and construct your sentences very tightly. Some people believe that in formal writing you must use very complex words and long sentences with many dependent and independent clauses. In fact, this is not true – good formal language is precise rather than complex. As you become more familiar with your discipline, you will feel more confident in using its vocabulary. This will happen gradually as you read books, articles and websites in your discipline, listen to lecturers, and talk to tutors and your fellow students.

Jargon (which we introduced in Chapter 6) is the term used to describe discipline-specific language. Some people consider it a critical term (as in the sentence 'This article is poorly written because it is full of jargon'), but shared language is very important for communications among people from the same profession: it provides them with a shorthand way of being understood. Remember, however, that when you communicate with people from other disciplines, you will need to use language you all understand.

Formal hint 2: Avoid strongly emotive language

Emotive language is inappropriate for the formal register, especially when you are expressing strong ideas you don't intend to develop or support. It is most commonly found (and highly appropriate) in feature articles and blogs, but is inappropriate in formal essays. The following 'How to spot and how to fix' table gives examples of overly emotive language, as well as suggestions for how to fix them.

🔧 How to spot and how to fix emotive language

How to spot overly emotive language	Problem	How to fix it with less emotive wording
The environment is being so badly destroyed by farmers taking water out of river systems in Australia.	The word 'so', used here to mean 'very', is one indication of overly emotive language. 'Destroyed' is also an emotive word, and one that cannot be backed up scientifically. (To what extent are the river systems 'destroyed'?)	▶ The environment is being damaged by farmers taking water out of river systems in Australia.
Australians have become so focused on sport that antiquated religious beliefs, values and ideologies are no longer relevant to them.	Again, the word 'so' is used emotively. 'Antiquated' is an emotive word that represents the writer's own emotional response to religious beliefs, but is not central to the argument about sport and religion. The sentence also refers to all Australians, which is inappropriate.	▶ Some Australians have become more focused on sport than traditional religious beliefs, values and ideologies, which they find no longer relevant.
Certain language is used to manipulate a group of people who are more interested in filling a shopping trolley than in worrying about whether the truth is being told.	This sentence uses an emotive image that is not central to the argument, which is about language and truth. The writer has depicted a group of people in society as more interested in shopping than in seeking truth, which may be a suitable image for a feature article, piece of fiction or reflective piece, but is inappropriate for formal academic writing.	▶ The language is manipulative; however, many people are not interested in questioning how language manipulates them or how truth is represented.

The writers of phrases like these may feel very strongly about particular issues, but cannot 'vent their feelings' in formal academic writing. They need to use less emotive language, and to develop and illustrate their ideas fully.

Formal hint 3: Avoid slang and colloquial language

Everything we said earlier about using clear, concise vocabulary and avoiding redundant phrases and clichés is also important when you're writing in a formal register. In fact, you are most likely to find redundant and clichéd phrases in colloquial or informal writing, which tends to be much looser in vocabulary and structure than formal writing.

Formal hint 4: Avoid phrasal verbs

Phrasal verbs are two-part verbs, in which a verb is followed by a preposition or an adverb. They are typical of an informal rather than the formal register. Notice in Table 11.3 how the meaning of the verb 'to look', for example, changes when it is followed by different words.

Table 11.3	Examples of phrasal verbs
Phrasal verb	**Example(s)**
to look up to	Mavis looked up to everyone who could do cryptic crosswords – they must be highly intelligent, she thought.
to look down on	Don't look down on me just because I left school before you – I've made a fortune from my business skills!
to look through	He looked through the bin of old vinyl records, searching for anything by Neil Young.
to look right through	He was so angry with Tom for stealing his girlfriend he looked right through him when they passed in town.
to look after	He looked after his wife for two weeks after she snapped her Achilles tendon playing netball.
to look forward to	The class of 2017 looked forward to their first year of university with great excitement.
to look back on	The class of 2017 looked back on their final year at school with great nostalgia.
to look like	It looks like it's going to rain today.
to look up	I suggest you look that up in a dictionary. *Or* I might look up those old friends because I haven't seen them since we were at school together.

All of the phrasal verbs shown in Table 11.3 can be replaced by more formal (but not particularly complex) equivalents; for example, to examine, to admire, to despise, to search, to ignore, to nurse, to remember, to anticipate, to resemble and to consult. But look back at the advice we gave earlier about keeping your verbs simple – choose a phrasal verb if the alternative is a very complex and pompous one.

ACTIVITY 11.4   Phrasal verbs

As an individual or with another student

This activity asks you to replace phrasal verbs with more formal alternatives in a piece of academic writing. You will find that, even though you will be able to use relatively simple verbs in your version, your register will sound much more formal than the original does.

Here is an annotation from a bibliography on sustainable architecture. Rewrite it, replacing the phrasal verbs with more formal verbs. Write as clearly and concisely as you can.

This introductory article from *The Weekly Architect* goes through the advantages of sustainable architecture. The author points out the damage caused by poor design and building techniques, and looks at alternatives that will help make the environment better. He lays out the history of sustainable architecture in Australia over the past fifty years, and makes it clear that the architectural profession is putting in a great deal of effort to fix up the problems. Unfortunately, there is a vast history of previous damage to live down. Ruling out the value of easy solutions, the author suggests that architects should not play down the problems, but should carry out a major review of their approach to residential and industrial design.

In a group or class

Share and discuss your answers.

Formal hint 5: Avoid using 'you' and 'we'

It is very informal to use 'you' to refer to people in general, and 'we' to refer to a community of people, whether local or national. 'You' actually refers to the person reading your writing, which is generally not what students mean when they use the word. 'We' refers to a small group of people, while students generally use it to refer to a much larger, more general group (e.g. Australians or New Zealanders, middle-class people, people who share the same values as me). The following 'How to spot and how to fix' table lists some of the typical kinds of phrases used by our students in the first drafts of their essays, followed by alternatives that avoid the problem.

How to spot and how to fix phrases that misuse 'you' and 'we'

How to spot the misuse of 'you' and 'we'	How to fix it with a more formal sentence
1 Since the Internet has advanced into one of the most used technological tools of the 21st century, it has become possible to do just about anything from the comfort of our own home office.	Since the Internet has advanced into one of the most used technological tools of the 21st century, people are now able to do just about anything from the comfort of their own home offices.
2 If you are able to create your perfect world with your perfect partner, then why would you choose to live in the 'real' reality?	If people are able to create their perfect world with their perfect partner, then why would they choose to live in the 'real' reality?
3 Although it is the twenty-first century, our transport system is still very underdeveloped, and we need to pressure our government to increase their budget to improve it.	Although it is the twenty-first century, the transport system of [X] state is still very underdeveloped, and citizens need to pressure the government to increase their budget to improve it.
4 This technology gives us the ability to change our own physical image.	This technology gives people the ability to change their own physical image.
5 In this article you get the feeling Australia lost its artistic talent to London because Australia was such a conservative place during the 1960s.	This article creates the impression Australia lost its artistic talent to London because Australia was such a conservative place during the 1960s.

You will have noticed there are several solutions to avoid the problem of using 'you' and 'we' to mean 'people in general':

- You can replace 'you' and 'we' with the word 'people' (or an equivalent word such as 'citizens'), followed by 'they', 'their' or 'them', as in sentences 1 to 4.
- If the sentence allows it, you can just leave out the word 'you', as in the first part of sentence 5.
- You can recast the sentence completely to avoid the need to use 'you' or 'we' at all. You can generally do this by turning the sentence on its head to find an alternative subject, as in sentence 5.

Formal hint 6: Avoid abbreviations

You should not use abbreviations in a formal piece of writing (although some people accept them in brackets or parentheses). The most common abbreviations used by our students are 'etc.', 'i.e.' and 'e.g.'.

Formal hint 7: Avoid contractions

Contractions are shortened words in which certain letters are replaced by apostrophes; for example:

- negatives such as 'can't', 'won't' and 'shouldn't'

- past-tense verbs such as 'should've' and 'might've'. (*Note:* Instead of this contraction, some students hear these phrases as 'should of' or 'might of' – an even worse mistake than the contraction because it makes no sense grammatically, and labels you as less competent than you are in using the English language. See the section on status marking and very serious mistakes in Chapter 12.)

When you write formally, you should write all of these words in full rather than as contractions.

Formal hint 8: Use informative adjectives

When we write and speak in the informal register, we tend to use non-specific adjectives like 'good', 'bad', 'interesting', 'boring' and 'difficult'. The formal register requires we use much more informative adjectives. For example:

- Is a piece of writing good because it is *thoroughly researched*?
- Is it bad because its examples are *inappropriate*?
- Rather than boring, are its ideas *unoriginal*, *repetitive* or *unchallenging*?
- Is it difficult to understand because it is *suitable* mainly for postgraduate students, or because its ideas are *undeveloped*?

> **The register of this book** {HINT}
>
> You might ask yourself about the register we have chosen to adopt in writing this book, and compare it to the registers we would have used if we were writing a guide for teachers or an academic article on the same subject for a peer-reviewed journal. Can you identify some of the characteristics that place this book well below formal on the language register scale (see Figure 11.3)? Think about our audience, our purposes and our context to give you some clues on this.

REVISION TOOLS

↘ Revision activity: Revise these ideas

1 Clear, concise English involves using strong, active verbs, without unnecessary adjectives, adverbs and redundant phrases.

2 Effective academic writing is clear, concise and formal.

3 Some people choose to write in complex, jargonistic ways in order to avoid responsibility or to create an impression of being intelligent.

4 Academic writing generally uses a highly formal register; it can take time to learn how to write academically in your discipline, but examining good models of academic writing can help.

5 Most forms of academic writing are detached, unemotional and impersonal. Academic writing is no more intrinsically valuable than any other form of writing, but you need to learn its conventions for your tertiary studies.

6 Reflective writing is generally less formal, and can include personal and emotional responses.

↘ Thinking activity: Critical and reflective questions

1 Do I receive feedback that my writing is too flowery or too informal? Am I aware of this tendency in my writing, and what do I want to do about it?

2 What approaches can I develop to help me adjust my language more quickly and smoothly for different contexts?

3 Do I notice over-complex language and jargon in political, business and educational communications? Why do I think this happens?

4 In an era that some people are labelling 'post truth', what might people do to help make communications at all levels clearer and less open to being contested? (Hint: In reflecting on this, consider your own influence, as well as that of your friends, colleagues, teachers, public figures and the media.)

↘ Useful websites

Watson, Don. 2013. *Bendable Learnings: Don Watson on the Wisdom of Modern Management.* YouTube video. 28.19. **https://www.youtube.com/watch?v=vz6QuKbEAsc** (You will find many other amusing and powerful speeches and interviews by Watson by entering his name in the YouTube site.)

Consult the following resources to explore the topic of academic writing further:

Monash University: 'Writing Clearly, Concisely and Precisely': **https://www.monash.edu/rlo/research-writing-assignments/writing/clear-communication/writing-clearly-concisely-and-precisely**.

Massey University (NZ): 'Introduction to Academic Writing': **http://owll.massey.ac.nz/academic-writing/introduction-to-academic-writing.php**.

Birmingham City University (UK) Centre for Academic Success: 'Academic Writing Style': **https://bcuassets.blob.core.windows.net/docs/120-academic-style-131921294445423769.pdf** (includes quizzes with answers).

REFERENCES

Fowler, Henry W., and Francis G. Fowler. 1973. *The King's English: The Classic Guide to Written English*, 3rd ed. Oxford: Oxford University Press.

Orwell, George. 1946. 'Politics and the English Language.' **http://www.orwell.ru/library/essays/politics/english/e_polit**.

Watson, Don. 2010. *The Invasion of Management Speak*. YouTube video. 3.10. **https://www.youtube.com/watch?v=RsVTDz6sunA**.

Watson, Don. 2004. *Death Sentence: The Decay of Public Language.* North Sydney, NSW: Random House Australia.

Watson, Don. 2004. *Watson's Dictionary of Weasel Words, Contemporary Clichés, Cant and Management Jargon*. Milsons Point, NSW: Knopf.

Watson, Don, and Helen Smith. 2015. *Worst Words*. North Sydney, NSW: Random House Australia.

CHAPTER 12

Grammar, punctuation and spelling

CONTENTS

The writing process

Before we start to look at English grammar and punctuation, we want to remind you about *the writing process*, which we discussed in Chapter 6. This is a multi-step process:

- *Step 1:* Writing your first draft, where you focus on your ideas.
- *Step 2:* Editing what you have written, where you reconsider how you develop, structure and present the ideas you have already written.
- *Step 3:* Proofreading your writing, where you focus on your grammar, punctuation and spelling.

However, it's not a simple process – you're not likely to go through each step in turn, and you'll often revisit previous steps as you work through your writing. Nevertheless, you may choose not to worry too much about getting your grammar perfectly correct while you're writing your first draft. Focusing strongly on grammar can limit your thinking and make your ideas a little stilted.

Why worry about grammar?

When you're ready to proofread your writing, the question might arise for you, 'Why should I worry about correcting my grammar?' There are three major reasons why you should worry about this:

- You write an academic assignment to communicate your ideas, and incorrect grammar might actually prevent your readers from understanding what you are saying.
- Even if your readers understand what you mean, they might need to do a lot of work to sort through confusing grammar. Having to do this will irritate them and detract from the power of your ideas. Remember that good writing involves you being considerate of your readers, and making it easy for them to understand what you want to say.
- Poor grammar may lead your readers to label you as less literate than you should be. At the moment, your readers are your lecturers and tutors, so poor grammar will mean you may get lower marks than your ideas deserve. After you graduate, your readers will be your employers, work colleagues and clients. Poor grammar in your communication with these people can affect your chances of promotion or of gaining important contracts.

Create a good impression

The impression you create on your readers is very significant, not just during your studies but also in your future professional life. The position of many employers is encapsulated by the title of an article by Kyle Wiens, CRO of iFixit, a global online repair community: 'I Won't Hire People Who Use Poor Grammar' (2012). He sums up his position clearly:

> ❝ I hire people who care about … details. Applicants who don't think writing is important are likely to think lots of other (important) things also aren't important. And I guarantee that even if other companies aren't issuing grammar tests, they pay attention to sloppy mistakes on résumés. After all, sloppy is as sloppy does. ❞

See the 'Useful weblinks' section at the end of this chapter, which lists articles from employers and other professionals who value good grammar.

Computer-table books

We strongly recommend that you buy several writing, grammar, punctuation and usage books to keep by your computer during the rest of your university and professional life. Below we list some of the books our students find most useful. We have grouped them under two categories: essay-type guides and ABC-type guides. It's a good idea to have at least one of each of these types of book, so that you can use the type that is most appropriate for the information you seek. Explore the books listed here, and others found at the same classification numbers in your library, to see which suit you best.

Essay-type guides

These guides are written in the form of short essays, or chapters, with each section devoted to aspects of writing and using the English language effectively. They are most appropriate if you want to understand a language concept, such as sentence structure, or a writing skill, such as paragraphing. Useful examples include the following:

Bate, Douglas, and Peter R. Sharpe. 1996. *Writer's Handbook for University Students*. Sydney: Harcourt Brace.

Bazerman, Charles, and Harvey S. Wiener. 2003. *Writing Skills Handbook*, 5th ed. Boston: Houghton Mifflin.

Strunk, William. 2004. *The Elements of Style*, new ed. Caboolture, QLD: KT Publishing.

Style Manual for Authors, Editors and Printers. 2002, 6th ed. Milton, QLD: Wiley.

Sword, Helen. 2012. *Stylish Academic Writing*. Cambridge, Mass.: Harvard University Press.

Zinsser, William Knowlton. 2006. *On Writing Well: The Classic Guide to Writing Non-fiction*, 30th anniversary ed. New York: HarperCollins.

ABC-type guides

These guides are organised alphabetically, like a dictionary or an encyclopaedia, with entries explaining the use of particular words, rules for individual punctuation marks and various concepts of language (e.g. inclusive language, clauses and phrases). They are most appropriate if you want to check specific information. See the following texts for good examples of guides of this type:

Hudson, Nicholas. 2015. *Modern Australian Usage: A Practical Guide for Writers and Editors*, 3rd ed. Crows Nest, NSW: Allen & Unwin.

Partridge, Eric. 1999. *Usage and Abusage: A Guide to Good English*, 3rd ed. rev. Janet Whitcut. Harmondsworth, Middlesex: Penguin.

Peters, Pam. 2007. *The Cambridge Guide to Australian English Usage*, 2nd ed. Leiden, Holland: Cambridge University Press.

Trask, R. L. 2002. *Mind the Gaffe: The Penguin Guide to Common Errors in English*. London: Penguin.

A grammar book

Although you need to understand only basic grammatical terms in order to improve your writing – and you will gain this understanding from the books listed above – some of you may want to learn more about grammar for its own sake. If so, we recommend the following quirky and beautifully presented book – a delight for the art lovers and creative writers among you, as well as for the hopeful grammarians:

Gordon, Karen Elizabeth. 1993. *The Deluxe Transitive Vampire: A Handbook of Grammar for the Innocent, the Eager and the Doomed*. New York: Pantheon.

Grammar

We can't cover every important aspect of grammar in this text, so we will focus just on those most of our students struggle with. Nor do we imagine that you will work through this chapter page by page; instead, you likely will focus on areas that you recognise are difficult for you.

Subject–verb agreement

Verbs can be singular (I sing, you sing, he/she/it sings) or plural (we sing, you sing – where 'you' refers to more than one person – they sing).

One significant marker of poor English is using a singular verb with a plural subject, or a plural verb with a singular subject. However, if you have been hearing and reading standard English since you were young you will probably make very few mistakes in subject–verb agreement. But a few areas of subject–verb agreement confuse even some experienced English users; see Table 12.1 for some examples.

> **Take care with two singular subjects linked together**
>
>
>
> Look out for the problem of the verb that follows two singular subjects. Our students often make the mistake of using a singular verb in situations like this: 'Safety and rehabilitation *is* the key to a healthy, modern and fair workplace'. The correct sentence is, 'Safety and rehabilitation are the keys to a healthy, modern and fair workplace'.

Table 12.1 Subject–verb agreement

Agreement rule	Examples
The words 'each', 'either', 'neither', 'everyone', 'everybody', 'anyone', 'anybody', 'no one', 'nobody', 'someone' and 'somebody' are singular, and you must use them with singular verbs.	• **_Each_** _of his articles_ **_was_** _very well supported by research._ • **_Anyone_** _who_ **_submits_** _the essay early will be given a chocolate frog._
The words 'some', 'none', 'any', 'all', 'more' and 'most' can refer to either singular or plural nouns, and therefore need either singular or plural verbs.	• **_Most_** _homes in Australian cities_ **_have_** _access to the broadband network._ • **_Most_** _inner-city development_ **_has_** _happened in the past decade._
Two singular subjects joined by 'and' take a plural verb. However, if you use the phrases 'as well as', 'in addition to' or 'along with' instead of 'and' to join two singular subjects, you do not use a plural verb. Singular subjects joined by 'or', 'nor', 'either … or', or 'neither … nor' take a singular verb.	• **_Aaron and James have_** _excellent oral presentation styles and always perform well in formal situations._ • **_Either Aaron or his friend James is_** _collecting the equipment for the presentation._ • **_Aaron, as well as James, has_** _gone to collect the equipment for the presentation._
When two or more subjects are joined by 'or', 'nor', 'either … or', or 'neither … nor', and one subject is singular while the other is plural, the verb agrees with the closest subject.	• **_Neither the tutor nor the students were_** _impressed by the quality of the presentation._ • **_Neither the students nor the tutor was_** _impressed by the quality of the presentation._
Group nouns such as 'the committee', 'the government', 'the orchestra' and 'the flock' take singular verbs, but when you specify individuals in the group you use plural verbs.	• **_The university senate opposes_** _voluntary student unionism._ • **_Members of the university senate have_** _spoken against voluntary student unionism._
Singular nouns that introduce plural nouns take singular verbs.	• **_The strength of her opinions was_** _impressive._ • **_The subject of all of these articles is_** _the future of sustainable development in Australia._
Some plurals of nouns that originated in other languages (particularly Latin and Greek) may appear to be singular, and some singulars may appear to be plural.	_The words 'data', 'media' and 'criteria' are all plural (their singulars are 'datum', 'medium' and 'criterion') and take plural verbs._

A 30-minute tour through sentence structure

In the next few pages, we are going to explain different types of sentences so that you can:

- understand when your own sentences are correct, and why
- understand when they are incorrect, and know how to correct them
- learn to vary your sentence structure to make your writing more interesting and powerful.

As we work through the explanation, we will define the basic terms you need to understand. When we explain a term for the first time, we will italicise it so that you can find it easily.

First, you need to understand the difference between a phrase and a clause:

- A *phrase* is a group of words that has no subject or verb. For example:
  - like a feather
  - with the exception of music
  - after the ball.
- A *clause* is a group of words that forms a complete idea, with a subject and a verb. It can be a complete sentence in itself, or part of a longer sentence. For example:
  - It floated to the ground as gently as a feather ...
  - For six weeks he gave up everything, with the exception of music.
  - ... and after the exhibition, she was inspired to change her approach to colour.

Simple sentences

A *simple sentence* has one subject and one verb – that is, it has one clause:

- The *subject* is the person or thing doing the action. It can be of any length, from a single word to a very long phrase.
- The *verb* describes the action of the subject. It can be one word (e.g. 'walks', 'described', 'saw') or several (e.g. 'will walk', 'has described', 'will have seen', 'has been described', 'will be seen').

In the following examples the subjects are bold-face and the verbs are italicised:

- **The candy-pink Monaro** *rolled* into the campus car park.
- **The population of the world** *is increasing* rapidly.
- **The first-year student** *arrived* an hour early for the first exam.
- **The concept of the circulation of the blood throughout the human body** *was* first *understood* by the Chinese several thousand years ago.

- **This article** *is* very accessible for first-year students.
- **The Swan River system** *will not survive* into the next century.

Notice that some of these verbs are in the present tense ('is' and 'is increasing'); the verb 'will not survive' is in the future tense; and the others are all in the past tense. These forms are all called *finite verbs* – they are 'finished' and strong enough to hold the action of the sentence. The word 'increasing' is called a *participle* – it's only one part of a verb and cannot be used as the only verb in a sentence. The finite verb 'is' must be added to complete it.

ACTIVITY 12.1 Generating sentences

With another student or individually

One excellent way of deepening your understanding of sentence structure is to generate your own sentences following sentence structure patterns. We suggest you stop reading now and write three or four simple sentences that you will build on as you read through the following pages. Vary the subjects from single words to longer phrases, and the verb tenses to include past, present and future.

_____

_____

_____

_____

_____

_____

In a group or a class

Share your sentences around the group to ensure you understand simple sentences.

Problem 1: The sentence fragment

The *sentence fragment* is a very significant sentence structure problem – it is one marker of someone who lacks the literacy skills needed for university writing. A sentence fragment starts with a capital letter and ends with a full stop, but it either does not have a verb at all or has a participle rather than a finite verb. The following 'How to spot and how to fix' table gives some examples of sentence fragments, with possible solutions. (The fragments are in italics in the left-hand column.)

How to spot and how to fix common redundant phrases

How to spot sentence fragments	How to fix sentence fragments
Global warming has been proved to be increasing throughout the world today. *Despite the doubts of a few global sceptics.* (*No verb*)	▶ *Connect the fragment to the preceding sentence with a comma:* Global warming has been proved to be increasing throughout the world today, despite the doubts of a few global sceptics.
The Australian film industry has not been strong in recent years. *Not since the Labor government economic support of the seventies.* (*No verb*)	The Australian film industry has not been strong in recent years, since the Labor government economic support of the seventies.
Sustainable architecture is an essential part of all university architecture courses. *Being the most important subject for training socially responsible architects.* (*No finite verb*)	▶ *Rephrase the sentence fragment (and often also the one before) to fit the situation:* Sustainable architecture is an essential part of all university architecture courses, since it is considered the most important subject for training socially responsible architects.
An interesting article discussing 'the Mozart Effect'. (*No verb*)	▶ *Add an extra phrase containing a verb to the beginning of the sentence:* This interesting article discusses 'the Mozart Effect'.

Why not write only in simple sentences?

Simple sentences are fine, but they aren't capable of explaining complex relationships among ideas, or of helping you develop your own thinking in sophisticated ways. For these purposes, you need compound and complex sentences, which describe relationships of time, cause and effect, comparison, purpose, illustration, exception and so on.

Compound sentences

A *compound sentence* is a combination of two simple sentences joined together in one of three ways:

1 by a coordinating conjunction
2 by an independent marker
3 by a semicolon.

The two sentences that are joined together to form a compound sentence are called *independent clauses* – each has a subject and a verb, and each could work independently to form a separate sentence.

The seven *coordinating conjunctions* are 'and', 'but', 'for', 'so', 'yet', 'or' and 'nor'. (Some people remember these by thinking of the invented word FANBOYS, formed from the first letter of each word.) When you use these words to join two independent clauses, you should include a comma after the first clause.

Independent markers include words like 'therefore', 'however', 'moreover', 'also', 'thus' and 'consequently'. When you use these words to join two independent clauses, you should include a comma immediately after the word itself and a semicolon after the first clause – although even some professional writers choose to leave out the comma. (We discuss how to use 'however' later in this chapter.)

Semicolons can be used on their own to join independent clauses. When you use a semicolon rather than a full stop, you are asking your reader to see the two clauses as very closely connected.

In each of the following examples of compound sentences, we have italicised the second independent clause. Notice that each second clause is a complete sentence, but we have chosen to connect it closely to its first clause to emphasise the relationship between the ideas.

- The candy-pink Monaro rolled into the campus car park, *and crowds of students stood and stared.*
- The population of the world is increasing rapidly, *and may reach 10 billion in 2050.*
- The first-year student arrived an hour early for the first exam; *however, the exam was postponed because the hall was flooded by a burst water main.*
- The concept of the circulation of the blood throughout the human body was first understood several thousand years ago by the Chinese; *yet many people believe it was discovered by the Englishman William Harvey in the 17th century.*
- This article is very accessible for first-year students; *it presents a clear and convincing argument for the use of geosequestration to store nuclear waste in Australia.*
- The Swan River system will not survive into the next century; *it will be choked by blue-green algae.*

ACTIVITY 12.2   Generating sentences

With another student or individually

Now combine each of the simple sentences you created in Activity 12.1 with an independent clause to create a compound sentence. Vary the ways you connect the two clauses within your sentences.

_____

_____

_____

_____

_____

_____

In a group or a class

Share your sentences around the group to ensure you understand compound sentences.

Problem 2: The run-on sentence (also called a comma splice)

Like the sentence fragment, discussed previously, the *run-on sentence* is a serious grammatical mistake, and is one of the most common errors our students make in their writing. It is also called a *comma splice* because you use commas to splice together simple sentences. Commas are not enough: you must use a conjunction, an independent marker or a semicolon to join simple sentences.

✂ How to spot and how to fix run-on sentences

How to spot a run-on sentence	How to fix a run-on sentence
Students held a large protest against the Vietnam War in Paris in March 1968, key members of the movement were arrested.	▶ Students held a large protest against the Vietnam War in Paris in March 1968, and key members of the movement were arrested. (*Conjunction*)
	Students held a large protest against the Vietnam War in Paris in March 1968; subsequently, key members of the movement were arrested. (*Independent marker*)
	Students held a large protest against the Vietnam War in Paris in March 1968; key members of the movement were arrested. (*Semicolon*)

Complex sentences

A *complex sentence* is a combination of a simple sentence and a *dependent clause*, which is a group of words that have a subject and a verb, but do not express a complete thought. This means that the dependent clause cannot be a sentence on its own.

The dependent clause is joined to the simple sentence by a participle, *pronoun* or *dependent marker*, along with a comma or a pair of commas. The clause can be placed before the simple sentence, after it or in the middle of it. Dependent markers include words and phrases that describe:

- a relationship of time, such as 'after', 'before', 'since', 'then', 'until', 'when', 'whenever' and 'while'
- a relationship of place, such as 'where' or 'wherever'
- a causal relationship, such as 'because', 'even if', 'in order to', 'since', 'so that' and 'unless'
- a comparison relationship, such as 'although', 'as', 'as if', 'even if', 'even though', 'if', 'though', 'whatever', 'whether' and 'while'.

Here are some examples of complex sentences. We have italicised the dependent clauses. Notice the placing of the commas to connect them to the main clauses (i.e. the simple sentences we started with). Notice also whether each dependent clause is connected to its main clause by a participle, a pronoun or a dependent marker:

- *Having been fitted with black leather upholstery*, the candy-pink Monaro rolled into the campus car park.
- *While it was estimated to have been 6.3 billion in 2000*, the population of the world is increasing rapidly.
- The first-year student, *who was not confident that she would pass any of her exams*, arrived an hour early for the first exam.
- The concept of the circulation of the blood throughout the human body was first understood several thousand years ago by the Chinese, *whose medical knowledge was highly developed*.
- *Although it is written by one of the leading authorities on the subject*, this article is very accessible for first-year students.
- The Swan River system will not survive into the next century *unless the State government provides a large grant to the Swan River Trust to support a major cleanup*.

An exception to the rule

In the last sentence in the above list, you will see the exception to the rule that you must connect a clause to the rest of its sentence with a comma. (There is always an exception to English grammar rules!) This exception states that when you join a dependent clause to the end of a sentence you often don't use a comma.

ACTIVITY 12.3 Generating sentences

With another student or individually

Now go back to the simple sentences you created in Activity 12.1 and add dependent clauses to generate complex sentences. Vary the position of the dependent clauses in your sentences and the ways you connect them to the main clauses.

_____

_____

_____

_____

_____

In a group or a class

Share your sentences around the group to ensure you understand complex sentences.

Compound–complex sentences

The last sentence pattern, the *compound–complex sentence*, is the combination of all three patterns we have already described. You will use this pattern regularly in your academic writing because it allows you to express the most complex relationship among ideas. You are also most likely to lose control of this pattern in your writing because it requires you to be very aware of what you are doing.

In the following list we have combined the sentences we have been working with throughout this section into compound–complex sentences. As you read each one, make sure you can identify the main clause (the simple sentence we started with), the independent clause and the dependent clause. We have added an extra independent clause to several of them to show that you do not have to limit yourselves to just three clauses. Notice the way the clauses are punctuated when they are combined:

- Having been fitted with black leather upholstery, the candy-pink Monaro rolled into the campus car park, and crowds of students stood and stared.
- While it was estimated to have been 6.3 billion in 2000, the population of the world is increasing rapidly, and may reach 10 billion in 2050.
- The first-year student, who was not confident she would pass any of her exams, arrived an hour early for the first exam; however, the exam was postponed because the hall was flooded by a burst water main.
- The concept of the circulation of the blood throughout the human body was first understood several thousand years ago by the Chinese, whose medical knowledge was highly developed; yet many people believe it was discovered by the Englishman William Harvey in the 17th century.
- Although it is written by one of the leading authorities on the subject, this article is very accessible for first-year students, and presents a convincing argument for the use of geosequestration to store nuclear waste in Australia.
- The Swan River system will not survive into the next century; it will be choked by blue-green algae unless the State government provides a large grant to the Swan River Trust to support a major cleanup.

ACTIVITY 12.4   Generating sentences

With another student or individually

Now, combine your main clauses, the independent clauses and the dependent clauses you added to them to create compound–complex sentences in a variety of structures.

_____

_____

_____

_____

_____

_____

In a group or a class

Share your sentences around the group to ensure you understand compound–complex sentences.

With another student or individually

If you still have problems understanding different sentence structures, here is some more practice with compound–complex sentences.

For each of these 10 sentences, follow this process:

1 Circle the main verb. (*Hint:* It may be more than one word.)
2 Underline the simple sentence.
3 Draw a wavy line under the independent clause.
4 Draw dotted lines under all dependent clauses.
The first is done for you.

1 Abbie knew thousands of people would be fighting for tickets to *Matilda*, so she put her phone on redial, hoping she might be one of the lucky ones to get through to the ticket office.

2 The IT executive chose his first home based on the suburbs that had access to the Broadband network; he didn't care whether these suburbs had schools, shops or cafés because these services weren't important to him.

3 Doubts about university study are very common, causing many students to struggle in their first semester, but by their second year most feel more settled.

4 The young nursing student has discovered he loves city life after living all his childhood in the bush, and spends hours walking around the streets revelling in the noise and crowds of people.

5 Battling the hordes of giant rats, the warrior queen felt her strength was failing, and she feared she would at last be defeated.

6 Ingrid loves watching game shows on TV, but feeling slightly embarrassed about this she has decided not to admit it to her friends.

7 Without her Dalmatian, who was always loyal and affectionate, Iris would have been very lonely; she didn't miss the so-called friends who had let her down so often.

8 If James had thought his car would be vandalised the first time he drove it, he would not have lashed out on a Ferrari; he would have bought a cheap second-hand car and saved his money for a trip to the Maldives.

9 When her tutorials were finished, she would have to push her way onto the train with dozens of others; that's when she most wished she had decided to study online.

10 After receiving the latest, multi-million-dollar, state-of-the art equipment, the clinic managers found that their requests for treatment grew exponentially; however, their nursing numbers did not increase, so they could not meet the extra demand.

In a group or a class

Share your sentences around the group to ensure you understand compound–complex sentences.

Modifiers

A *modifier* is a word, a phrase or a clause that gives you more detail about one part of a sentence. Many modifiers are, in fact, dependent clauses (discussed in the earlier 'Complex sentences' section). Here are some complex sentences, with the modifiers in italics:

- *Hoping to finish her essay on time*, she stayed up all night.
- *Excited at the prospect of seeing a new Harry Potter movie*, Jessica and her friends queued in the rain.

In each of these cases, the modifier is placed at the beginning of the sentence and followed by a comma. It relates to the subject of the sentence ('she' or 'Jessica and her friends'), which comes immediately after the comma. The modifier can also be placed elsewhere in a sentence, as in these examples:

- She stayed up all night to finish that design, *which won her the First-Year Design Award.*
- The female king penguin hatches one egg each year. She rears her young, *which is born with soft down rather than feathers, and thus cannot swim in the cold Antarctic waters*, by placing it on her feet and covering it with her abdomen skin to keep it warm.

Misplaced modifiers

A modifier must always be placed next to the phrase it modifies. If you put it in the wrong place in a sentence, you say something different from what you actually mean. Sometimes the result can be amusing, sometimes incomprehensible, as the following 'How to spot and how to fix' table demonstrates.

How to spot and how to fix misplaced modifiers

How to spot a misplaced modifier	How to fix a misplaced modifier
Overloaded with statistics and percentages in the first couple of paragraphs, the reader may seem to get a little lost among them. (*Does the writer really want to say the reader is overloaded with statistics? She has said this by placing the modifier next to the words 'the reader', but she perhaps means something else.*)	Since the first couple of paragraphs are overloaded with statistics and percentages, the reader may seem to get a little lost among them.
Possessing a tensile strength 10 times greater than steel and yet weighing a considerable amount less, we can only imagine the new structures and buildings we will be able to construct from nanotubes. (*We must be Supermen!*)	Since nanotubes possess a tensile strength 10 times greater than steel and yet weigh a considerable amount less, we can only imagine the new structures and buildings we will be able to construct from them.
With beady eyes, a piercing scream and a huge black wingspan, the woman was terrified of the swooping bat. (*We heard this sentence on a recent radio program about the cliffs of northern France – and the speaker certainly didn't mean what she said!*)	With beady eyes, a piercing scream and a huge black wingspan, the swooping bat terrified the woman.

'Not only/not just ... but also ...'

One way our students frequently misplace modifiers is in the phrase 'not only ... but also' (or 'not just ... but also'). To place this correctly, you need to identify the stem of the sentence – that is, the phrase common to both parts of the sentence. (The phrase won't be written in full in both parts of the sentence, but it will be implied.) You then place 'not only ...' immediately after this stem. Look at these examples:

- *Wrong stem:* 'The student not only won the Design Prize but also the Top Student of the Year prize.'
- *Correct: 'The student won not only* the Design Prize but also the Top Student of the Year prize.'
- *Wrong stem:* 'Cyberspace not only provides a site where physical limitations can be transcended but also where social boundaries can be eradicated.'
- *Correct: 'Cyberspace provides a site not only where* physical limitations can be transcended but also where social boundaries can be eradicated.'

When you place 'not only' incorrectly, you usually place it too close to the beginning of a clause, not including enough words in the stem. In these examples, not only 'the student' and 'cyberspace' are common to both parts of the sentences but also the complete phrases 'the student won' and 'cyberspace provides a site where'.

Dangling modifiers

A *dangling modifier* is a modifier that, rather than being misplaced as the previous examples were, is left dangling because its subject has been omitted. When you write a dangling modifier, your reader can generally imagine what your subject might be, but you shouldn't expect the reader to do this work – you should state the subject explicitly. Look at the examples in the following 'How to spot and how to fix' table.

⚒ How to spot and how to fix dangling modifiers

How to spot a dangling modifier	How to fix a dangling modifier
Written in the first person, the author outlines the importance of ...	▶ This article is written in the first person, and the author outlines the importance of ...
In researching for this essay, the group of keywords 'copyright' and 'copyright and the Internet' were all significant.	▶ In researching for this essay, I found the group of keywords 'copyright' and 'copyright and the Internet' were all significant.
Very popular in TV series in the past decade, many students are now applying to study forensic science courses at university.	▶ Since TV series based on forensic science have been very popular in the past decade, many students are now applying to study forensic science courses at university.

Parallel construction

When you have more than one phrase or clause in a sentence, you should make sure they are all constructed in the same way – that is, they are *parallel*. For example, if you use the infinitive form of the verb in your first clause, you should also use it in all other clauses in that sentence. We have chosen a range of examples to demonstrate unbalanced and parallel constructions for you in the following 'How to spot and how to fix' table. The important phrases for the parallel construction have been italicised.

✂ How to spot and how to fix unbalanced constructions

How to spot an unbalanced construction	How to fix it by creating a parallel construction
Good managers evaluate the costs of the presentations, the quality of the presenters and whether the programs are worthwhile.	▶ Good managers evaluate *the costs of* the presentations, *the quality of* the presenters and *the worth of* the programs.
The Mitchell article attempts to go beneath the surface results of the survey to analyse the choices the pollsters made, and discussing the limitations of these choices.	▶ The Mitchell article attempts to go beneath the surface results of the survey *to analyse* the choices the pollsters made, and *to discuss* the limitations of these choices.
The author explains why students cheat; what teachers or lecturers can do to educate themselves about plagiarism; what approaches students can develop to prevent plagiarism; and strategies of detection to be used.	▶ The author explains why students cheat; *what* teachers or lecturers *can* do to educate themselves about plagiarism; *what approaches* students *can* develop to prevent plagiarism; and *what strategies* teachers *can* adopt to detect it.
Cyberspace allows individuals to adopt both feminine and masculine attributes, to assume another race or national identity, or change their physical characteristics.	▶ Cyberspace allows individuals to adopt both feminine and masculine attributes, *to assume* another race or national identity, or *to change* their physical characteristics.

Punctuation

We discussed commas and full stops earlier, in relation to sentence structure. Now let's look at some of the other punctuation you might find difficult: apostrophes, colons, semicolons and dashes.

Apostrophes

Apostrophes have two purposes:

1 to replace a missing letter
2 to show possession.

Missing letter

This use of the apostrophe is very easy – you replace a letter, or several letters, with an apostrophe. The resulting word is called a *contraction*.

Sometimes you need to combine two words into one to create the contraction, and should take care to place the apostrophe where the letter is left out, not where the words are joined (e.g. 'should not' becomes 'shouldn't', not 'should'nt'); in other cases, you need to change some of the letters to create the new word (so, for example, 'will not' becomes 'won't').

Possession

In English we show possession by adding -'s after the person or thing doing the possessing; for example:

- the *student's* assignments
- the *experiment's* results.

The easiest way to decide how to add the apostrophe is to write down who or what is doing the possessing (in the examples above, 'the student' and 'the experiment'), then add an apostrophe and an 's' to the end of that word. If the final letter of this word is already an 's', then there are two different possible approaches:

1 If the word ending in 's' is a singular noun or a person's name, then add the apostrophe and another 's', just as for the basic rule.

2 If the word is a plural noun, or an ancient name (e.g. names from The Bible such as Jesus and Moses, and names from the classical era such as Achilles and Sophocles), add just the apostrophe – you don't need to add another 's'.

These rules will help you with tricky possessions like the following:

- the students' assignments (the assignments of more than one student)
- the policy's implications (the implications of one policy)
- the policies' implications (the implications of two or more policies)
- Prince Charles's interest in town planning
- *Bridget Jones's Diary*
- Moses' 10 commandments
- Achilles' heel.

Beware of false possessives

Don't start to imagine all words that end in an 's' are possessives. In English there are two other main reasons why a word might end in an 's': it could be a plural (e.g. two assignments), or it could be the third-person singular of a present-tense verb (e.g. he writes his assignments carefully). To add an apostrophe before the 's' in either of these situations would mark you as less literate than you should be as a university student.

Decade numbers

Many people make mistakes with the punctuation of the words for decades – such as 'the 1960's'. You must write the names of decades without an apostrophe – that is, 'the 1960s'. After all, what would an apostrophe stand for in these words? They are plural nouns – there is no missing letter and they are not possessives. To remind yourself about this when you're writing, write the name in your mind in words – 'the nineteen sixties' – and notice there is no apostrophe.

Place names

In Australia we omit the apostrophe from place names; for example:

- Kings Road
- St Georges Terrace
- Queens Gardens.

Don't be confused when you see such names written with apostrophes, as some British place names do include apostrophes (so you will see both 'Queen's Road' and 'Queens Road' in British texts).

A confusion – 'its' and 'it's'

Now let's look at the situation when you should have to use an apostrophe for both a missing letter and possession in the same word – the case that so often confuses our students:

- 'it's' and 'its'
- 'you're' and 'your'
- 'they're' and 'their' (not to mention 'there', which is unrelated but often confuses students, too)
- 'who's' and 'whose'.

The rule here is that when you need to use an apostrophe to replace a missing letter and to show possession in the same word, *the missing letter takes precedence*. For example:

- It's a very easy book to read – its language is colloquial and its sentence structure is simple.
- You're going to find your assignments difficult to finish if you don't start now.
- They're always hesitant to explain their presence there in that building.
- Who's asking about that lost dog? The man whose car is parked outside.

To check whether apostrophes are correct in any situation, see if the sentence reads correctly when you substitute missing letters for the apostrophe; for example, 'it is', 'you are', 'they are', 'who is'.

HINT

'Its' and 'it's'

Lynne Truss, a journalist who wrote a best-selling book on punctuation called *Eats, Shoots and Leaves*, describes her reaction to people who confuse 'its' and 'it's': 'No matter that you have a PhD and have read all of Henry James twice. If you still persist in writing "Good food at it's best", you deserve to be struck by lightning, hacked up on the spot and buried in an unmarked grave' (Truss 2003, 44). This is, of course, a humorous exaggeration, but it also suggests the intense reaction some readers have to incorrect apostrophes. It's worth keeping these readers happy!

ACTIVITY 12.6 Apostrophes

With another student or as an individual

Rewrite the following sentences using apostrophes correctly. In some cases this will mean you omit an apostrophe; in others you will choose not to use one. *(Note: You will need to correct some grammatical errors, too!)*

1   Every year the five students borrowed their families cars and drove to Kings Park for a picnic on the anniversary of they're first meeting.

_____

_____

2   Dickens most famous novel is *Great Expectations*. Students appreciation of this novel is based on it's believable characters.

_____

_____

3   'We should'nt be late for that lecture today. Its the last one for the semester and were going to do an evaluation.' 'Your kidding! Those evaluations dont give us any chance to say what we want! We should of stayed home today anyway.'

_____

_____

4   James friend, whose an artist, designed the huge painting over the mantelpiece their. Its blues and greens are powerful but the lighter colours arent soft enough, so it's background is too obtrusive.

_____

_____

In a group or class

Share your answers to ensure you all understand how to use apostrophes.

Colons

The *colon* introduces the next part of a sentence. You can generally replace it with 'that is' or 'as follows', or, in the informal register, with 'i.e.'. You will find colons used in many different situations, as shown in Table 12.2.

Table 12.2	Uses of the colon
Situation where you use a colon	**Example(s)**
Introducing a quotation	Smith et al. (2003) claim that an effective early warning system for tsunamis can be introduced into the Indian Ocean region within the next decade: 'Scientists have collaborated successfully to develop such a system, and with support from the governments in the region it will be highly effective.'
Introducing a list	Developments in nanotechnology have introduced some amazing new types of material: nanotubes, superconductors and superfluids.
Explaining, developing or elaborating the idea of the first part of the sentence	The Italians were not the first people to appreciate coffee: it was popular in Ethiopia as early as AD1000.
	Fossils have been found of primates that share the attributes of modern apes: flat chests, relatively flat faces and shoulder blades that are fixed at the back.

Be careful when you use a colon to introduce a list

⟨ HINT ⟩

When you use a colon to introduce a list, the part that comes before the colon must be a complete clause. For example, you cannot write a sentence like 'The students handed in: their assignments, their portfolios and their reading journals.' The sentence is correct without the colon. If you want to use a colon here, you have to make the phrase before the colon a complete clause. For example, you could write 'The students handed in everything that was due: their assignments, their portfolios and their reading journals'.

Semicolons

Like commas, *semicolons* work to separate clauses from the rest of their sentence; however, they are stronger than commas – that is, they make a stronger break from the rest of the sentence. This is demonstrated in Table 12.3.

Table 12.3	Uses of the semicolon
Situations where you use a semicolon	**Example**
Joining two complete sentences you want to associate closely in your reader's mind	Already discussed in the section on compound sentences earlier in this chapter.
Separating items in a list, where each item is a complete clause or a long phrase, and/or some items have internal commas	Many reasons are given for the increased popularity of inner-city living in Australia, including the ageing of the Baby Boomers, who no longer need large houses and gardens; the increase in disposable income of young professional people, who can now afford to live in expensive city apartments; the improvements in public transport in many Australian cities; and the recent rise in petrol prices, which are seen as likely to remain high indefinitely.

Two uses of 'however'

You can use 'however' in two ways, but you need to understand how the punctuation is different for each of them. The first method is to use it as an adverb, where it expresses a contrast between one idea and another:

> The student handed in his assignment. He had forgotten, however, to attach a reference list, so his tutor returned it to him.

When you use 'however' as an adverb you must surround it with commas – unless it is at the beginning or end of a sentence, of course. The clue to its being used as an adverb is that you can place it in more than one position without changing the sense of the sentence. (See how many positions you can discover in the second sentence of the previous example.)

The other method is to use it as a conjunction, where it joins two sentences:

> The student handed in his assignment; however, he had forgotten to attach a reference list to it.

When you use 'however' like this, you must precede it with a semicolon to connect it more closely with the second clause than the first, and then follow it with a comma. You can't move it to any other position in the sentence because you are using it to join two sentences into one. You could replace the semicolon with a full stop, but would lose the implied connection between the ideas.

Dashes

Dashes are common in informal register – you will see them throughout this book, which is an informal presentation for students, but we would not use them as often in a formal text such as an academic essay. They generally introduce a second thought within a sentence, and are therefore a more casual version of the colon we explained above. For example:

> Dashes can be very effective – they help make a text sound conversational.

You can use dashes in formal writing, too, but mainly in pairs when you want to set off an idea from the rest of the sentence that surrounds it. For example:

> Dashes can be very effective – in both formal and informal writing – to set a phrase off from the rest of a sentence.

When you use a pair of dashes, they act like a pair of commas or a pair of parentheses. They separate a phrase from the rest of the sentence more strongly than a pair of commas would, but less strongly than a pair of parentheses. This makes sense if you think about the punctuation marks visually and consider their relative effect on your eyes – the dash is more visually dramatic than the comma, but less than the parenthesis.

HINT

Make sure your sentence is complete

When you use just one dash in a sentence, the part that comes before the dash must be a complete clause – that is, it must have a subject and a complete verb. You can't rely on the part after the dash to complete your main thought – it acts only as an afterthought. When you use a pair of dashes, the part outside the dashes must be a complete sentence.

Spelling

When most people write in languages they are very familiar with, they think about their spelling only occasionally. They instinctively know how to spell thousands of words, recognising patterns of letters and syllables without having to think consciously about them. So what is the difference between successful spellers and those who struggle with spelling? This difference is clear when the two groups of spellers come to words they're unsure of. Weak spellers are either unaware they are spelling a word incorrectly, or realise they're not sure but don't know what to do about this. They might ask someone else, or guess the correct spelling. Some of our students even spell the same word in three or four different ways throughout an assignment, reasoning that at least one of them will be correct! The following sections give advice for working on your spelling.

Computer spell-checkers

Some students think they no longer need to learn how to spell because their computer spell-checker will automatically correct all their mistakes. There are three problems with this approach:

1 You won't do all your university written work on a computer. How will you handle spelling problems during in-class writing exercises and exams?

2 Your spell-checker will generally offer you several alternatives to your misspelled words. How will you choose the correct ones?

3 Your spell-checker won't identify a mistake if your misspelling is, in fact, a correct word (even if the wrong one for your purposes).

Don't let the spell-checker do the work for you. One of our colleagues recently marked a thesis in which the student had clearly misspelled the word 'organic' each time she used it; she had allowed the spell-checker to correct it automatically, and it became 'orgasmic' throughout the thesis.

This doesn't mean you should avoid using spell-checkers. In fact, you must remember to check the words highlighted by your spell-checker after you have finished editing your written assignments – it's especially good at picking up your typing mistakes.

Strategies for successful spelling

Successful spellers use a combination of strategies to arrive at the correct spelling of words they're doubtful about – different strategies suit different words:

- *They use visual techniques.* They write all the alternatives they can think of, either in their own handwriting or on a computer, to see which one looks correct. They look at the patterns of letters and how syllables are combined, and recognise the correct spellings visually.

- *They use aural techniques.* They say the word aloud, listening to each syllable, because they've trained themselves to recognise how to spell a word by its sound. (Be careful with this one, however – English syllable sounds are highly irregular, so most people prefer to write down spellings and use their visual memory. Aural memory is a useful 'second string', but you shouldn't rely on it alone.)

- *They think about how words are put together.* They understand how syllables are added to words, and how spellings change when these syllables are added. For example, they know how prefixes and suffixes affect spelling, and how verbs change to show different tenses.

- *They divide words into syllables (in their mind or on paper), and think about each syllable separately.* This avoids problems of running syllables together. For example, students wouldn't make the common mistake 'intresting' if they divided the word into its syllables – 'int-er-est-ing'.

- *They focus on the part of each word they have always found difficult.* For example, many students find the words 'separate', 'sentence' and 'definite' difficult to spell, and they all make mistakes on the same syllables – they misspell the words as 'seperate', 'sentance' and 'definate'. When these students try to learn the correct spellings, they should focus their learning on the difficult syllables.

- *They pay particular attention to double letters and how these relate to sound (especially short and long vowels – see below).* They think carefully about when to use double letters and when not to. Some of our students have problems with the different forms of the verb 'to write', for example. They would find it helpful to remember that 'write' and 'writing' have a single 't', while 'written' has a double 't' (and the two different pronunciations of the vowel 'i' would help them remember this).

- *They think about spelling rules.* Successful spellers understand that, although there are many exceptions to most spelling rules, the rules can be useful. We're sure you've been taught these spelling rules in your primary schooling, but will remind you about some of the best-known rules:
  - 'i' before 'e' except after 'c' – so 'relief' and 'pier', but 'receive' (common exceptions include 'height' and 'their')
  - some prefixes and suffixes are formed with double letters (see the sections on prefixes and suffixes on the following pages)
  - if singular nouns end in 'y' preceded by a consonant ('-ly', '-ty' and so on), their plurals end in '-ies' ('families', 'treaties'), but if they end in a vowel before the 'y' ('-ay', '-ey', '-iy', '-oy', '-uy'), then they end in '-ys' (monkeys, buoys)
  - if singular nouns end in '-is', their plurals end in '-es' ('synopses', 'syntheses').

- *They learn how to use a dictionary efficiently.*

- *They invent 'word tricks' to help them with difficult spellings.* For example, we still use the phrase 'the car is stationary' to distinguish that spelling from 'stationery' (i.e. pens and pencils). Other common spelling word games include 'the principal is a pal' (to distinguish it from 'principle') and 'there's a bus in business' to help remember that difficult spelling.

Spelling rules for plural nouns

We have included just the rules about plural nouns that most affect our students' writing. For a longer list, look at one of the grammar books recommended earlier in this chapter, or type 'spelling rules for plural nouns' in your preferred search engine.

Short and long vowels

The sounds of all vowels can be described as either *short* or *long*. Short vowels are pronounced like this (the ˘ symbol is one way of representing a short sound in pronunciation guides):

- ă as in battle
- ĕ as in expansion
- ĭ as in written
- ŏ as in frond
- ŭ as in uphold.

Long vowels are pronounced like this (the − symbol is one way of representing a long sound in pronunciation guides):

- ā as in debate
- ē as in revalue
- ī as in write and writing
- ō as in oppose (the second o here - the first is short)
- ū as in overrule.

Some students have problems spelling related words that have different vowel sounds, such as 'written', 'write' and 'writing'. If you understand that a double letter makes the preceding vowel short, while a final silent 'e' makes it long, then this will help you spell all these words correctly. Think also about 'precede' and 'precedent', and 'reveal' and 'revelation'. The rules governing how vowels are pronounced are too complex to discuss in full in this book, but we encourage you to notice words as you read them, and start to build a list of rules of how letter combinations affect the pronunciation of vowels.

You can learn to spell well

It's never too late to improve your spelling. Unless you have a specific learning difficulty that affects your ability to spell, you can train yourself to be a good speller – it just needs effort.

Prefixes

Prefixes are syllables placed on the front of words to alter their meaning. Prefixes are most commonly used to make a word negative; for example:

- *'un-'* ('un*important*', 'u*nn*ecessary')
- *'im-'* ('impolite', 'i*mm*obile')
- *'in-'* ('inactive', 'i*nn*umerate')
- *'mis-'* ('misinform', 'mi*ss*hapen')
- *'dis-'* ('disappoint', 'di*ss*atisfy')
- *'il-'* ('illogical', 'i*ll*egible').

Notice the words from this list that have double consonants in the middle. When the last consonant of the prefix and the first consonant of the main word are the same, you need to write them both in the final word.

This rule will help you remember when to use double letters and when to use single letters when you add a prefix to a word.

Other common prefixes include *'syn-'*, *'sym-'* and *'com-'* (all meaning 'together' or 'with'), *'pre-'* (meaning 'before') and *'pro-'* (meaning 'on behalf of').

Suffixes

Suffixes are placed on the end of words, and have several roles. First, they are added to verbs to change the tenses:

- *'-ed'* ('experimented', 'chatted', 'rated') for a past-tense verb
- *'-ing'* ('experimenting', 'chatting', 'rating') as part of a present-tense verb.

If you're unsure about when to double the last consonant before a suffix and when to keep it single, focus on the pronunciation of the word. Notice you must double the consonant before adding a suffix to verbs like 'to chat' (single-syllable verbs ending in consonants), but not to verbs like 'to rate' (single-syllable verbs ending in a silent 'e'). The sounds of these verbs can also help you remember when to double the consonants (see the comment on short and long vowels earlier in this chapter).

Second, the suffixes *'-ible'* and *'-able'* help form adjectives. Many students have problems remembering which words take the suffix *'-ible'* and which take *'-able'*, so we offer you the following handy guide, which works in most cases:

- If the base word is a complete word in itself, add *'-able'* ('laughable', 'admirable').
- If the base word is not a complete word, then add *'-ible'* ('dirigible', 'terrible'). (The exceptions to this rule include 'irritable', 'contemptible' and 'flexible'. You'll just have to learn such exceptions – write them on your personal spelling list if you find them difficult.)

Other suffixes include *'-less'* (as in 'harmless' and 'regardless'), *'-er'* and *'-est'* (which are also called *comparatives* and *superlatives*, as in 'prettier', 'prettiest' and 'bigger', 'biggest'). Notice what happens to these base words when you add comparative and superlative endings – see if you can think of other words that work like these ones.

Understanding these syllables and how they are added to the fronts or ends of words helps you to spell more words correctly.

Homophones

Homophones are words that sound like each other but are spelled differently. The following 'How to spot and how to fix' table shows some homophones that often confuse our students.

⚒ How to spot and how to fix homophones

How to spot a homophone	How to fix homophones
there/their/they're	▶ In that group there you'll find the most thoughtful students at the university. Their questioning attitudes and ability to reflect on their learning mean that they're most likely of all to succeed.
where/we're/were/wear	▶ 'I'm sorry we're late for dinner. We were on time, but then my son couldn't decide what to wear; and then my husband forgot where he'd put your address. But we're here at last. Hope there's some food left!'
here/hear	▶ 'Do you hear the tractor roaring down the road? I'm sure it'll be here within a few moments.'
its/it's	▶ 'It's great that the new Australian film has just won an Academy Award for its cinematography.'
your/you're	▶ 'Lost your whistle, Ump?' yelled the angry football mum. 'You're a disgrace to the game!'
whose/who's	▶ 'Who's going on the site visit tomorrow?' 'It depends whose bus they're using – if it's MetroBus most of us will refuse to go.'
to/too/two	▶ Two of you students will have to carry these models to the display hall, and I'll need some volunteers to take the data projector and laptop, too. Why aren't you helping, Jenny?' 'Because I don't want to!'
weather/whether/wether	▶ The old farmer wondered whether his sheep would survive the coming storm. He had 200 sheep, of which 50 were wethers, and he worried for them all because of the weather forecast.
know/no	▶ 'Do you think we can all pass this unit?' 'I know of no reason why any of you should fail!'

For more information about the correct use of any of the words in the table, look them up in a dictionary (particularly an online learner's dictionary, which includes many sentences in which each word is used correctly). Our favourite is the *Cambridge Advanced Learner's Dictionary* (see **http://dictionary.cambridge.org**). The 7ESL website (**https://7esl.com/homophones**) contains a list of hundreds of homophones.

Severe spelling problems

Of course, a small number of people have severe spelling problems. However hard they work and whatever they do, they can't recognise when they have made a spelling mistake. Some people know they always misspell a particular word, but can't remember which alternative they generally use, and therefore which one is wrong. Some people can look at two different versions of a word without being able to see that they are different.

Spelling problems of this severity are very uncommon. If you have such a problem, you will probably have been diagnosed already by an educational psychologist, and have developed ways of dealing with it that allow you to succeed in your studies. Make sure you make yourself known to a university counsellor, so that this person can represent your interests to your lecturers and tutors, who will most likely give you special consideration for assignments and exams.

If you haven't been diagnosed with specific language problems but still find spelling very difficult, apply some of the techniques in this chapter you haven't tried before. If you're still struggling, make an appointment to talk to a university counsellor – they are trained to help you in situations like this.

> **Why bother about spelling?**
>
> Poor spelling sometimes makes your meaning confusing, but more often it creates a bad impression on your readers. If you make mistakes in a formal written communication, people may consider you less literate than you would like to appear. It's particularly important to give a professional impression of your communication skills to your employers, lecturers, colleagues and clients, so it's worth perfecting your spelling skills.
>
> HINT

Common difficulties for students for whom English is an additional language

If English is an additional language for you, you may experience some of the grammar problems we discussed earlier in this chapter. But you are also likely to have problems with particular aspects of English that more experienced English speakers don't have to think about.

Below we will discuss briefly the most common language problems we see among our first-year international students. We don't have space here to explain the relevant grammatical issues in depth, so we will just mention briefly some of the problems you may have. We recommend you consult grammar books or websites (many of which include exercises with answers). We have listed some useful books and websites at the end of this chapter.

Verb tenses

In some languages, verbs can't be conjugated into different tenses, so some of our international students find verb tenses confusing. If you experience difficulty with verb tenses, there may be two kinds of problem:

1 You may forget how to construct particular verb tenses, which is understandable because English contains lots of irregular verbs. Your only solution to this problem is to consult a grammar book or website and learn the verb forms.

2 You may misunderstand how to vary the verb tenses in particular situations. When you have this problem, you should think about the time sequence of what you are describing, and about how the individual parts relate to each other. You will need to read about verb sequencing in a grammar book.

Incorrect verb tenses are likely to confuse your reader more than many other grammar mistakes, so it is worth working hard to fix up this problem.

Writing about a work of art

If you are analysing a written text, film, painting or other work of art, you must write in the present tense (e.g. 'Season 4 of *Twin Peaks* is a pleasant surprise for long-time fans of the show'); but if you are writing about the history of its creation you must write in the past tense (e.g. 'Season 1 of *Twin Peaks* was shot on location in the Pacific Northwest'). It's easy to understand why you must use the present tense for analysis if you consider that you're analysing the text as a construction that still exists now.

Subject–verb agreement

We have already discussed some of the complexities of subject–verb agreement. Some of our students for whom English is an additional language have difficulties with the basic concepts of subject–verb agreement. If this is a problem for you, you must work on improving it through a grammar book or reputable online resource. Poor subject–verb agreement is a significant indicator of poor English-language skills, and will affect your grades at university.

The use of articles

We have already explained the different types of noun: proper nouns, common nouns and abstract nouns. Common and abstract nouns may seem easy to understand. However, they can cause problems, especially if you are learning English as an additional language, because of the differences between *count nouns* (i.e. nouns in which the individual items can be counted, such as 'table' and 'flock of pelicans') and *non-count nouns* (i.e. nouns for things that cannot be counted, such as 'water', 'happiness' and 'gravity'). Count nouns always take the *definite article* ('the') or the *indefinite article* ('a' or 'an'), while in some situations non-count nouns do not. You need an article for a non-count noun only when you are talking about a particular example of it. For example:

- The overseas visitors watched in awe as *a* flock of pelicans soared from *the* surface of *the* water.
- Water covers 70 per cent of *the* surface of *the* planet.
- The rocket escaped from *the* gravity of Earth and set off towards Mars.
- The gravity of *the* Earth is six times stronger than *the* gravity of the moon.

For more information about articles, see the following websites:

- About.com: 'English as 2nd Language. Articles: The/a/an', http://esl.about.com/od/beginningenglish/ig/Basic-English/Articles.htm.
- Frankfurt International School: 'Articles', http://esl.fis.edu/grammar/rules/article.htm.
- Online Writing Lab (OWL) at Purdue University: 'Using Articles', https://owl.purdue.edu/owl/general_writing/grammar/using_articles.html.

Strategies for developing your language

If English is an additional language for you, you may find the strategies suggested in Chapter 6 useful to help you develop your English skills.

REVISION TOOLS

↘ Revision activity: Revise these ideas

1 Writing with correct grammar makes your ideas easy to understand, creates a good impression with your readers and labels you as appropriately literate to be a tertiary student and professional. Some grammar mistakes are particularly likely to see you labelled as not literate enough for study and professional work.

2 It is important to have a collection of books and/or online resources to help you write correctly, and to get used to consulting them regularly.

3 Sentence structure is the foundation of grammar – if you understand how sentences work, you can write correctly and fix any problems that might occur in your writing. Sentences can be simple, compound, complex or compound–complex.

4 Good punctuation is related to sentence structure, but it is also good to master other punctuation such as apostrophes, semicolons, colons and dashes.

5 Correct spelling is also important in good communication, so that your meaning will be clear, and you will create a good impression. There are many strategies and rules that will improve your spelling. You must pay attention to errors indicated by your computer's spell-checker before submitting assignments.

6 If English is an additional language for you, you may make certain grammar mistakes because of your previous experience with other languages. You can focus on these areas when working on your English.

↘ Thinking activity: Critical and reflective questions

1 How clear and correct is my written English? Am I committed to improving it during my studies, and what approaches can I use to help me do this?

2 Can I instinctively feel when my writing is awkward or incorrect? How can I adapt my strategies to help me be more aware when my writing is awkward?

3 How did I feel about my writing when I finished my previous education? In what ways are those feelings changing as I begin my university studies?

4 Why do people care about writing clearly and correctly? What differences would it make if people didn't bother about how we write?

↘ Useful weblinks

Articles that promote good grammar in business

Dikson, Karen. 2019. 'The Importance of Good Grammar Skills in Business.' BusinessTown. **https://businesstown.com/importance-good-grammr-skills-business**.

Click Here Labs. 2016. 'Good Grammar Is Crucial to Creating a Good First Impression.' **https://clickherelabs.com/blog/good-grammar-is-crucial-to-creating-a-good-first-impression**.

Scaros, Cecile. 2016. "The Importance of Good Grammar in Business Communications." LinkedIn, May 2, 2016. **https://www.linkedin.com/pulse/importance-good-grammar-business-communications-cecile-scaros**.

Online language labs and grammar exercises

Griffith University's wonderful website, 'EnglishHELP', is aimed at international students but relevant for everyone; see **https://www.griffith.edu.au/international/englishhelp**, and scroll to the end of the homepage to find the grammar and writing headings.

The Learning Centre at the University of New South Wales publishes a website called 'Online Academic Skills Resources'. One of its pages deals with punctuation, and includes many example sentences; there are also pages on referencing, critical thinking, time management, making notes, giving oral presentations and a range of other useful topics. See **https://student.unsw.edu.au/skills**, and scroll down the page to the heading 'Resources'.

An online version has been created of William Strunk's *The Elements of Style* (one of the essay-type guides mentioned in this chapter); see **http://www.bartleby.com/141**.

Capital Community College in Hartford, Connecticut (US) publishes a detailed website called 'Guide to Grammar and Writing', which includes a wide range of information sheets, grammar quizzes, PowerPoint slides and essays; see **http://grammar.ccc.commnet.edu/grammar**.

For an extremely comprehensive list of homophones, with explanations, see the 7ESL website at the following URL: **https://7esl.com/homophones**.

Jack Lynch's 'Guide to Grammar and Style' website provides a detailed alphabetical list of grammatical problems and issues, with clear explanations; see **http://jacklynch.net/Writing**.

Paul Brians's 'Common Errors in English Usage', published on the Washington State University website, is equally useful; see **https://brians.wsu.edu/common-errors-in-english-usage**. See also Paul Brians's list of common misspellings at **https://brians.wsu.edu/common-errors**.

The 'Learn English' website includes information for elementary and intermediate learners of English, along with more than 400 language quizzes and games; see **http://www.learnenglish.be/index.htm**.

Purdue University's 'Online Writing Lab (OWL)' is the original of all online language labs, and contains handouts and exercises on a wide range of language issues, along with more general guides to writing, referencing and writing in different disciplines; see **http://owl.english.purdue.edu/owl**.

The Internet TESL Journal's 'Self-Study Grammar Quizzes' provide grammar exercises with answers; see **http://a4esl.org/q/h/grammar.html**.

The 'Literacy Education Online' website of St Cloud State University, Minnesota (US) provides links to pages on basic grammar, punctuation and sentence structure, all with clear examples; see **http://leo.stcloudstate.edu/catalogue.html**.

Online dictionaries and thesauruses

Cambridge Advanced Learner's Dictionary: **http://dictionary.cambridge.org**.
Longman Dictionary of Contemporary English: **http://www.ldoceonline.com**.
Merriam-Webster's dictionary and thesaurus: **http://www.merriam-webster.com**.
Oxford Advanced Learner's Dictionary: **http://www.oup.com/elt/catalogue/teachersites/ oald7/?cc=global**.
Thesaurus.com (an online version of *Roget's Thesaurus*): **http://thesaurus.reference.com**.

REFERENCES

Truss, Lynne. 2003. *Eats, Shoots and Leaves: The Zero Tolerance Approach to Punctuation*. London: Profile Books.
Wiens, Kyle. 2012. 'I Won't Hire People Who Use Poor Grammar.' *Harvard Business Review*, July 20, 2012. **https://hbr.org/2012/07/i-wont-hire-people-who-use-poo**.

PART FIVE

FACE-TO-FACE COMMUNICATION

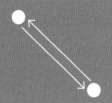

In the 'real world' the importance of establishing and maintaining effective face-to-face communication cannot be overstated. Even though much of your assessment at university level will be written work, some of your tasks will include face-to-face communication, and you will probably experience a higher proportion of this kind of task as you progress through your course. Once you graduate, your professional success may depend on how well you communicate face-to-face with clients, employers and peers.

For now, as a first-year student, use the information in this section to help you improve and challenge your 'non-written' communication practices. Part 5 includes four chapters:

→ **Chapter 13:** Interpersonal skills

→ **Chapter 14:** Intercultural communication

→ **Chapter 15:** Teamwork

→ **Chapter 16:** Presentations

In Chapter 13 we focus mainly on the communication skills you will use in your professional workplace. Those of you preparing for professions in which you will have significant direct interaction with clients should apply these skills to those workplaces. We hope you will appreciate, however, that you can also apply them to your student life.

In the other three chapters we focus on the first-year experience: communicating with students and staff members from a range of cultures, working in student teams to complete written and oral tasks, and making oral presentations as part of your course. Of course, all of these skills are also relevant to your future professional lives.

CHAPTER 13

Interpersonal skills

CONTENTS

Active listening

Perhaps the most significant aspect of interpersonal communication is listening. Listening may appear to be a one-way process, in which the listener is passive; but it should, in fact, always be an active process in which the listener is as engaged as the speaker. (See Chapter 4 for a detailed discussion of actively listening to lectures and videos.)

Listening in small groups

In this section we will focus on the listening skills you need for effective communication in pairs, small groups and small-classroom situations (that is, seminar, tutorial or workshop groups).

Non-verbal language

The most important factor that makes you a good (or not-so-good) listener in a small group is your body language or non-verbal language – that is, your posture, gestures, eye contact with the speaker and your facial expressions as you listen.

You are all experts in the non-verbal language of the culture you have grown up in, even though, at the moment, you may not be able to articulate what you know. You may not realise the powerful impact the body language of a listener has on the person speaking. Activity 13.1 is designed to help you to understand both sides of the speaker–listener relationship.

A word of caution before you do the activity, however: remember that the way people use non-verbal language is strongly affected by their culture. For example, in Western cultures all listeners – whatever their age, gender and educational level – are expected to maintain eye contact with people they are listening to. On the other hand, people in some other cultures are required to avoid eye contact with their elders, people of the opposite sex or people of a different social background, even when these people are speaking directly to them. For more discussion of intercultural communication issues, see Chapter 14.

ACTIVITY 13.1   Listening role-play

This activity is designed to help you articulate what you already know about the effects of non-verbal language in a verbal communication, and will lead you to see the communication from the points of view of both the listener and the speaker.

Working with a partner, assign one person the role of the listener and the other the role of the speaker. Work through the following process:

1   The speaker speaks for two minutes on a given subject, whatever the listener is doing. The listener must use body language to block and disengage from the communication.
2   Reverse your roles and repeat step 1.

---

3   All pairs join in a class discussion. First, the listeners describe what they did to block the communication. The speakers then describe how they felt about continuing to speak while the listeners were blocking, and the techniques they used to try to re-engage their listeners.

4   Return to your pairs and repeat the entire role-play, this time adopting the body language typical of an engaged, interested listener. (Don't 'ham it up' – just be genuine.)

5   Reverse roles and repeat the role-play.

6   In a class discussion talk about the experience of being both listeners and speakers in the two situations.

ACTIVITY 13.2   Listening in different cultures

This activity is just a brief look at intercultural communication issues associated with listening. See Chapter 14 for more intercultural communication activities.

If you have students from different cultures in your class, discuss the differences in the speaking–listening relationship in all of your cultures. Consider how the age, gender, family and social background of both listeners and speakers affect verbal communications in your culture. (For example, who is allowed to speak to whom in your culture? How would your listening behaviour differ depending on the background of the person speaking to you?)

Communicating online

Even if you are studying online, you are probably involved in some personal communications with other students. You will learn best if you play a part in building an online learning community with your fellow students. If a discussion board is provided in the unit, do as much you can to participate, even if there are no marks attached to this activity. You may also be able to discuss ideas with your fellow students in live online classrooms, by email, by video-call, or in a WhatsApp or Discord group chat. Many units ask you to share files with each other and to work on projects together.

It may seem impossible for students to engage in group work and teamwork online. However, most universities have learning outcomes such as 'the ability to communicate with others in writing and orally' and 'the ability to work in teams/groups and to develop leadership skills'. University leaders believe that all their students, whether studying face-to-face or online, deserve equal educational opportunities, so they encourage their teaching staff to find ways for online students to work productively in groups. If you are an online student, you will experience a range of personal communication opportunities – we urge you to take them as much as you can! Chapter 2, Chapter 10 and Chapter 15 each have more advice about how to get the most out of using the online space in your learning.

You don't have to be an online extrovert!

Your lecturers and tutors understand that some students enrol in online learning because they would prefer not to engage with other students. If this is your situation, look for ways that you can engage with others without feeling uncomfortable – teachers don't expect everyone to be extroverted and talkative, but they do hope that their students will find ways to share ideas and work with each other.

Many websites offer advice for successful online learning, often centering around personal and communication qualities. For examples, see the 'Useful weblinks' list at the end of Chapter 1.

Personal space

Another important aspect of your face-to-face listening skills is your understanding of *personal space*. This is the amount of space you need to keep around you so that you don't feel uncomfortable and 'invaded'. To help you understand this concept better, work through Activity 13.3.

Edward T. Hall, in his *Theory of Proxemics*, which was first published in 1966, defined four concentric circles or zones of personal space, which Nina Brown (2011) summarises as follows:

66 • *Intimate space:* The closest 'bubble' of space surrounding a person. Entry into this space is acceptable only for the closest friends and intimates.

• *Social and consultative spaces:* The spaces in which people feel comfortable conducting routine social interactions with acquaintances as well as strangers.

• *Public space:* The area of space beyond which people will perceive interactions as impersonal and relatively anonymous. **99**

ACTIVITY 13.3   Personal space

With another student or as an individual

Draw three concentric circles, and position yourself in the centre. Label the circles 'Intimate space', 'Social and consultative spaces' and 'Public space'. Write the names or titles/positions of your friends, family, acquaintances and work colleagues or clients in these circles, representing where you feel comfortable for each of them to be when you relate to them. Show the distance to the edge of each of these circles (i.e. how far you choose to be from each of these groups of people).

In a group or a class

Compare your diagram to those of other students in your class, and discuss the similarities and differences.

The size of these zones varies in different cultures – in some cultures, for example, people approach acquaintances quite closely while they are communicating with them, while people in other cultures keep even family and friends at some distance. This can create difficult situations. For example, you may be in a business meeting with someone from another culture whose social zone is much smaller than yours. As this person listens to you, they may sit too close for your comfort, and you may start to feel awkward. On the other hand, you may sit close to a business associate, and may even put your hand on their arm as you speak, but feel ill at ease because this person seems cold and unresponsive. Perhaps this is due to the fact that this person's social zone is much larger than yours and you are intruding on their personal space.

So what can you do about personal space issues?

- Be sensitive to other people's non-verbal language.
- If you feel uncomfortable because someone is too close to you, understand that she or he may have smaller zones of personal space than you. If you need to step back or push back your chair, do this gently.
- If other people move away from you slightly as you talk to them, don't 'follow them in' – allow them to find their comfortable distance. And don't feel insulted – it's not a criticism of you, but an issue of personal space.
- When you're in a meeting with people from different cultures, take your cue about distances from the other members of the group. Allow them to place the furniture, or to move it if they are uncomfortable. Do not touch other people unless you are sure that they are comfortable with this. If working with people from other cultures, be careful even about shaking hands – although you might consider this gesture very formal and non-invasive, people from some cultures are uncomfortable about even this form of touching. Once again, take your cue from other people.
- When you first work in a new environment, be careful about intruding on other people's territories. Some people protect their personal space by having their own seats or their own mugs in the lunchroom, for example, and feel very threatened if you take these things. If you're in any doubt, ask.
- You can delineate your own space at work, at home or anywhere else by placing personal objects, such as photos and wall hangings, appropriately to 'claim' the space.

If you are interested in reading more about this subject, you will find many articles on proxemics online. You might also read more about Hall's ideas on how different cultural contexts influence interpersonal communication (see the 'Useful weblinks' section at the end of this chapter).

Encroaching on personal space

Be aware that some people knowingly encroach on your personal space – they might move close to you, stand over you or touch you on the shoulder, for example. Their aim might be to intimidate you, to demonstrate their power over you, to support you or to move your relationship to a more intimate level – only you can decide which is the case and how best to respond. If you are uncomfortable about someone's behaviour, it is OK to say 'I'd rather you didn't do that'. If the behaviour continues or escalates, it is a good idea to seek advice and support. Most universities and workplaces now have services that can provide advice on dealing with such situations, and we urge you to consult them.

Feedback

Throughout your life at university and in the workforce you will be asked to give feedback to peers, subordinates and superiors. The feedback may be on documents they have written, their performance on particular tasks, the way they handle clients, their plans for your course or department or many other things. Before you give feedback, think about what kind of feedback you would like yourself. The following are some generalised rules about feedback:

- It should be detailed and specific. It may feel good to hear someone say, 'Everything is wonderful; I have no suggestions for improvement,' but this leaves you with nowhere to go.
- It should be positive. This doesn't mean you want to hear only praise, but you do want to be acknowledged for your effort and the care you put into a project.
- If it offers criticism, it should focus on *how* you could improve things.

When people ask for your feedback, make sure you understand what areas they want you to focus on. Often they will have particular questions, or they may be unsure about particular areas of their product. They are more likely to be receptive to your ideas if you start with the issues they asked you to look at. You can go on to other areas later, if you need to.

You must also consider the possible long-term effects of your feedback. You are often in a continuing relationship with the people you are responding to, and need to preserve or enhance a good working relationship.

In the context of all of these comments, here are some general suggestions for giving feedback that will help your listeners to improve, and will not deflate or dispirit them:

- Start with what you liked about the project. This will give your listeners a sense of being valued, and will create a springboard for the rest of the discussion.

- Acknowledge your listeners' aims in the project. This will show that you are 'on the same wavelength'. You might also find you misunderstood the purpose of the project, and you may change your response.

- Acknowledge any problems or hindrances that the people might have had in the project – there is no value in criticising people for things they had no control over. Listen carefully to their explanation about these hindrances.

- Focus on suggestions and alternatives, rather than on destructive criticism. If appropriate, help your listeners set timelines for anything they need to do in response to your feedback.

- Try to explain your reactions in unemotional terms, so that your feedback is descriptive rather than evaluative. Be sensitive to any intense reactions to your feedback from your listeners, and discuss these openly.

- Don't overload your listeners with unnecessary details – if you give too much detail, they may not be able to absorb it all.

Listening to feedback

As we stated above, all interpersonal communication is a two-way process. As well as thinking about how you can give feedback constructively, you need to consider how to listen effectively to feedback from other people. Feedback may take place in a formal one-to-one meeting, but in university contexts it is most likely to happen in a classroom, studio or professional practice setting. This feedback is often given in a group context, by your lecturer, supervisor, peers and group members, and this public environment may add to the stress you experience in listening to it. Here are some general suggestions:

- Try not to feel threatened or defensive. If you are aware that you are starting to react in this way, avoid the temptation to interrupt the speakers, to justify yourself or to 'go on the attack'. Try to remain still and quiet until you have heard what the speakers are saying.

- Rephrase or clarify the meaning of anything you are doubtful about. (Say something like, 'So what you are saying is …'.) If you do this, you will sometimes find you have the wrong impression of what the speakers mean, or they realise they are being unfair and soften their criticism.

- If the speakers ask for specific changes in the project, in the product or in your behaviour, work with them to write down exactly what you will do, what they will do and the deadlines for all of this.

- After you leave the feedback meeting, you may decide you want to make a written record of what was said. Write it clearly and simply, make sure you date it and – if appropriate – send it to the people who gave you the feedback. You might check this document with a colleague who was not involved in the situation before sending it.

Receiving online feedback

Most online teachers feel concerned about the impact of their feedback on their students. Since these teachers have no experience of their students face to face, they don't know how each student will respond to feedback, and they're not able to mitigate the difficult aspects of critique with their eye contact, tone of voice and body language.

If you have received feedback online that disturbs or confuses you, take a few deep breaths, then follow some basic steps:

- Re-read the feedback several times, trying to focus on what the teacher is guiding you to do.
- If you're still unsure after this time, email your tutor (or contact them in one of the ways set out for your unit).
- Resist the temptation to start by being aggressive or accusatory – you will achieve more if you ask for further information, clarification or support than you will by being confrontational.

Small talk

People need to engage in small talk when they are with people they don't know very well. *Small talk* is exactly that: it is about small subjects, so it is not deep or probing enough to intimidate anyone. It helps people feel safe enough to communicate together. Whether you need to establish some rapport so that you can work on an assignment, or you need to complete an activity together, those of you who can listen well and engage in conversations about everyday things (i.e. those who are good at small talk) will achieve more success in your first year than those who find this type of communication difficult.

The content of small talk is insignificant. It consists of things that are both easy to say and easy to respond to. Discussing the weather is the classic example. For you, this may consist of talking about the fact that you have no air-conditioning in your car and so are really hot, or discussing the weather the previous weekend and how it affected what you had planned to do. Or you might chat about the type of food at the campus canteen or café, the state of the lecture theatre you are in, or the weird layout of your department building. Small talk invites the other person to give an opinion, but it's about a subject that is neither intimate nor controversial, so it's not intimidating.

In your professional practice you may want to put your client at ease at the beginning of a meeting, particularly if this person is likely to feel uncomfortable initially; for example, if you are a healthcare professional working with a patient or a lawyer greeting a nervous client for the first time. In such cases, the ability to engage in small talk with your client will make the situation easier.

So, while you are in your first year of study, take any opportunity that requires you to make a quick link with another person and practise your small talk.

ACTIVITY 13.4 Small talk

With a partner

Have one student assume the role of an elderly patient and the other the role of a young resident doctor, nurse or medical imaging scientist. Suppose you are waiting together for the moment when a specialist will arrive to take the patient through a stressful procedure. The student who is the young professional must initiate and maintain relevant small talk with the patient for two minutes.

In a group or a class

Think of real-life situations that could require you to successfully engage in small talk with another person (especially situations that could arise in your future profession). Share with the others in your group what sort of small-talk subjects you could talk about, and how you could discuss these topics.

Working with people with a disability

The term 'people with a disability' has now replaced the term 'disabled people', in order to emphasise the *people* rather than the disability or the condition of being disabled. The Commonwealth *Disability Discrimination Act* was established in 1992 and is overseen by the Australian Human Rights Commission. This Act defines disability as:

> • total or partial loss of the person's bodily or mental functions; or
> • total or partial loss of a part of the body; or
> • the presence in the body of organisms causing disease or illness; or
> • the presence in the body of organisms capable of causing disease or illness; or
> • the malfunction, malformation or disfigurement of a part of the person's body; or
> • a disorder or malfunction that results in the person learning differently from a person without the disorder or malfunction; or
> • a disorder, illness or disease that affects a person's thought processes, perception of reality, emotions or judgment or that results in disturbed behaviour (Australian Government 1992, 5). 99

During your time at university and in your future professional life you will certainly communicate face-to-face with people with a disability – at university these people might be your lecturers, your peers or people you work with in professional-practice situations; in your professional life they might be bosses, colleagues, clients or (if you are a health professional) patients. You should take opportunities to talk to these people about their experiences of living with a disability because the more you understand their perspectives and life experiences, the more effective you will be in your interpersonal communications with those who live with a disability. Do not feel embarrassed if you initially feel awkward in these communications, but focus on developing your interpersonal communication capacities. Remember, also, that not all disabilities are visible. Be alert to possibilities that people have disabilities you were not initially aware of, and that less visible disabilities can sometimes increase the pressures on people in face-to-face situations rather than decreasing them.

It is very important that you think carefully about the way you speak with and about people with a disability, not just to protect them from discrimination but also to protect yourself against developing prejudices – the link between using discriminatory language and the way we see the world is very strong. (See the Queensland Government Department of Communities, Child Safety and Disability Services 2012 document *A Way with Words: Guidelines for the Portrayal of People with a Disability* at **https://www.qld.gov.au/disability/documents/community/way-with-words.pdf** and the Australian Network on Disability at **https://www.and.org.au/pages/inclusive-language.html** for excellent discussions of language use.)

Students with a disability

You, the reader, may have a disability, and if so we hope that your university experience will be a positive one. All universities have specific support areas that are there to assist you in your studies – if you choose to use them. We understand that you may want to start your university studies without the 'label' of a disability, but if you are able to speak to your university's counsellors, support services or equivalent, they can put in place processes that will support your studies.

Negotiation

When you negotiate, you work with other people to reach an agreement or settlement about an issue that affects you all. *Negotiation* has a number of implications:

- It usually refers to a multi-step process in which the people or groups of people involved set down their positions on the issue, then come together to reach some kind of settlement. We do not generally use the term 'negotiation' for a dispute that arises suddenly and is then resolved 'on the spot'.
- It suggests that some kind of transaction or bargaining takes place, and that the two or more people involved are equally powerful, or at

least have something to offer each other. We do not use the term for a situation in which one person has power over the other. For example, you do not negotiate with an employer who has decided to sack you, or with a lecturer whose unit you have just failed. In these situations, you might request they reconsider their decision, but you have no bargaining position for a negotiation.

Negotiation has become a popular term in business disciplines, but is as important in other disciplines. Look for opportunities to develop your negotiation skills during your university studies.

Tone

Be aware of the *tone* of your negotiation – you must come over as reasonable and willing to listen to the other side and to work for some kind of consensus. If you are very aggressive, you may achieve what you want in the short-term, but you may also alienate the people you are negotiating with and cause them to avoid working with you in the future.

Try not to consider the other person or people involved as 'the enemy'. This is difficult when much of our language encourages us to see people with whom we must negotiate as opponents or 'the other side'.

Assertiveness and aggression

To be a successful negotiator, you need to learn to be assertive. Don't confuse this with being aggressive. Being *assertive* means stating clearly what you want and standing up for your rights without attacking other people.

In many cultures, women are socialised into being unassertive. Assertive women can be seen as not being feminine, and be labelled as 'stubborn', 'bossy', 'aggressive' or 'hormonal' when they behave in ways seen as normal in men. For female students, this can be made worse when they study in courses in which they are in the minority. Some universities encourage women to enrol in science and engineering courses in an attempt to alter the gender imbalance in these courses.

One way women and girls may respond to negative labelling is by being passive. Female students in a university may defer to male students and academics, choose to be silent and unobtrusive in classrooms and fail to participate in class activities. We challenge all of you – male and female students – to develop your assertiveness, without becoming aggressive, in the following ways:

- Stand up for your opinions and rights.
- Be honest and concise. This doesn't mean you have to say everything you are thinking, but that you should give the information that you think everyone needs to achieve a good outcome.

- Be focused. Stay on the subject, without degenerating into being critical or abusive. When people are being aggressive to you, you might try a technique some people call 'broken record', where you continually repeat your main point calmly and unemotionally.
- If a situation becomes untenable – for example, if the other person continues to be abusive or aggressive – walk away. You can resume negotiations later.

Tip for improvement

If your voice is usually quiet or high-pitched, practise lowering its pitch a little. A lower pitch can help you feel calmer and more confident, and thus prompt your audience to listen more closely.

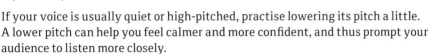

ACTIVITY 13.5   Assertiveness role-play

Five participants are required for this role play: a lecturer, an ignored student, a supportive student, an aggressive student and an observer.

Role-play the following situation: Three students in your discipline have completed a group project, and are explaining it to their lecturer and answering questions about it. The lecturer focuses attention on the first two students (A and B), directing all questions their way and completely ignoring the third student (C). The third student is assertive, trying repeatedly to participate. The supportive student (A) is aware that one of them is being ignored and tries to include them. The other student (B) becomes aggressive, trying to force the lecturer to look and listen only to them.

After the role-play, hold a debriefing session in which the participants discuss how they behaved, how they responded to each other and how the other participants' behaviour affected their reactions. The observer gives feedback on the role-play and on the debriefing session.

Successful negotiation

Consider the following techniques to achieve successful formal negotiations, whether at university or in your professional life.

Take your time

Try to allow enough time in meetings for all parties to present their position fully. Be careful about setting very short deadlines. If a deadline is unavoidable, schedule enough meetings before that date to make sure all people have been heard.

Bargaining

Think of the negotiations as a series of acts of bargaining. If you have prepared your negotiating priorities thoroughly, you will have a clear idea of the basis from which you can bargain.

Dealing with deadlocks

If you reach a deadlock in the negotiations, try to give them a renewed impetus by employing any of the following tactics:

- Refer back to what both parties have to offer to the issue to reignite the sense of goodwill.
- Summarise the position you have already reached in the negotiations. This can clarify any misunderstandings, and can sometimes allow either party to see a way through the deadlock.
- Ask the other group to suggest a way out of the deadlock, or suggest one yourself.
- Close this meeting, and agree to come back together in a different way in the near future – for example, if there are more than two people involved, one of you from each negotiating team might meet in an informal setting; or each team might invite one new person with a different perspective or a different skill to the next meeting.

Win–win solutions

Sometimes it is possible to rephrase the two negotiating positions so that both sides gain from the negotiation. Negotiating groups may think they are arguing for two opposing positions, whereas their positions can both be achieved in the same solution. This requires that you listen carefully to what the other people say they want, and that you phrase your position as precisely as possible.

Face-saving solutions

Sometimes members of the other party can see the value of your position, but have problems accepting it because this would mean they would lose face with their colleagues, clients, fellow students and so on. You will reach a solution in this situation if you find a way to help the other side save face while accepting your position.

You might be able to do this, for example, by writing a public statement that adopts some of the wording of the other side's position to present your own case.

Conflict resolution

The term *conflict resolution* is used commonly in the professions, particularly in the business professions, and is a synonym for 'successful negotiation'. Many websites list useful strategies for conflict resolution, and most of them incorporate the negotiation strategies listed above. See the 'Useful weblinks' section at the end of this chapter for links on conflict resolution.

Some negotiations fail

Sometimes, despite your best efforts, negotiations fail – that is, you are unable to agree on a plan that meets your requirements; or members of the other group are not convinced that they want what you have to offer at the 'price' you are asking. Don't assume this is a permanent situation, however, especially in a work context – you may be able to reignite the negotiations at another time, perhaps when the personnel of the other group changes. If negotiations fail, make a note to yourself to revisit the proposal at some time in the future.

ACTIVITY 13.6   Negotiation role-play

This role-play requires groups of at least three people: one community group member, one representative of an appropriate professional body and one observer. Other group members can take the roles of extra community members or extra professional people. The negotiation is between the community group and a professional body that is seen as negatively influencing the community – for example, an urban planning group keen to provide high-density housing for a large number of people in a particular community; an engineering organisation responsible for constructing a tunnel under the community's land; or a juvenile justice organisation seeking to build a youth detention facility in a particular community.

Conduct the role-play, with the observer making notes on the negotiation techniques, tone and approach of the participants.

After the role-play, all members debrief by discussing how they felt about their own behaviour and responses, what made them want to cooperate and what made them resist the other members' suggestions. The observer feeds back comments to the group about the role-play itself and about the debriefing.

Successful meetings

Meetings can range from very formal business meetings to less formal planning meetings. As a student, you are most likely to be involved regularly in less formal meetings; however, for your future professional life, it's also important for you to understand how to create effective formal meetings. Much of this section applies specifically to formal meetings, but it will be easy for you to adapt this information to suit informal group-project meetings. (You will find more on successful group work and teamwork in Chapter 15.)

Meetings conducted via online platforms such as Webex, Zoom and Microsoft Teams are becoming more common as people increasingly take advantage of flexible working arrangements. It can be easy to forget that you are in a formal meeting when online – if you are in need of some humour, you can search for 'awkward video conference moments' or similar to find some very funny stories!

Remember that when you're online, turn-taking and eye contact can be even more important than when you are meeting in person. Think about where you have your camera located so that you are naturally looking at others when you are watching other speakers on-screen. As tempting as it may be, avoid multi-tasking such as writing emails – this usually results in you appearing to be disengaged with the proceedings and you may miss important information. If you are working from home, talking with your family or housemates about avoiding interruptions will help to ensure that you maintain a professional appearance during these calls, whether they are for work or for study.

Student reflection 13.1   Meeting in the online space

As someone with a very busy schedule – working, parenting, and all that goes with these roles – being able to have meetings with my supervisor online has lots of benefits. I don't have to spend an hour in the car each way travelling to campus, I don't have to find babysitting for my children, and I can more easily fit the session in around my other jobs. However, I do sometimes feel like I'm missing something... a personal connection, perhaps. It's harder to make small talk with someone when you're seeing them through a computer screen, and sometimes it feels like the meeting is less important because I'm sitting in my bedroom rather than being in a more formal space. I'm grateful that the technology is available to meet face-to-face this way though, as without it I would struggle to progress my studies at the moment.

Katie Fielding, Education PhD student

However formal your meeting will be, you need to consider three separate stages, as described below.

Before the meeting

How well you prepare for a meeting will control how successful it is likely to be. You need to consider issues including:

- your purpose and the outcomes you hope for
- attendees
- venue, date and time to suit the purpose and attendees
- negotiation strategies you will employ if disagreement arises.

Creating an agenda

For most meetings, it is wise for the chairperson to create a written agenda and circulate this to attendees before the meeting, so that they will know what to expect and can prepare their positions and any necessary documents. The agenda might be no more than a list of topics to be discussed; it might also note which attendees will take responsibility for particular items. You can see examples of agendas on many of the useful websites listed at the end of the chapter.

Representing an organisation

Often you will attend a formal meeting on behalf of a particular organisation. In these cases it is your responsibility to speak to relevant line managers before the meeting to prepare your position.

Beginning the meeting

In Australia, professional meetings are increasingly introduced with an Acknowledgement of Country, where the chairperson acknowledges the local Indigenous group, caretakers of the land where the meeting will take place. This acknowledgement can be a single sentence such as 'I acknowledge that this meeting is being held on the traditional lands of the [appropriate group] people', or 'I acknowledge that this meeting is being held on Aboriginal land and recognise the strength, resilience and capacity of Aboriginal people in this land.'

On the other hand, here is the more detailed acknowledgement published by Curtin University's Centre for Aboriginal Studies:

66 Acknowledgement to Country (Boodja)

Curtin University would like to pay our respect to the Aboriginal and Torres Strait Islander members of our community by acknowledging the traditional owners of the land on which the Bentley Campus is located, the Wadjuk people of the Nyungar Nation; and on our Kalgoorlie Campus, the Wongutha people of the North-Eastern Goldfields. **99**

(Curtin University n.d.)

During the meeting

In almost all situations your meeting will be run by the chairperson, whose role is to welcome attendees, introduce the agenda and then keep the meeting on track. Usually the meeting secretary will make notes about what has been discussed, and will document the decisions made and the attendees who will take responsibility for implementing them. This person will later create and circulate a document called the *minutes* of the meeting. If finances are relevant to your meeting, a treasurer will present a budget, which will be discussed at the meeting.

If conflicts arise during the meeting, the chairperson can initiate any of the negotiation strategies outlined earlier in this chapter.

After the meeting

The chairperson needs to review each meeting after it has been conducted, reflecting on its success and on what needs to be followed up before the next meeting. If you are a committee member, you may have been set a task for the next meeting, and you must consult with relevant colleagues so that you can represent their interests in that next meeting. Before the next meeting, you will receive the minutes created by the secretary, and you should check to ensure these reflect what was discussed. If amendments are necessary, you can request them at the next meeting.

ACTIVITY 13.7 Agenda, meeting and minutes

This activity for a group of about six people starts with a shared task that requires at least one meeting. In your group, choose an appropriate situation or have one set by your tutor. One person must take on the role of the chairperson, one the secretary and one the treasurer (if relevant). All other members are meeting attendees. Work through the following process:

1 All members work together as a group to create an agenda for a meeting on your chosen situation.
2 Conduct the meeting, with the chairperson coordinating, the secretary taking the minutes, the treasurer taking charge of the budget (if relevant) and the other attendees participating.
3 Have all members work together to create the minutes.
4 After the meeting, reflect as a group on what you did well; what problems you faced and how you resolved them; what you would do differently next time; and what you have learned about conducting successful meetings.

REVISION TOOLS

↘ Revision activity: Revise these ideas

1   Listening is an active rather than a passive activity. By being actively engaged in listening, you will improve your own understanding of the information and ideas presented, and remember them better, as well as encourage the speakers to be livelier in their presentation styles.

2   Your own cultural background and personality influence the amount of space you feel comfortable maintaining between yourself and others.

3   In all study and work situations, you are likely to communicate with people with a disability, and you need to understand how to relate respectfully to these people.

4   Giving and receiving feedback can be very challenging; you need to practise doing both effectively. This can be particularly difficult for those studying online.

5   Negotiation involves individuals or groups of people who have some bargaining power with each other. It will be valuable for your future professional life to develop your negotiation skills in many situations.

6   Meetings can range from informal to formal, but all require that you understand your purposes and the processes you will adopt.

↘ Thinking activity: Critical and reflective questions

1   In what ways do I communicate successfully face to face, and in what ways do I need to improve my communications?

2   What issues need to be considered when conducting meetings in an online space, such as via Webex or Zoom? What are some of the benefits of having meetings using such platforms, and what are some of the disadvantages?

3   How may interpersonal communications be important in my future professional life?

4   When considering face-to-face communications in classrooms and professional situations, we often notice the extroverted people first. However, in what ways can introverted people be successful in interpersonal communications? Thinking about people I know who are introverted, what makes them successful? If I consider myself introverted, how can I enhance my capacities to communicate well in face-to-face situations?

↘ Useful weblinks

Consult the following resources for extensive further information about face-to-face communication:

Proxemics

Jenkinson, P. 2017. *Nonverbal Code: Proxemics (Space)*. YouTube video. **https://www.youtube.com/watch?v=a-mZ7EDO_38**.

Working with people with a disability

Queensland Government Department of Communities, Child Safety and Disability Services: 'A Way with Words: Guidelines for the Portrayal of People with a Disability': **https://www.qld.gov.au/disability/documents/community/way-with-words.pdf**.

Australian Network on Disability: 'Inclusive Language': **https://www.and.org.au/pages/inclusive-language.html**.

Negotiation and conflict resolution

Fisher, Fred. 2013. *Building Bridges between Citizens and Local Governments to Work More Effectively Together Through Managing Conflict and Differences*: **http://www.gdrc.org/decision/BuildingBridges.pdf** (Chapter 5 focuses on negotiation).

Helpguide.org: 'Conflict Resolution Skills': **https://www.helpguide.org/articles/relationships/conflict-resolution-skills.htm**.

Society for Human Resource Management: 'How to Resolve Workplace Conflicts': **https://www.shrm.org/hr-today/news/hr-magazine/pages/070815-conflict-management.aspx**.

University of Notre Dame: 'Conflict Resolution Skills and Techniques in the Workplace': **https://www.notredameonline.com/resources/negotiations/6-simple-workplace-conflict-resolution-techniques**.

Successful meetings

Charles Sturt University: *'Club Starter Guide'*: **http://www.csu.edu.au/__data/assets/pdf_file/0010/148546/CSU-Club-Starter-Guide.pdf**.

University of South Australia: 'Managing your Project Meetings and Making Them Worthwhile': **https://lo.unisa.edu.au/mod/book/view.php?id=424250&chapterid=69982**.

University of Western Australia: 'Guide to Effective Committee Meetings': **http://www.governance.uwa.edu.au/committees/principles/meetings**.

REFERENCES

Australian Government. 1992. *Disability Discrimination Act 1992* s 37. Canberra: Federal Register of Legislation. Full text is available at **https://www.legislation.gov.au/Details/C2018C00125/Download**.

Brown, Nina. 2011. 'Edward T Hall: Proxemic Theory, 1966.' **https://escholarship.org/content/qt4774h1rm/qt4774h1rm.pdf?t=o0wtd6**.

Curtin University Centre for Aboriginal Studies. n.d. 'Acknowledgement to Country (Boodja).' Accessed July 16, 2020. **https://karda.curtin.edu.au**.

Intercultural communication

CONTENTS

> 66 My advice to international students is to always keep an open mind and be respectful by first honoring the culture and values of the people of that land. Expose yourself to various experiences and diverse peoples. Do not to make assumptions of others by relying too much on your own cultural and ethical background. Also, when you feel unsure, it's always best to check that you really do understand what your peers are trying to say by questioning them, repeatedly and using different methods if needed; this will help avoid misunderstandings. 99
>
> *Mortigou Labunda, MBA (International) graduate from Sabah (Borneo)*

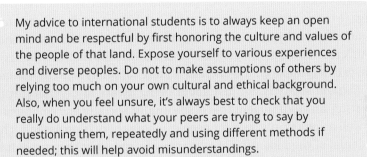

Key concepts

As a student in the higher education community you have opportunities to develop not only capabilities associated with your chosen discipline, but also your *intercultural capabilities* – or what some label 'cultural competence'. (The term 'intercultural capabilities' is broader than 'cultural competence', but the latter is also used.)

A central component of these capabilities is your ability to communicate with empathy and respect with people from various cultures. When we refer to intercultural capabilities in this higher education context, we include your:

- awareness and understanding of your own cultural perspectives
- knowledge of other cultures
- level of cultural responsiveness to others
- skills and confidence in cross-cultural interactions.

A reference to 'intercultural capabilities' will be included in your institution's list of graduate outcomes, which you are expected to achieve by the time you complete your studies, no matter what course you are studying. For example, Monash University (2019) names two all-encompassing graduate capabilities, one of which states that the University prepares its graduates to be 'responsible and effective global citizens who: engage in an internationalised world; *exhibit cross-cultural competence*; and demonstrate ethical values.' As a student you should work on enhancing your 'cross-cultural competence' or capabilities so that when you graduate you can help make your workplace a more *culturally safe* environment.

Cultural safety is not just about being aware of diversity; it is about creating 'an environment that is spiritually, socially and emotionally safe, as well as physically safe for people; where there is no assault, challenge or denial of their identity, of who they are and what they need. It is about shared respect, shared meaning, shared knowledge and experience of learning together' (Williams 1999, 213).

Here are some other concepts specifically relevant to investigating communication in a culturally diverse tertiary environment. The idea of *culture* is very broad but for this text, we define it as the shared set of beliefs, knowledge, history, world views, values, traditions and protocols for behaviour of a particular group of people. Your culture is influenced by many aspects of your lived experience, including ethnicity, gender, sexuality and class. Many of these factors are visible to others – such as skin colour, facial features, dress and language– and this can lead to members of dominant cultural groups discriminating against minorities. Whether you identify yourself as belonging to one of the dominant *majority* cultural groups or you are a member of one of the many *minority* groups, as a student studying in an Australian tertiary institution remember that we are all of equal status and we are all expected to communicate with each other in a respectful, inclusive manner. Even if you already know how to do this, explore this chapter further to see if maybe you could do this better.

In addition to becoming 'culturally capable', today there is also a greater commitment in Australian educational institutions to developing students' *Indigenous cultural capabilities* (ICC). ICC is about how proficient you are when working with Indigenous Australians and in addressing issues related to Indigenous Australians. Your institution may refer to this in its list of graduate capabilities with words similar to those used by Universities Australia (2016):

> **66** Through interactions with Aboriginal and Torres Strait Islander classmates and staff, and understanding more about our history and its continuing legacies in Indigenous communities, the skills and capabilities of the nation's future service providers, planners and professionals can be strengthened. **99**

Your institution may have a plan to achieve this. See the YouTube video *GA5 Culturally Capable When Working with First Australians*, created by Griffith University in 2018, explaining what this is all about (see the 'References' section at the end of this chapter for details). Curtin University was the first university to have a Reconciliation Action Plan (RAP), which has as one of its aims to 'develop a greater understanding of how our different pasts and cultures are part of our shared history and shared future' (Curtin University 2020).

Last, we include the term *diversity*, which is used loosely to label the way we are all different to each other. These differences include aspects of our identity that are fixed (such as race and ethnicity) and aspects that can change during our lives (such as language and religion). This chapter focuses on improving communication skills among people of diverse races and ethnicities, with an aside section on non-sexist communication.

The communication process is dynamic

Appropriate protocols for communication change over time, so use current, reliable local resources that offer guidelines on how to communicate with Indigenous Australians. For example, use resources from the Reconciliation Australia website; and, especially for health students, we suggest resources on the Australian Indigenous Health Infonet website. (See the 'Useful weblinks' list at the end of this chapter for details.)

Intercultural communication describes the communication process among people from a range of cultural groups that enables them to reach a shared understanding that is acceptable to everyone in those groups. The term is complex and you will find various explanations but for this text, we like the simple definition that 'it is the interaction of people from different cultural backgrounds' (Alexander et al. 2014, 28).

Because people often use the term 'intercultural communication' to refer to communication among people of diverse ethnic/racial backgrounds, and since this is very significant in multicultural Australia, this is the focus for most of the chapter. But please don't forget the many other subcultural groups we mention.

ACTIVITY 14.1   Strategies to challenge prejudice and discrimination

You can work on this activity alone, with another student or in a group.

Read the following statement in a paper published by UNESCO and discuss what it means:

'Many who encourage intercultural competences are coming to understand that people either are competent jointly, or are incompetent, but there is no such thing as one person being interculturally competent alone' (Leeds-Hurtwitz, 2013, p. 38).

The tertiary environment

Opportunities

As stated, Australian tertiary institutions comprise students and staff members from a wide range of cultural groups. This culturally diverse environment is a source of great richness – intellectually, emotionally and spiritually. At its best, it gives us opportunities to broaden our sense of who we are, develop our understanding of others and increase cultural competency, and thus to make good relationships across our communities.

In an academic context, working with culturally diverse groups can bring many advantages. For example, it gives you opportunities to experience:

- different ways of engaging with academic processes (e.g. writing and researching) that are culturally competent
- different approaches to problem solving
- different perceptions about issues
- a variety of experiences to apply to discussion
- new professional and interdisciplinary links with people and organisations outside your current experience.

Wherever you have come from before you started your tertiary studies, you want to eventually feel like the student in Student reflection 14.1.

 Student reflection 14.1 **Growing to meet the challenge**

I went from a high school that had 200 students to a university with 20 000. It was a bit weird and lonely at first, but I made friends with people in my units and after that I really started to love uni. It can be really fast-paced and difficult to keep up with, but you grow to meet the challenge and after each semester there's a sense of accomplishment for how far you've come.

Kaylene Schutz, Bachelor of Psychology student

Check the World Economic Forum website

Watch the *Davos 2017: Maintaining Innovation* video on YouTube (see **https://www.youtube.com/watch?v=zd6J_AweAjQ**, or search this title), which emphasises the importance of collaborating with people from different cultures and working among people of other cultures to inspire innovation. Professor Alice Gast, President of Imperial College, London, states in the forum that, since 1940, around 40 per cent of those who won Nobel Prizes for physics and chemistry were living in a foreign country at the time they won the prize.

Challenges

On the other hand, a multicultural environment also creates possibilities for confusion and misunderstanding that are not present in a monoculture. Some people may respond with fear to those who look different from them, and this fear may be heightened by linguistic and behavioural differences.

If you are a recent migrant to Australia or a student visiting from another country, or perhaps an Indigenous Australian student from a remote community, we encourage you to be actively involved in higher education even if your culture is very different from the dominant culture. Also, if English is an additional language for you, then you have much to offer your fellow students and teachers – even if the communication process is challenging. You will gradually develop both your Standard Australian English language skills and your knowledge of the local student culture (note the advice from Mortigou, the international student who is quoted at the beginning of this chapter). The more opportunities you take to communicate with people of other cultures, the more easily your English-language skills will develop.

Avoid making assumptions

Remember that making assumptions about others based on how they look is always fraught. The key is to always be respectful and friendly, and to try to get to know the other person. This doesn't mean you have to become 'best mates'. However, if you must work or study together, exchanging a few simple details about your backgrounds will help you start to get to know this person. Focus on trying to communicate with another *person*, not on trying to get to know another 'culture'.

If you are a student who speaks Standard Australian English only and who is part of the dominant, majority local culture, be aware that you are likely to be in a more comfortable, powerful position in comparison with students from minority cultures. Your institution will have in place diversity policies or principles to guide the behaviour of both staff members and students. Here is one example from the Student Code of Conduct at Edith Cowan University (2020):

> 66 Respect the opinions and diversity of fellow students, lecturers, tutors and other professional staff, including refraining from using offensive or derogatory language. 99

Case study: Australia's First Nations

As a tertiary student who is part of a culturally diverse community, communication is about more than respecting the rights of different people; it is an opportunity to challenge and educate yourself in a variety of worldviews, including the different ways people communicate. In Australia, especially during the past few decades, in our schools and places of higher education we have become more aware of the richness of Indigenous knowledges. Many descendants of Australia's Aboriginal and Torres Strait Islander, or First Nations, who have survived colonisation are sharing or rediscovering the knowledges of their ancestors, which enhances our learning – and how we communicate.

At this point, note that Australia's First Peoples usually prefer to be identified by their distinct 'nation' or language group, just as people from, for example, Italy would prefer to be known as 'Italians' rather than 'Europeans'. For example:

- Australian National University is situated in the country of the Ngunnawal and Ngambri peoples. For information about what the university offers First Nation students, see **https://www.anu.edu. au/students/information-for/indigenous-students**.
- Curtin University's Bentley campus is on Whadjuk Noongar country. The Whadjuk people are one of the 14 groups that make up the Noongar nation, which covers the south-western area of Western

Australia (see South West Aboriginal Land and Sea Council, 2020 for more information).

However, if you are a First Nation student, or if you have worked or studied with people who belong to a First Nation, you may be aware that many people do not know the names of the various nations or language groups and are often unsure about how to refer to them. If you want to refer to the wider group, many of Australia's First Nations prefer the words 'Aboriginal and Torres Strait Islander peoples' to distinguish the many peoples on the mainland and Tasmania, from those of the Torres Strait Islands. When speaking, it is also common practice to use the term 'Aboriginal' as a noun, because the word 'Aborigine' has negative historical connotations for many people. If you're unsure about the correct conventions, ask your lecturer or your First Nation friends, or do further research by exploring the useful weblinks listed at the end of this chapter. Student reflection 14.2 shares the experiences of Yamatji Elder, Richard Nelly, on the continuing experiences of racism in Australia.

Student reflection 14.2 — Racism still exists, so reflect on what you can do to address this

The following reflection comes from Kathleen Nelly, a Yamatji Amungu woman born in Perth, Western Australia. Kathleen quoted words from her grandfather to add to her argument that everyone needs to still keep working at making the society more fair and just – especially for First Nations. These sentences were the powerful conclusion to her Communications, Culture and Indigenous Perspectives in Business case study report entitled, 'The Case of Mr Ward':

'My grandfather Richard Nelly is a Yamatji Elder, he once told me that "At 60 years of age I have experienced more discrimination as an Indigenous Elder, than I ever did as a young Indigenous footy player in the 1970s; racism has changed exponentially." (Richard Nelly, unpublished 'interview', 2016). Although he said this to me four years ago, it reminds me that Aboriginal people have fought racial discrimination for many years, and still do'.

Kathleen Nelly, Commerce student

Capitalisation

The terms 'Indigenous Australian' and 'Aboriginal' are both used, and it is accepted protocol to always write these with an upper-case 'I' and 'A', respectively, if you are referring specifically to the First Peoples of Australia. Use the excellent information from the Gulanga Good Practice Guides at the ACT Council of Social Service (ACTCOSS) (2016) website. See details in the 'Useful weblinks' list at the end of this chapter.

Inclusive communication

Inclusive language is language that aims to embrace everyone who could find a particular message or words relevant to them. Using inclusive language is relevant to successful intercultural communication, and is also crucial to your wider communication skills. Inclusive language does not label people according to their gender, race, religion, sexuality or other cultural group; nor does it label a whole group according to the behaviour of individual members of that group. That is, it is language that does not use stereotypes.

The value of inclusive communication

Universities, professional groups, employers, governments and many other organisations have published policies insisting that their members use inclusive language. You will almost certainly find an inclusive language policy on your institution's website.

On their website, The Centre for Universal Design Australia (2020) quotes and promotes the advice of Hemsley et al. (2018), who in an article in *The Conversation* tell us how to be inclusive in our communication with people who have a disability, which in turn results in us being more inclusive of all people. The website notes these authors have explained useful information under each of the following headings: Remove communication barriers – meaning everyone has a right to communicate with others and deserves respect; Prepare for communication success; and Build a conversation together. The *Conversation* article also adds a fourth condition, that you should 'use communication aids and alternative strategies when you talk.' (Read the short, helpful article online.)

Some cynical words have been written in past decades about inclusive language, which is often called 'politically correct' language, by critics who claim it is unnecessary and that it makes the English language tortuous. Even if you have heard such gripes, we hope that, as you read this text, you will appreciate the importance of inclusive, accurate language. Both as a tertiary student and as a worker in your future profession, you will be expected to adapt your language to be inclusive of all people. By using inclusive language, you:

- present a more accurate and sophisticated view of a situation
- connect with everyone in your audience and don't marginalise anyone
- avoid offending people who belong to minority groups, as well as those who do not share your values
- avoid the risk of developing an 'us-and-them' mentality in your audience, or of positioning anyone as more powerful than another; we are all equal and we need our language to reflect this
- help develop your audience's (and your own) intercultural capabilities, since language and thought are inextricably linked.

Finally, remember that you are working in an academic context, and that inclusive language is considered to be the most appropriate language.

Verbal communication

Communicating with peers who speak languages other than the language(s) you understand will probably be your greatest challenge. This is likely to be the case whether you speak only English or if English is your second (or third, fourth or fifth) language.

Because you are studying at an Australian higher education institution, everyone is expected to be able to communicate in Standard Australian English. However, different levels of proficiency, different accents and different cultural backgrounds might make communication challenging at times. Have you ever heard someone trying to translate a word or phrase from their language into English and struggling because they can't find the equivalent concepts? Such experiences make our dialogue with people from other cultures both exceptionally interesting and potentially frustrating.

Our suggestions

Apart from words, issues such as accents, grammar, colloquialisms and turn-taking are all associated with language differences. Here are some strategies to help intercultural communication exchanges. Some of them may be particularly useful if you are doing a team project (see Chapter 15) with peers who have language backgrounds different to yours:

- Listen carefully, giving the other person your full attention.
- When you listen to, and speak with, others, expect that you will understand them. Avoid immediately putting up a 'block' inside your head when you hear the other person speaking English differently to you.
- It's okay to ask someone to repeat what they have told you (even if you do this more than once).
- Write down any keywords or decisions. Writing or printing words will help everyone clarify or even reiterate what has been spoken.
- Exchange text messages, emails or use social media. Talking face-to-face or using synchronous chat can be daunting if you don't feel confident in English, whereas text messages, emails and using social media, such as Messenger, give you time to check what you have written (and you can practise writing English).
- The way we talk and leave spaces in between our responses in a spoken exchange is referred to as *turn-taking*. Australians with a European ancestry generally leave very little time when responding to each other. They may even start talking before other people have finished what they are saying. In informal settings this is usually okay, but in more formal settings – such as business meetings – such overlaps in people speaking are not as acceptable. However, the variations in turn-taking

among people of different cultures can be quite marked – in some cultures interrupting someone is unacceptable in all situations. If this is true for you, and if you also find speaking Standard Australian English difficult, then you may find it initially challenging to have conversations with local students. In a multicultural group, a good rule is to take your cues from the slowest speaker, and adjust your pace and turn-taking accordingly. Here are some more suggestions:

- *If Standard Australian English is your first language:* If you have spoken at your normal pace and your colleague indicates he or she is experiencing difficulty understanding you, try to speak a little slower and enunciate your words clearly. Your intonation patterns, accent or use of colloquialisms may make conversations with a person for whom English is a second (or third) language a bit more difficult.
- *If Standard Australian English is not your first language:* Some of your peers may not be familiar with your accent, so you, too, may find initial conversations challenging. Don't worry if you use incorrect grammar while you are speaking – keep talking and occasionally ask your listeners if they've understood what you have said.

Non-verbal communication

Dress and general appearance

Differences in dress and gestures may seem only superficial, but dress – including hairstyle, accessories and makeup – along with the way we use our bodies to communicate are expressions of who we are. As previously noted, dress is a visible marker of one's culture, and it may create a barrier between you and other people even before you talk to them. This can also be true of the way people express themselves with their bodies – especially their hands and eyes (e.g. not making eye contact).

Our suggestions

Be open-minded and accepting of everyone. It is inappropriate to comment on someone's appearance, even if the person is a classmate. Non-verbal cues (such as hand gestures) can also add complexity to communication. Refrain from making any negative non-verbal signs in front of people you don't know because these cues may be more offensive than you realise. If you are offended by particular non-verbal signs made by people from another culture, and if this person is one of your friends, then discuss this together.

Even if you don't make comments about another person's behaviour, your non-verbal reactions may create a barrier. Respond to every person as an individual, rather than as a representative of a culture that may be different from yours. Actively challenge and change your view, so that you see visible differences as interesting rather than threatening.

Different concepts of time

Organising group meetings can be an interesting opportunity for exploring different understandings of time. There can be differences in concepts of time not only among individuals but also in different cultures. Definitions of a 'brief meeting' or 'finishing on time' can vary markedly among individuals, and sometimes this can be linked to different understandings within an ethnic group. One Australian example provided by student Tomzarni Dann is of 'Broome Time': where a meeting lasts for as long as you need or want it to.

Our suggestions

When you organise to meet your peers, specify what time you are meeting and for how long. When you talk about doing some 'quick' research on a subject, nominate how many hours you are thinking about. Until you know each other, and given there are many ways to understand time, be flexible, don't make assumptions and keep talking to each other about this subject.

ACTIVITY 14.2 An intercultural communication experience

This activity will be useful for first-year classes as a combined ice-breaking and intercultural communication activity.

As an individual or with another student

Talk to someone whose cultural heritage is different from yours.

1 Share information with each other about your name(s). Discuss the history of your family name, and share stories about your given first name.

2 Share information about what you consider to be important about the following aspects of life. Also discuss the attitudes of your close family members, since these may differ from your own attitudes. For example:
   - *Language:* Which languages can you speak? Do your family and culture value being able to speak more than one language?
   - *Family:* What definition of family have you learned at home?
   - *Work:* What occupations do people in your family have? What jobs are regarded in your family as 'being successful'?
   - *Study:* What attitudes do you have towards education? What would your family consider a 'good education'?
   - *Relationships:* What are your family's ideas about marriage?
   - *Beliefs:* Have you grown up with knowledge of a particular belief system or religious tradition? What is this tradition, and what are some of its key beliefs and practices?
   - *Food:* Which foods have special meaning in your culture and/or family?
   - *Gender roles:* What are your attitudes towards gender and sexuality? (For example, are there expectations about gender specific roles?)
   Politics: What political traditions did your parents or grandparents follow?

3 Based on your answers to Question 2, identify two similarities and two differences between you and your colleague.
   - Discuss two values, beliefs or practices you admire in each other's culture.

- Discuss two values, beliefs or practices you would find most challenging if you were to live in the same household as the person you are talking to.

In a class or a group

Record the names of the various countries of origin of each class member, then note the countries of origin of class members' parents and grandparents. Now partner with one or more people who have different ancestry to you, and work through the questions above. Share the group's outcomes with each other.

ACTIVITY 14.3 Reconciliation in action

In a class or a group

Discuss your responses to the following questions.

1 What is the name of the First Peoples of the land where your institution is situated?
2 Is your institution involved in any activities with that group of people? Find examples.
3 Does your institution do anything associated with 'reconciliation'? Perhaps it has a special reconciliation strategy or a plan – such as a 'Reconciliation Action Plan' (RAP). Go to the 'Who has a RAP' link on the Reconciliation Australia website (**http://www.reconciliation. org.au**) to see if your educational institution has a RAP. Whether or not it has a RAP, find out what your institution is doing in relation to reconciliation and what you can do to be involved.

An important aside: inclusive language and gender references

As you have probably noted, we enjoy exploring how we use the English language within an academic context, and we believe it a powerful tool to do good. We also ask that you be aware people can feel offended by language that presents them as inferior to the dominant group, or that stereotypes them, ignores them completely or refers to issues in their lives that would not be considered relevant in the dominant group. For example, people can be offended by:

- words such as 'girls', 'love' and 'honey'
- references to their appearance – including weight, clothing and facial features – in situations in which such references are irrelevant
- phrases such as 'you're being a girl' or 'what an old woman!' being applied to men in a derogatory way
- the use of the words 'man' and 'men' to mean people in general
- phrases that focus on their family and home life more than on their achievements in their professional world – for example, a non-binary senior executive being described as a wife and mother first, rather than being acknowledged for their professional experience.

Be accurate

If you're referring to a group of people and you know they are all men, then you can use the word 'men'. If you're referring to a group that includes men, women and non-binary people – or you are unsure who you are addressing – then simply use an appropriate inclusive term such as 'people', 'humans' or 'human beings'.

Be relevant

If, for example, you're writing about the career of a female executive, focus on her professional achievements, not her appearance, family circumstances, behaviour or relationships with co-workers.

Avoid gender-specific terms

Find substitutes for gender-specific labels (but avoid clumsy words such as 'waitperson'). If you can't think of an appropriate term, write your sentence in another way. Here are some useful alternatives (if you look up 'inclusive language' in a search engine you will also find many options):

- 'humans' – not 'mankind'
- 'staff the office' – not 'man the office'
- 'supervisor' – not 'foreman'
- 'executive' – not 'businessman'
- 'police officer' – not 'policeman'.

Many career groups today label men, women and other genders with the same word (e.g. 'author', 'priest', 'manager').

Be careful how you use pronouns

The English language contains mainly male and female pronouns when using the singular form. However, as there are several gender identities, and some people are non-binary in how they identify themselves, remember to be respectful and inclusive, especially as has already been noted, when communicating with a mixed group of people you don't know. There are several resources available to help you. This clear, user-friendly website by Minus18 provides instructions and examples on the respectful use of personal pronouns: **https://pronouns.minus18.org.au**. They also have a downloadable language guide on their website. Here are a few methods used by professional writers:

- They make sentences plural, which avoids this problem because 'they' is inclusive of male, female and all non-binary people; for example, 'Psychology students need to have open minds and must be inquisitive yet accepting in their approach.'
- They rewrite sentences to leave out the pronouns; for example, 'A psychology student needs to have an open mind and be inquisitive yet accepting in approach.'.

- They always replace 'he', 'his' and 'him' with 'they', 'their' and 'them', even when talking about one person: 'A psychology student needs to have an open mind and they must be inquisitive yet accepting in their approach.'

A final word on respect

You may be part of a specific local community of university students, but, more significantly and more overtly than ever before, you are also a member of the global community. The growing use of technology in higher education has changed the way this community functions, as the authors of The New Media Consortium's 2017 *Horizon Report* note:

66 The advent of educational technology is spurring more collaborative learning opportunities; at the most basic level, wikis, Google Docs, social media and messaging apps enable seamless sharing and communication (Adams Becker et al. 2017, 20). 99

No matter how challenging your communications with people who are different to you might be, however, it is your responsibility, as a citizen of this global community, to always show respect.

As Curtin University Emeritus Professor, Simon Forrest, Whadjuk, Ballardong Noongar Elder said to one of the authors in 2017:

66 Students sometimes ask me, 'Simon, why do you focus on our differences instead of our commonalities?' My answer is, 'It is easy to talk about stuff we have in common; the challenge is talking about our differences. We need to learn how to do this and acknowledge our differences – and to do this with respect. 99

ACTIVITY 14.4 Language that offends

As an individual or with another student

1 List phrases or words that were considered highly offensive in your grandparents' generation but no longer seem offensive today.
2 Conversely, list phrases or words that were not considered offensive in your grandparents' generation but are now highly offensive.

In a class or a group

Share these lists with the class and compile group lists of phrases and words. Discuss what these lists suggest about changing values in society.

REVISION TOOLS

↘ Revision activity: Revise these ideas

1 While studying, you need to develop your intercultural communication capabilities to a level where you are self-aware about using inclusive language in all areas of life. The paramount principle for inclusive communication is respect for everyone.

2 Being able to communicate with others with empathy and respect begins with having awareness of your own cultural background and the various cultural groups you belong to.

3 Knowing the name of, and developing awareness about, the First Peoples of the land where you are living is a useful foundation for developing your intercultural communication skills.

4 Using inclusive, accurate language when referring to people is paramount in academic writing and presenting

5 Language, because it is part of culture, is dynamic, so keep informed and continually check in with people about the meaning of words and the best choice of words to use for various situations.

↘ Thinking activity: Critical and reflective question

1 During the past year, when have I heard/read some non-inclusive, offensive language and what action did I take to respond?

2 What is the story of my ancestry, going back to my great-grandparents' generation?

3 Which cultural groups do I belong to?

4 What can I do to learn more about the land area and the First Nations who lived/live where I was born?

5 What are my thoughts about what Prof. Simon Forrest, the Elder in Residence at Curtin University, said about respect? (See page 320.)

6 What two things can I do as a student to build inclusivity and respect among my peers?

7 Do I know about the United Nations' Declaration on the Rights of Indigenous Peoples (or UNDRIP)? (If not, go to **http://www.un.org/esa/socdev/unpfii/documents/DRIPS_en.pdf**.)

8 What is one culturally safe practice that I think would enhance the workplace of my future profession?

↘ Useful weblinks

Australian Institute of Aboriginal and Torres Strait Islander Studies (AIATSIS) is the premier website for current information about how to research Australia's First Nations, as well as relevant, ethics and language. See **https://aiatsis.gov.au**.

The Australian Human Rights Commission website has a range of information on Aboriginal and Torres Strait Islander people and issues related to them; see **https://humanrights. gov.au/our-work/aboriginal-and-torres-strait-islander-social-justice**.

The Australian Indigenous Health Infonet offers a range of excellent resources, which will be especially useful for students studying in the health sciences. The site is maintained by staff members at Edith Cowan University. See **http://www.healthinfonet.ecu.edu.au**.

Newcastle University's 'Inclusive Language Guidelines' provide an example of how one educational institution offers specific, useful suggestions for words to avoid, and words to use to help us be more inclusive; see **https://policies.newcastle.edu.au/document/view-current.php?id=140**.

Twelve Canoes. 2008. This remains one of the best online basic resources available for people who want a brief and meaningful overview of the history of Australia's First Peoples. The website was created by people from Indigemedia Incorporated, Christensen Fund, South Australian Film Corporation and Screen Australia. See **http://www.12canoes.com.au**.

Flinders University's inclusive language guide can be found here: **http://www.flinders.edu.au/equal-opportunity/tools_resources/publications/inclusive_language.cfm**.

Minus18 (**https://www.minus18.org.au**) is a website with extensive information. We suggest you download their language guide from the 'Resources' section of the website.

The State Government of Victoria's 'Aboriginal Cultural Competence Framework' can be found at: **http://www.dhs.vic.gov.au/__data/assets/pdf_file/0006/580848/cultural_competence_matrix_2008.pdf**.

This University of Queensland blog discusses topics and issues relating to LGBTIQ+ (lesbian, gay, bisexual, transgender, intersex and queer+) people. See 'What does LGBTIQ+ mean?': **http://www.uqu.com.au/blog-view/what-does-lgbtiq-mean-29**.

The University of Western Sydney's 'Study Smart' website has useful information about several relevant topics, including cultural literacy; see **https://www.westernsydney.edu.au/studysmart/home**.

University of Wisconsin–Milwaukee's (2020) website on gender-neutral pronouns is simply formatted and easy to navigate; see **https://uwm.edu/lgbtrc/support/gender-pronouns**.

What is Standard Australian English, and why is it 'standard'? See this Board of Studies, Teaching and Educational Standards NSW (BOSTES) webpage to find out: **https://ab-ed.nesa.nsw.edu.au/go/aboriginal-english/what-is-standard-australian-english**.

REFERENCES

ACT Council of Social Service (ACTCOSS). 2016. *Gulanga Good Practice Guide: Preferences in Terminology When Referring to Aboriginal and/or Torres Strait Islander Peoples.* **https://www.actcoss.org.au/publications/capacity-building-resource/gulanga-good-practice-guides**.

Adams Becker, S., Cummins, M., Davis, A., Freeman, A., Hall, Giesinger, C., and Ananthanarayanan, V. 2017. *NMC Horizon Report: 2017 Higher Education Edition.* Austin, Texas: The New Media Consortium. **https://www.unmc.edu/elearning/_documents/NMC_HorizonReport_2017.pdf**.

Bryant Keith Alexander, Lily A. Arasaratnam, Roberto Avant-Mier, Aisha Durham, Lisa Flores, Wendy Leeds-Hurwitz, S. Lily Mendoza, John Oetzel, Joyce Osland, Yukio Tsuda, Jing Yin & Rona Halualani. 2014. 'Defining and Communicating What "Intercultural" and "Intercultural Communication" Means to Us', *Journal of International and Intercultural Communication* 7:1: 14–37, DOI: 10.1080/17513057.2014.869524

Curtin University. 2020. *Curtin's Reconciliation Action Plan 2014–2017.* Bentley, Western Australia: Curtin University. **https://about.curtin.edu.au/values-vision-strategy/indigenous-commitment/aboriginal-reconciliation-plan**.

Curtin University. 2017. 'Inclusive Language Procedures.' **http://policies.curtin.edu.au/local/docs/policy/Inclusive_Language_Procedures.pdf**.

Edith Cowan University. 2020. 'The Student Code of Conduct'. **https://intranet.ecu.edu.au/__data/assets/pdf_file/0010/853885/ECU-Student-Code-of-Conduct.pdf**. (PDF is downloadable from **https://intranet.ecu.edu.au/student/overview**.)

Griffith University. 2018. *Griffith Graduate Attribute: Culturally Capable When Working with First Australians.* YouTube video. **https://www.youtube.com/watch?v=L_-OkJv6qeo&feature=emb_logo**.

Hemsley, B., H. Turnbull, J. Steel, L. Bryant, and M. Brunner. 2018 'We Can All Help to Improve Communication for People with Disabilities.' *The Conversation*. **https://theconversation.com/we-can-all-help-to-improve-communication-for-people-with-disabilities-101199**.

Johnston, M., and S. Forrest. 2020. *Working Two Way: Stories of Cross-cultural Collaboration from Nyoongar Country*. Singapore: Springer Nature.

Leeds-Hurtwitz, W. 2013. *Intercultural Competences: Conceptual and Operational Framework*. UNESCO (United Nations Educational Scientific and Cultural Organization). **https://en.unesco.org/interculturaldialogue/resources/132**.

Monash University. 2019. *Aligning Course Outcomes Educational Standards Frameworks*. **https://www3.monash.edu/pubs/2019handbooks/alignmentofoutcomes.html**.

South West Aboriginal Land and Sea Council. 2020. 'Language', *Kaartdijin Noongar – Noongar Knowledge: Sharing Noongar Culture*: **https://www.noongarculture.org.au/language/**.

Universities Australia. 2016. *Indigenous Strategy 2017–2020*. **https://www.universitiesaustralia.edu.au/policy-submissions/diversity-equity/indigenous-higher-education/**. Canberra: Universities Australia.

Williams, Robyn. 1999. 'Cultural Safety – What Does it Mean for Our Work Practice?' *Australian and New Zealand Journal of Public Health* 23 (2): 213–14. **http://onlinelibrary.wiley.com/doi/10.1111/j.1467-842X.1999.tb01240.x/epdf**.

World Economic Forum. 2017. *Maintaining Innovation*. Filmed January 2017 at the World Economic Forum Annual Meeting, Davos. YouTube video, 56:05. **https://www.youtube.com/watch?v=zd6J_AweAjQ**.

↘ CHAPTER 15

Teamwork

CONTENTS

Teams and groups

Theorists, particularly in the business disciplines, have written a lot in the last few decades about the differences between groups and teams. The word 'team', according to some writers, suggests a tighter, more focused collection of people than the word 'group'. The members of a *team* have shared goals and work together to achieve them. The term *team building* is used in the business world in discussions of how people might improve their work environment – a successful company needs to build a team rather than just a loose group of people.

On the other hand, some studies use the term group rather than team because it is seen as a more inclusive term, and one less focused solely on the business world. *Groups* can include family, friendship, social, cultural and sporting groups we all belong to in various parts of our lives, very few of which we would label teams.

In this chapter we use the term 'team', since we are concerned with groups structured to complete formal collaborative tasks with shared goals. Teams might be self-selected or placed together by a lecturer. (Note that most of the ideas we discuss do not relate to informal groups, such as those formed for a specific, brief tutorial or workshop activity.)

Research into teamwork

At first-year level you are unlikely to need to research teamwork issues in depth, so this chapter is designed to give you just a taste of some of the theory and practice of teamwork, which you may delve into in more detail in future years of study within your particular disciplinary context. Many of our colleagues comment to us that they teach classes on teamwork in their courses (e.g. business, planning, psychology, project management, medical imaging, education and so on) to second- and third-year students, but are happy that we give students a general introduction in our classes. For these reasons we have chosen not to focus in depth on any of the current research, but instead to just mention one of the main figures in this area, Dr R. Meredith Belbin. If you want to read more widely in the area, we suggest you start with this author.

Friendship teams and organised teams

Teams can be self-selecting – that is, individual members may choose to work together because they're friends or because they think they'll be able to collaborate well together. On the other hand, some of you will be placed in teams by your lecturers or tutors, either randomly or in order to create a particular mix of people (e.g. a blend of genders, young and mature-aged, people from different cultures or people majoring in different disciplines).

If you are placed in a team of people you hardly know and initially feel uncomfortable, take heart: most of our students begin by wanting to work with friends, but finish their organised collaborative experience feeling happy they were placed with individuals they knew less well as it gave them the opportunity to see new perspectives and meet different people.

Benefits of working in teams

Many of you will choose to work with others in an informal way (e.g. sharing resources, studying together for exams or discussing ideas over coffee). We urge you to look out for fellow students you can collaborate with in these ways. Doing so will make your university life a more positive experience than if you remain solitary, and your marks are likely to be higher because your fellow students will develop and challenge your ideas.

There will be times, however, when you are forced to work with others in a formal team, often to produce work that will be assessed (e.g. writing a team report, making a team oral presentation). You can enter into this as a positive experience, since team collaboration can have many advantages.

ACTIVITY 15.1 Working in a team – benefits

With another student or as an individual

Think of a past experience you have had as a member of a team, in work, study, or within an organisation. (Resist the urge to focus on horror stories!) List the benefits you gained from these experiences, both in team outcomes and in your personal development. Remember that even difficult experiences can have beneficial outcomes!

In a group or a class

Compile a list of the benefits your group or class members have gained from teamwork. Were there any unexpected benefits?

Working in teams does not come easily to many people, but you can learn to do it better by understanding how you behave when you are in a team, as well as what makes teams succeed and fail. The more practice you get in teamwork at university, the better you are likely to become in doing it for your future professional life (or, at least, the more you are likely to learn what *not* to do next time!).

Student voices – benefits of teamwork

Our students speak in the reflections following of some of the benefits they have gained from working in teams. Even though she generally prefers to work alone, the student in Student reflection 15.1 recognised many different benefits, both for herself and for the quality of the work the team produced.

Student reflection 15.1   The benefits of teamwork

I was surprised at how well I worked with the group, as I often consider myself more apt to perform in solitude. I felt that a lot of ideas I offered helped to develop not just my own role, but those of others in the group, and the depth of the project as a whole. I suspect it was beneficial for the ingenuity of the project that I could bring relevant personal experiences to the table, something I never imagined would be appropriate in an academic setting. The group responding so positively to my ideas has changed how I perceive my capabilities where group projects are concerned. This is a big positive for me because, despite my anxieties surrounding it, I recognise learning to work in a group is important in this setting, as it will prepare me for working with others in my professional life. I also have realised how helpful it is in terms of generating ideas; it often seemed each team member's ideas would spark those of another.

Kathleen Ward, Communications student

Even students studying online are often required to work in teams. Don't be afraid of this – the online environments used by educational institutions have come a long way in recent years. While they may not completely mimic the face-to-face communication we are used to, online environments can still provide opportunities for meaningful teamwork, as can be seen in Student reflection 15.2.

Student reflection 15.2   Teamwork and studying online

Overall, I enjoyed the process, the work and interacting with the other group members. I can see the value in group work in university, especially when studying online. It adds another dynamic which I find more engaging. Personally, when motivation can be waning, I found having the responsibility to the group to at least check and answer any questions beneficial. I was happy with how the others reacted to my statements and questions so I think these negotiations have reinforced my approach to collaboration.

Sean Dixon, Construction Management student

Conflicts in teams

No one claims, however, that teamwork is always easy and rewarding. You need to be aware of some of the difficulties that might arise, and of techniques to deal with them. Experience and research indicate that, even if you choose your own team members rather than being placed in a team by a lecturer or tutor, your team is likely to experience some conflicts working together.

ACTIVITY 15.2   Working in a team – difficulties

With another student or as an individual

Look back over your past experiences as a member of a team, in work, in study and/or within organisations. List the difficulties you have experienced in these situations, both in the team outcomes and in your personal development.

In a group or a class

Compile a complete list of the difficulties your group or class members have experienced in teamwork. Are there issues that seem to come up frequently? Why do you think this might be?

Student voices – some difficulties of teamwork

Both our online and our on-campus students experience the full range of difficulties you are likely to have identified in Activity 15.2. For example, Student reflection 15.3 discusses the common problem of team members not pulling their weight.

Student reflection 15.3   Teamwork doesn't always go smoothly

I understand that not everyone is available at the same time but, unfortunately, I believe that certain team members really let us down and we missed out on their contributions, suggestions and expertise because they didn't make an effort to communicate and work together as a team. They barely, if ever, made a contribution and it was as though they were not even there. Is it really that hard? Did they not realise that we were supposed to be working as a team? I found this to be frustrating and disappointing because if we were creating this [project] in a real work environment, they would have left the rest of the team to pick up the slack and caused a lot of unnecessary stress. I have learnt that you can't always rely on others, especially in a team environment, because there is always going to be someone who either doesn't participate as much as others or not at all.

Marcia Doolan, Fine Art student

Student reflection 15.4 highlights the importance of everyone in the team having clear and compatible expectations, of 'being on the same page'.

Student reflection 15.4   The importance of clear expectations when working in teams

Upon reflecting, I realise my vision of this project was larger than the other team members. This highlights the importance of clear communication in the early stages and discussing all the specifics to ensure that the vision shared is equal across the board.

A challenging aspect for me, however, was communication. I did not feel that all of our team members were equally engaged. Communicating over a discussion board felt stilted as there were often 'days' (or never) before certain group members responded and even when I tried to motivate people to respond by suggesting a deadline, it didn't work! Having only four active team members didn't help and I understand that people have different life circumstances but the discussion board often felt more like a void than a group environment. Perhaps my expectations were too high.

Alina Morelli, Professional Writing student

Dealing with team conflicts

Different types of problems might affect the progress of your team; however, you might be able to solve a simple problem by simply expressing yourself calmly. For example, if some members don't contribute to discussion, you could encourage them to speak; if others have not completed particular required tasks, you could ask them why not, and then perhaps organise a group member to coordinate tasks and remind everyone when each deadline approaches.

But what can you do to resolve major conflicts of the kind that seriously interrupt the team's work and cause emotional distress among its members? The first step is to recognise that conflict is a common feature of any extensive team experience, and that working through the conflict leads to more flexible relationships and responses to the team tasks. Note that your team is not a therapy or self-help group, and you are not qualified to analyse each other's personal issues, but you need to work together to complete a task. The following sections provide some actions you can take to resolve conflict.

For additional detail about how to deal with team conflicts, look at the section on negotiation in Chapter 13.

Advice for working in online groups

Following is a range of advice from our online students about working in teams. The contexts of the advice vary, and some ideas contradict others, but we hope you can find some useful suggestions for enhancing your own online teamwork.

Take opportunities to speak to each other synchronously if they arise

Online groups often work together on discussion boards. This can be for a variety of reasons: this is the method available through the Learning Management System (LMS); a record of communication is required to award marks; the organisation wishes to be able to have a degree of control over the content; and so on. However, some students choose to communicate in additional ways outside of the LMS. If you do choose to take part in conversations outside the official spaces provided by your course, do so with care. Chapter 10 has some advice about communicating through social media.

In some units, students are asked to submit oral presentations. This can be a daunting prospect, particularly if you have chosen to study online because you would prefer not to have to work face-to-face with others. However, Student reflection 15.5 highlights the value of hearing fellow students speaking.

Student reflection 15.5   The value of oral presentations

Listening to the oral presentations was a huge turning point for me regarding group dynamics and how I perceived my fellow group members. It reminded me of Margaret Heffernan's mention of 'social capital'. Having that audio connection helped me to relate to everyone in a more humane context. This was something which surprised me. I previously hadn't thought it would play such a vital role in relating to the group and also had not realised how detached I had been until I genuinely connected through their voices.

Barbara Bozsik, Fine Art student

If you are working online without listening to formal voice recordings, it can be valuable to use FaceTime, Skype or a similar communication platform as a collaborative tool, as the student from Student reflection 15.6 recommends.

Student reflection 15.6   Some limitations of the discussion board

Only being able to communicate with other members over the discussion board imposed limitations on the group. The discussion board requires frequent checking to see if there have been additional posts or replies, which is not easy for students with full-time work commitments. This led to some tension in our group with some members starting work on an idea and then returning to the board to find the concept had changed as a discussion had taken place in the interim. For group work, particularly in the ideas stage, conference calls, Skype calls or face-to-face meetings would have helped to clarify the concept without misunderstandings and in a more productive manner.

Simon Blyth, Business student

Use asynchronous communication to defuse difficult situations

On the other hand, the student from Student reflection 15.7 found value in the discussion board – she struggled to work with a student who was becoming hostile, but found the distance in time and space created by the discussion board helped defuse the conflict.

Student reflection 15.7   **A benefit of using discussion boards**

Working as a group of three, it seemed apparent one member constantly felt a loss of power in this format. As a group, we made every effort to explain, engage and negotiate, however, when communication became hostile I found it difficult to respond. For me, this is where I benefited from the use of the discussion board as it allowed time for a careful, considered and respectful response.

Kristie Foenander, Fine Art student

Keep communication respectful and semi-formal, where appropriate

Student reflection 15.8 contains advice on communicating respectfully and in a semi-formal register that may be helpful to any team member.

Student reflection 15.8   **Respectful communication**

Working with people I barely knew, I was careful to keep the conversations semi-formal, to minimise offending or upsetting anyone, and maintain a sense of fairness during the negotiations. There were many different personalities in our group: some aggressive, others assertive. Some were timid and required encouragement to become involved. Maintaining the semi-formal environment was key in the positive development of these group discussions. I was aware that once this activity was over, I still have another three and a half years to spend with these students – I wanted it to be pleasant!

Geoff Barnes, Architecture student

Team roles

Think about how you have behaved and responded in a range of teams or groups you have worked within during your life so far. Although you may have held a variety of positions in these groups, research suggests that you will have tended to behave and respond in similar ways in most of them. For example, if you are a practical organiser and like to work efficiently to achieve your goals, or if you are enthusiastic and full of new and creative ideas, then you will have shown these tendencies in all your group experiences. Researchers describe these tendencies as your team or group *roles*.

A great deal of research has been devoted over the past decades to defining the various roles people adopt in teams. One of the best-known sets of roles has been developed by Dr R. Meredith Belbin and his team from Henley Business School (Part of the Henley Management College) in the UK, who claim that all team members adopt combinations of nine roles, as shown in the Belbin team role chart (reproduced in Table 15.1).

| Table 15.1 | The nine Belbin team roles |

Belbin Team Role	Contribution	Allowable weaknesses
Plant	Creative, imaginative, free-thinking. Generates ideas and solves difficult problems.	Ignores incidentals. Too preoccupied to communicate effectively
Resource investigator	Outgoing, enthusiastic, communicative. Explores opportunities and develops contacts.	Over-optimistic. Loses interest once initial enthusiasm has passed.
Coordinator	Mature, confident, identifies talent. Clarifies goals. Delegates effectively.	Can be seen as manipulative. Offloads own share of the work.
Shaper	Challenging, dynamic, thrives on pressure. Has the drive and courage to overcome obstacles.	Prone to provocation. Offends people's feelings.
Monitor evaluator	Sober, strategic and discerning. Sees all options and judges accurately.	Lacks drive and ability to inspire others. Can be overly critical.
Teamworker	Cooperative, perceptive and diplomatic. Listens and averts friction.	Indecisive in crunch situations. Avoids confrontation.
Implementer	Practical, reliable, efficient. Turns ideas into actions and organises work that needs to be done.	Somewhat inflexible. Slow to respond to new possibilities.
Completer finisher	Painstaking, conscientious, anxious. Searches out errors. Polishes and perfects.	Inclined to worry unduly. Reluctant to delegate.
Specialist	Single-minded, self-starting, dedicated. Provides knowledge and skills in rare supply.	Contributes only on a narrow front. Dwells on technicalities.

Source: Belbin Associates. 2017. 'The Nine Belbin Team Roles.' Reproduced with kind permission of Belbin. http://www.belbin.com/about/belbin-team-roles.

Understanding your roles

No one adopts one role at all times; however, most of us tend to adopt just a few roles, with one perhaps being stronger in some situations, while another is more dominant in others. Think, for example, what happens to you when you begin to work with a team of students in which no one has been appointed leader. Do you find yourself organising and coordinating the team? What if no one else takes up the organising role – would you then, however reluctantly, begin to do this?

It is very useful to explore these roles and build some sense of your tendencies. Here are some things to think about:

- First, realise that no one role is superior or inferior to the others – they are descriptions rather than judgements. Remember that each role makes contributions to the team, but also introduces weaknesses.
- Think of each role as a continuum – you will feel you are in the centre of some, while you are strongly at one end for others.

ACTIVITY 15.3   Team role activity

Look at the lists of contributions and weaknesses associated with the Belbin team roles (see Table 15.1). Rank the list from one to nine, with one being the role you feel most represents you, and nine the least.

Share your list with the class and discuss:

- Which role(s) comes up most frequently in your class? Which one the least? What problems or benefits might this present if you needed to work on a task together?
- Do you feel that this list accurately represents the roles you have observed people taking when you have participated in group work? What would you add or take out of the list?

View the TED Talk *The Power of Introverts*, by Susan Cain. Reflect on the ideas she presents about some of the problems she sees with the assumption that being an extrovert is better than being an introvert.

You can find this presentation by going to **https://www.ted.com** and searching for the title. (See the 'Useful weblinks' section at the end of the chapter for the direct URL.)

Successful teams

No role is more useful to a team than any other, and a successful team needs to include a combination of different roles. According to Dr Belbin's researchers, these roles can be grouped in three clusters, and teams are most likely to be successful when their members adopt roles from across the three clusters:

- *Action roles:* 'Completer finisher', 'Implementer' and 'Shaper'
- *Social roles:* 'Coordinator', 'Resource investigator' and 'Teamworker'
- *Thinking roles:* 'Monitor evaluator', 'Plant' and 'Specialist' (Belbin 2012).

Working in teams

The process of working in a team is similar whether your task is written, oral, performance-based or a combination of these, and whether it will take several weeks or an entire semester. This process involves having regular meetings, agreeing on goals, ensuring group members oversee particular aspects of the task and setting deadlines. Example 15.1 highlights some of the joys and frustrations of working in a group to complete a task.

In Chapter 16 we outline an appropriate process for working in teams to develop an oral presentation. When faced with a team writing task or performance-based task, you will go through the same process, so adapt our advice for the different focus of the task. For written tasks, make sure you also plan the writing process in conjunction with the relevant chapter in this book (report, essay, case study and so on).

Example 15.1 Teamwork: a student's experience of group work 'Sanditecture'

On 17th February 2020, before the pandemic hit, the first-year interior architecture students arrived at orientation day to be told that their first assignment for the year would be to build a sand sculpture. At our first official class we were separated into 20 groups and were designated a famous building to influence our concept for our final sand sculpture design. The following week, we were required to have our final design ready so that we could focus on our 2-day venture starting with an intensive sand sculpture training day and ending with a 5 ½ hour building and construction day.

Successes and challenges

Starting the semester off with a group project was a great way to build quick relationships, especially when you're just finding your feet. The project was a very fun and exciting way of starting conversation and bonding. Our group started with sharing all our own ideas for the assignment and how we were going to build this sand structure. We were all nervous about the reality of what we had to accomplish in such a short time, which brought us closer together as we had common ground. Naturally we all had different strengths and weaknesses, which we worked through respectfully by allocating duties that we all agreed upon. Communication was difficult as we didn't have a lot of time together to hash things out in person; however, making a digital group chat really helped us to discuss further ideas outside of class hours. On the day it was a very exciting time; it really brought out our true colours and the roles we naturally embodied such as the director, the organiser, the design developer, the support team, etc. We learnt that in every group there will be different work ethics, personalities, abilities and motivations and it's about working with all these factors to create an environment that ends successfully for each of us.

Sanditect challenged us in a new environment that most of us are not familiar with anymore which is the physical side of working. Instead of desks and chairs we had grass, sand and hot weather, instead of pens it was shovels and diggers, and the sore eyes from a screen turned into sore arms from pounding sand. It was a wonderful change as it really pulled forward the sense of building relationships by working through problems together immediately as there wasn't any other time due to our 5-hour deadline. Working so closely to the next group (who were technically our competitors) we were forced to share equipment

Figure 15.1 Courtnee's team sand sculpture, inspired by the Chrysler Building, in progress

and that simple interconnection brought out discussion. It was funny how quickly community was created and how quickly a lot of us were motivating other groups and helping with problems that we might have previously encountered. The best part was learning not only about these people that were similar yet different in many ways, but learning more about yourself and how you must adapt, compromise and maybe be uncomfortable. You realise at the end how much you have grown in learning, thinking and behaving in such a small space in time.

Advice for teamwork

If I was to give advice to the next group of first years it would be to try and be honest about your own abilities and thoughts up front, as this will help you and hopefully encourage others to create an open and responsible environment. By doing this you will be able to plan a clear path of expectations and work through problems that arise quicker, as you all already know where you stand on the project.

Courtnee Nichols, Interior Architecture student

REVISION TOOLS

↘ Revision activity: Revise these ideas

1 The term 'team' suggests a more formal, structured organisation than the term 'group'. Teams can be structured in order to create a particular mix of members, which can have many benefits for members and for the work produced.

2 By completing an assignment in a team, students can create a more diverse, thoughtful assignment than they would by working alone. In addition, they often develop their own personal qualities.

3 In contrast, students may struggle to communicate with other team members, may find others are not pulling their weight and may not share the hopes and expectations of their fellow members.

4 Online learning creates particular difficulties, but students can adopt a range of strategies to enhance their experience.

5 People consistently adopt certain roles in team situations. Teams require a balance of roles in order to be successful.

6 Whether a team assignment is oral, written, performance-based or a combination of these, students will need similar approaches to organising their teams.

↘ Thinking activity: Critical and reflective questions

1 What attitudes do I have towards group work in educational settings? Where do these attitudes come from? Have my past experiences in group assignments led me to make unfair assumptions about others?

2 How do I feel about group tasks or teamwork in situations outside of study? (For example, at work or in social situations.) If I feel differently than I do in a study situation, why might this be?

3 Referring to the team roles described by Belbin (see Table 15.1), which one would I like to develop further, and why did I choose this role? How do I feel about the 'weaknesses' that Belbin's roles suggest I might demonstrate when taking on a particular role?

4 At the end of a team project, how effective has my team been? What qualities have I noticed in myself, and what examples of my contribution illustrate each of these qualities?

↘ Useful weblinks

TED Talks: *The Power of Introverts*, by Susan Cain: **https://www.ted.com/talks/susan_cain_the_power_of_introverts?utm_campaign=tedspread&utm_medium=referral&utm_source=tedcomshare**.

University of Queensland: 'Group Work': **http://www.uq.edu.au/student-services/learning/group-work**.

University of New South Wales: 'Guide to Group Work': **https://student.unsw.edu.au/groupwork**.

University of Southern Queensland: '15 Tips for Effective Group Work at Uni': **https://social. usq.edu.au/study-tips/2014/08/group-work-tips**.

University of Melbourne: 'Working in Groups': **http://services.unimelb.edu.au/__data/assets/ pdf_file/0010/529777/Working_in_Groups_Update_051112.pdf**.

REFERENCES

Belbin Associates. 2012. 'A Little Bit Me, a Little Bit You.' **https://teamrolesbelbin.wordpress. com/category/team-role-reports**.

Belbin Associates. 2017. 'Belbin Team Roles.' **http://www.belbin.com/about/belbin-team- roles**.

CHAPTER 16

Presentations

CONTENTS

Presenting in tertiary environments

As a tertiary student, you will be required to deliver presentations in a variety of learning spaces. This chapter focuses on guiding you to make successful formal academic presentations in any learning space where speaking is integral to the presentation. It does not offer technical advice about software or learning management systems (LMSs); rather, it contains guidelines and strategies that will help you to give effective formal oral presentations in online and face-to-face environments.

Audience

As with all communication, you must first consider your audience, purpose and context. Apart from this golden rule, carefully check the instructions for your presentation assignment before using advice in this chapter. During the first years of tertiary study, your audience is likely to be your peers and lecturer. Think about what you know about the audience and what this will mean for your presentation. Consider the following questions:

- *What register (i.e. degree of formality) should I use?* It is unlikely that you will need to be very formal in a class consisting of peers (unless you are instructed to role-play). If, however, you are presenting to a broader group, adjust your presentation style to suit that audience. In this instance, you may be expected to speak more formally.

- *How does this audience influence what I say?* What content do you need to explain or define? What would interest your audience, and what might they already know? Do not assume everyone is as passionate about your subject as you are. For example, an engineering student who uses an entire presentation to explain a circuit diagram of a very complex, expensive car sound system may fascinate some class members, but others, including the lecturer or tutor, may become bored.

- *How will I maintain the audience's attention, and what interaction strategies will I use?* Few people are able to concentrate for more than 10 minutes without a change in pace and activity, so plan some audience interaction.

- *How will this audience affect how I look and speak?* How will this audience influence the non-verbal aspects of your presentation, including where you position yourself, how you dress and how you use your voice?

Purpose

You are likely to have more than one purpose for your presentation. You may wish your audience to be:

- educated (probably about a subject related to your discipline)
- convinced of a particular argument

- persuaded or challenged to change attitudes or viewpoints
- entertained
- active participants in the presentation.

Context

The primary context for a formal oral presentation is an academic one. You are usually being assessed, and are thus expected to have considered the assessment instructions carefully. Even if you are friends with people in your class, and however informal the register you choose to adopt, do not be too casual, and show evidence you are prepared by keeping to the allotted time and focusing on communicating clearly about the subject.

Also consider any specific instructions for the presentation. Here are some possibilities:

- *You are the subject 'expert' who must present ideas and inspire discussion.* This is a common tutorial presentation format, where everyone is expected to have done some preparatory work but you are the person who identifies the main ideas, provokes discussion and guides the class. In this context a successful presentation depends on you helping your peers to actively participate, while making sure the key ideas or facts are covered; so prepare questions, and answers, that will do this.

- *You are required to instruct your peers about a particular skill, such as referencing, evaluating a text or mastering a particular point of English grammar.* In this context the most successful presentations will be the ones that teach the skill most clearly, using the best examples and appropriate detail.

- *You must reflect on a site visit, case study, professional practicum or lecture by a visiting speaker.* This will require a brief description of the event; but this will depend on the type of reflection requested.

- *You are required to do an oral presentation of a written report.* Here, speak about something you (and perhaps your team) have completed in a written format. Do not simply read the report, but instead decide what elements of the report you will share, and how you will share (e.g. perhaps using visuals).

Content

Now you have the audience, purpose and context for your presentation, it is time to explore – research – and decide upon the content. You need to decide what content you want to include and what content you want to omit. As you do your research, keep reminding yourself about your audience, purpose and context (including the amount of time you have been allocated for the presentation).

Effective presenters have a range of strategies to keep on track during a presentation, depending on their personal style and skills in oral delivery. Here are some strategies for you to consider using while preparing for your presentation:

- Most presentation software has note-making capabilities, so use these notes on a mobile device, such as your smartphone or tablet, and position them where they will be easily visible. Practise scrolling through the points while you present. Make sure you can see the points easily when you glance at and scroll through them – this advice is also applicable if you choose to use printed notes. Include several visuals in your presentation (see the discussion of presentation aids later in this chapter), and use these as prompts as you deliver the content.

- Finally, whatever you do, do *not* write your speech in full and then read it aloud. This technique prevents you from maintaining eye contact and engaging with your listeners. It doesn't matter if you need to check notes or make a mistake – remember that the audience is expecting you to *present*, not read.

Structure

Just as in a formal written assignment, your oral presentation needs a structure that, unless you have been instructed otherwise, will consist of an introduction, a body and a conclusion.

Introduction

This is the place where you will establish your audience's expectations. Start confidently by doing the following:

- Entertain or interest your audience from the beginning. Start with a provocative idea, some interesting information, a personal anecdote or an entertaining quotation. (For ideas, see the section on audience interaction later in this chapter.)

- Appear relaxed and be prepared. Your classmates will forgive you for being nervous, but they will not be impressed if you are disorganised.

- Explain your central idea(s). In most cases, give a preview of the main points you will cover. It is often helpful to have these points in a visual format so everyone can read them. (Occasionally, you might choose not to provide a preview as part of a planned strategy.)

Body

Present your main points, explain them and give examples. Do not try to tell your audience everything you know about the subject – select the information appropriate for this audience.

How you structure this part of the presentation will vary depending on your purpose, and on the assignment instructions. For example, if you are instructed to:

- *present an argument*, then centre your presentation on your thesis statement. Progress logically through your ideas, using examples to demonstrate and prove the thesis
- *be the 'expert' on a particular topic* and lead the rest of the class in exploring the relevant issues, focus on providing a range of challenging thoughts and questions to guide further discussion
- *report on a practicum, site visit or professional experience*, organise your ideas chronologically, but make sure you include reflections on what you have learned from the experience
- *persuade your audience*, choose examples and use language designed to encourage them to accept your position. You might even use humour to establish a rapport with them, so they will be happy to be persuaded.

It is usually helpful to make the structure of the presentation clear to the audience, since it is easy to lose track of the main ideas when listening to an oral presentation. Refer back regularly to the notes or slide where you have outlined the key points, and make strong organisational comments such as 'And the third reason why ...'.

Your illustrative examples could include:

- personal anecdotes or stories
- historical events
- current events happening anywhere in the world
- ideas from primary or secondary research
- statistics
- graphics.

Conclusion

The conclusion to a presentation is very similar to one you will write for a formal essay; that is, it usually:

- signals you are about to finish your communication
- summarises the main points you have made
- makes sure your central idea, or thesis, is clear
- leaves your audience feeling positive about your presentation (e.g. by finishing with an interesting idea or question).

Use correct language and acknowledge your sources

Ask someone to check your spelling and grammar. If you have a spelling mistake on a projected slide it can look worse than if it was hidden in a paragraph in a long essay!

Always cite your sources within the presentation, and include a reference list towards the end. Be prepared to make this list available if requested.

Present with confidence

Now you have some ideas about content and structure, we will look at the crucial aspects of *how* the presentation will be delivered. First, we have a few comments about the idea of having 'confidence'.

Some of us are always comfortable in front of an audience, but for most of us, there will be times when such experiences make us feel nervous. This is normal, and most of us manage this nervousness and succeed in giving effective presentations. The trick we have learned is that, even if we feel nervous, we *appear* confident. So if you feel nervous, we advise you to practice pretending to be confident in front of your phone or laptop camera (or use a mirror), and remember: your audience can't see what you are thinking or feeling! When it is time to give your presentation, take three deep breaths before starting, make eye contact with the audience and smile. These simple actions should have two effects:

- They will help your audience feel connected and ready to listen to you.
- They will 'trick' you into feeling more confident.

Are you still feeling anxious about public speaking?

There are a number of useful resources online on this subject. Try using the strategies outlined under the heading '30 Ways to Manage Speaking Anxiety' on the University of Iowa (2020) website: **https://counseling.uiowa.edu/self-help/30-ways-to-manage-speaking-anxiety**. If these are not helpful, check your institution's counselling support services, since most universities offer free courses on overcoming presentation anxiety (for students and staff).

Audience interaction

In most presentations you will be assessed on how well you involve your audience, as Joel Kandiah, an accounting and education student, noted in Student reflection 16.1.

A good presentation uses a multi-sensory approach. It can incorporate questioning techniques, visual aids (e.g. PowerPoint, video or pictures) and other activities such as games or separating the audience into groups for a task. The more you get the audience involved in a presentation, the more likely they will respond positively to it.

Joel Kandiah, Accounting and Education student

Here are some suggested techniques to help you:

- Acknowledge your nervousness, or, very occasionally, you might need to explain any problems you might have with your voice or presentation techniques (e.g. 'I hope you can hear me OK during this presentation because I've got a sore throat'). However, you should *never* apologise in advance for problems with your content, organisation or preparation. Some of our students have started their presentations with statements like 'This talk is going to be really boring, but I hope you'll be able to sit through it.' Never do this, even if you think it – it will only put off your audience before you start!

- Ask your audience at the beginning what they know about the topic. (Be careful with this technique, though, since you will then need to respond very briefly to what is said without getting sidetracked or using up too much of your allotted time.) Whatever you decide, never assume you are the only person present who knows your topic; be humble, and acknowledge and involve the audience in exploring the subject. Introduce a brief initial audience activity. For example, you might poll people's opinions or backgrounds on a relevant issue using an app, showing the results on the screen before you begin, then repeating the poll at the end and comparing the results.

- Announce at the beginning that you will have a quiz at the end and, again, consider using an interactive app.

- Be aware of how everyone is responding to your presentation. If people seem confused, stop and ask them if they understand. If people are losing interest, change your position, or the pace or pitch of your voice.

- Be prepared for questions. Try to pre-empt questions when you rehearse with your peers. If you don't know the answer to a question, either ask other audience members to help out or acknowledge that you don't know and follow up later. You could also prepare some provocative comments for the audience at the end of the presentation to stimulate discussion.

- Become comfortable in how to use the presentation software of your institution's LMS. Find out what is available to support you both to prepare and deliver the presentation well before the date of your presentation.

Humour

One important aspect of audience interaction is the relationship you establish with the audience, and the use of humour can be a good way to establish this relationship. You can do this by using some of the many amusing cartoons, photographs and other visuals available on the Web, many of which can be used without seeking copyright permission. These can be particularly useful as 'attention grabbers' to be used at the beginning of a presentation.

Humour, however, can also be problematic. It is often culturally specific, and your jokes or 'funny' remarks may offend someone. As always, consider your audience carefully – your whole audience, including your lecturer or tutor – and think about whether what you plan to say might be offensive to any of them. Being aware of and expressing empathy towards people from backgrounds (e.g. race, ethnicity, religion, gender) different to yours is part of your tertiary education, as we discussed in Chapter 14. Be especially aware of the sensitivities expressed by minority groups in your class (e.g. a small number of women in a predominantly male class). Unless you are very familiar with everyone in your audience, be careful with your use of humour. Check Chapter 14 for further discussion about this.

ACTIVITY 16.1 Telling a story: an alternative way to get your audience's attention

With another student

Discuss how you might use storytelling in a presentation. Here, we are referring to telling your stories – not re-telling stories that belong to other people. You may have to consider similar issues about respect to those mentioned about humour, but storytelling is usually easier and more authentic. Discuss this with people who are good storytellers, then practise telling each other stories relevant to your topic. Critique how the content of the story and the way you told it enhanced your presentation. Note that there are several websites and instructive YouTube videos on how to use stories to enhance presentations. Two examples are *How to Use a Story to Start a Presentation* (see **https://www.youtube.com/watch?v=T7bk5csUzUo**), and a blog by Sarah Denholm that includes a section on 'Using stories in presentations' (see **https://improveyourpublicspeaking.com.au/are-stories-in-presentations-always-persuasive**).

Non-verbal language

When we discuss *non-verbal language* in a presentation, we are usually referring to anything about you that isn't related to words. This includes:

- voice quality
- eye contact
- posture, gesture and facial expressions
- appearance and dress.

Voice

When people say, 'It's not *what* you say but *how* you say it,' this often refers mostly to your voice. Here are important aspects about how you use your voice to help you deliver a more successful presentation:

- *Volume:* Do you speak too quietly? Is there a microphone for you to use if the venue makes it necessary?
- *Pitch:* Is your voice too high-pitched or low-pitched?
- *Pace:* Do you vary your pace to keep your audience interested and to add emphasis to important ideas?
- *Modulation:* Does your voice rise and fall as you speak, or is it monotonous?
- *Clarity:* Have you checked the pronunciation of keywords with someone who knows them? If you speak Standard Australian English as an additional language, will you feel more confident if you check your pronunciation with a native speaker?
- *Fluency:* Do you hesitate as you speak? Do you often include 'ums', 'ahs', 'you knows' and 'likes' (i.e. words and phrases that can be considered non-verbal because they usually don't add meaning to what you say)?

Do you speak fluent Australian English?

If your first language is not Standard Australian English and you are feeling anxious about presenting, use visuals and handouts to help you, so that you can be more confident your audience understands what you are saying. Refer to the section on handouts and links later in this chapter for further advice.

Eye contact

Maintaining *eye contact* during an oral presentation or looking directly into the camera (if you're presenting in online environments) can be difficult, but it is also important. For most presentations in an Australasian academic context, there is a direct correlation between the amount of eye contact you have with your audience and your presentation's success. Your listeners will stay interested if they feel you are talking to them directly.

Here are some suggestions about eye contact:

- Before you start speaking, force yourself to glance all around the classroom or lecture room. You don't need to look at each person separately – just move your eyes slowly to all parts of the room. If you feel intimidated by looking directly at one person, look at small groups of people instead.
- As you start talking, scan the room slowly, making eye contact with everyone as you go, but not holding any one person's eye, which will make this person uncomfortable (unless you want to silence someone who is not being attentive, of course!).
- Be careful not to focus your eyes only on the lecturer. It's understandable that you would feel the need to impress this person, or to check out their reaction to what you're saying, but force yourself to look at everyone equally.
- Don't ignore one side of the room or any audience members at other locations (e.g. whose presence is visible on a monitor or screen), since people who feel excluded may become restless. You may need to adopt some kind of pattern the first few times you give a presentation to make sure you move your eyes over all your audience. For example, you might look first at your online audience, then to each corner of the room, then into the middle, then back to the edges, and so on, to make sure you include everyone.
- When you need to look at notes or at a screen, return your eyes to the audience as quickly as possible. Do not talk to a screen; unless, of course, the presentation is being distributed online. Even then, remember to regularly look at the audience in the room as well as those who are online.
- If you find it particularly difficult to maintain eye contact, practise doing this before you make your next oral presentation.

Body language

How you use your body will vary slightly depending whether you are presenting online or face-to-face. For more specific information on presenting online, see the excellent advice on the website created by the University of Melbourne (details in the 'Useful weblinks' list at the end of this chapter). In all contexts, your audience and the aim of the presentation will influence your body language. Figure 16.1 presents some body language tips.

Finally, remind yourself that your peers and lecturers want you to succeed.

Figure 16.1   Some body language tips

Stance

Adapt the level of formality in your stance that will suit your audience – if you are speaking to a group of peers in a small room, for example, it may be appropriate to sit on the edge of a desk; if you are making a formal presentation to 200 people, on the other hand, you may need to be on a raised platform. If you are speaking to a camera and cannot see the audience, imagine people smiling back at you. If you are standing, aim not to move too much, since if you move around in a frenetic way your audience will be more involved in watching you move than in listening to your presentation.

Posture

Aim to stand, or sit, in a confident 'strong' way and avoid putting your hands in your pockets and looking too casual, even for a small group of your peers.

Gestures

Your gestures need to be natural ones. If you normally use your hands or arms to emphasise points when you are talking, continue to do this. However, avoid any gestures that will attract your audience's attention to what you are doing rather than to your ideas.

Facial expressions

Smile and try to have a natural, friendly facial expression as you begin your presentation. If you feel nervous, take two or three deep breaths and relax your jaw. Focus on what you want to say rather than on any feelings of nerves or embarrassment.

Appearance and dress

You need to consider your clothing and the way you present yourself (e.g. hair, jewellery) for your presentation. Sometimes your lecturer will require you to dress in a particular way (e.g. to wear business clothing). If you are not given specific instructions, you should appear neat, clean and tidy, and avoid any distracting clothing that will take your audience's attention away from the rest of your presentation – unless, of course, your clothing is integral to the presentation. Dirty clothes, as well as T-shirts with provocative words or designs, can be unnecessarily distracting. While these might be acceptable for normal classes, they are not appropriate when you are presenting to a group.

Presentation aids

For most presentations, using complementary visual or audio materials is valuable, since these:

- help you organise the content you are presenting
- allow you to present your words in an additional medium (some people learn better by reading the words they are hearing and seeing complementary visuals).

Before we discuss presentation aids, consider the physical or online environment where you are presenting.

Environment

You may not be able to choose the room or online learning platform where you will be presenting, but you should be able to control some aspects of the layout. If you're unfamiliar with the room, assess it before the presentation and think through any potential problems. Even if you are familiar with the room, and even if it is in your home (if you are presenting online), consider the following questions from your perspective as the presenter:

- Do you know how to use the equipment available? If you're unsure, check online for instructions or ask your lecturer to support you – especially if you are unfamiliar with new technology. If you are using your own devices, are they compatible with equipment in that classroom?
- Is the room of an appropriate size? If it is large and your audience is a small group, consider asking them to gather in one area so they can hear you (and so it will feel more welcoming).
- Will your presentation be distributed to locations other than the room you are presenting from? If so, how will you interact with people in the audience who are not physically in the same room but who you can see on a monitor?
- Can you control the lighting for projecting to any screens, or will you project to monitors on tables (if they are available)?
- You may be presenting in a classroom that is a collaborative learning space with a central podium and several monitors and tables around the room. However, you may also be in an old-fashioned lecture theatre or at your home desk. Wherever you are, remember that you – and maybe your group – need to hold the audience's attention, so become familiar with the space and, if possible, adjust the surroundings to make everyone comfortable.
- If you are showing a poster or a visual artefact, have you checked where to place it or how to project it so that it will be seen clearly by all audience members? For example, do you need to adjust the size and amount of text on your poster or slides? Note Example 16.1, showing one slide from Janelle Brown, who uses readily available stock library

graphics plus some simple text to help her explain key points in her PowerPoint presentation on 'Facilitation processes in Indigenous Australian Context'.

Example 16.1 PowerPoint presentation

The Need for Group Facilitation

To share knowledge, idea and concepts

To resolve issues

To obtain a shared vision for the future

Student reflection 16.2 includes some recommendations and tips for presenting online from your home.

Student reflection 16.2 — Presenting from your home desk

If presenting online and the audience can see you, be especially mindful about your background. Though you can often choose a virtual background, these may not always be suitable so make sure you check your camera before the presentation starts and are happy with what your audience will see behind you. Even more important can be what the audience can – or cannot – hear! Note what Kathleen learned from her experience as a first-year student:

I was at home for my online presentation and noise was a big impact, I recommend turning off all background noises such as phones and apps not in use on your laptop to prevent noises during your presentation. During the COVID-19 lockdown everyone was home, our neighbours and their kids were also home, I constantly had to speak extra loud to go over the children's noise next door and neighbours mowing lawns, etc. I recommend either recording at night or choose an alternative location to do your presentation if you have loud noises around you. My group recorded our presentation five times – in the end we recorded our final presentation after a group member's kids were asleep after 8pm! The more we did the presentation out aloud the better we got with public speaking and better at controlling the whole presentation.

Kathleen Nelly, Commerce student

Best use of software

There are many presentation software options, so, unless you are instructed to use particular ones, choose whatever you like. Whichever software you choose, we remind you that if you are delivering a presentation, it is always useful to have a back-up plan as to the technology you use, since no technology is foolproof. Below we have included a few hints that are most relevant to slides or fixed images:

- For projected images, use minimal text and include only keywords or main ideas. If you have several sentences you want the audience to read, consider the option of sending audience members a link or giving them a handout. Animating slides can make a presentation dynamic, easy to watch and engaging; however, use your discretion regarding the amount and style of animation. Look at the sample presentation in Figure 16.2 for an example of how you can achieve this.
- Always aim to implement the Principles of Universal Design so as to be as inclusive as possible of your audience (see **http://universaldesignaustralia.net.au**).
- Don't read slides aloud to the audience; instead, use them as prompts while you talk through details. Even if there are several monitors in the room and/or your presentation can be viewed on mobile devices, use 24-point (minimum) simple sans serif fonts (as per Universal Design principles). Also use a consistent background and font to allow space between lines and in margins, so that the content will not look cluttered. If you include a graphic, make it easy to read – enlarge it if necessary and, as already noted, always include a citation unless you created the graphic. Consider using a wireless mouse so you can move away from the computer and stand in the most appropriate places in the room.
- If the presentation is being distributed to other locations, check instructions about positioning for the cameras.

Example of presentation software

Figure 16.2 shows part of a presentation created by Megan Goerke for a first-year digital media production marketing unit. Megan chose tools that best created movement, using software she thought was more visually stimulating than other software she had used and that best suited the requirements of her assignment. Her assignment was to create a marketing pitch to a band for a music video. The dynamic, holistic view afforded by the software, along with its 'zooming' feature, helped her focus the audience's attention. The initial view of all the slides provides a hint of what you will see during the presentation. You can experiment with other software, compare the animation, sound and navigation to see what you prefer to use for your presentation subject.

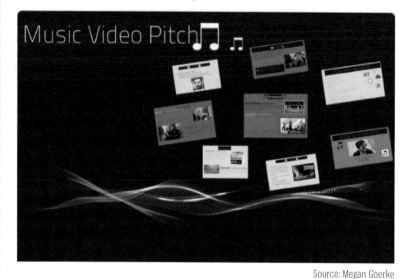

Figure 16.2 A screenshot of the Prezi created by Megan Goerke, Behavioural Science student. (All slides are visible.) The complete presentation can be viewed at https://prezi.com/stfaiyyurlvj/music-video-pitch

Source: Megan Goerke

There are several presentation examples of the cloud-based presentation software Megan chose at the Prezi website (**http://prezi.com**).

Movies and digital stories

If you want to show a movie segment created by others, such as a YouTube clip, always introduce it, explaining its context and what you want your audience to notice as they watch it.

Never show a long, unedited segment from a movie; you cannot afford to allow someone else's performance to dominate your presentation. Including a small section to support your argument, however, can be useful.

When utilising a movie, make sure you have the relevant clip ready to go at the appropriate point of your presentation so that your audience will not have to wait while you find the segment. Edit and organise the movie, and know how to operate the equipment in the space where you will upload or deliver your presentation.

Be creative in your presentation assignments, though always remember to check the assignment instructions for any restrictions about the content and format. If you have created a digital story or film as your presentation, audience and purpose are still key to how you shape it. Example 16.2 shows an instance of a student being creative with a presentation to great effect.

Example 16.2 Using film to engage your audience

Here is an example from part of a presentation by student, Sharon Beale (see Figure 16.3). This is a screen grab from her film entitled 'The Eastern Curlew', where the text appears while you listen to Sharon presenting. The film is narrated (presented) by Sharon as the audience gets to watch engaging film clips of the presentation topic – the Eastern Curlew. Occasionally, Sharon has included a slide with a graph or table, but otherwise we are given some key points during the film as shown in Figure 16.3, where the audience always gets to watch the bird being discussed.

Figure 16.3   **A screenshot of the film created by Sharon Beale, Bachelor of Education student**

Timestamp: 0:22

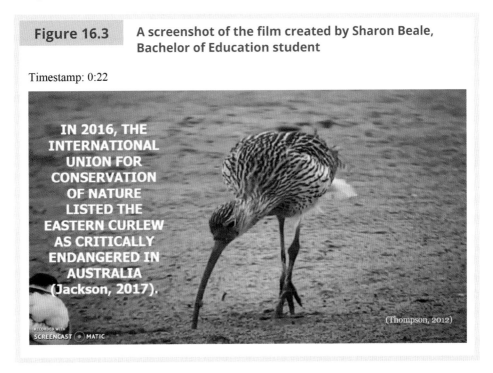

Do you need to include a 'warning'?

It is important to consider if *any* information contained in your presentation requires a warning before it is shown. For example, whenever you give a presentation where you are naming or showing graphics of individuals who may be from Australia's First Nations, you need to include a warning (see ACT Council of Social Service, 2016). The reasons for including this type of warning are often, but not always, connected to respect for people who are deceased. Example 16.3 shows an in-presentation warning about hearing about traumatic events created by Centre for Aboriginal Studies student, Jacqui Holub. In exploring the policies over Australia's colonial history that have ongoing impact on First Nations in Australia, Jacqui created a digital story focused on the story of one senior Noongar woman, Brenda Larsen.

The presentation was uploaded onto her university's LMS. Jacqui included a slide with the warning at the start of the presentation – *before* she showed a photo of her interviewee, Ms Larsen.

Example 16.3   Wording from an in-presentation warning

Aboriginal and Torres Strait Islander viewers please be warned this presentation may cause distress as the impacts of historical events and government Acts are discussed throughout Brenda's story.

Jacqui Holub, Centre for Aboriginal Studies student

Jacqui created a warning that is specific to the context for her presentation. We suggest if your presentation ever requires a similar warning you get advice from websites named in Chapter 14 and from the one named in the references at the end of this chapter.

Student reflection 16.3   **Presenting to an online audience: some helpful ideas**

This reflection is from online student, Sharon Beale, who had to have her presentation uploaded ready for an audience who will watch it at a time that suits them.

I really enjoy creating presentations – introducing ICT as part of our online learning gives us the opportunity to show our creativity as well as demonstrate our knowledge. However, online presentations do have their issues. The absence of an audience provides no feedback on the content delivery, nor any indication if something has not been understood or heard clearly. To help overcome this, I assume my audience has no prior knowledge on the topic, and always include an explanation of the subject. This ensures the presentation can be understood by all audiences. Furthermore, I limit the amount of text used on each slide. It's extremely difficult to both listen to audio and read text at the same time. Hence, I restrict my slide text to reiterating my speech rather than providing new information. For example, using keywords from the script to reinforce my point, rather than additional information not spoken. Also, I have found the use of topic related images and/or videos assist in retaining the audience's attention. If the audience doesn't enjoy the presentation, they will fail to recall any of the information given.

Sharon Beale, Bachelor of Education student

Handouts and supporting information

Handouts, whether electronic or hardcopy, can be useful if you want people to remember complex information, and including *links* can be especially useful if you want to give people the opportunity to explore the subject and references further.

If you choose to distribute or upload a document, decide whether to make it available before, during or after the presentation. If you distribute it before you present, you may lose your audience's attention, since they might focus on the information in the document instead of you. On the other hand, if students have the document in hand, you can direct them to specific points, and they can highlight or make notes.

If you distribute information after the presentation, it is helpful to inform the audience that you intend to do this during the presentation so that they know what to expect.

Here are some things that you might include if you give a handout or distribute supporting information:

- information related to your topic
- key takeaway points
- detailed graphics
- references to sources used
- discussion questions.

If you distribute printed handouts, pay attention to making them attractive and easy to read. For example:

- Allow plenty of white space so your audience can easily add notes.
- Your headings should be in larger font than the rest of the text.
- Make your graphics large enough to see clearly, labelling them if necessary, and include references.

Objects

Don't forget that there can be much value in showing *objects* relevant to your presentation. For example, one of our students allowed his audience to touch meteorite samples during his presentation on meteorites. Document cameras are often available and are useful tools to project large images not only of documents but also of any object small enough to be placed under the camera lens.

Posters

Posters are often used for presentations, though creating a good poster can take time. Note the following suggestions:

- Brainstorm and write down key ideas before starting on your poster.
- Make the poster easy to read:
  - Use a large font that is legible from several metres away (see the Universal Design websites listed at the end of this chapter).
  - Include reasonable-sized, clearly labelled and correctly referenced graphics.
  - Avoid excessive use of upper-case letters or underlining, since both are difficult to read.
- Make it attractive:
  - Don't overfill the poster with information.

- Leave a reasonable amount of 'white space'.
- Don't use too many different colours, layout styles and fonts. Most professional graphic artists suggest you use no more than two different fonts, and vary these by using different sizes, bolding and italics.
- Don't use a very 'busy' background that will detract from the information being shown.
- Draw your viewers' eyes to a few key areas on the poster:
  - Focus on your main ideas.
  - Place related ideas together, and use visual techniques (e.g. boxes, similar colours, arrows and lines) to suggest relationships.
- Use consistent, concise language throughout:
  - Think carefully before changing from active to passive verbs, from past tense to present tense or from 'we' to 'you' in different sections. (It may be okay to do this, but ask others to check in case it makes the poster confusing.)
  - If this is a team poster, organise for one person to be responsible for editing the language, so that there will be a consistent voice.
  - Double-check your spelling.
- Check that you have the required equipment and a suitable place to hang the poster.
- If you are using a poster as part of an oral presentation, make sure it will be visible to everyone wherever you and the audience are positioned; ideally, it will be able to be projected onto monitors and screens.

Team presentations

We covered working as a team (rather than a group) in Chapter 15, but here we suggest a good process for creating a team presentation. The process outlined below can be applied to situations where you are completing written group assignments just as well as when you are preparing for an oral presentation.

Planning your presentation

First, check the marking guide and note how your team's oral presentation will be assessed:

- Will you be assessed on the creation process as well as the final product (i.e. the presentation)?
- Will you all share the same mark, or is there also an individual assessment component?
- Has the lecturer or tutor stated clear processes to be followed in case a team member is unable to complete their contribution?

- Are all team members expected to make *the same* contribution to the task (e.g. each member must speak for five minutes), or do the instructions allow you to all make *equivalent* contributions? In the latter case, one member might be responsible for formatting the presentation, for example, and thus speak for less time than the rest of the team.

As soon as you are given your group assignment, meet briefly to work through the following steps at the first meeting.

First meeting

Step 1

Introduce yourselves, and exchange contact details – this is essential.

Step 2

Do an initial quick brainstorm of the assignment task. Clarify together the purpose of the presentation. Discuss and debate until you all agree on the objective and the requirements. If the instructions are ambiguous, check in with your lecturer or tutor.

Step 3

Use Table 15.1 in the previous chapter, which describes the Belbin team roles, to talk about the roles each of you tends to play in a team, and consider the balance of roles you have in this new team. Given the combination of roles you have, talk about the strengths and challenges you anticipate your team might have.

Step 4

Now share with each other what you consider are the skills you can bring to this particular assignment. For example:

- 'I am good at researching databases and getting the details correct.'
- 'My critical reading skills are good – I give useful feedback on other people's ideas.'
- 'I'm good at managing an audience' (e.g. during a question-and-answer session).

Try to be open about your capabilities and your expectations for the assignment. However, note that all team members must do an equal amount of work. (Look back at the section on teamwork and conflict resolution in Chapter 15.)

This is also the time to discuss what result you are hoping to achieve. If there are discrepancies in the group, try to resolve these in a respectful way. For example, if you are the only group member aiming for a High Distinction grade, consider these questions:

- What are you prepared to do to make this more likely to happen?
- How will you feel if other team members get a higher mark than they deserve thanks to your efforts?
- Are the other team members prepared to meet you halfway?

Step 5

Plan – and record – all the tasks and responsibilities for the assignment. If you are being assessed on process as well as product, good record keeping is important evidence. Assign tasks to everyone, but plan to review this together regularly, since requirements may change as you start working on the assignment.

If this is your first team assignment, accept that the process may be imperfect; however, as you become more familiar with each other, you will learn each other's strengths and weaknesses. Also, try to use consensus when making decisions.

Step 6

Organise at least two meeting dates at the outset, and decide on some deadlines. Make the next time you meet soon – within the next seven days. Discuss how and where you will meet (online or on campus). Again, there are so many ways to meet and share work and we do not want to recommend any one application, except to advise you to decide together how, when and where you will next meet.

Student reflection 16.4

Get to know each other as soon as possible

Make friends with people in your group. Find out what you have in common with each other first before working together as this will make you all comfortable to talk and express your thoughts openly. My group had met up after our class and introduced ourselves before we started our assignment; we all became friends on Instagram and created a group chat to talk through stuff. This also helped track who was contributing and arranging meetings. This helped our group collaborate better.

Kathleen Nelly, Commerce student

Second meeting

At this meeting, reconsider your roles and tasks. By now, you will have all had a chance to do some work on the assignment, and so should have a clearer sense of what is required. Now is the time to clarify and reassign tasks, as well as to establish deadlines. At this meeting, make the following decisions:

- Who will collate the presentation? Even though *everyone* must provide the material for the final product, the format, language and structure in which you choose to present that material could be different. Your presentation will be more coherent if one or two members take responsibility for finalising the presentation. Organise the deadline for submitting the material to whoever is doing that task, so that there will be enough time for everyone to check and suggest edits.

- Decide who will introduce and conclude the presentation. These sections are vital for a successful presentation, so don't leave them to chance. Here are options for organising this:
  - Choose one person to do both of these sections, and leave the body to the others.
  - Assign the introduction to the person who is likely to speak most fluently, so the presentation will start strongly. This person could also present the conclusion and manage audience activities.
  - Assign the introduction to the least-confident speaker because it will be shorter than the other parts and may not involve as much technical detail. This person could do other tasks, such as formatting, so that he or she does an equivalent amount of work. This person could sometimes also present the conclusion, but should not coordinate audience activities.
- Decide how to shape the body of the presentation. Are there alternatives to having each person speak separately, one after another? (Sometimes this is the most effective method, but plan this carefully.) How will you move from one section to another?

Be aware that, even when you have done your research and prepared your presentation, you have still completed only half of your preparation – the other half is to rehearse the presentation. *Do not skip this stage!* During your meeting, decide together when you will be ready to meet for this rehearsal.

Rehearse, rehearse, rehearse!

If you feel uncomfortable about the prospect of giving your presentation with your fellow team members, rehearse alone as often as you can. Film your rehearsal, share with a friend and work on improving your efforts before the team rehearsal meeting.

Other meetings

At each meeting, all team members need to report back to the team about what they have – or have not – done since last communicating. Be aware that completing a team project is a complex activity, and aim to be honest with each other about your progress– whether you are happy with it or not. As soon as you have done your work, send it to the people responsible for collating the presentation. Do not leave this to the last minute. Also discuss any potential costs that may be entailed in creating this presentation and agree how you will share these. Talk to your lecturer or tutor if this is a problem.

As soon as possible, start rehearsing the presentation. Even if it is not finalised, start practising, giving each other feedback on your non-verbal language skills (as described earlier in this chapter) to help improve your delivery. Remember that, since some, if not all, of the final mark will depend on the overall quality of the presentation, it will be valuable to help each other perform as well as possible (see Student reflection 16.5).

Student reflection 16.5 | **Advice about team presentations from a past student**

… in a successful team presentation, team members are able to support each other throughout the presentation, especially if one presenter loses their place or forgets what they are saying. This shows that they all know what they're talking about and have researched the topic together.

Melissa Settineri, Law student

Check that you have at least one team member who is confident using any hardware or software you will be using. If you are using equipment from different sources, make sure everything is compatible.

Final meetings

Your presentation should be completed in time for the penultimate meeting so that you can make some last-minute changes. If you plan to use a variety of audio-visual materials and/or artefacts, check that everything is complementary. Run through the entire presentation and make any necessary adjustments. Organise to help any member who needs extra support with visual aids or delivery style.

At your final meeting, practise the entire presentation again from beginning to end, timing each person's part. Make sure you're all happy and clear about how the presentation is going to work. As Megan Goerke says, 'You don't want your audience to feel the awkward vibe from the people presenting being very unorganised and all over the place with their presentation.'

Finally, you could use the assessment rubric shown in Figure 16.3 as a checklist to help you prepare. (After delivering your presentation, you can re-use the checklist to reflect on what worked and what you might do differently the next time you present.)

Figure 16.3	Oral presentation checklist

Presenters' names: _____

Feedback by: _____

Subject knowledge and relevance

Subject uninteresting and irrelevant	|--------------|	Presenters had extensive knowledge of subject, which was highly relevant and thought-provoking
Language too complex or too simple for the audience	|--------------|	Appropriate language was used for the audience

Group dynamics

People presented as individuals rather than as a group; little connection among speakers	|--------------|	Evidence of preparation, with people making clear connections between each part of presentation
No evidence of teamwork	|--------------|	Team members appeared to support each other and presented as a team

Organisation of ideas and content

Presentation was poorly structured	|--------------|	Presentation was well structured, with strong introduction and conclusion
Organisation of ideas clashed with team's purposes, or group didn't seem to have considered the aim(s) of their presentation	|--------------|	Team ideas were well organised and the aims were clear (e.g. to entertain, to challenge, to inform)

Use of technology/multi-media

Technology chosen and aids used were incoherent, and format, language and style differed among speakers	|--------------|	The team chose technology and aids that were coherent and consistent in format, language and style
Presenters appeared unprepared and were unable to use technology and/or other presentation aids	|--------------|	Presenters were capable and prepared in how they used technology and/or other presentation aids
Layout and design of slides, images or other audio-visual materials were unattractive or illegible	|--------------|	Layout and design of slides, images or other audio-visual materials were clear and attractive
Sources (including images and sounds) were not referenced	|--------------|	All sources (including images and sounds) were correctly referenced
Multi-media aids used were inappropriate or badly integrated	|--------------| *(If no other aids were used, write 'NA')*	Slides, images or other audio-visual materials were appropriate and well integrated

Audience interaction		
Presenter(s) failed to interact with or engage audience in activities	|---------------|	Presenter(s) were interacting and audience was interested throughout the presentation, or the presentation included appropriate techniques to engage audience
Presenter(s) did not respond effectively to audience questions	|---------------|	Presenter(s) listened and responded effectively to audience questions

Comments:

REVISION TOOLS

↘ Revision activity: Revise these ideas

1   The three most important things to consider for a presentation is to know as much as you can about your audience; be explicit about the purpose; and be aware of the particular context for that presentation.

2   A presentation must have a clear structure, which usually includes an introduction, a body section and a conclusion.

3   Team presentations require more planning than individual presentations, along with several team meetings, in order to be successful.

4   *How* you present is almost as important as *what* you present. Find out about the presentation environment (e.g. Will the presentation be available only online?) and be familiar with the technology you will be using.

↘ Thinking activity: Critical and reflective questions

1   Have I asked a friend to listen to me practising my presentation?

2   Am I confident with the technology I need to use for this presentation?

3   Am I ready to present my work to an audience? (Use the checklist in Figure 16.3 to help answer this question.)

4   Do I know how to present in a distributed learning environment?

5   If I'm presenting online, what is my background going to look like and does it suit the context of my presentation?

6   Will my presentation be inclusive of all my peers, wherever in the world they are?

7   What three things have worked well for me in past presentations?

8   What three things do I need to work on to improve my future presentations?

↘ Useful weblinks

Australian Catholic University has a comprehensive website on how to create a successful oral presentation; see **http://dlibrary.acu.edu.au/research/orals/index.htm**.

James Cook University has some excellent library guides, including one that names TED Talks about public speaking (see **https://libguides.jcu.edu.au/ba3000/TED-Talks**) and another with student examples, including a PowerPoint video. See **https://libguides.jcu.edu.au/ba3000/digitalpresentation**.

Monash University's Research and Learning Online website has information on how to prepare for presentations (go to the 'Online presentations tab): **https://www.monash.edu/rlo/research-writing-assignments/assignment-types**.

Library Study Smart at the University of Western Sydney have created some useful guides on presentations and posters. See **https://www.westernsydney.edu.au/studysmart/home/assessment_guides/presentations_and_posters**.

Library Study Smart have also made several helpful downloadable guides on group work. See **https://www.westernsydney.edu.au/studysmart/home/assignment_help/group_work**.

The University of Washington (US) provides instructions about equal access and your presentation – based explicitly on Universal Design principles; see **http://www. washington.edu/doit/equal-access-universal-design-your-presentation**.

On the Centre for Universal Design Australia website, note, especially, the downloadable PDF entitled 'Universal Design Principles Checklist'; see **http://universaldesignaustralia.net.au**.

University of Melbourne. 2020. 'Presenting Online.' **https://students.unimelb.edu.au/ academic-skills/explore-our-resources/learning-online/presenting-online**.

REFERENCES

ACT Council of Social Service (ACTCOSS) 2016. 'Gulunga Good Practice Guide: 'Aboriginal and/or Torres Strait Islander "Warning".' **https://www.actcoss.org.au/publications/ capacity-building-resource/gulanga-good-practice-guides**.

↘ CHAPTER 17

How far you've come!

CONTENTS

Where to from here?

When our students begin their first-year studies, many of them feel disoriented and unsettled. Some of this results from the new on-campus or online environment in which they find themselves – one much larger and more confusing in its organisation than their previous educational worlds. You may share this response. It may be the first time that you – rather than your parents – are getting yourself started in your studies. You have to enrol in a course, register in classes, find your way around campus or around complex online environments and learn to navigate learning management systems such as Blackboard, WebCT and Moodle. Even people who have studied before or who feel quite accomplished and capable in their professional lives can struggle with this!

Are you an online student?

Are you beginning online study and feeling overwhelmed by your first experience of an online environment, whether Blackboard or a similar system? It's worth reminding yourself that such disorientation is normal – you would probably feel equally disoriented if you were going onto any university campus for the first time. Allow yourself some time to find your way around your learning sites, and click on all the links to see how the site is structured and what is available, just as you would have to find your way around all the relevant buildings if you were studying on a campus. Even if you participate in social media frequently, or use various software and platforms at work, the online systems you will be engaging with for your study are likely to be new to you. Make the time to explore your new online campus in those early days of your course.

Reflective and critical thinking

The other area that unsettles many of our first-year students is the way they are asked to think at university. It's not unusual for our students to plead with us in the first half of semester, 'Just tell us the answers – everyone keeps asking us questions!' Or, more difficult for them, 'Our lecturers are all contradicting each other in their opinions. What's the right answer?' By the end of semester, though, they're beginning to realise that open, reflective and critical thinking will be valued throughout their studies and in their future professional lives, as shown in Student reflection 17.1.

Student reflection 17.1   The value of reflective thinking

I have in this brief time learnt the importance that skills such as reflective thinking have in helping me to deepen my understanding of any topic or concept – this can only be an asset in my new chosen field because it helps me to always challenge the way I see the industry I will work in and my place in it; as built environment professionals if we all do that, it can only be beneficial to the industry as a whole.

Alex Zuniga, Architecture student

Student reflection 17.2 is by Engineering students who wrote about the impact of working in a team on their thinking.

Student reflection 17.2   The benefits of working in a team

It influenced us to think outside-of-the-box, and thus ultimately as engineers. We also realised which design processes work better than others. We experimented with several processes and also things like graphs, tables, Systematic Approach to Refinement, SWOT analysis, drafts and several other forms of evaluation. Therefore, we greatly improved our creative and critical thinking methods.

Marelize Venter, Cameron Broad, Dawit Tesfaye, Lane O'Rafferty, Robert McLeod
and Wei Wei, Engineering students

Time management

Another area our students comment on frequently is *time management*. This will become more important to you as your studies continue – as your assignments become longer and more complex, and you are usually working on several at the same time. In Student reflection 17.3, a student expresses surprise that being prepared in advance can be satisfying.

Student reflection 17.3   Preparation leads to satisfaction

Managing time is extremely important for future job prospects and I learnt it here first. The idea of getting an assignment finished before the due date has never crossed my mind. I think I loved the adrenalin caused by being such a procrastinator in the past but this unit has taught me to embrace what needs to be done and possibly even enjoy the process. It gives me such satisfaction to complete assignments that I haven't rushed and thrown together and I think this comes from this unit's ability to make me want to learn ways to improve and do well.

Anna Dewar-Leahy, Construction Management student

One good way of helping you to plan ahead is to build an informal study group of fellow students who meet regularly to discuss ideas, assignments and problems in their studies. We can't emphasise enough how important this will be for your future successes. As suggested in Chapter 1, whether you are studying exclusively online, exclusively on-campus or in a mixed-delivery mode, making connections with other students and building your learning community will enable you to thrive as a tertiary student.

Engagement

As well as building informal relationships with students outside the classroom, it is important to engage in classroom activities – the more active you are, the more you will learn. This does not mean that every student needs to be extroverted. The important thing is that, rather than sitting back as a passive receptor, you should shape your learning by sharing your understandings and involving yourself in problem solving, discussion and other classroom activities. In Student reflection 17.4, a student reflects on some of the internal roadblocks they would like to overcome to engage more fully in their studies.

Student reflection 17.4 — Recognising internal roadblocks

When I enrolled in university this time around, I decided to not tell anyone that I was doing it as I didn't want the pressure of disappointing or letting those people down … upon reflection, it was actually myself I was scared of letting down, because I've always prided myself on being completely self-sufficient and not requiring any help or assistance. So, something I've struggled with has been reaching out for help. Although I don't find it hard communicating in person, I do find it challenging doing it via text or online. Maybe it's because there would be a record of me needing help? Something I need to work on is reaching out for guidance and support, and finding ways to build trust so that I am more comfortable with relying on others for assistance.

Ebba Collinson, Architecture student

Student reflection 17.5 offers further advice from another student.

Student reflection 17.5 — Some advice to help you succeed

Be confident and don't feel intimidated to speak up in a tutorial. You need 'everyday' communication skills with people in your class – it's how you make new friends who can help you get through all of your work.

Melissa Settineri, Law student

Confidence

Self-confidence can often be elusive – in some situations you might feel very confident, and in others your confidence may seem to evaporate. One useful strategy is to reflect regularly on the situations in which you do feel confident. What characteristics of these situations enhance your confidence, and what can you do to 'fan' that feeling? For example, are you most confident in small classes where you know the other students? Why is this, and how can you take that confidence into larger groups? Sometimes, if you can build confidence in one area of your communications, the feeling will translate into other areas, too. Student reflection 17.6 is from a student who found spending time establishing their academic skills, such as those we discuss in this book, to be helpful in building their confidence.

6ᓮ Student reflection 17.6   Building academic skills for confidence

The learning journey is a long road trip of discovery. I have found it is important to lay a solid foundation for my studies to ensure I set myself up to achieve my goals. I have found university study to be a daunting task and having the opportunity to work on my academic skills has enabled me to build confidence in my ability to study at this level and achieve all I aspire to be.

Steve Trudgian, Fine Art student

Making use of all the resources available to you is also important in building your confidence. Remember, the staff in the unit are there to help, as noted in Student reflection 17.7.

6ᓮ Student reflection 17.7   Using resources to build academic skills and confidence

As a mature aged student, restarting my academic education was a big challenge. The first three weeks were like climbing a steep hill. However, the support provided was exceptional. The biggest confidence builder was the assurance that help was always at hand. Every question was answered promptly and the textbook was helpful in giving me the confidence that my work was on the right track. Confidence is the basis for all communication and mine has developed by completing the weekly activities and through the forum interaction with tutors and peers. When I started, I had no idea where I was going with my future studies but now, I think I have the confidence to consider a degree in Creative Writing.

Lala Sheikh, Humanities student

Two final notes from us

First, don't forget the processes you developed in your communications unit (or component of a unit). In future semesters you may not study a language process unit, but you will be expected to apply what you have learned in this one. Even if your future lecturers do not emphasise the same things as your communications lecturers and tutors did (e.g. essay and report structures, referencing, and clear and correct written expression), assume that they still value them. The processes that you have been working on throughout this book have been developed by communications specialists working with disciplinary lecturers, so you can assume they are what your lecturers want.

Second, as you were advised in Chapter 1, make sure you know where to go in your institution to get help for everything to do with your studies. Whether you want to change your course, are feeling stressed or are still unsure how to find journal articles, go to the university's website and spend some time checking where and how you can survive and thrive during and beyond this first year. There will usually be a specific section for students, with lots of helpful resources. For example, Curtin University's 'Current Students' page: **https://students.curtin.edu.au**.

You are living in an era of unprecedented change, and so it is as important that you learn to adapt to these changing circumstances as it is that you learn current ideas and information. Many of your lecturers and tutors will focus more on helping you develop the approaches you'll need to cope with changes than on teaching you content. For example, the following hint box is an extract from a conversation with a Curtin University Architecture lecturer.

Learning enables you to be dynamic

'Learning is a lot about development for change, getting the skills and information and knowledge that allows you to shift your current position, or develop it, to accommodate what is only ever going to be changing around you anyway ... You can't just dig your feet in the sand and refuse to move – you'll just get buried.'

Lara Mackintosh, Architecture lecturer

A student reflects on this rapid change and the importance of adapting in Student reflection 17.8.

Student reflection 17.8 **Rapid change and the importance of being adaptive**

I am not sure about what will help my communications in my future life. Will taking the lessons I have learned in this unit be enough? Unlikely. It seems like these things will be the ones that I'll need to adapt and grow throughout my time at university and in the professional world, with new requirements for each new situation. By staying attentive to what is required and keeping an open mind, I think I will be able to achieve at least some of what is required for good communication.

Alex Cardell-Oliver, Urban and Regional Planning student

And final words from three students

Most students survive their first year and continue studying until they complete one or more courses. Many students are now studying at least some units online, and with the rapidly changing educational and social climates in Australia, more students are likely to study exclusively in this environment in future years. The advice given in Student reflection 17.9 is particularly valuable to online students, but is applicable to anyone studying at university.

 Student reflection 17.9 **Studying online**

If someone were to ask me for advice on how to study online I would tell them to really emphasise questioning yourself and questioning everything else. Why? Because I found this way the best way to learn and develop, even giving me a sense of empowerment over my own work. I would also encourage someone to engage constantly with their lecturer and peers, as I found things were so much easier and satisfying when you know you have the support to help you. The more questions you ask your lecturer, and yourself, the faster and easier you will develop. This really gave me the passion and drive to work through this unit.

Matt Hunter, Construction Management student

To conclude, we remind you of a suggestion we gave in the first chapter of this book: make a friend! This is the most common piece of advice we have heard from successful first-year students. In Student reflection 17.10 it is reiterated by two students.

Making friends will help you to succeed

Make friends with people in your year group and people in the year group above you (studying the same course as you). The people in your year group will help you get through your studies, and the people a year older will give you invaluable advice about what you should and shouldn't do.

Megan Goerke, Behavioural Science student

To survive at uni, you need other people going through the same things with you. To make friends you just need to TALK and say hi, and uni will be a much better experience! So, talking would be a communication skill you need to survive at uni; as obvious and silly as that sounds!

Sarah Edminston, Nursing student

As you look back on everything you have learned about communications from this book, and from your course so far, take a moment to remind yourself how far you've come in this new world of university studies. And enjoy the feeling of achievement!

↘ INDEX

A

abbreviations 72, 250
ABC-type guides 256
Aboriginal and Torres Strait
  Islander students 7, 313
abstract nouns 233
abstracts 60, 168–70, 212
academic calendars 7
academic essays 189–90
academic honesty 99–107
academic integrity 78–104
academic learning
  support 8
academic paragraphs 97–8
academic scholarship 99
academic skills 369
academic texts, reading
  59–74, 116
academic writing/principles
  112–35, 139–58, 162–85,
  189–206, 210–25, 230–51
accents 315
accuracy 52, 84–5, 319
acknowledgement 79, 99,
  343
Acknowledgement of
  Country 303
action roles 333
active listening 289–93
active verbs 235
active voice 198, 235
adjectives 251
adverbs 274
agenda 302–3
aggression 298–9
agreement (subject–verb)
  257–8, 282
alphabetical order 84
analysis 69, 122, 127, 129,
  189–90, 218–20
analytical essays 189–90,
  199
analytical reports
  compiling 165–79
  types of 162–5

animation 351
annotated bibliographies
  213–17
  language 216–17
  writing 214–16
annotation 68, 73–4,
  213–15
APA system 80
apostrophes 269–72
appeal 17, 23
appearance 316, 348
appendices 179
argument 63, 193–5, 342
  developing 192–7
  reading for 60–3
argumentative essays 190
arrows 73
artefacts 42
articles 48–50
  headings; subheadings
    64–5
  structure 64
  uses 282–3
assertiveness 298–9
assessment
  dissatisfaction with 17
  due dates and tips 8
  LMS submission 4, 6
assessment guides 17
assessment rubric 361–2
assignments 10, 23
  backing up 33
  post-entry 14
  requirements 7, 210,
    342
  submission 33
assumption 35, 112–13,
  140, 312, 344
  questioning 139, 143
asynchronous
  communication 330–1
asynchronous study
  modes 24–5
audience 16, 213, 218,
  221–2, 339, 343–5, 349,
  351, 355

audio-visual
  communication 69
audio-visual scholarly texts
  68–70
aural techniques 276
Australian Standard
  English 14, 311, 315–16,
  346
authenticity 79, 145
author–date citations 82,
  91
authority 52, 93
authors/names 97
  name order 40, 84
  original words see
    quoting/quotations
avoidance 66–7

B

bargaining 299
Belbin team role chart 332,
  357
beliefs 141
bias 25, 52, 112–13
bibliographic details 40, 71
bibliographies 83–4, 179
  annotated 213–17
  reference lists
    comparison 83
Blackboard 4
block indentations 90
blogs 54, 210
  writing 221
body (presentation) 341–2,
  359
body (report) 173, 175–6
body language 29, 289,
  316, 347–8
'bookending' references
  97–8, 203
books 48
brainstorm 357
browsers 34
'by' 235

C

calendars 7–9
campus 22, 366
    on campus *versus* online
      study 27–8, 34
    familiarising oneself
      with 9
Canvas 4
capitalisation 313
case study analysis 218–20
census 18
challenge (idea) 122
change 133
    adapting to 370–1
    educational 22
charts 181, 332, 357
cheating 100–1
    see also plagiarism
checklists 113, 130–1, 183–
  5, 361–2
Chicago referencing
  system 80
citations 79–82, 90, 94–5
clarity 346
classes 116
    'flipped' 12
    virtual and physical
      formats 11–12
clauses 259, 261–3
    unbalanced 269
clichés 232, 247
    avoiding 240
clothing 348
code-switching 244–5
collaboration 24, 221, 325–
  7, 330, 349
    versus collusion 101
colloquial language 243,
  247, 315
    see also informal
      registers
collusion 100–1
colonisation 312
colons 272–3
colour 223, 308
colour coding 120
comma splices 263

commas 82, 261–3, 274
common knowledge 89
common nouns 232
communication 13–16, 114,
  148, 289–91, 294, 308–17,
  330–1, 368, 370, 372
    audience, purpose and
      content 16
    dynamic nature 309
    formal 16
    forums 4
    virtually 30–2
communication barriers
  314, 316
community 320
  of learners 32
complex sentences 263–4
compound sentences
  261–2
compound–complex
  sentences 264–5
computer literacy 29–30
computer spell-checkers
  276
computer-table books
  256–7
concessive argument
  194–6
conclusion 60, 176–7, 190,
  193, 205, 342
confidence 343, 369
conflict 327–31
conflict resolution 300–1,
  330–1
conjunctions 261, 263, 274
connections 4–11, 60
connectives 129–30, 181,
  205
consensus 358
content 130, 214, 217, 339
  restrictions 352
  source drivers 202–3
content pages 170, 171,
  219
context 16, 145, 180
contractions 250–1, 269–70
conventions 134–5, 189
    see also rules

coordinating conjunctions
  261
coordinators 17–18, 26
core values 12–13
'correspondence courses'
  24
counselling 8, 11, 18
course content 18
course outlines 7
coursework, delivery
  modes 24
COVID-19 182, 350
credits 18
critical and reflective
  thinking 139, 366–7
critical reflection 140
critiques 122
cues 316
cultural artefacts 42, 191
cultural groups 310
cultural safety 308
culture 14, 308
currency 52

D

dangling modifiers 268
dashes 275
data 64
databases 40, 44–5
deadlines 358
deadlocks 300
decade numbers 271
decimal notation 119,
  165–6, 181
decision making 358–9
degrees 28
delivery modes 24
dependent clauses 263–6
dependent markers 263
description 189–90
descriptive reports 162
detail, reading for 64–6
development (idea) 122
dictionaries 67, 139, 277,
  280
digital devices 11–12
digital footprint 225

visual techniques 276
visuals 181, 349
vocabulary 134, 190, 238
    clear, concise and
        discipline-specific 246
voice 94, 133–5, 141, 145,
    198, 235–6, 344,
    346
volume 346
vowels 277–8

W

warnings 353–4
'we' 249–50
webpages 53
websites 4, 6–7, 18, 50, 94,
    117, 221
weekly activities 27
weekly study plans 7
welcome packs 4
wikis 222
win–win solutions 300
women 26
word counts 211
word tricks 277
words 65–7, 72, 81, 217,
    318
    construction 276
    discipline-specific 134

own words *see*
    paraphrasing
parts 277
quote omissions/
    changes 91
see also connectives
work environments 325
workload 5, 13, 148
works cited 83
workshops 11
work/working 5–6, 22, 29,
    330
    own work 90, 130, 134,
        146–8
    with people with a
        disability 296–7
    reflecting on 146
    in teams 334
    versus 'winging it' 8
world wide web (web) 41,
    45–6
writing 112–35, 139–58,
    162–85, 189–206, 210–25
    annotated
        bibliographies 214–16
    approaches 112–35,
        198–9
    blogs 221
    case study analyses
        218–20

clumsiness 132
develops thinking 230–2
essays 189–206
formality in 246, 343–51
importance of 140–1
improving 113–18
informally 145–6
'muscles' 113–14
online 114
refining 230–51, 255–83
reflectively 139–58
reports 180–2
summaries 210–12
tertiary genres 210–25
for thinking 114–15
writing process 118–33,
    255
written reports 340
written texts 59–74, 340
WYSIWYG website builders
    221

Y

years (in citations) 93
'you' 249–50
YouTube videos 69, 352